THE

COMPLETE CATALOGING REFERENCE SET

Collected manuals of the Minnesota AACR 2 Trainers

VOLUME II

EDITED BY

NANCY B. OLSON and EDWARD SWANSON

Minnesota Scholarly Press

1988

Published by:

MEDIA MARKETING GROUP /
        MINNESOTA SCHOLARLY PRESS, Inc.
P.O. Box 611
DeKalb, Illinois 60115

ISBN 0-933474-44-X

Layout and design by Sharon Olson / Apple Blossom Books

This book was produced using an Apple Macintosh Plus computer;
Microsoft Word 3.01 program; Altsys Fontographer program; Aldus
PageMaker 2.0a program; and an Apple LaserWriter printer.

Chapter 11

COMPUTER FILES

Introduction

This chapter is based on *A Manual of AACR 2 Exmaples for Micro-computer Software*, second edition, with examples added from several other manuals.

All examples have been revised to reflect the *Anglo-American Cataloguing Rules, second edition, Chapter 9, Computer Files*, draft revision, 1987.

The general material designation for all material cataloged by this revised chapter is "computer file." The GMD "machine-readable data file" is no longer valid.

All types of computer files may be cataloged, whether available by remote access or directly. Unpublished and published files are cataloged by the same rules.

The revised chaper 9 lists a hierarchy of sources to be used as the chief source of infromation. A note must be made giving the source used.

Edition information is interpreted very broadly in the revised chapter 9.

An area 3 is added to the rules. This area is required if no area 5 is used. For bibliographic records including an area 5, the use of area 3 depends on the information available to the cataloger.

Area 5 uses physical description as in all other chapters of *AACR 2*. If the computer file is available by remote access, area 5 is omitted.

A "system requirements" note is one of the first notes, and must be used. Source of cataloging information must also be named in a note.

Because the Library of Congress began cataloging these materials very recently, they have not yet issued any rule interpretations on this chapter.

By Paul Lutus

(C) 1980 Apple Computer, Inc.

Example 358

```
Lutus, Paul.
    MusiComp [computer file] / by Paul Lutus.
-- Computer program. -- Cupertino, Calif. : Apple
Computer, c1980.
    1 computer disk : sd., col. ; 5 1/4 in. + 1
manual (22 p. ; 22 cm.). -- (Special delivery
software)

    System requirements: Apple II.
    Title from title screen.
    Summary: Uses the Apple's sound generating
capability to play music and displays the musical
notes on the screen. Also allows user to program
in compositions.


    I. Apple Computer, Inc.  II. Apple II.  III.
Title.  IV. Title: Music comp.  V. Series.
```

This is one of many programs with an author clearly named on the title screen.

In area 3, the word "computer" is optional if a GMD is used.

Example 359

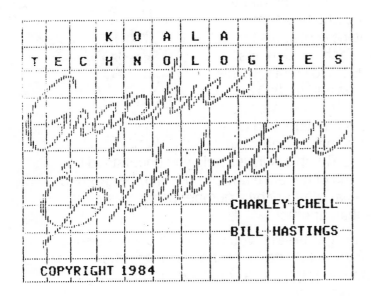

```
Chell, Charley.
    Graphics exhibitor [computer file] / Charley
Chell, Bill Hastings. -- Santa Clara, CA : Koala
Technologies, c1984.
    1 computer disk : col. ; 5 1/4 in. + 1 guide.

    System requirements: Apple II or higher;
KoalaPad touch tablet; printer.
    Title from title screen.
    Summary: Program allows user to combine parts
of pictures, add text, program them into a se-
quence, and/or print them.


    I. Hastings, Bill.  II. Koala Technologies
(Firm).  III. Apple II.  IV. Title.
```

Note use in the System requirements note of "Apple II or higher". This phrase is found on the item. It is a useful expression which could be used in many of these examples.

The Library of Congress has decided not to use area 3 unless it provides information not available elsewhere in the bibliographic record.

```
1. Trap and Guess
2. Bumblebug
3. Hidden Treasure
4. Bumble Art
5. Roadblock

6. Sound on/off
7. End
```

WELCOME TO BUMBLE PLOT

Meet Bumble, a friendly creature from the planet Furrin, who has some challenging games for you. Each game helps you learn to identify points on lines and grids. You will need this skill to find places on maps and to read or make charts and graphs. Bumble will also help you understand the meaning of negative and positive numbers and to see what is meant by a number being greater or less than another.

Play the games and you will become a powerful number-pair plotter! You can also learn about computer graphics as you draw pictures with your computer.

If this is the first time you have used Bumble Plot, start at the beginning and take your time. Play each game in order so you can learn everything step by step.

P.S. Some people may think that Bumble Plot is just for fun. To see what you are learning, turn to THE LEARNING LIST on page 18.

Example 360

```
Grimm, Leslie.
     Bumble plot [computer file] / by Leslie Grimm
; artist, Corinne. -- V. 1.1. -- Programs. --
Portolo Valley, Calif. : The Learning Company,
c1982.
     1 computer disk : sd., col. ; 5 1/4 in. + 1
manual. -- (Computer learning games)

     System requirements: Apple II.
     Title from title screen.
     Summary: Five games to help user (age 8-13)
identify points on lines and grids.
     Contents: 1. Trap and guess -- 2. Bumblebug
-- 3. Hidden treasure -- 4. Bumble art -- 5. Road-
block.


     I. Learning Company.  II. Apple II.  III.
Title.  IV. Title: Trap and guess.  V. Title: Bum-
blebug.  VI. Title: Hidden treasure.  VII. Title:
Bumble art.  VIII. Title: Roadblock.  IX. Series.
```

Descriptions of the separate games are not needed for this cataloging as the single summary sufficiently describes the subject matter of the
package.

Example 361

<u>Level 1</u>

Hefter, Richard.
    The stickybear ABC. -- Optimum Resources,
c1982.
    1 computer disk.

    System requirements: Apple or Apple II+; 48K;
DOS 3.3.
    With: The strawberry look book / by Richard
Hefter. McGraw-Hill, c1980.

    I. Optimum Resources, Inc. II. Apple. III.
Title.

Example 362

Hefter, Richard.
    The strawberry look book -- McGraw-Hill,
c1980.
    [32 p.]

    With: The stickybear ABC / Richard Hefter.
Optimum Resources, c1982.

    I. Title.

D: (first) 1.0D1, 1.1B1, 9.0B1, 9.7B15, 1.7B31
D: (second) 1.0D1, 2.5B7, 1.7B21
ME: 21.1A1:CSB25
AE: 21.30E, 24.1

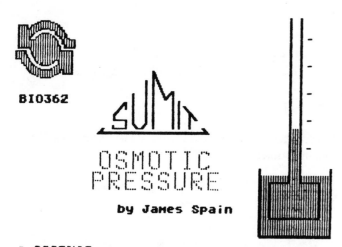

BIO362

A CONDUIT reviewed and tested program.
(C)Copyright 1983, Michigan Tech. Univ.

Second title frame

S	Single-concept
U	User-adaptable
M	Microcomputer-based
I	Instructional
T	Technique

<u>Your First Run</u>

   Simply respond to the program prompts, referring to the <u>User's Notes</u> as needed. Note that you may have to adjust the color controls on your monitor. (As a reference, the fluid in the osometer should be blue-green.)

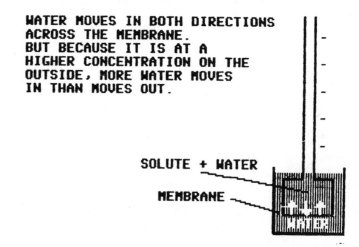

WATER MOVES IN BOTH DIRECTIONS ACROSS THE MEMBRANE. BUT BECAUSE IT IS AT A HIGHER CONCENTRATION ON THE OUTSIDE, MORE WATER MOVES IN THAN MOVES OUT.

SOLUTE + WATER

MEMBRANE

WATER

PRESS <SPACE BAR> TO CONTINUE.

Example 363

```
Spain, James.
    Osmotic pressure [computer file] / by James
Spain. -- Iowa City, Ia. : CONDUIT, c1983.
    1 computer disk : col. ; 5 1/4 in. + user's
notes. -- (SUMIT)

    System requirements: Apple II.
    Title from title screen.
    "A CONDUIT reviewed and tested program."
    Contents: Osmotic pressure simulations --
Molecular model for osmosis.
    "BIO362A".


    I. CONDUIT (Firm).  II. Apple II.  III. Se-
ries.  IV. Title.
```

"SUMIT" was considered to be a series statement. The last note is the number which appears on the title screen.

Example 364

```
SUPER-TEXT ™ FORM LETTER MODULE

COPYRIGHT {C} 1981 BY E.ZARON
     ALL RIGHTS RESERVED


1. COPY PRINTER PARAMETERS

2. CHANGE DISPLAY FORMAT
   {CURRENTLY UPPER CASE ONLY}

3. EXIT TO BASIC

OR PRESS RETURN TO CONTINUE >■
```

MUSE SOFTWARE ™

Zaron, E. (Ed).
    Super-text form letter module [computer
file]. -- Baltimore, MD : Muse Software, c1981.
    1 computer disk ; 5 1/4 in. + 1 manual (50 p.
: ill. ; 26 cm.)

    System requirements: Apple II; printer.
    Title from title screen.
    Copyright and manual by E. Zaron.
    To be used with form letter file created
using the Muse program, Super-text, or address
file created using the Muse program, Address book.

    I. Muse Software (Firm).   II. Apple II.   III.
Title.

    The author of the program is named in the copyright statement but not on the title screen. He is also the author of the manual as shown on its title page. Note is made of this relationship and he is used as main entry. Note the form of name is the main entry. E. Zaron appeared in the copyright statement and on the title page of the manual, but he was listed elsewhere as Ed Zaron.

Example 365

```
Cutter, Mark.
     MacDraw [computer file] / by Mark Cutter.
-- Version*91. -- Cupertino, Calif. : Apple Com-
puter, 1985.
     1 computer disk ; 3 1/2 in. + 1 manual (120
p. : ill. ; 23 cm.)

     System requirements: Macintosh; 128K;
printer.
     Title from title screen.
     Summary: Allows user to create precise, com-
plex drawings that can be changed and modified.


     I. Apple Computer, Inc.  II. Macintosh.  III.
Title.
```

The edition statement includes an asterisk, just as in the chief source of information.

Example 366

MacPaint version 1.5

written by Bill Atkinson

Copyright 1985, Apple Computer Inc.

OK

```
Atkinson, Bill.
     MacPaint [computer file] / written by Bill
Atkinson. -- Version 1.5. -- Cupertino, Calif. :
Apple Computer, c1985.
     1 computer disk ; 3 1/2 in. + 1 manual (32 p.
: ill. ; 23 cm.)

     System requirements: Macintosh; 128K;
printer.
     Title from title screen.
     Summary: Allows user to do art work of all
types.


     I. Apple Computer, Inc.  II. Macintosh.  III.
Title.
```

Example 367

```
MacTerminal
MacTerminal Version 2.0 of December 6, 1985
```

```
--by Mike Boich and Martin Haeberli


© 1983, 1984, 1985 by Apple Computer, Inc.


0 characters are stored off top.

3223552 characters are free on the disk.        [ OK ]
```

```
Boich, Mike.
    MacTerminal [computer file] / by Mike Boich
and Martin Haeberli. -- Version 2.0. -- Cupertino,
Calif. : Apple Computer, c1985.
    1 computer disk ; 3 1/2 in. + 1 manual (116
p. : ill. ; 23 cm.)

    System requirements: Macintosh; 128K; modem;
MacWorks program.
    Title from title screen.
    Summary: Allows user to connect the Macintosh
computer with other computers by cable or phone
lines.


    I. Haeberli, Martin.  II. Apple Computer,
Inc.  III. Macintosh.  IV. Title.
```

This also needs a phone line, but this should be understood by the user. Any program calling for a modem assumes the modem is connected to a phone or phone line.

Encore Systems

MacWrite, the Macintosh Word Processor

Written by Randy Wigginton, Ed Ruder, and
Don Breuner of Encore Systems.

Version 4.5, April 4, 1985.

Document occupies 1K on disk,
with 3117K remaining. Saving the
document may change these values.

OK

© 1985 Encore Systems
© 1985 Apple Computer Inc.

Example 368

Wigginton, Randy.
    MacWrite [computer file] : the Macintosh word
processor / written by Randy Wigginton, Ed Ruder,
and Don Breuner of Encore Systems. -- Version 4.5.
-- Cupertino, CA. : Apple Computer, c1985.
    1 computer disk ; 3 1/2 in. + 1 manual (143
p. : ill. ; 23 cm.)

    System requirements: Macintosh; 128K;
printer.
    Title from title screen.

    I. Ruder, Ed. II. Breuner, Don. III. Encore
Systems (Firm). IV. Apple Computer, Inc. V.
Macintosh. VI. Title. VII. Title: MacWrite, the
Macintosh word processor.

    No summary is needed for this bibliographic record as the other
title information tells the user this is a word processing program.

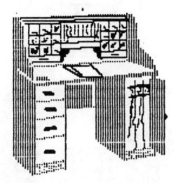

INFORMATION MASTER™

By: James A Cox and Stephen M Williams

© COPYRIGHT 1979

James A Cox & High Technology, Inc.

Second title screen

```
        Information Master

   Version 5.2      Ser #3882



              By
         James A. Cox
             and
      Stephen M. Williams
       Copyright © 1979
 High Technology Software Products, Inc.
```

Example 369

```
Cox, James A.
     Information master [computer file] / by James
A. Cox and Stephen M. Williams. -- Version 5.2. --
Oklahoma City, OK : High Technology Software
Products, c1979.
     1 computer disk : sd., col. ; 5 1/4 in. + 1
user's manual.


     System requirements: Apple II; printer.
     Title from title screen.
     Summary: Allows user to organize and print
mailing lists, reports, etc.


     I. Williams, Stephen M.  II. High Technology
Software Products, Inc.  III. Apple II.  IV.
Title.
```

The added entry for the corporate name uses the form shown because this form is used in the copyright statement.

First title screen

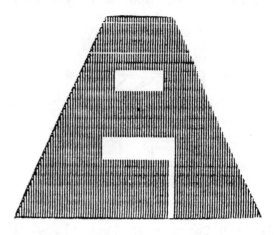

EDUCATIONAL ACTIVITIES

Second title screen

MATHEMATICS SERIES

MISSING FACTS

BY
ROBERT WILLIAMS

© 1980 ACTIVITY RECORDS INC.

Example 370

```
Williams, Robert.
     Missing facts [computer file] / by Robert
Williams. -- Freeport, N.Y. : Educational Activi-
ties, c1980.
     1 computer disk : col. ; 5 1/4 in. -- (Mathe-
matics series).

     System requirements: Apple II.
     Title from title screen.
     Also called: Missing math facts.
     Copyright by Activity Records Inc.
     Summary: Includes examples for addition, sub-
traction, multiplication, and division with four
levels of difficulty for each process.


     I. Educational Activities (Firm).  II. Activ-
ity Records Inc.  III. Apple II.  IV. Title.  V.
Title: Missing math facts.
```

The copyright note is included here because this firm is noted prominently on the title screen, and an added entry should be included for them. A person or body must be named somewhere in the bibliographic record to justify an added entry, thus the note.

IBM-PC
and Major Compatibles

AUDITING THEORY

BUSINESS LAW

PRACTICE

CPA

EXAMINATION REVIEW

MICROCOMPUTER DIAGNOSTICS 1985 EDITION

Irvin N. Gleim
Patrick R. Delaney

ISBN 0-471-82338-4

WHAT IS CPAMD?

CPAMD is a software program that provides you with a flexible environment in which you can interact with sets of multiple-choice questions drawn from the last four years. The design of the program is to give control over the questions and the process of interacting with them.

You should view the operation of the program as having three levels. At the top level, you select a question set by reviewing the description of the contents of each. At the next level, having selected a question set, you can then rearrange the questions in that set and, on demand, select questions that you want to view. Finally, at the lowest level, having selected a question you can select an answer to it and optionally view the rationale for that answer.

The program allows you to interact with the questions in either a STUDY/REVIEW mode or an EXAM mode.

WHAT DOES CPAMD CONTAIN?

Your CPAMD package contains the following:

- Disk I—Auditing and Accounting Theory
- Disk II—Business Law
- Disk III—Accounting Practice
- User Manual
- Registration Card and Licensing Agreement
- Key Command Card

Example 371

```
Gleim, Irvin N.
    CPAMD [computer file] / Gleim & Delaney. --
1985 ed. -- New York : J. Wiley, c1985.
    3 computer disks ; 5 1/4 in. + 1 manual (30
p. ; 23 cm.).

    System requirements: IBM PC; MS-DOS 2.0.
    Title from title screen.
    Manual: CPA examination review : microcom-
puter diagnostics / Irvin N. Gleim, Patrick R. De-
laney.
    Summary: Includes sets of questions on audit-
ing, accounting theory, business law, and account-
ing practice, the four main topics of the CPA
examination.


    I. Gleim, Irvin N. CPA examination review.
II. Delaney, Patrick R. CPA examination review.
III. IBM PC.  IV. Title.
```

This IBM PC example had a title screen, which was used as the chief source of information. Note the wording and punctuation of the note referring to the accompanying manual, which was by the same publisher as the disk (1.7B11, 1.7A3).

Catlab

A Genetics Simulation

J. F. Kinnear
Melbourne State College, Australia

A CONDUIT Reviewed and Tested Package
Copyright 1982 by J. F. Kinnear

© 1982 Judith Kinnear, Melbourne State College

CATLAB is published by CONDUIT, P.O. Box 388, Iowa City IA 52244.

Apple Computer, Inc. makes no warranties, either express or implied, regarding the computer software associated with the CATLAB package, its merchantability or its fitness for any particular purpose. "Apple" or "Apple II" is the registered trademark of Apple Computer, Inc.

Partial support for preparation of this material for distribution was provided by the Fund for the Improvement of Postsecondary Education, Grant G007905216. Any opinions, findings, conclusions, or recommendations expressed or implied here do not necessarily reflect the views of the Foundation.

BIO391A: CATLAB
APPLESOFT 48k, DOS 3.3

CONDUIT

COMPUTING IDEAS FOR EDUCATION

If for any reason you cannot read this diskette, contact CONDUIT immediately for authorization to exchange (319-353-5789). Replacement will be made free of charge, if requested within 30 days of data shipped.

© CONDUIT P.O. Box 388, Iowa City, IA 52244
 Duplicate for backup only

Example 372

```
Kinnear, J. F. (Judith F.)
    Catlab [computer file] : a genetics simula-
tion / J.F. Kinnear. -- Iowa City, Ia. : CONDUIT,
c1982.
    1 computer disk : sd., col. ; 5 1/4 in. + 8
col. slides + 1 student guide (29 p. : ill. ; 21
cm.) + instructor manual (39 p. : ill. ; 21 cm.)

    System requirements: Apple II; slide projec-
tor.
    Title from title screen.
    Slides show cat coat colors and patterns.
    Summary: Teaches principles of genetics
through a simulation in which cats of different
coat color and pattern are mated.


    I. CONDUIT (Firm)  II. Apple II.  III. Title.
```

This item has slides to be used with it. It is not a kit because the computer material is the dominant item; the slides are accompanying material.

On some software packages the name of the firm is given as "CONDUIT", on others as "Conduit". The first form seems to be predominant.

INTERACTIVE MICROWARE, INC.
P.O. Box 139 • State College, PA • 16804 • (814) 238-8294

QUICK-SEARCH LIBRARIAN™

BY TERRY CORL AND PAUL K. WARME   COPYRIGHT © 1982   INTERACTIVE MICROWARE, INC.

INSTRUCTION MANUAL

A Data Base Journal Reference System for APPLE II Series Microcomputers

INTERACTIVE MICROWARE, INC.
COPYRIGHT (C) 1982
VERSION 1.1

QUICK-SEARCH LIBRARIAN

BY TERRY CORL &
PAUL K. WARME

Example 373

```
Corl, Terry.
    Quick-search librarian [computer file] / by
Terry Corl & Paul K. Warme. -- Version 1.1. --
State College, Pa. : Interactive Microware, c1982.
    1 computer disk ; 5 1/4 in. + 1 instruction
manual.

    System requirements: Apple II; printer.
    Title from title screen.
    Summary: Allows user to create a personal
data base containing references to journals. Ref-
erences can be entered, edited, searched, sorted,
and printed.


    I. Warme, Paul K.  II. Interactive Microware,
Inc.  III. Apple II.  IV. Title.
```

Note the transcription of the statement of responsibility exactly as it appears on the title screen, with the "&".

```
%%%%%%%%%%%%%
% Eating for %
%             %
% Good Health %
%%%%%%%%%%%%%
```

Aquarius Publishers
Inc. 1982

Written by: Dee Surette & P.C. Hutinger

(Copyright 1982)

SURVIVAL SKILLS

A UNIQUE APPROACH TO READING COMPREHENSION

This series of programs is designed to improve your students' reading and thinking abilities. The use of 'Real World' topics and a unique branching technique make these lessons especially suitable for the older, basic student.

Each lesson is written on both a fifth and third grade level.

Students first read a fifth grade level paragraph and are given a comprehension question. A correct student response is met with a short explanation which tells why the response is wrong. The same concepts are then presented in a paragraph written on a third grade level, and the student is again questioned.

Survival Skills Series

PERSONAL CONSUMERISM
Tips on Buying a Used Car
Reading an Advertisement
Consumerism and You
Shopping in a Comparative Way
Laws for Consumers
Consumer Fraud
Consumer Help
Understanding Labels

WORK SERIES
How to Get and Hold a Job
The Job and You
Self-Concept and Your Work
Part-Time Jobs
New On the Job
Interviewing

PERSONAL FINANCE
How to Finance a Car
Money
All About Interest
Metrics and You
Eating for Good Health
You and Insurance
Credit

CONTEMPORARY LIVING
Friends and You
The Age of Responsibility
Map Reading
Succeeding
Decision Making
The Law

Example 374

```
Surette, Dee.
     Eating for good health [computer file] /
written by Dee Surette & P.C. Hutinger. -- Indian
Rocks Beach, FL : Aquarius Publishers, 1982.
     1 computer disk ; sd., col. ; 5 1/4 in. + 1
teacher's guide. -- (Survival skills) (Personal
finance).

     System requirements: Apple II.
     Title from title screen.
     "A unique approach to reading comprehension"
--Teacher's guide.
     Summary: Designed to improve reading skill
and thinking ability; lessons written on 3rd and
5th grade levels.


     I. Hutinger, P. C.  II. Aquarius Publishers,
Inc.  III. Apple II.  IV. Title.  V. Series.  VI.
Series: Personal finance.
```

Example 375

Roos, T.B.
    Life+ [computer file] : life, death, and
change / T.B. Roos. -- Wentworth, N.H. : COMPress,
c1980.
    1 computer disk ; col. ; 5 1/4 in. + 1 manual
+ 1 student booklet. -- (Biobits ; 1)

    System requirements: Apple IIe.
    Title from title screen.
    Student booklet: Tribbles : an introduction
to the scientific method / Ruth Von Blum and
Thomas Mercer Hursh. Iowa City, Ia. : CONDUIT,
c1976.
    Summary: Elements in a grid reproduce, main-
tain, or extinguish themselves, according to a set
of formal rules, as proposed in "Conway's game."

    I. Von Blum, Ruth. Tribbles. II. Hursh,
Thomas Mercer. Tribbles. III. COMPress (Firm).
IV. CONDUIT (Firm). V. Apple IIe. VI. Title:
Life plus. VII. Title: Life, death, and change.
VIII. Series.

    This title screen is very confusing. There are several "Biobits"
packages, so this was used as the series title.

```
MIDWEST SOFTWARE ASSOCIATES present  TM
================WRITE AWAY
A WORD PROCESSING/COMMUNICATIONS SYSTEM
COPYRIGHT 1984 by DOUGLAS B. STINSON
                  217 VICTORY LANE
                  ST CHARLES, MO  63303

  ALL RIGHTS RESERVED

 DUPLICATION FOR OTHER THAN SINGLE-
 SYSTEM BACKUP PURPOSES IS EXPRESSLY
 PROHIBITED.

 ========WRITE AWAY is published by:
  MIDWEST SOFTWARE ASSOCIATES
        1160 APPLESEED LANE
        ST. LOUIS, MO  63132
```

Stinson, Dougas B.
   [Write away]
   Midwest Software Associates present Write away [computer file] : a word processing /communications system . -- St. Louis, MO : Midwest Software Associates, c1984.
   1 computer disk ; 5 1/4 in. + 1 manual + 1 command card.

   System requirements: Apple II; 80 column card; modem; printer.
   Title from title screen.
   Copyright and manual by Douglas B. Stinson.

   I. Midwest Software Associates. II. Apple II. III. Title: Write away.

Stinson was chosen as main entry because he has the copyright on the software and is the author of the manual. One may consider him "chiefly responsible for the creation of the intellectual or artistic content of a work" as in rule 21.1, even though he is not named as author on the title screen. We may use information from the copyright statement in this fashion, but must include the information in a note, as shown above, rather than in the statement of responsibility.

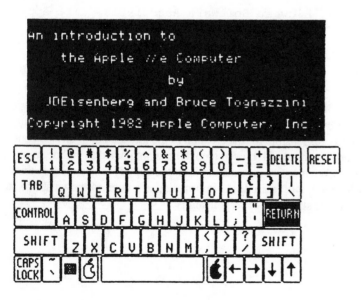

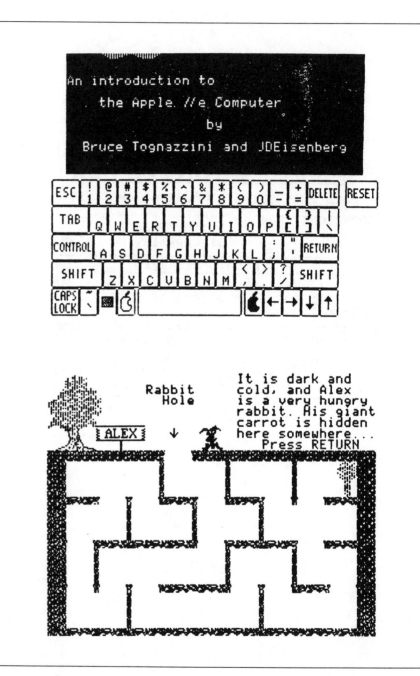

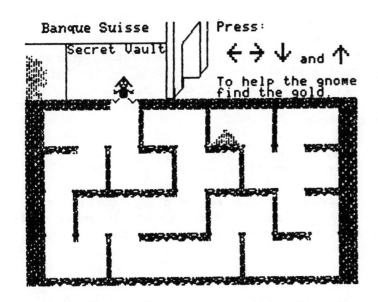

Example 377

```
Eisenberg, J. D.
    Apple presents Apple [computer file] : an in-
troduction to the Apple IIe computer / by J.D.
Eisenberg and Bruce Tognazzini. -- Cupertino,
Calif. : Apple Computer, c1982.
    1 computer disk : sd., col. ; 5 1/4 in.

    System requirements: Apple IIe.
    Title from title screen.
    Includes two maze games: Alex the rabbit
hunting a carrot, and gnome seeking gold in secret
vault of Swiss bank.


    I. Tognazzini, Bruce.  II. Apple Computer,
Inc.  III. Apple IIe.  IV. Title.  V. Title: In-
troduction to the Apple IIe computer.
```

The names of the two authors of this program appear in random order; Eisenberg will appear first some times, Tognazzini first other times. I used as main entry the name which appeared first when I was running this to catalog it.

This title proper also includes "presents". I did not make a uniform title or title added entry for "Apple" because users seem to know this item by the title "Apple presents Apple".

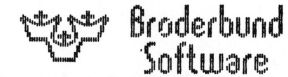

Presents

Lode Runner

By

Doug Smith

(C) Copyright 1983

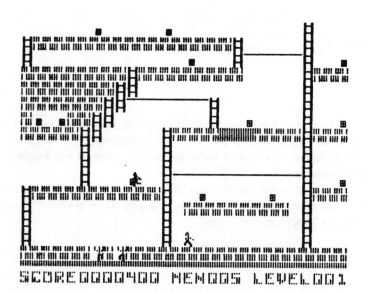

Example 378

```
Smith, Doug.
    [Lode runner]
    Broderbund Software presents Lode runner
[computer file] / by Doug Smith. -- San Rafael,
Calif. : Broderbund Software, c1983.
    1 computer disk : sd., col. ; 5 1/4 in. + 1
directions.

    System requirements: Apple II.
    Title from title screen.
    Title in manual: Loderunner.
    Summary: Action game and game generator; for
one player. Game has sequence of 150 mazes. Game
generator permits user to design puzzles and
scenes.


    I. Broderbund Software (Firm).  II. Apple II.
III. Title: Lode runner.  IV. Title: Loderunner.
```

This example also has "presents" in the title proper. I have chosen here to use a uniform title, and have not traced the title proper but have traced the uniform title and the variant form which appears in the manual.

```
    STRATEGIC SIMULATIONS INCORPORATED


              PROUDLY PRESENTS
```

```
C A R T E L S   &   C U T T H R O A T S
= = = = = = = = = = = = = = = = = = = = =

        THE BUSINESS STRATEGY GAME
                [ 1981
            by Dan & Bill Bunten
```

Example 379

Bunten, Dan.
      [Cartels & cutthroats]
      Strategic Simulations Incorporated proudly
presents Cartels & cutthroats [computer file] :
the business strategy game / by Dan & Bill Bunten.
-- Mountain View, CA : Strategic Simulations,
c1981.
      1 computer disk : sd., col. ; 5 1/4 in. + 1
manual + 1 pad of business planning sheets + 1
short rules card.

      System requirements: Apple II.
      Title from title screen.
      Summary: A management simulation game incor-
porating environment, production management, and
market forces.

      I. Bunten, Bill. II. Strategic Simulations
Incorporated. III. Apple II. IV. Title: Cartels
& cutthroats. V. Title: Cartels and cutthroats.

A uniform title was used here because of the wording of the title proper. Note the use of an added entry for the title with the word "and" replacing the "&". The added entry for the company includes the word "Incorporated" spelled out in full because that is the form used by the corporate body (24.5C1, B.2).

The Power® Of: Construction Management Using Lotus 1-2-3™

by
Jay C. Compton

Edited by:
Estelle Phillips
Theresa Simone

Management Information Source, Inc.

First Printing

ISBN 0-943518-17-2

Lotus 1-2-3 is a trademark of Lotus Development Corporation
Cambridge, Mass.
(617) 492-7171

The Power Of:® is a trademark of Management Information Source, Inc.

ONE OF A SERIES OF INSTRUCTIONAL MANUALS ON THE USE AND APPLICATION OF COMPUTER PROGRAMS

**CONSTRUCTION MANAGEMENT
USING LOTUS 1-2-3**
961

File Names:

EquipCos	BidUnit1	ECosting
HaulUnit	BidUnit2	JCosting
EstUnit	BidLump1	PaySched
EstLump	BidLump2	CashMan

```
The IBM Personal Computer DOS
Version 2.10 (C)Copyright IBM Corp 1981, 1982, 1983

A>dir

 Volume in drive A is VOLUME 961
 Directory of  A:\

COMMAND  COM    17792   10-20-83   12:00p
EQUIPCOS WKS     2944    1-01-80   12:15a
HAULUNIT WKS     2432    1-01-80   12:17a
ESTUNIT  WKS     5376    1-01-80   12:19a
ESTLUMP  WKS     4096    1-01-80   12:20a
BIDUNIT1 WKS     7936    1-01-80   12:21a
BIDUNIT2 WKS     5760    1-01-80   12:23a
BIDLUMP1 WKS     6400    1-01-80   12:25a
BIDLUMP2 WKS     7296    1-01-80   12:26a
ECOSTING WKS     7936    1-01-80   12:30a
JCOSTING WKS    15616    1-01-80    4:22a
PAYSCHED WKS     4992    1-01-80   12:35a
CASHMAN  WKS    13056    1-01-80   12:37a
       13 File(s)     232448 bytes free
```

Example 380

```
Compton, Jay C.
   The power of construction management using
Lotus 1-2-3 / by Jay C. Compton ; edited by
Estelle Phillips, Theresa Simone. -- Portland, Or.
: Management Information Source, c1984.
   v, 300 p. : ill. ; 28 cm. + 1 computer disk.

   System requirements: IBM PC; Lotus 1-2-3
computer program.
   "Disk contains worksheets with labels and
formulas already entered"--Instructions.
   ISBN 0-943518-17-2.

   I. Phillips, Estelle, 1928-       II. Simone,
Theresa.  III. Management Information Source, Inc.
IV. IBM PC.  V. Title.  VI. Title: Construction
management using Lotus 1-2-3.
```

In this case, the disk is considered to be accompanying material to the text, rather than the dominant item. This package is cataloged as a book accompanied by a computer disk rather than as a computer disk accompanied by a book.

ALPHABET ZOO

ABC TIME
LETTER GAME
SPELLING ZOO

Example 381

```
Disharoon, Dale.
     Alphabet zoo [computer file] / by Dale Disha-
roon ; artwork by Bill Groetzinger. -- Cambridge,
Mass. : Spinnaker Software Corp., c1983.
     1 computer disk : sd., col. ; 5 1/4 in. + 1
user's guide. -- (Early learning series)

     System requirements: Apple II.
     Title from title screen.
     For children 3 to 8 years old.
     Contents: ABC time [letters of alphabet] --
Letter game [first letter of pictured item] --
Spelling zoo [association of letters with sounds].


     I. Groetzinger, Bill.  II. Spinnaker Software
Corp.  III. Apple II.  IV. Title.  V. Title: ABC
time.  VI. Title: Letter game.  VII. Title: Spell-
ing zoo.  VIII. Series.
```

The contents notes has information about each program added in brackets. This is clearer to the user than writing a separate summary which would refer to "the first program", "the second program", etc. We can use this technique of combining contents note with descriptions, but must use brackets around the information we have supplied; the contents note is information transcribed directly from the item. If, however, we are making a contents note to which we add number of filmstrip frames per title, or playing time for music selections, those additions are supplied in parentheses because the information is taken directly from the item.

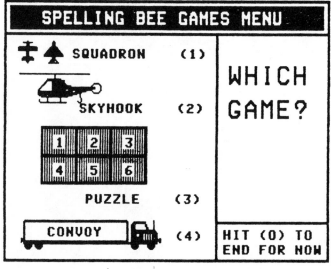

EDU-WARE SERVICES INC.
P.O. Box 22222
Agoura Hills, California 91301-0522

ACKNOWLEDGEMENTS

JOHN CONRAD created the basic program and was the computer artist for all of the screen drawings for the Apple version of *Spelling Bee Games*.

DAVID MULLICH designed revisions to bring this program up to DragonWare quality.

PETER HUNZIKER programmed final system modifications for the Apple version.

JIM WOOTTON was the primary playtester for all versions of *Spelling Bee Games*.

RAY ALCAZAR programmed the Atari disk and cassette version.

TRACY SMITH was the computer artist for the Atari version.

SANDY BLUMSTROM conducted system testing, recommended needed changes, and wrote this manual.

PAM POLLOCK edited and designed this manual.

Example 382

Conrad, John R.
    Spelling bee games [computer file]. -- Ver-
sion 1.0. -- Agoura, CA : Edu-ware Services,
c1981.
    1 computer disk : sd., col. ; 5 1/4 in. + 1
guide (20 p. : ill. ; 22 cm.). -- (DragonWare)

    System requirements: Apple II; game paddles.
    Title from title screen.
    Copyright and guide by John R. Conrad.
    Summary: Word and letter games for early
spelling and reading readiness skills.
    Contents: Squadron -- Skyhook -- Puzzle --
Convoy.

    I. Edu-Ware Services, Inc. II. Apple II.
III. Title. IV. Title: Squadron. V. Title:
Skyhook. VI. Title: Puzzle. VII. Title: Convoy.
VII. Series.

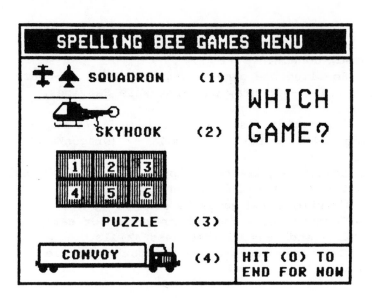

```
                                        Example 383


Conrad, John R.
     Spelling bee games [computer file]. -- Ver-
sion 1.1.2. -- Agoura, CA : Edu-ware Services,
c1981.
     1 computer disk : sd., col. ; 5 1/4 in. + 1
guide (20 p. : ill. ; 22 cm.). -- (DragonWare)

     System requirements: Apple II; game paddles.
     Title from title screen.
     Copyright and guide by John R. Conrad.
     Summary: Word and letter games for early
spelling and reading readiness skills.
     Contents: Squadron -- Skyhook -- Puzzle --
Convoy.


     I. Edu-Ware Services, Inc.  II. Apple II.
III. Title.  IV. Title: Squadron.  V. Title:
Skyhook.  VI. Title: Puzzle.  VII. Title: Convoy.
VII. Series.
```

Cataloging of two versions of this package.

𝕭ookends

© 1983
Jonathan D. Ashwell

SENSIBLE
SOFTWARE

Second screen

```
               Bookends
  The Reference Management System
           Copyright 1983
                 by
          Jonathan D. Ashwell
        Sensible Software, Inc.
```

Version information on second screen

```
- - - - - - - - - - - - - - - - - - -
        BOOKENDS Extended
- - - - - - - - - - - - - - - - - - -

  The Reference Management System
         Copyright 1983-1985
                 by
          Jonathan D. Ashwell
        Sensible Software, Inc.
```

Bookends™ Extended

Sensible Software, Inc.

© 1985 Jonathan D. Ashwell
© 1983 Apple Computer, Inc.

BOOKENDS™

EXTENDED

Sensible Software, Inc.

© 1983 by Jonathan D. Ashwell
© 1983 by Apple Computer, Inc.

Example 384

Ashwell, Jonathan D.
    Bookends [computer file] : the reference
management system. -- Computer program. -- Oak
Park, Mich. : Sensible Software, c1983.
    1 computer disk ; 5 1/4 in. + 1 manual (79 p.
; 23 cm.)

    System requirements: Apple II, printer.
    Title from title screen.
    Copyright and manual by Jonathan D. Ashwell.
    Summary: Designed to save, retrieve, and
format references, and to print bibliographies.

    I. Sensible Software, Inc. II. Apple II.
III. Title. IV. Title: Bookends, the reference
management system.

Example 385

Ashwell, Jonathan D.
    Bookends extended [computer file] : the ref-
erence management system. -- V2.08. -- Computer
program. -- Birmingham, Mich. : Sensible Software,
c1985.
    2 computer disks ; 3 1/2-5 1/4 in. + 1 manual
(107 p. ; 23 cm.)

    System requirements: Apple IIe with 80 column
card or Apple IIc; 128K; ProDOS; printer.
    Title from title screen.
    Copyright and manual by Jonathan D. Ashwell.
    Contents of disks are identical.
    Summary: Designed to save, retrieve, and
format references, and to print bibliographies.

    I. Sensible Software, Inc. II. Apple IIe.
III. Apple IIc. IV. Title.

    Cataloging of two editions of a program. The new version has disks for each of the two sizes of Apple disk drives. The added entry for the company uses the form shown because that is the form of name used by the company on the item (24.5C1, B.2).

Broderbund Software PRESENTS...

THE PRINT SHOP™

BY DAVID BALSAM & MARTIN KAHN

COPYRIGHT 1984 PIXELLITE SOFTWARE
ALL RIGHTS RESERVED

Broderbund Software

PRESENTS

A
PIXELLITE
PRODUCTION

FEATURING
ARTWORK
BY

GINI SHIMABUKURO

THE PRINT SHOP

GRAPHICS

LIBRARY

DISK ONE

COPYRIGHT 1984 · BRODERBUND SOFTWARE

COMPUTER IMAGERY

BY
MARTIN KAHN

Example 386

Balsam, David.
    [Print shop]
    Broderbund Software presents-- The print shop
[computer file] / by David Balsam & Martin Kahn.
-- Data and program. -- San Rafael, Calif. : Broderbund Software, c1984.
    1 computer disk : col. ; 5 1/4 in. + 1 refer-
ence manual.

    System requirements: Apple II; printer; op-
tional joystick or koala pad.
    Title from title screen.
    Copyright: Pixellite Software.
    Summary: Allows user to design and print
signs, letterheads, greeting cards, logos, etc.
Includes demonstration program.

    I. Kahn, Martin. II. Broderbund Software
(Firm). III. Pixellite Software (Firm). IV.
Apple II. V. Title: Print shop.

Example 387

The Print shop graphics library [computer file] /
    featuring artwork by Gini Shimabukuro ... [et
al]. -- Data and program. -- San Rafael, CA :
Broderbund Software, c1984.
    2 computer disks : col. ; 5 1/4 in. + 1
graphics card.

    System requirements: Apple II; program Print
shop; printer.
    Title from title screen.
    Includes demonstration: Computer imagery / by
Martin Kahn.
    "Broderbund Software presents A Pixellite
production"--First screens.
    Summary: Additional graphics to be used with
the program Print shop in printing signs, letterheads, greeting cards, logos, etc.

    I. Kahn, Martin. Computer imagery. II. Bal-
sam, David. Print shop. III. Broderbund Software
(Firm). IV. Apple II. V. Title: Computer im-
agery.

An illustration of related materials. It is very common to find software packages designed to be used with other programs.

Example 388

Switcher

by Andy Hertzfeld

Version 4.4 -- August 12, 1985

© 1985 Apple Computer, Inc.

Helpful Hints:

Use ⌘[and ⌘] to rotate between applications.
Use ⌘\ to return back to the switcher.
Use the option key to transport the clipboard between applications (or not).
Use ⌘-shift-option-period as an "emergency exit" to exit hung applications.
The Finder can be run under the Switcher; open Switcher to quit from the Finder.
Click on the screen of the Mac icon to toggle saving screen bits to save 22K.

Thanks to John Markoff and Bud Tribble.

```
Hertzfeld, Andy.
    Switcher [computer file] / by Andy Hertzfeld.
-- Cupertino, Calif. : Apple Computer, c1985.
    on 1 computer disk : 3 1/2 in. + 1 manual (21
p. : ill ; 22 cm.)

    System requirements: Macintosh; 512K.
    Title from title screen.
    Manual: Using Switcher with Microsoft appli-
cations. Bellevue, WA : Microsoft Corp., c1984.
    Summary: Turns Macintosh into a multi-program
workstation. Allows user to have up to 8 programs
in memory and switch between them and share infor-
mation.
    With: Microsoft excel.


    I. Apple Computer, Inc.  II. Microsoft Corp.
III. Macintosh.  IV. Title.  V. Title: Using
Switcher with Microsoft applications.
```

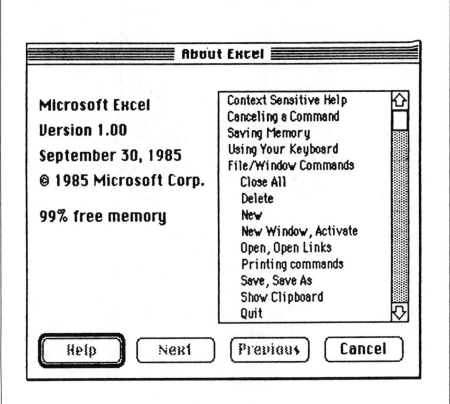

Example 389

Microsoft excel [computer file]. -- Version 1.00.
     -- Bellevue, WA : Microsoft Corp., c1985.
     2 computer disks : 3 1/2 in. + 1 manual (365
p. : ill ; 24 cm.) + 1 quick reference guide (20
p. : ill. ; 18 cm.) + 1 manual (207 p. : ill. ; 22
cm.)

     System requirements: Macintosh; 512K; 2 disk
drives; printer optional.
     "Complete spreadsheet program with business
graphics and database"--Manual.
     Title of second manual: Arrays, functions,
and macros.
     With: Hertzfeld, Andy. Switcher.

     I. Microsoft Corp. II. Macintosh. III.
Title: Arrays, functions, and macros. IV. Title:
Excel.

     This is an example of "with" cataloging (1.17B21). The two items
come together, but there is no collective title.

DLM ✲✲✲✲✲
ARCADEMIC SKILLBUILDER
Alien Addition

COPYRIGHT, 1982
DEVELOPMENTAL LEARNING MATERIALS
ONE DLM PARK
ALLEN, TEXAS 75002 U.S.A.

PRODUCED BY
EDUCATIONAL INFORMATION SYSTEMS INC.
LAWRENCE, KANSAS 66044
AUTHORS: JERRY CHAFFIN & BILL MAXWELL

DLM Alien Addition

DEVELOPMENTAL
LEARNING MATERIALS
One DLM Park • Allen, Texas 75002   APPLE II+/IIe
© 1984 DLM   L1111

DLM
Alien Addition
Educational Software
USER'S GUIDE

Example 390

Level 1

Alien addition. -- Developmental Learning Materi-
      als, c1982.
      1 computer disk + 1 user's guide.

      System requirements: Apple II+ or IIe; 48K.
      Summary: Computer game designed to increase
student's skill in adding numbers 0 through 9.
      ISBN 0-89505-135-4.

      I. Developmental Learning Materials (Firm).
II. Apple II.

D: 1.0D1, 1.1F2, 9.0B1, 9.7B15, 9.7B17.

Example 391

About Microsoft Chart

100 Percent Free

57320 Bytes Maximum

Chart Version 1.0

August 8, 1984

© 1984 Microsoft Corp.

Menus

Commands I

Commands II

Creating a New Series

Types of Series

Entering Data

Editing Data

Help   Cancel

```
Microsoft chart [computer file] -- Version 1.0. --
     Bellevue, WA : Microsoft Corp., c1984.
     1 computer disk ; 3 1/2 in. + 1 manual (184
p. : ill. ; 23 cm.)

     System requirements: Macintosh; 128K; printer
optional.
     Title from title screen.
     "Tool for translating numeric data into
graphic form"--Manual.


     I. Microsoft.  II. Macintosh.  III. Title:
Chart.
```

The Library of Congress name authority file now lists "Microsoft" as the correct form of the added entry.

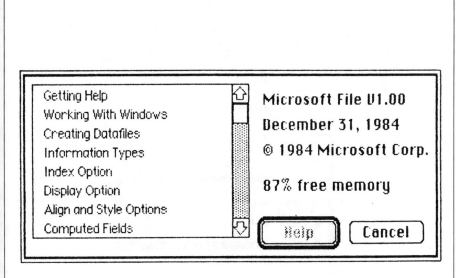

Example 392

```
Microsoft file [computer file] -- V1.00. --
     Bellevue, WA : Microsoft Corp., c1984.
     1 computer disk ; 3 1/2 in. + 1 manual (246
p. : ill. ; 23 cm.)

     System requirements: Macintosh; 128K; printer
and second disk drive optional.
     Title from title screen.
     Summary: Designed to store, retrieve, and
process information and prepare reports.


     I. Microsoft.   II. Macintosh.
```

Study Guide
RRT008

Fahrenheit 451

**Microcomputer Courseware
for Language Arts
and Literature**

MEDIA BASICS COURSEWARE

LARCHMONT PLAZA • LARCHMONT NEW YORK 10538

Return to Reading

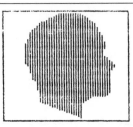

MEDIA BASICS

Presents

Return to Reading

An Exclusive

MEDIA BASICS

Courseware
Program

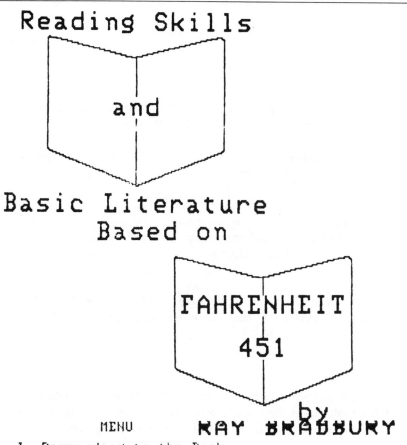

Reading Skills and Basic Literature Based on FAHRENHEIT 451 by RAY BRADBURY

MENU

I. Responding to the Book

  A. Exploring Feelings
  B. Making Connections

II. Understanding the Book

  A. Literary Appreciation
  B. Comprehension
  C. Critical Thinking
  D. Vocabulary Skills

III. Going Beyond the Book

  A. Activities
  B. Enjoying Other Books

Press RETURN

Example 393

```
Fahrenheit 451 [computer file] -- Larchmont, N.Y.
   : Media Basics Courseware, c1983.
   1 computer disk ; 5 1/4 in. + 1 study guide.
-- (Return to reading)

   System requirements: Apple II.
   Title from guide.
   "Based on Fahrenheit 451 by Ray Bradbury."
   Summary: Evaluates reading skills and meas-
ures comprehension.


   I. Bradbury, Ray, 1920-    Fahrenheit 451.
II. Media Basics Courseware (Firm).   III. Apple
II.   IV. Series.
```

    This has such confusing title screens the title from the guide was used as title proper.

Example 394

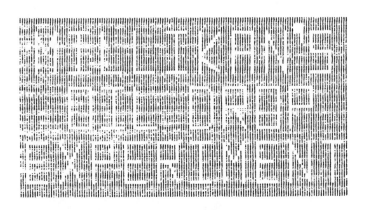

```
Millikan : [computer file] Millikan's oil drop ex-
    periment. -- Anoka, MN : Mentor Software,
    c1979.
    1 computer disk : col. ; 5 1/4 in. + 1 guide
(5 p. : ill. ; 28 cm.).

    System requirements: Apple II.
    Title from title screen.
    Summary: Simulation to determine the funda-
mental electrical charge.


    I. Mentor Software, Inc.  II. Apple II.  III.
Title: Millikan's oil drop experiment.
```

The title proper chosen was the title that appears on the first screen. This information on the second screen was used as other title information (this famous experiment is known by the name of its originator).

Example 395

PageMaker™
Version 1.1, 4-nov-85

OK

Written by Jeremy Jaech, Mike
Templeman, Dave Walter, Mark
Sundstrom, and John Nelson.

```
PageMaker [computer file] / written by Jeremy
    Jaech ... [et. al.]. -- Version 1.1. -- Se-
    attle, Wash. : Aldus, 1985.
    2 computer disks ; 3 1/2 in. + 1 manual.

    System requirements: Macintosh; 512K;
external disk drive or hard disk drive;
ImageWriter or LaserWriter printer or phototype-
setter.
    Title from title screen.
    Summary: Formats pages of newsletters, news-
papers, documents for printing.


    I. Jaech, Jeremy.  II. Aldus Corporation.
III. Macintosh.  IV. Title: Page maker.
```

Second title screen

Version 04.13.84
c1983 Hartley Courseware

Capitalization Practice

Copyright (c) 1982
Hartley♦ Courseware, Inc.
All rights reserved

Capitalization

Test

Hi! Type your name and press return.

_____

(name)

Capitalization

Skill Level 2-6

Reading Level 2-3

This two-disk program received the
"Best Software of the Year" Award
from _Learning_ Magazine and
Curriculum Product Review!

The **Practice Disk** introduces the basic rules of capitalization. Each rule is followed
by examples and a series of randomly presented practice sentences. The student
works with each sentence until (s)he believes it is correct. If there is an error, the
corrected sentence is presented directly below the student's work. The student
may compare the two sentences before proceeding.

Lessons include the following:
1 - First word in sentence and I
2 - Proper personal names
3 - Days of the week & months
4 - Holidays, A.M. & P.M.
5 - Proper place names
6 - Titles
7 - Misc. (including capitalization of mom, dad, etc.)

his aunt mary is from boston.

Press C to capitalize.
Press : to erase.
Press SPACEBAR to move the line.

The **Test Disk** has a ten item mastery test for each of the lessons on the Practice
Disk. The teacher may **MODIFY THE SENTENCES** on both disks. This allows the
teacher to personalize the content of the lessons. Complete record-keeping on the
Test Disk.

©**Hartley**♦ Courseware, Inc.

15-01

15-01 Capitalization-Practice #911

Hartley'

Hartley'Courseware, Inc. Dimondale, MI 48821   (517) 646-6458

15-01 Capitalization-Test #911

Hartley'

Hartley'Courseware, Inc. Dimondale, MI 48821   (517) 646-6458

Example 396

Capitalization [computer file]. -- / Version
    04.13.84. -- Dimondale, MI : Hartley Course-
    ware, c1983.
    2 computer disks ; 5 1/4 in. + 1 guide (19 p.
; 22 cm.)

    System requirements: Apple II.
    Title from guide.
    Summary: Includes practice disk that intro-
duces basic rules of capitalization in 7 lessons.
Test disk includes test for each lesson. Teacher
may modify sentences on either disk, keep records
for up to 50 students.

    I. Hartley Courseware, Inc.   II. Apple II.

    Note the version number here that is obviously a date. Nevertheless,
it is transcribed as an edition statement.

```
┌─────────────────────────────────────────────┐
│ ▣▤▤▤▤▤ Omnis 3 Database Manager ▤▤▤▤▤▤ │
├─────────────────────────────────────────────┤
│                                             │
│                                             │
│   Version number: 3.10.MAC                  │
│                                             │
│   Serial number:  Shown on disk label       │
│                                             │
│   Supplied to:                              │
│     Olson                                   │
│                                             │
│   Supplied by:                              │
│     BLYTH SOFTWARE INC                      │
│     2655 CAMPUS DRIVE #150                  │
│     SAN MATEO, CA 94403                     │
│                                             │
│   (C) BLYTH SOFTWARE LIMITED  1985          │
│                                             │
└─────────────────────────────────────────────┘
```

Example 397

```
Omnis 3 database manager [computer file]. --
    Version number 3.10.MAC. -- San Mateo, CA :
    Blyth Software, c1985.
    4 computer disks ; 3 1/3 in. + 1 manual + 1
pocket reference guide.

    System requirements: Macintosh; 512K; hard
disk drive; printer.
    Title from title screen.
    Title in manual: Omnis 3, the database man-
ager.
    One disk is backup.


    I. Blyth Software Limited.  II. Macintosh.
III. Title: Omnis three database manager.  IV.
Title: Omnis 3, the database manager.
```

The form of name chosen for the first added entry was that used in the copyright statement.

The Bank Street writer
Developed by
Intentional Educations, Inc.
Franklin E. Smith and
(C) 1982 The Bank Street College
of Education
Programmer: Gene Kusmiak

BRODERBUND SOFTWARE, INC.

Example 398

The Bank Street writer [computer file] / developed
    by Intentional Educations, Inc., Franklin E.
    Smith, and the Bank Street College of Educa-
    tion ; programmer, Gene Kusmiak. -- San Ra-
    fael, Calif. : Broderbund Software, c1982.
    1 computer disk ; 5 1/4 in. + 1 manual.

Word processing system.
System requirements: Apple II; printer.
Title from title screen.

    I. Smith, Franklin E. II. Intentional Educa-
tions, Inc. III. Bank Street College of Education. IV. Broderbund Software (Firm). V. Apple
II.

    The nature and scope note is the only note to precede the system
requirements note.

Example 399

```
▤□▭▭▭▭▭▭ About MacInTax™ ▭▭▭▭▭▭
```
MacInTax™ 1985, Version 1 (Initial Release).

Copyright © 1985, 1986 by **SoftView,** Inc.
315 Arneill Road, Suite 215
Camarillo, CA 93010;

Technical Support: (800)MACNTAX (outside CA) or (800)MACVIEW (from CA).

Developed by Michael W. Morgan with a lot of help from Darlene DuVarney, Tehani Stocks, Richard Hinson, Keith Golden, and Alan Wootton.

QUICK REFERENCE GUIDE

This Reference Guide lists most of the commands or actions you may want to perform, followed by the steps used to perform ther

OPEN / ACTIVATE

—New Tax File (Section 2.2)

MacInTax 1985 [computer file] / developed by
    Michael W. Morgan with a lot of help from
    Darlene DuVarney ... [et al]. -- Version 1
    (initial release). -- Data and programs. --
    Camarillo, CA : SoftView, 1986.
    1 computer disk ; 3 1/2 in. + 1 manual (41 p.
: ill. ; 20 cm.)

    System requirements: Macintosh; 512K;
printer.
    Title from title screen.
    Summary: For preparing federal income tax
returns; includes all the basic schedules.

    I. Morgan, Michael W.   II. DuVarney, Darlene.
III. SoftView, Inc.   IV. Macintosh.   V. Title:
MacInTax.

A second disk is available as a supplement; contains business schedules. This package does all calculations, transfers numbers from one schedule to another, and prints out the complete filled in schedules all ready to sign.

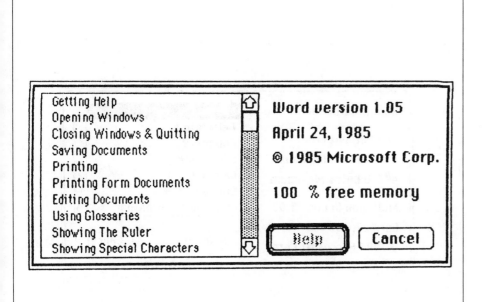

Example 400

```
Word [computer file]. -- Version 1.05. --
    Bellevue, WA : Microsoft Corp., c1985.
    1 computer disk ; 3 1/2 in. + 1 manual (283
p. : ill. ; 23 cm.) + addendum.

    System requirements: Macintosh; 128K;
printer, external drive recommended.
    Word processing program.
    Title from title screen.
    Title on manual: Microsoft word.


    I. Microsoft.  II. Macintosh.  III. Title:
Microsoft word.
```

Note the inconsistency of the publisher between this title proper and that of Microsoft file or Microsoft chart.

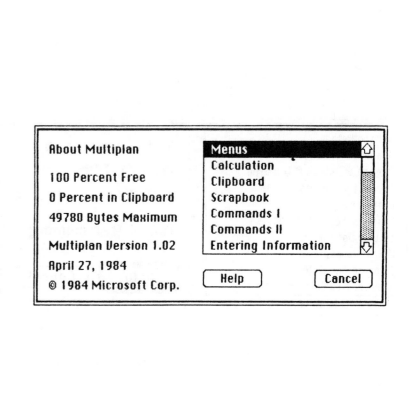

About Multiplan

100 Percent Free
0 Percent in Clipboard
49780 Bytes Maximum

Multiplan Version 1.02
April 27, 1984
© 1984 Microsoft Corp.

Menus
Calculation
Clipboard
Scrapbook
Commands I
Commands II
Entering Information

Help   Cancel

Example 401

```
Multiplan [computer file]. -- Version 1.02. --
     Bellevue, WA : Microsoft Corp., c1984.
     1 computer disk ; 3 1/2 in. + 1 manual (172
p. : ill. ; 23 cm.)

     System requirements: Macintosh; 128K; printer
optional.
     Title from title screen.
     Title on manual: Microsoft multiplan.
     Summary: Spreadsheet program.


     I. Microsoft Corp.  II. Macintosh.  III.
Title: Microsoft multiplan.
```

```
                    Word Juggler IIe
                    version 2.5
                    c1983 Quark Engineering
```

```
                    Word Juggler

                    version 2.8


        (C) Copyright 1981-84 Quark Incorporated

        _____


                            Word Juggler (version 2.8)
Options:

    1. NEW - Erases all text and goes to text
       entry mode.

    2. CATALOG - Lists all files in a directory.

    3. LOAD - Loads a document from disk and
       goes to text entry mode.

    4. STORE - Stores document on disk.

    5. DELETE - Removes a file from disk.

    6. FORMAT - Allows a diskette to be format-
       ted.

    7. PREFIX - Defines the prefix to be used
       for disk access.

    8. EDIT CONFIGURATION - Allows printer and
       default parameter selection.

    9. QUIT - Exits Word Juggler.

Which option (Press RETURN to edit text)?
```

Example 402

```
Word juggler IIe [computer file]. -- Version 2.5.
    -- Denver, Co. : Quark Engineering, c1983.
    1 computer disk ; 5 1/4 in. + 1 user's manual
+ 1 hardware package.

    Word processing system.
    System requirements: Apple IIe; proDOS 1.0;
printer.
    Title from title screen.
    Hardware package includes a keyboard enhancer
circuit card that must be installed in the Apple
IIe. Replacement keycaps, keyboard template, and
tools also included.


    I. Quark Engineering (Firm).  II. Apple IIe.
```

Example 403

```
Word juggler [computer file]. -- Version 2.8. --
    Denver, Co. : Quark c1984.
    1 computer disk ; 5 1/4 in. + 1 user's man-
ual.

    Word processing system.
    System requirements: Apple IIe or IIc; proDOS
1.1.1; printer.
    Title from title screen.


    I. Quark Incorporated.  II. Apple IIe.  III.
Apple IIc.
```

Two editions of the same word processing package. Note change in name of the company.

The newer version does not require any modification of the Apple IIe.

IBM

PC APPRENTICE

PERSONAL COMPUTER LEARNING SERIES

dBASE II

ASHTON·TATE™

Deborah Stone

A PRENTICE-HALL/CHAMBERS TUTORIAL WORKBOOK

PRENTICE-HALL, INC., Englewood Cliffs, N.J. 07632

Example 404

dBASE II [computer file]. -- Ver. 2.41A. --
    Englewood Cliffs, N.J. : Prentice-Hall,
    c1984.
    1 computer disk ; 5 1/4 in. + 1 workbook (231
p. : ill. ; 24 cm.). -- (IBM PC Apprentice. Personal computer learning series)

    System requirements: IBM PC; printer.
    Title from title screen.
    Software copyright: Ashton-Tate.
    Workbook by Deborah Stone.
    Summary: Tutorial on use of computer program,
dBASE II.

    I. Stone, Deborah. II. Prentice-Hall, Inc.
III. Aston-Tate (Firm). IV. IBM PC. V. Series.

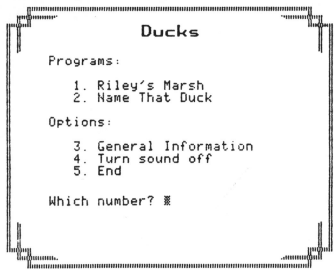

Ducks

Programs:

    1. Riley's Marsh
    2. Name That Duck

Options:

    3. General Information
    4. Turn sound off
    5. End

Which number? ▓

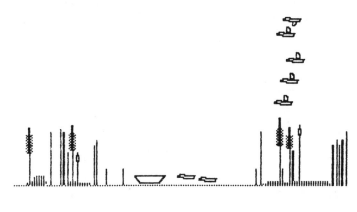

Press SPACE BAR to shoot

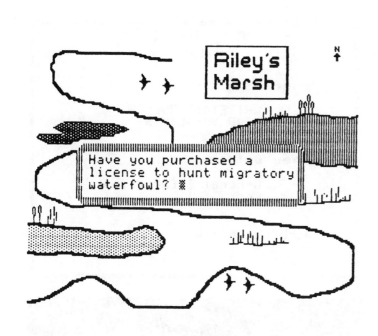

Example 405

Ducks [computer file] / Minnesota Educational Computing Corporation. -- Version 1.0. -- St. Paul, Minn. : MECC, c1984.
    1 computer disk : sd., col. ; 5 1/4 in. + 1 guide. (40 p. : ill. 28 cm.)

    System requirements: Apple II.
    Title from title screen.
    Summary: Teaches hunting ethics, federal and Minnesota hunting laws, hunting safety practices, and identification of waterfowl.
    Contents: Riley's marsh -- Name that duck.

    I. Minnesota Educational Computing Corporation. II. Apple II. III. Title: Riley's marsh. IV. Title: Name that duck.

    Note this item is from MECC, a well-known supplier of educational software. The corporate name changed in 1984 from "Consortium" to "Corporation".

Example 406

```
Oh, deer! [computer file] / Minnesota Educational
     Computing Consortium. -- Version 1.0. -- St.
     Paul, Minn. : MECC, c1983.
     1 computer disk : sd., col. ; 5 1/4 in. + 1
manual. (38 p. : ill. 28 cm.)


     System requirements: Apple II.
     Title from title screen.
     Manual includes instructions, role-playing
cards, management report form, and 6 readings.
     Summary: Simulation on controlling population
of a herd of deer in an urban environment.
     Contents: Whitetail Hollow. -- Herd manage-
ment.



     I. Minnesota Educational Computing Corpora-
tion.  II. Apple II.  III. Title: Whitetail Hol-
low.  IV. Title: Herd Management.
```

   This is one of the many items produced by MECC for use in
Minnesota schools. The name of the company, used in full in the statement
of responsibility, can then be given in the abbreviated form in the publication, distribution, etc. area.

Example 407

FISH

A tutorial-based simulation on blood circulation in an animal ... chambered heart.

MINERALS

An identification guide for 29 minerals commonly studied in ...

ODELL LAKE

A simulation on the food chain for fish.

QUAKES

A simulation on locating the epicenter of an earthquake.

```
Science. Volume 3 [computer file]. / Minnesota
    Educational Computing Consortium. -- Version
    4.5. -- St. Paul, Minn. : MECC, c1980.
    1 computer disk ; 5 1/4 in. + 1 manual (61 p.
: ill. ; 28 cm.).

    System requirements: Apple II.
    Title from title screen.
    Contents: Fish [simulation on blood circula-
tion] -- Minerals [ identification guide for 29
minerals] -- Odell Lake [simulation involving food
web of fish] -- Quakes [simulation, locating epi-
center of earthquake] -- Ursa [tutorial on con-
stellations].

    I. Minnesota Educational Computing Consor-
tium.  II. Apple II.  III. Title: Fish.  IV.
Title: Minerals.  V. Title: Odell Lake.  VI.
Title: Quakes.  VII. Title: Ursa.
```

This shows the cataloging of one of the MECC multi-program disks. Contents and summary information are combined as shown (see earlier example Alphabet zoo).

Example 408

Science. Volume 2 [computer file] / Minnesota Edu-
    cational Computing Corporation. -- Version
    3.1. -- St. Paul, Minn. : MECC, c1980.
    1 computer disk ; 5 1/4 in. + 1 manual (84
p. : ill. 28 cm.)

    System requirements: Apple II.
    Title from title screen.
    Contents: Cell membrane [simulation of inter-
action within cell] -- Collide [simulation, collision of two bodies, momentum and kinetic energy]
-- Diffusion [simulation, relative diffusion rates
of gases] -- ICBM [simulation, calculations for
interception] -- Nuclear simulation [illustrates
radioactive decay of 9 isotopes] -- Pest [simula-
tion, interactions between pesticides and environ-
ment] -- Radar [educational game, interception of
ICBM] -- Snell [simulation, refraction of light
waves].

    I. Minnesota Educational Computing Corpora-
tion. II. Apple II. III. Title: Cell membrane.
IV. Title: Collide. V. Title: Diffusion. VI.
Title: ICBM. VII. Title: Nuclear simulation.
VIII. Title: Pest. IX. Title: Radar. X. Title:
Snell.

This is another volume in the MECC science series.

CELL MEMBRANE

a simulation of the interaction between a cell and six factors in its internal and external environments.

COLLIDE

a simulation of the collision of two bodies which displays the outcome in terms of momentum and kinetic energy.

DIFFUSION

a simulation on the relative diffusion rates of gases.

ICBM

a simulation of the interception of an ICBM which involves students in the underlying mathematical calculations.

NUCLEAR SIMULATION

a simulation which illustrates the radioactive decay of nine different isotopes.

PEST

a simulation of interactions which occur between pesticides and the environment.

RADAR

an educational game which simulates the interception of an enemy ICBM.

SNELL

a simulation of the refraction of light waves as they pass between two mediums.

Example 409

```
Cell membrane [computer file].-- on 1 computer
    disk ; 5 1/4 in. + 1 guide (8 p. : ill. ; 28
    cm.).

    In Science. Volume 2, [computer file] / Min-
nesota Educational Computing Consortium. -- Ver-
sion 3.1. -- St. Paul, Minn. : MECC, c1980.

    System requirements: Apple II.
    Title from title screen.
    Summary: Simulates the interaction between
cell and its environment. User controls six fac-
tors of the environment.


    I. Minnesota Educational Computing Consor-
tium.  II. Apple II.
```

Example 410

Snell [computer file]. -- on 1 computer disk ; 5
    1/4 in. + 1 guide (7 p. : ill. ; 28 cm.).

    In Science. Volume 2, [computer file] / Min-
nesota Educational Computing Consortium. -- Version 3.1. -- St. Paul, Minn. : MECC, c1980.

    System requirements: Apple II.
    Title from title screen.
    Summary: Simulates refraction or change of
direction that occurs when light waves pass between two media. Also considers reflection when
critical angle is reached. Users control angle of
incident ray and index of refraction for the
media.

    I. Minnesota Educational Computing Consor-
tium. II. Apple II.

Example 411

Pest [computer file]. -- on 1 computer disk ; 5 1/
    4 in. + 1 guide (7 p. : ill. ; 28 cm.).

    In Science. Volume 2 [computer file] / Minne-
sota Educational Computing Consortium. -- Version
3.1. -- St. Paul, Minn. : MECC, c1980.

    System requirements: Apple II.
    Title from title screen.
    Summary: Simulates the interactions which
occur between pesticides and the environment. User
controls variables which affect life forms within
treated area.

    I. Minnesota Educational Computing Consor-
tium. II. Apple II.

The preceding examples, Cell membrane, Snell, and Pest, show individual cataloging of programs on a disk, as "In" analytics (see AACR2 Chapter 13, rule 13.5). This technique is useful when each of the programs on one disk are distinctly different, and when patrons would benefit from having appropriate summary and subject headings for each program. Each of the programs, or only selected programs, could be cataloged as "In" analytics. Note the punctuation of the "In" statement.

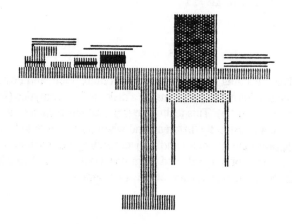

Example 412

```
Parrot Software presents Select [computer file] :
    hearing aid selection using the Berger tech-
    nique. -- State College, PA : Parrot Soft-
    ware, c1983.
    1 computer disk : sd. ; 5 1/4 in. + 1 manual
(6 p. ; 22 cm.)


    System requirements: Apple II; optional pro-
gram, Hearing aid manager.
    Title from title screen.
    Manual: Select a hearing aid / Gary J. Glas-
coe.
    Summary: Uses the Berger technique to gener-
ate data needed to select the correct hearing aid
from a number of specifications.



    I. Glascoe, Gary J. Select a hearing aid.
II. Parrot Software (Firm).  III. Apple II.  IV.
Title: Select.  V. Title: Hearing aid selection
using the Berger technique.
```

This item has a "presents" title proper. In an LCRI for 7.1B1 (CSB 13) we are told to ignore this information in the case of motion pictures and videorecordings. We are not, however, to ignore it for other materials, but to transcribe the complete grammatically connected information as title proper.

```
                STONEWARE'S

          =>   DB MASTER   <=


             (REV. 3.02!)


           SERIAL # 44267A




     (C) 1980,1982 DB MASTER ASSOCIATES
            ALL RIGHTS RESERVED   2222


   PRESS 'RETURN' TO CONTINUE ...
```

Example 413

```
Stoneware's DB master [computer file] -- Version
    3.02. -- San Rafael, Calif. : Stoneware,
    c1982..
1 computer disk ; 5 1/4 in. + 1 manual.

    System requirements: Apple II+ or IIe; 2 disk
drives; printer.
    Title from title screen.
    Summary: Allows creation, storage, manipula-
tion, and preparation of reports based upon input
files.



    I. Stoneware Incorporated.  II. Apple II+.
III. Apple IIe.  IV. Title: DB master.  V. Title:
D B master.
```

Here we have a title proper which includes a possessive. A new LCRI (Appendix A.4A, CSB 31) would have us use a lower-case letter beginning the word following the possessive. I did not in this case because the item involved used upper-case letters for "DB".

The added entry for the company uses the form of name found on the item itself.

Screen 1

Example 414

APPLE BARREL II
THE MONEY BARREL
FROM CDS

MASTER MENU

1 CHECKBOOK

2 LOAN CALCULATOR

3 FUTURE VALUE CALCULATOR

4 DAYS BETWEEN DATES

5 CALENDAR

Screen 4

APPLE BARREL II
THE MONEY BARREL
FROM CDS

MASTER MENU

16 THINK

17 DYNAMITE

18 LUNA C T OR L

19 MOUNTAIN

20 ALIEN

```
Dynamite [computer file]. -- no. 17 on 1 computer
    disk ; 5 1/4 in.

    In Apple Barrel II. -- Logan, Utah : Soft-
WareHouse, Inc., 1981.
    System requirements: Apple II.
    Title form title screen.
    Summary: Game for one player, in which player
and computer alternately remove up to three
sticks of dynamite at a time, the one taking the
last stick being the loser.
```

Example 415

```
Bibliofile [computer file]. -- Washington, D.C. :
     The Library Corp., 1985-
     1 compact laser optical disk ; 12 cm.

     LC MARC database.
     System requirements: IBM PC; CD-ROM player;
index/program disk.
     Title from disk label.
     Cumulative replacement disk issued weekly and
quarterly.


     I. Library Corporation.
```

Example 416

MSUS/PALS
Online Circulation Control System
Release v. 02.10 04 Mar 86

COPYRIGHT: 1979 U.C. Regents;

1986 Pecan Software Systems, Inc.; 1986 PALS

Loading Program. Please wait...

Online circulation control system [computer file]
/ MSUS/PALS. -- Release v. 02.10. --
[Mankato, Minn.] : PALS, c1986.
1 computer disk ; 5 1/4 in. + user's guide.

System requirements: Sperry PC (or IBM com-
patible); p-system operating system.
Title from title screen.
Summary: The circulation control module of
the Minnesota State University System Project for
Automated Library Systems statewide online catalog.

I. Minnesota State University System. Project
for Automated Library Systems.

THE
SYSTEM USERS MANUAL

FOR THE
SUBJECT KEYWORD AND
GEOGRAPHICAL NAME
INDEXES TO THE

LIBRARY OF CONGRESS
CLASSIFICATION SCHEDULES

PREPARED BY GERALD WOODWARD
AUGUST 74

A SPECIAL PROJECT
DIRECTED BY
MRS. NANCY B. OLSON
SYSTEMS ANALYST, MEDIA SYSTEM
MANKATO STATE COLLEGE
MANKATO, MINNESOTA 56001

Example 417

Library of Congress indexes [computer file]. --
    Data (4 files : 122,072, 141,419, 45,420,
    124,051 records) and programs (9 files). --
    1974-75.
    7 computer reels ; 12 in. + program documen-
tation manual + system users manual.

    System requirements: Univac; COBOL.
    Title from system users manual.
    Project director, Nancy B. Olson ; program-
mers, Gerald Woodward, Dale Houg, Michael S.
Barnett.
    Prepared for and funded by U.S. Historical
Documents Institute; project performed at Mankato
State University.
    Programs and data used to prepare: Combined
indexes to the Library of Congress classification
schedules / Nancy B. Olson. Washington, D.C. :
U.S. Historical Documents Institute, 1975.

    I. Olson, Nancy B. Combined indexes to the
Library of Congress classification schedules. II.
Woodward, Gerald. III. Houg, Dale. IV. Barnett,
Michael S. V. Mankato State University. VI. U.S.
Historical Documents Institute.

Chapter 12

MICROFORMS

Introduction

This chapter is based on *A Manual of AACR 2 Examples for Microforms* by Edward Swanson, with examples added from several other manuals.

Probably no part of the *Anglo-American Cataloguing Rules, second edition (AACR 2)*, has engendered more discussion and controversy than has chapter 11, the chapter dealing with the cataloging of microforms.

Two major groups have been involved, those wishing to follow the provisions of chapter 11 as written and describe all microfoms on the basis of the microforms, and those wishing to describe microforms of previously existing works on the basis of the original item. The questions raised have been the subject of lengthy debates within the United States, mainly within the American Library Association.

At its midwinter meeting in 1980, ALA's Committee on Cataloging: Description and Access (CC:DA) forced a task force to look into the question. The task force conducted its work during the spring of 1980 using a computerized teleconferencing system.

The task force reported at the 1980 annual conference of ALA in New York. Rather than putting forth a single report, the task force presented three proposals:

1) Describe microreproduction of previously existing works in terms of the original, giving details of the microreproduction in a note.

2) Describe microreproductions of previously existing works in terms of the original, giving details of the manufacture of the microreproduction in area four of the description as place of manufacture, name of manufacturer, and date of manufacture.

3) Describe microreproductions in terms of the microreproduction, giving details of the original in a note, as prescribed by chapter 11. This proposal also included the provision for expanding the use of uniform titles to collocate the microreproduction and the original in cases where the title proper as it appeared on the microreproduction differed from the title proper of the original. As the author of this proposal, I can say that perhaps it was overly detailed as presented. However, it did preserve one of the cardinal principles of AACR 2 as presented in rule 0.24, "the starting point for description is the physical form of the item in hand, not the original or any previous form in which the work has been published." The rules for uniform titles were revised by the Joint Steering Committee for Revision of AACR (JSC) at its July 1981 meeting, and the rules now cover such use of uniform titles.

At the 1981 midwinter meeting of ALA, the CC:DA conducted open hearings on the matter. At the 1981 annual conference of ALA, the CC:DA considered a proposal from the Library of Congress for the addition of an option to chapter 11 permitting the description of a microreproduction in terms of the original. The committee voted 5-4 in favor of the ALA representative to the JSC supporting this proposal when it was presented to the JSC. The JSC met following the 1981 ALA conference and decided not to make any changes in chapter 11 at that time, but to permit the national libraries to issue rule interpretations for the use of chapter 11. The Library of Congress in September 1981 issued its rule interpretations for chapter 11, which prescribed the description of a microreproduction of a previously existing work in terms of the original.

This chapter includes microform publications that have not been issued in another form previously, in other words original microfom publications. Several of the examples include microreproductions of previously published works, but they are works that have been collected and published as a unit for the first time in microform. In addition, there are examples of analytical cataloging for individual title.

This chapter also includes microform reproductions of previously existing works. It includes monographic publications, manuscript items, and a collection without a collective title.

In some of the examples the cataloging has been done on the basis of the rules in chapter 11 as originally written. Two examples of cataloging are given for several items: using the rule interpretations for chapter 11 as issued by the Library of Congress in September 1981; and using the rules in chapter 11 as originally written.

Several examples also include the uniform title that would be used for the item to collocate all manifestations of the item if one were using chapter 11 as originally written and the uniform title proposal that was presented to the CC:DA.

A problem arises when cataloging an item using the provisions of the Library of Congress rule interpretations. The rule interpretations do not address this problem, nor have I found a solution elsewhere. This problem is that of describing the microreproduction of only a part of a previously published work (in these cases, a serial of which only a part was reproduced in microform). Because I believe that all information that relates only to the microreproduction should be included in a single note (as in chapter 11 all information relating only to the original is included in a single note) I have included this information in that note, preceding the place, etc., of publication, etc.

I still believe that the rules in chapter 11 of AACR 2 are the appropriate ones for the cataloging of microforms. I would guess that a large part of the whole controversy is the difficulty people are having in treating as separate activities the two actions in descriptive cataloging: first describing a physical item, and only after that has been done providing access to the intelluctual content of that physical item. The arrangement of AACR 2 itself illustrates these separate actions: one first uses the rules in part 1 to describe the item and only then goes to part 2 to find the rules for choosing and formulating the access points that enable the user to find the intellectual content of that item.

As we move toward more sophisticated machine methods of access to the intellectual content of physical items, I believe that it is appropriate for the user to be able to separate out records for specific physical manifestations of a work. The records that are retrieved through specific access points should enable the user to tell immediately from the main part of the description what the physical format of the item is. This is possible when describing the item on the basis of the rules in chapter 11. It is not possible when using the Library of Congress rule interpretations.

The question of the international nature of AACR 2 also arises. The last information I have is that the National Library of Canada and the British Library were planning to follow the rules in chapter 11. In the spirit of international cooperation, should we not do the same? If not, we must present a much more convincing argument to the JSC than we have so far for rewriting chapter 11 to reflect the policies now being followed by libraries in the United States. I do not see that such an argument is possible.

Please note that the views expressed this introduction are my own and do not necessarily reflect those of the other members of the Minnesota AACR 2 Trainers.

Every effort has been made to prevent errors in the cataloging presented in this manual. We would appreciate being informed of any that may have crept in.

MINNESOTA CONSERVATION

OR

RESOURCE MANAGEMENT IN MINNESOTA

A Thesis

Submitted to the Graduate Faculty

of the

University of Minnesota

By
JULIUS FREDERIC WOLFF, JR.

In Partial Fulfillment of the Requirements

For The

Degree of

DOCTOR OF PHILOSOPHY

JULY

1949

Example 418

Wolff, Julius Frederic, 1918-
    Minnesota conservation, or, Resource manage-
ment in Minnesota [microform] / by Julius Frederic
Wolff, Jr. -- 1949.
    x, 500 leaves ; 28 cm.

    Typescript (carbon copy).
    Thesis (Ph.D.)--University of Minnesota,
1949.
    Bibliography: leaves 472-493.
    Microfilm. [Saint Paul, Minn. : Minnesota
Historical Society, 1974]. 1 microfilm reel ; 35
mm.

    I. Title. II. Title: Minnesota conservation.
III. Title: Resource management in Minnesota.

```
Type: a Bib lvl: m Govt pub:    Lang: eng Source: d illus:
Repr: a Enc lvl: I Conf pub: 0 Ctry: mnu Dat tp: r M/F/B: 10
Indx: 0 Mod rec:    Festschr:    Cont: b
Desc: a Int lvl:    Dates: 1974,1949
```

```
        010
        040     XXX $c XXX
        007     h $b d $d a $e f $f u--- $g b $h u $i c $j u
        043     n-us-an
        090
        049     XXXX
        100 10 Wolff, Julius Frederic, $d 1918-
        245 10 Minnesota conservation, or, Resource manage-
ment in Minnesota $h microform / $c by Julius Frederic
Wolff, Jr.
        260 0  [Saint Paul, Minn. : $b Minnesota Historical
Society, $c 1974].
        300     1 microfilm reel ; $c 35 mm.
        504     Bibliography: leaves 472-493.
        500     Microreproduction of: 1949. x, 500 leaves ;
28 cm. Typescript (carbon copy). Thesis (Ph.D.)--Univer-
sity of Minnesota, 1949.
```

Example 419

```
Wolff, Julius Frederic, 1918-
     Minnesota conservation, or, Resource man-
agement in Minnesota [microform] / by Julius
Frederic Wolff, Jr. -- [Saint Paul, Minn. :
Minnesota Historical Society, 1974].
     1 microfilm reel ; 35 mm.

     Title from 1st frame.
     Bibliography: leaves 472-493.
     Microreproduction of: 1949. x, 500 leaves ;
28 cm. Typescript (carbon copy). Thesis (Ph.D.)
--University of Minnesota, 1949.
     Microfilm.


     I. Title.  II. Title: Minnesota conserva-
tion.  III. Title: Resource management in Minne-
sota.
```

```
Type: a Bib lvl: m Govt pub:    Lang: eng Source: d illus:
Repr:    Enc lvl: I Conf pub: 0 Ctry: mnu Dat tp: r M/F/B: 10
Indx: 0 Mod rec:    Festschr: 0 Cont: b
Desc: a Int lvl:    Dates: 1974,1949

    010
    040     XXX $c XXX
    007     h $b d $d a $e f $f u--- $g b $h u $i c $j u
    043     n-us-an
    090
    049     XXXX
    100 10  Wolff, Julius Frederic, $d 1918-
    245 10  Minnesota conservation, or, Resource manage-
ment in Minnesota $h microform / $c by Julius Frederic
Wolff, Jr.
    260 1   $c 1949.
    300     x, 500 leaves ; $c 28 cm.
    500     Typescript (carbon copy).
    502     Thesis (Ph.D.)--University of Minnesota,
1949.
    540     Bibliography: leaves 472-493.
    533     Microreproduction: $b [Saint Paul, Minn. :
$c Minnesota Historical Society, $d 1974]. $e 1 micro-
film reel ; 35 mm.
```

922.273   Seton, Elizabeth Ann, Mother, 1774.   BX 4705
Melville, Annabelle (McConnell) 1910.   [Card 1 (of 11) numb 1. i-ix, 1-25]
. . . The life of Elizabeth Bayley Seton, 1774-1821 . . . Washington, D. C.,
The Catholic Univ. of America [c.] 1949. (ix, 477 numb. l. 28cm. (Catholic Univ. of America. Studies
in American church history, v. 39) Thesis (Ph.D.)–Catholic Univ. of America.   Bibliography: numb.
l. 468-477.

Example 421

Melville, Annabelle M. (Annabelle McConnell),
     1910-
     The life of Elizabeth Bayley Seton, 1774-1821
[microform] / Melville, Annabelle McConnell. --
Washington, D.C. : Catholic Univ. of America,
1949.
     11 microopaques ; 8 x 13 cm. -- (Studies in
American church history / Catholic University of
America ; v. 39)

     Bibliography: leaves 468-477.
     Micro Card Fo-49 5629--Fo-49 5639.
     Microreproduction of: 1949. ix, 477 leaves ;
28 cm. Typescript. Thesis (Ph.D.)--Catholic University of America, 1949.

     I. Title.   II. Series: Studies in American
church history (Catholic University of America) ;
v. 39.

Example 422

Melville, Annabelle M. (Annabelle McConnell),
      1910-
      The life of Elizabeth Bayley Seton, 1774-1821
[microform] / by Annabelle M. Melville. -- 1949.
      ix, 477 leaves ; 28 cm.

      Typescript.
      Thesis (Ph.D.)--Catholic University of Amer-
ica, 1949.
      Bibliography: leaves 468-477.
      Microopaque. Washington, D.C.: Catholic Univ.
of America, 1949. 11 microopaques ; 8 x 13 cm.
(Studies in American church history / Catholic
University of America ; v. 39). Micro Card Fo-49
5629--Fo-49 5639.

      I. Title. II. Series: Studies in American
church history (Catholic University of America) ;
v. 39.

Type: a Bib lvl: m Govt pub: Lang: eng Source: d illus:
Repr: c Enc lvl: I Conf pub: 0 Ctry: dcu Dat tp: r M/F/B: 10b
Indx: 0 Mod rec: Festschr: 0 Cont:
Desc: a Int lvl: Dates: 1949,1949

      010
      040   XXX $c XXX
      007   h $b g $c r $d a $e l $f u--- $g b $h u $i c
$j u
      090
      049   XXXX
      100 10 Melville, Annabelle M.
      245 14 The life of Elizabeth Bayley Seton, 1774-
1821 $h microform / $c by Annabelle M. Melville.
      260 0 Washington, D.C. : $b Catholic Univsity of
America, $c 1949 $e ([Middletown, Conn.] : $f Micro-
card).
      300   11 microopaques ; $c 8 x 13 cm.
      490 0 Studies in American church history / Catho-
lic University of America ; $v v. 39
      504   Includes Bibliography.
      500   Micro Card Fo-49 5629--Fo-49 5639.
      500   Microreproduction of typescript: 1949. ix,
477 leaves ; 28 cm. Thesis (Ph.D.)--Catholic University
of America, 1949.

929.2 Bucklin family CS71
Cooper, Hattie B. comp. [Card 1 (of 2)—p. [3], 1-23]
[*Bucklin Fam.*] Squire Bucklin of Foster, R.I. His ancestors back to
William Hingham Buckland of Hingham, Mass., 1635, and his descendants.
[Roxbury, Mass.] 1944. *[iii] 45, 5, [2], 3 p. plate, drawing, 27cm.
Typewritten manuscript. Bracketed title entry is key abbrev. of Amer. Gen.
Index.*

GL-57
1071
MICRO CARD

Example 423

Cooper, Hattie B. (Hattie Bartlett), 1862-
     Squire Bucklin of Foster, R.I. [microform] :
his ancestors back to William Hingham Buckland of
Hingham, Mass., 1635, and his descendants, Buckland, Bucklen, Bucklin, Bucklyn / compiled by
Hattie B. Cooper. -- 1944.
     45, 5 leaves : ill. ; 28 cm.

     Typescript.
     Microopaque. [United States] : Micro Card,
[1957]. 2 microopaques ; 8 x 12 cm. At head of
title: Bucklin fam. Publisher's no.: GL-57 1071--
GL-57 1072. Includes: Additions and corrections to
the manuscript history of the Bucklin family filed
by Hattie B. Cooper/ [C.A. Bucklin]. 1946. 3
leaves ; 28 cm.

     I. Bucklin, C.A. (Clyde A.). Additions and
corrections to the manuscript history of the
Bucklin family filed by Hattie B. Cooper. 1957.
II. Title.

Example 424

Cooper, Hattie B. (Hattie Bartlett), 1862-
     Squire Bucklin of Foster, R.I. [microform] :
his ancestors back to William Hingham Buckland of
Hingham, Mass., 1635, and his descendants, Cooper,
Hattie B., comp. -- [United States] : Micro Card,
[1957].
     2 microopaques : ill. ; 8 x 12 cm.

     Title from header.
     At head of title: Bucklin fam.
     Includes: Additions and corrections to the
manuscript history of the Bucklin family filed by
Hattie B. Cooper/ [C.A. Bucklin]. 1946. 3 leaves ;
28 cm.
     Publisher's no.: GL-57 1071--GL-57 1072.
     Microreproduction of: 1944. 45, 5 leaves, 28
cm. Typescript.

     I. Bucklin, C.A. (Clyde A.). Additions and
corrections to the manuscript history of the
Bucklin family filed by Hattie B. Cooper. 1957.
II. Title.

[Title page]

Medical Student Financing and
the Armed Forces Health
Professions Scholarship Program

Victoria Daubert, Daniel Relles, Charles Roll, Jr.

January 1982

Prepared for the
Office of the Assistant Secretary of Defense/Health Affairs

Rand
Santa Monica, CA 90406

[Microfiche header]

ED 220 004   MEDICAL STUDENT FINANCING AND THE
              ARMED FORCES HEALTH PROFESSIONS
              SCHOLARSHIP PROGRAM
              DAUBERT, VICTORIA, AND OTHERS
              RAND CORP., SANTA MONICA, CALIF.
              JAN 82

Example 425

Daubert, Victoria.
    Medical student financing and the Armed
Forces Health Professions Scholarship Program
[microform] / Victoria Daubert, Daniel Relles,
Charles Roll, Jr. -- Santa Monica, CA : Rand,
[1982].
    ix, 88 p. ; 28 cm.

    Microfiche. [Arlington? Va.] : ERIC, 1983. 1
microfiche ; 11 x 15 cm. "ED 220 004."
    Final report. 1977-1978
    Sponsored by the Office of the Assistant
Secretary of Defense for Health Affairs. MDA-903-
77-C-0273.

    Summary: The impact of the Health Professions
Educational Assistance Act of 1976 (P.L. 94-484)
was assessed. The 1977 survey of a sample of first
and second year medical students evaluated their
preferences regarding alternative medical education financing methods. Attention is directed to
implications of the results for current and future
anticipated changes in AFHPSP participation, given
no program changes, and cost-effective program
changes to attain a goal of about 1,200 physicians
per year.
    "R-2414-HA."

    I. Relles, Daniel, 1943- II. Roll, Charles.
III. Rand Corporation. IV. United States. Office
of the Assistant Secretary of Defense for Health
Affairs. V. Title.

```
Type: a Bib lvl: m Govt pub:    Lang: eng Source: d Illus:
Repr: b Enc lvl: I Conf pub: 0 Ctry: vau Dat tp: r M/F/B: 10
Indx: 0 Mod rec:    Festschr: 0 Cont: t
Desc: a Int lvl:    Dates: 1983,1982
     010
     040     XXX $c XXX
     007     h $b e $d a $e m $f c042 $g b $h u $i c $j u
     037     ED 220004 $b ERIC $f microfiche $c $0.97
     088     R-2414-HA
     090
     049     XXXX
     100 10 Daubert, Victoria. $u Rand Corp.
     245 10 Medical student financing and the Armed
Forces Health Professions Scholarship Program $h micro-
form / Victoria Daubert, Daniel Relles, Charles Roll,
Jr.
     260 0   Santa Monica, CA : $b Rand, $c [1982].
     300     ix, 88 p. ; $c 28 cm.
     302     90
     533     Microfiche. $b [Arlington? Va.] : $c ERIC,
$d 1983. $e 1 microfiche ; 11 x 15 cm. "ED 220 004."
     513     Final report. $b 1977-1978
     536     Sponsored by the Office of the Assistant
Secretary of Defense for Health affairs. $b MDA-903-77-
C-0273.
     520     The impact of the Health Professions Educa-
tional Assistance Act of 1976 (P.L. 94-484) was as-
sessed. The 1977 survey of a sample of first and second
year medical students evaluated their preferences re-
garding alternative medical education financing methods.
Attention is directed to implications of the results for
current and future anticipated changes in AFHPSP par-
ticipation, given no program changes, and cost-effective
program changes to attain a goal of about 1,200 physi-
cians per year.
     500     "R-2414-HA."
     700 10 Relles, Daniel, $d $u Rand Corp.
     700 10 Roll, Charles. $u Rand Corp.
     710 20 Rand Corporation. $u Santa Monica, CA $4 org
```

```
     710 10 United States. $b Office of the Assistant
Secretary of Defense for Health Affairs. $4 fnd
     776 0   Daubert, Victoria. $t Medical student fi-
nancing and the Armed Forces Health Professions Schol-
arship Program $c (paper copy) $w (OCoLC)nnnnnnn
```

"What brings so many Irish to America!"

A Pamphlet

WRITTEN BY HIBERNICUS:

one part of which
Explains the Many Causes
of
IRISH EMIGRATION;

the other

The consistency or Inconsistency
of
Native Americanisms ...

Published for the author

New York, February 5, 1945

Example 426

Hibernicus.
    "What brings so many Irish to America!"
[microform] : a pamphlet, one part of which explains the many causes of Irish emigration, the
other the consistency or inconsistency of "native
Americanism" as it is / by Hibernicus.
-- New York : Published for the author, 1845.
    78 p. ; 22 cm.

    Microfilm. [New Haven, Conn.] : Yale Univer-
sity Library, Photographic Service, 1954. on 1
microfilm reel : negative ; 35 mm. No. 8 in a
microfilm collection with title: Catholic pamphlets.

    I. Title.

Example 427

Hibernicus.
    "What brings so many Irish to America!" [mi-
croform] : a pamphlet, one part of which explains
the many causes of Irish emigration, the other the
consistency or inconsistency of "native Americanism" as it is / by Hibernicus. -- [New Haven,
Conn.] : Yale University Library, Photographic
Service, 1954.
    on 1 microfilm reel : negative ; 35 mm.

    Title from first frame of item.
    No. 8 in a microfilm collection with title:
Catholic pamphlets.
    Microreproduction of original published: New
York : Published for the author, 1845. 78 p. ; 22
cm.

    I. Title.

Example 428

```
AD 696 200    DEFENSE DOCUMENTATION CENTER
              ALEXANDRIA VA
              MACHINE-AIDED INDEXING. (U)
              KLINGBIEL, PAUL N. ;
              JUN 69  DOC-TR-69-1
UNCLASSIFIED                     FLD/6P 5/2  NL
```

Klingbiel, Paul H.
   Machine-aided indexing [microform] : technical progress report for period January 1967-June 1969 / Paul H. Klingbiel (Directorate of Development). -- Alexandria, Va. : Defense Documentation Center, [1969].
   v, 24 p. : ill. : 28 cm.

   Microfiche. Springfield, Va. : Clearinghouse for Federal Scientific & Technical Information, [1969]. 1 microfiche, negative ; 11 x 15 cm. "AD 696 200."
   "June 1969."
   Progress report. Jan. 1967-June 1969.
   Sponsored by U.S. Office of Naval Research.
   Later report issued as: DDC-TR-71-3.

   Summary: A partial syntactic analysis is used to detect words and phrases in contexts that make them useful for indexing purposes. At least 500,000 words of text will be processed to obtain statistics to determine whether the system is competitive with manual indexing.
   Includes references.
   "DDC-TR-69-1."

   I. Defense Documentation Center (U.S.). II. United States. Office of Naval Research. III. Title.

```
Type: a Bib lvl: m Govt pub: f Lang: eng Source: d Illus: a
Repr: b Enc lvl: I Conf pub: 0 Ctry: vau Dat tp: r M/F/B: 10
Indx: 0 Mod rec:    Festschr: 0 Cont: t
Desc: a Int lvl:    Dates: 1969,1969
     010
     040    XXX $c XXX
     007    h $b e $d b $e m $f c042 $g b $h u $i c $j u
     037    AD 696 200 $b Clearinghouse for Federal
Scientific and Technical Information $f microfiche
     088    DDC-TR-69-1
     090
     049    XXXX
     100 10 Klingbiel, Paul H. $u Defense Documentation
Center $4 org
     245 10 Machine-aided indexing $h microform : $b
technical progress report for period January 1967-June
1969 / $c Paul H. Klingbiel (Directorate of Develop-
ment).
     260 0  Alexandria, Va. : $b Defense Documentation
Center, $c [1969].
     300    v, 24 p. : $b ill. ; $c 28 cm.
     302    28
     533    Microfiche. $b Springfield, Va. : $c Clear-
inghouse for Federal Scientific & Technical Information,
$d [1969]. $e 1 microfiche, negative ; 11 x 15 cm. "AD
696 200."
     500    "June 1969."
     513    Progress report. $b Jan. 1967-June 1969.
     536    Sponsored by U.S. Office of Naval Research.
     580    Later report issued as: DDC-TR-71-3.
     520    A partial syntactic analysis is used to
detect words and phrases in contexts that make them
useful for indexing purposes. At least 500,000 words of
text will be processed to obtain statistics to determine
whether the system is competitive with manual indexing.
     504    Includes references. $b 5
     500    "DDC-TR-69-1."
```

```
     710 20 Defense Documentation Center (U.S.). $b
Alexandria, Va. $4 org
     710 10 United States. $b Office of Naval Research.
$4 fnd
     776 1  Klingbiel, Paul H. $t Machine-aided indexing
$g (June 1969) $c (hard copy) $r DDC-TR-69-1 $w
(OCoLC)nnnnnnn
     785 13 $r DDC-TR-71-3 $g Mar. 1971
```

AD 721 875   DEFENSE DOCUMENTATION CENTER
              ALEXANDRIA VA
              MACHINE-AIDED INDEXING. (U)
              KLINGBIEL, PAUL N. ;
              MAR 71 DDC-TR-71-3
UNCLASSIFIED   FLD/6P 5/2 NL

Example 429

Klingbiel, Paul H.
    Machine-aided indexing [microform] : techni-
cal progress report for period July 1969-June 1970
/ Paul H. Klingbiel (Directorate of Development).
-- Alexandria, Va. : Defense Documentation Center,
[1971].
    iii, 152 : ill. ; 28 cm.

    Microfiche. Springfield, Va. : National Tech-
nical Information Service, [1971]. 3 microfiches,
negative ; 11 x 15 cm. "AD 721 875."
    "March 1971."
    Progress report. July 1969-June 1970.
    Sponsored by U.S. Office of Naval Research.
    Earlier report issued as: DDC-TR-69-1.

    Summary: Progress is reported on the develop-
ment of a partial syntactic analysis technique for
indexing text. Although over 500,000 words of text
have been indexed, this report is limited to the
analysis of results at the 115,000 word level.
    Includes references.
    "DDC-TR-71-3."

    I. Defense Documentation Center (U.S.). II.
United States. Office of Naval Research. III.
Title.

```
Type: a Bib lvl: m Govt pub: f Lang: eng Source: d Illus: a
Repr: b Enc lvl: I Conf pub: 0 Ctry: vau Dat tp: r M/F/B: 10
Indx: 0 Mod rec:    Festschr: 0 Cont: t
Desc: a Int lvl:    Dates: 1971,1971
    010
    040    XXX $c XXX
    007    h $b e $d b $e m $f c042 $g b $h u $i c $j u
    037    AD 696 200 $b National Technical Information
Service $f microfiche
    088    DDC-TR-71-3
    090
    049    XXXX
    100 10 Klingbiel, Paul H. $u Defense Documentation
Center $4 org
    245 10 Machine-aided indexing $h microform : $b
technical progress report for period July 1969-June 1970
/ $c Paul H. Klingbiel (Directorate of Development).
    260 0  Alexandria, Va. : $b Defense Documentation
Center, $c [1971].
    300    iii, 152 ; $c 28 cm.
    302    148
    533    Microfiche. $b Springfield, Va. : $c Na-
tional Technical Information Service, $d [1971]. $e 3
microfiches, negative ; 11 x 15 cm. "AD 721 875."
    500    "March 1971."
    513    Progress report. $b July 1969-June 1970.
    536    Sponsored by U.S. Office of Naval Research.
    580    Later report issued as: DDC-TR-69-1.
    520    Progress is reported on the development of a
partial syntactic analysis technique for indexing text.
Although over 500,000 words of text have been indexed,
this report is limited to the analysis of results at the
115,000 word level.
    504    Includes references. $b 12
    500    "DDC-TR-71-3."
```

```
    710 20 Defense Documentation Center (U.S.). $b
Alexandria, Va. $4 org
    710 10 United States. $b Office of Naval Research.
$4 fnd
    776 1  Klingbiel, Paul H. $t Machine-aided indexing
$g (Mar. 1971) $c (hard copy) $r DDC-TR-71-3 $w
(OCoLC)nnnnnnn
    785 13 $r DDC-TR-69-1 $g Mar. 1969
```

```
Minnesota Post Offices
Aabye, Norman Co. 1776
Aarhus, Lac Qui Parle Co. 2534
Aastad, Otter Tail Co. and Grant Co. 1522
Abel, Hennepin Co. 1257
Acoma, McLeod Co.   2200
Acton, Meeker Co.   417
Ada, Norman Co. (late
Macdonaldville, Polk Co.) 1210
Adair, Freeborn Co. 2159
1
```

```
Minnesota Post Offices
Zumbro, Olsted Co. 253
Zumbro Falls, Wabasha Co. 429
Zumbrota, Goodhue Co. 352
Zuzu, Cass Co. 2473

434
```

```
Post Offices               Minnesota

Fort Snelling, Hennepin Co. (late Dubuque Co.,
Wis.)
Established May 9, 1828.
Elias T. Laugham, first P.M.
1
```

```
Post Offices               Minnesota

Redore, St. Louis Co.
Established Nov. 26, 1917.
Daniel F. Ryan, first P.M.
3369
```

INDEX OF MINNESOTA POST OFFICES

Compiled by Newton D. Mereness

Microfilm made for original card file

in the Minnesota Historical Society

Example 430

```
Mereness, Newton D. (Newton Dennison).
    Minnesota post offices [manuscript]. -- [ca.
1917-1921].
    434, 3369 cards ; 8 x 13 cm.

    Typescript.
    Title from index cards.
    Compiled by Newton D. Mereness.
    Summary: Consists of 434 index cards with
names of post offices in alphabetical order refer-
ring to the 3369 cards for individual post offices
that are arranged chronologically by date estab-
lished. Cards for individual post offices include
name of post office, county of location, date
established, and name of first postmaster.


    I. Title.


D:    4.7B3; 4.7B17
ME:   21.4A; 22.16
AE:   21.30J
```

Example 431

```
Mereness, Newton D. (Newton Dennison).
    Index of Minnesota post offices [microform].
/ compiled by Newton D. Mereness. -- [St. Paul,
Minn. : Minnesota Historical Society, 1974].
    1 microfilm reel ; 35 mm. -- (A Minnesota
Historical Society microfilm publication)

    "Microfilm made from original card file in
the Minnesota Historical Society."
    Summary: Consists of 434 index cards with
names of post offices in alphabetical order refer-
ring to the 3369 cards for individual post offices
that are arranged chronologically by date estab-
lished. Cards for individual post offices include
name of post office, county of location, date
established, and name of first postmaster.
    Microreproduction of: Minnesota post offices.
[ca. 1917-1921]. 434, 3369 cards ; 8 x 13 cm.
Typescript.


    I. Title.


D:    11.4D; 11.5D4; 11.6B1; 11.7B
ME:   21.4A; 22.16
```

Example 432

Standard Bibliographic Microfilm Target

Section I

Author(s) _Henry Hastings Sibley_____ Date(s) _1811-1891_

Title _Henry Hastings Sibley Papers_____

Publisher, if a book _____

Publication date(s) _1815-1930___ Volume of material _15 linear ft._
or period covered

Holder of original material _Minnesota Historical Society___

Bibliographic references_____

External finding aids _Manuscript Microfilm Publications Guide_

Restrictions, if any, on use_____

Editor and publisher of microfilm edition _Jane Spector Davis, Ed._

Holder of master negative _Minnesota Historical Society___

Section II

Producing laboratory _Dakota Microfilm Service_ Date _June, 1968_

Film size:35mm(✓) 16mm( )   Reduction ratio:14X( ) 20x( ) 12x(✓)

Image placement: IA( ) IIA( ) IIB(✓) Duplex( ) Duo( )

Note that this form is to be used for books, manuscripts, records,
periodicals, and newspapers interchangeably.

Sibley, Henry Hastings, 1811-1891.
    Henry Hastings Sibley papers [microform] /
Jane Spector Davis, editor. -- [St. Paul, Minn.]
: Minnesota Historical Society, 1968.
    32 microfilm reels ; 35 mm. (A Minnesota
Historical Society microfilm publication)

    Fur trader, politician, territorial delegate
to Congress (1849-1853), governor of Minnesota
(1858-1860), and businessman. Correspondence and
miscellaneous papers, undated and 1815-1899;
records of the Grasshopper Relief Committee,
1873-1874; fur trade records; 1823-1855; Fort
Snelling sutler store records, 1836-1839; letter
books, 1849-1859; and miscellaneous records,
1836-1930, all in the Minnesota Historical Society. Also included are letters loaned by the
Burton Historical Collection of the Detroit Public Library, letters and other materials loaned
by the Sibley House Association, and translations
of letters from Joseph N. Nicollet, Joseph
Laframboise, and other fur traders.
    Low reduction.
    Partial calendar of the papers for the years
1815-1890 and an alphabetical list of correspondents available in the Minnesota Historical Society.
    Described in: Guide to a microfilm edition of
the Henry Hastings Sibley papers / Jane Spector
Davis. St. Paul : Minnesota Historical Society,
1968.
    Also available in negative microfilm.

Microreproduction of: Papers / Henry Hastings
Sibley. 1815-1930. 15 ft. Gift of the Sibley
family, 1893-1955, and gifts of other donors and
purchases, 1869-1967.

I. Davis, Jane Spector.   II. Title.

Example 433

Sibley, Henry Hastings, 1811-1891.
    Papers [microform] / Henry Hastings Sibley.
-- 1815-1930.
    15 ft.

Fur trader, politician, territorial delegate
to Congress (1849-1853), governor of Minnesota
(1858-1860), and businessman. Correspondence and
miscellaneous papers, undated and 1815-1899;
records of the Grasshopper Relief Committee, 1873-
1874; fur trade records; 1823-1855; Fort Snelling
sutler store records, 1836-1839; letter books,
1849-1859; and miscellaneous records, 1836-1930.
    Gift of the Sibley family, 1893-1955, and
gifts of other donors and purchases, 1869-1967.
    Partial calendar of the papers for the years
1815-1890 and an alphabetical list of correspondents available in the repository.
    Microfilm. [St. Paul, Minn.] : Minnesota
Historical Society, 1968. 32 microfilm reels ; 35
mm. (A Minnesota Historical Society microfilm
publication). Also included are letters loaned by

the Burton Historical Collection of the Detroit
Public Library, letters and other materials loaned
by the Sibley House Association, and translations
of letters from Joseph N. Nicollet, Joseph Laframboise, and other fur traders. Jane Spector Davis.
Also available in negative microfilm.

    I. Davis, Jane Spector.

Additional added access points could be made for the various
correspondents, etc.,

Photographs by the Wright Brothers

Prints from the Glass Negatives in the Library of Congress

A Micropublication Commemorating the Seventy-fifth Anniversary of the First Flight by the Wright Brothers, December 17, 1903

Library of Congress Washington 1978

1D3 Orville Wright aloft, Kitty Hawk, Oct. 1911
LC–USZ62–66609

Library of Congress Cataloging in Publication Data

Wright, Wilbur, 1867–1912.
Photographs by the Wright Brothers.

Reproduced from the collection in the Prints and Photographs Division at the Library of Congress.

1. Aeronautics—United States—History—Pictorial works. 2. Wright, Wilbur, 1867–1912. 3. Wright, Orville, 1871–1948. I. Wright, Orville, 1871–1948, joint author. II. United States. Library of Congress. Prints and Photographs Division. III. Title. Microfiche TL521 629.13′0092′4 78–606137 ISBN 0–8444–0266–4

Cover

1B10 Starting Orville Wright in glider, Oct. 10, 1902. Wilbur Wright at left, Dan Tate at right.
LC–USZ62–56227.

For sale by the Superintendent of Documents,
U.S. Government Printing Office, Washington, D.C. 20402
Stock Number 030–014–00003–1

☆ U.S. GOVERNMENT PRINTING OFFICE : 1978 O—275–332

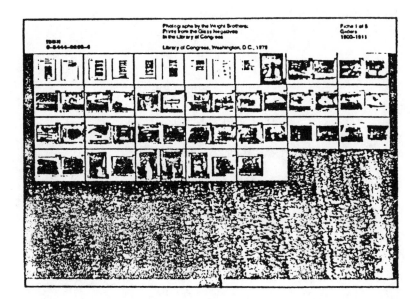

Example 434

Wright, Wilbur, 1867-1912.
    Photographs by the Wright brothers [micro-
form] : prints from the glass negatives in the
Library of Congress. -- Washington, D.C. : Library
of Congress , 1978.
    5 microfiches (162 fr.) : chiefly ill. ; 11 x
15 cm. + 1 pamphlet (20 p. : ill. ; 19 cm.)

    "A micropublication commemorating the sev-
enty-fifth anniversary of the first flight by the
Wright brothers, December 17, 1903."
    Reproduction of 301 photographs and other
items in the collection of the Prints and Photographs Division of the Library of Congress.
    Contents: fiche 1. Gliders, 1900-1911 --
fiche 2. Powered flights, 1903-1915 -- fiche 3.
Portraits and informal photographs -- fiche 4.
Kitty Hawk and other locales -- fiche 5. Memora-
bilia.
    ISBN 0-8444-0266-4.

    I. Wright, Orville, 1871-1948. II. Library
of Congress. III. Library of Congress. Prints and
Photographs Division. IV. Title.

LINDAU, RUDOLPH

OUR LITTLE WORLD

TRANSLATED FROM THE
GERMAN BY
CORNELIA DAY WILDER

Example 435

Lindau, Rudolf, 1829-1910.
    [Die kleine Welt. English]
    Our little world [microform] / translated
from the German of Rudolph Lindau by Cornelia Day
Wilder. -- St. Paul : Price, McGill & Co., 1889.
    149 p. ; 17 cm.

    Translation of: Die kleine Welt.
    Microfilm. [Saint Paul, Minn.] : Minnesota
Historical Society, [1973?]. 1 microfilm reel ; 35
mm. (A Minnesota Historical Society microfilm
publication)

    I. Wilder, Cornelia Day, 1868-1903. II.
Title.

Example 436

Lindau, Rudolf, 1829-1910.
    [Die kleine Welt. English]
    Our little world [microform] / Lindau, Rudolf
; translated from the German by Cornelia Day
Wilder. -- [St. Paul, Minn.] : Minnesota Historical Society, [1973?].
    1 microfilm reel ; 35 mm. -- (A Minnesota
Historical Society microfilm publication)

    Translation of: Die kleine Welt.
    Microreproduction of: St. Paul: Price, McGill
& Co., 1889. 149 p. ; 17 cm.

    I. Wilder, Cornelia Day, 1868-1903. II.
Title.

Woolf, B.E.
Off to the War

Boston
1861

Matthews, B.

This Picture and That

New York
1894

Triplet, J.
A Supper in Dixie

New York
1865

FILM MADE BY
THE NEW YORK
PUBLIC LIBRARY
RATIO 15 1963

Example 437

Woolf, Benjamin Edward, 1836-1901.
    Off to the war! [microform] : an original
farce for the times in one act / by Benjamin
Edward Woolf. -- Boston : W.V. Spencer, 1861.
    23 p. ; 20 cm.

    On cover: Spencer's Boston theatre.
    Microfilm. [New York, N.Y.] : New York Public
Library, 1963. 1 microfilm reel ; 35 mm. Low re-
duction. With: This picture and that / by Brander
Matthews ; A supper in Dixie / by James Triplet.

    I. Title.

Example 438

Woolf, Benjamin Edward, 1836-1901.
    Off to the war! [microform] / Woolf, B.E.
-- [New York, N.Y.] : New York Public Library,
1963.
    1 microfilm reel ; 35 mm.

    Low reduction.
    With: This picture and that / Matthews,
B. ; A supper in Dixie / Triplet, J.
    Microreproduction of: Boston : W.V. Spencer,
1861. 23 p. ; 20 cm. On cover: Spencer's Boston
theatre.

    I. Title.

Example 439

Matthews, Brander, 1852-1929.
    This picture and that [microform] : a comedy
/ by Brander Matthews. -- New York : Harper, 1894.
    76 p. : ill. ; 14 cm.

    Microfilm. [New York, N.Y.] : New York Public
Library, 1963. on 1 microfilm reel ; 35 mm. Low
reduction. With: Off to the war! / by Benjamin
Edward Woolf.

    I. Title.

Example 440

Matthews, Brander, 1852-1929.
    This picture and that [microform] : a comedy
/ Matthews, B. -- [New York, N.Y.] : New York
Public Library, 1963.
    on 1 microfilm reel ; ill. 35 mm.

    Low reduction.
    With: Off to the war! / Woolf, B.E.
    Microreproduction of: New York : Harper,
1894. 76 p. ; 14 cm.

Example 441

Triplet, James.
    A supper in Dixie [microform] : a farce in
one act / by James Triplet. -- Acting ed. -- New
York : S. French, 1865.
    16 p. ; 19 cm. -- (French's minor drama ; no.
296)

    Microfilm. [New York, N.Y.] : New York Public
Library, 1963. on 1 microfilm reel ; 35 mm. Low
reduction. With: Off to the war! / by Benjamin
Edward Woolf.

    I. Title. II. Series.

Example 442

Triplet, James.
    A supper in Dixie [microform] / Triplet, J.
-- [New York, N.Y.] : New York Public Library,
1963.
    on 1 microfilm reel ; 35 mm.

    Low reduction.
    With: Off to the war! / Woolf, B.E.
    Microreproduction of: Acting ed. -- New York
: S. French, 1865. 16 p. ; 19 cm. -- (French's
minor drama ; no. 296)

    I. Title. II. Series: French's minor drama ;
no. 296.

Example 443

These examples could also be cataloged as a unit:

Woolf, Benjamin Edward, 1836-1901.
    Off to the war! / Woolf, B.E. This picture
and that / Matthews, B. ; A supper in Dixie /
Triplet, J. [microform]. -- [New York, N.Y.] : New
York Public Library, 1963.
    1 microfilm reel : ill. ; 35 mm.

    Low reduction.
    Microreproduction of: Off to the war! : an
original farce for the times in one act / by
Benjamin Edward Woolf. Boston : W.V. Spencer,
1861. 23 p. ; 20 cm. On cover: Spencer's Boston
theatre ; This picture and that : a comedy / by
Brander Matthews. New York : Harper, 1894. 76 p. ;
14 cm. ; and, A supper in Dixie : a farce in one
act / by James Triplet. Acting ed. New York : S.
French, 1865. 16 p. ; 19 cm. (French's minor drama
; no. 296).

    I. Matthews, Brander, 1852-1929. This picture
and that. 1963. II. Triplet, James. A supper in
Dixie. 1963. III. Title: Off to the war! IV.
Title: This picture and that. V. Title: A supper
in Dixie.

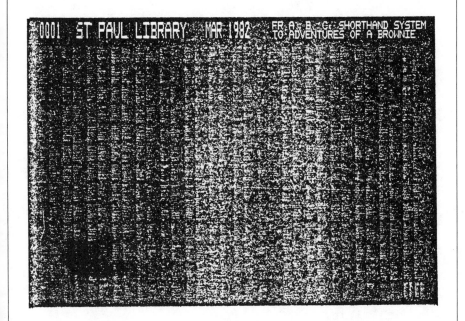

Example 444

Treated as an individual publication:

```
Saint Paul Public Library.
    St. Paul Library [microform] : [catalog].
-- Mar. 1982. -- [Saint Paul, Minn. : Saint Paul
Public Library], 1982 (Monterey Park, Calif. :
Autographics, Inc.)
    126 microfiches ; 11 x 15 cm.

    Title from header.


    I. Title.
```

Example 445

Treated as a serial publication:

```
Saint Paul Public Library.
    St. Paul Library [microform] : [catalog].
-- [Jan. 1981]-    .  -- [Saint Paul, Minn. :
Saint Paul Public Library, 1981-   (Monterey Park,
Calif. : Autographics, Inc.)
        microfiches ; 11 x 15 cm.

    Quarterly (somewhat irregular).
    Title from header.
    Each issue supersedes the previous one.


    I. Title.
```

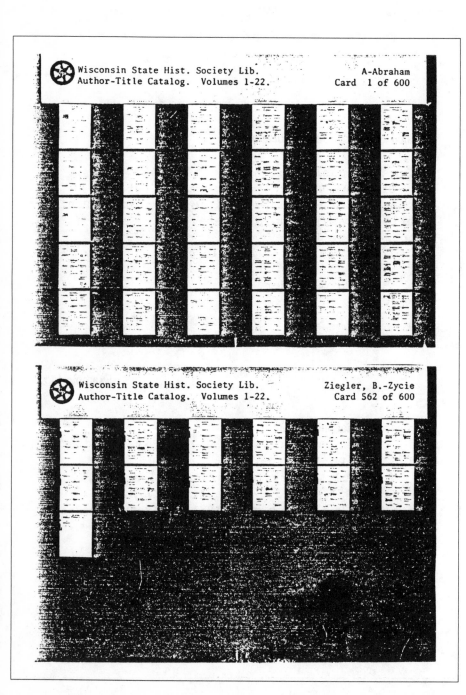

Example 446

State Historical Society of Wisconsin. Library.
     Author-title catalog, volumes 1-22 [micro-
form] / Wisconsin State Hist. Society Lib. --
[Westport, Conn.] : G[reenwood] P[ress,
197-].
     on 562 microfiches of 600 ; 11 x 15 cm.

     Microreproduction of the library's card cata-
log.
     With: City directory catalog / Wisconsin
State Hist. Society Lib. ; Atlas catalog (Publishers) / Wisconsin State Hist. Society Lib. ; Atlas
catalog (Geographic) / Wisconsin State Hist.
Society Lib. ; Newspaper catalog / Wisconsin State
Hist. Society Lib. ; and, Newspaper catalog (Labor) / Wisconsin State Hist. Society Lib.

     I. Title.

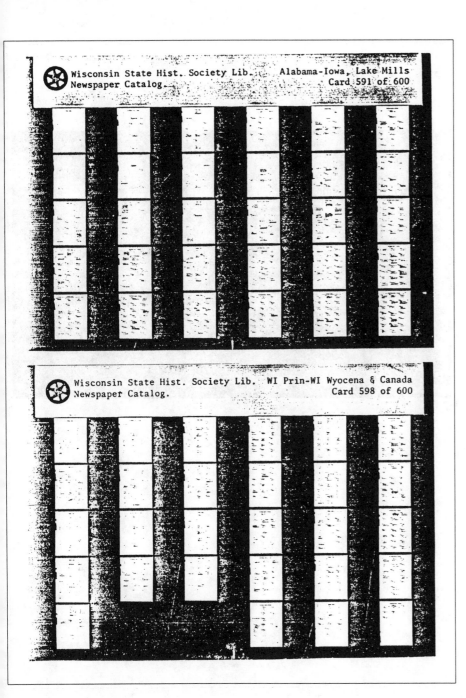

Example 447

State Historical Society of Wisconsin. Library.
     Newspaper catalog [microform] / Wisconsin
State Hist. Society Lib. -- [Westport, Conn.] :
G[reenwood] P[ress, 197-].
     on 8 microfiches of 600 ; 11 x 15 cm.

     Microreproduction of the library's card cata-
log.
     With: Author-title catalog, volumes 1-22 /
Wisconsin State Hist. Society Lib.

     I. Title.

Example 448

```
Oberlin College. Library.
    A classified catalogue of the collection of
anti-slavery propaganda in the Oberlin College
Library [microform] / compiled by Geraldine
Hopkins Hubbard ; edited by Julian S. Fowler. --
[Oberlin, Ohio : The Library], 1932.
    x, 84 p. ; 26 cm. -- (Oberlin College Library
bulletin ; v. 2, no. 3)

    Microfiche. Louisville : Lost Cause Press,
1966. 3 microfiches : negative ; 8 x 13 cm. LCP
24,722.


    I. Hubbard, Geraldine Hopkins.  II. Fowler,
Julian S.  III. Title.  IV. Series.
```

Example 449

```
Oberlin College. Library.
    A classified catalogue of the collection of
anti-slavery propaganda in the Oberlin College
Library [microform]. Louisville : Lost Cause
Press, 1966.
    3 microfiches : negative ; 8 x 13 cm.

    Publisher's no. LCP 24,722.
    Microreproduction of: Compiled by Geraldine
Hopkins Hubbard ; edited by Julian S. Fowler.
[Oberlin, Ohio : The Library], 1932.  x, 84 p. ;
26 cm. (Oberlin College Library bulletin ; v. 2,
no. 3)


    I. Hubbard, Geraldine Hopkins.  II. Fowler,
Julian S.  III. Title.  IV. Series: Oberlin Col-
lege Library bulletin ; v. 2, no. 3.
```

Minnesota (Ter.) Constitutional Convention, 1857.
[Mn 1] Journal. 1857.   CARD 1 of 3

Example 450

```
Minnesota. Constitutional Convention (1857 ;
     Democratic).
   Journal of the Constitutional Convention of
the territory of Minnesota [microform] : begun and
held in the city of Saint Paul, capital of said
territory, on Monday, the thirteenth day of July,
one thousand eight hundred and fifty-seven. --
Saint Paul : E.S. Goodrich, state printer, 1857.
     209 p. ; 23 cm.

   Microfiche. [Westport, Conn.] : G[reenwood
P[ress, 1973]. 3 microfiches ; 11 x 15 cm. ([State
constitutional conventions ; series 2], Mn 1).
Title on header: Journal.


   I. Title.  II. Title: Journal.  III. Title:
Journal.  IV. Series: State constitutional conven-
tions ; series 2, Mn 1.
```

Example 451

```
Minnesota. Constitutional Convention (1857 ;
     Democratic).
   Journal [microform] / Minnesota (Ter.) Con-
stitutional Convention, 1857. -- [Westport, Conn.]
: G[reenwood P[ress, 1973].
   3 microfiches ; 11 x 15 cm. ([State constitu-
tional conventions ; series 2], Mn 1)

   Title on header: Journal.
   Microreproduction of: Journal of the Consti-
tutional Convention of the territory of Minnesota.
Saint Paul : E.S. Goodrich, state printer, 1857.
209 p. ; 23 cm.


   I. Title.  II. Title: Journal of the Consti-
tutional Convention of the territory of Minnesota.
III. Series: State constitutional conventions ;
series 2, Mn 1.
```

Using a uniform title, the heading would be:

```
Minnesota. Constitutional Convention (1857 ;
     Democratic).
   [Journal of the Constitutional Convention of
the territory of Minnesota]
     Journal [microform] ...
```

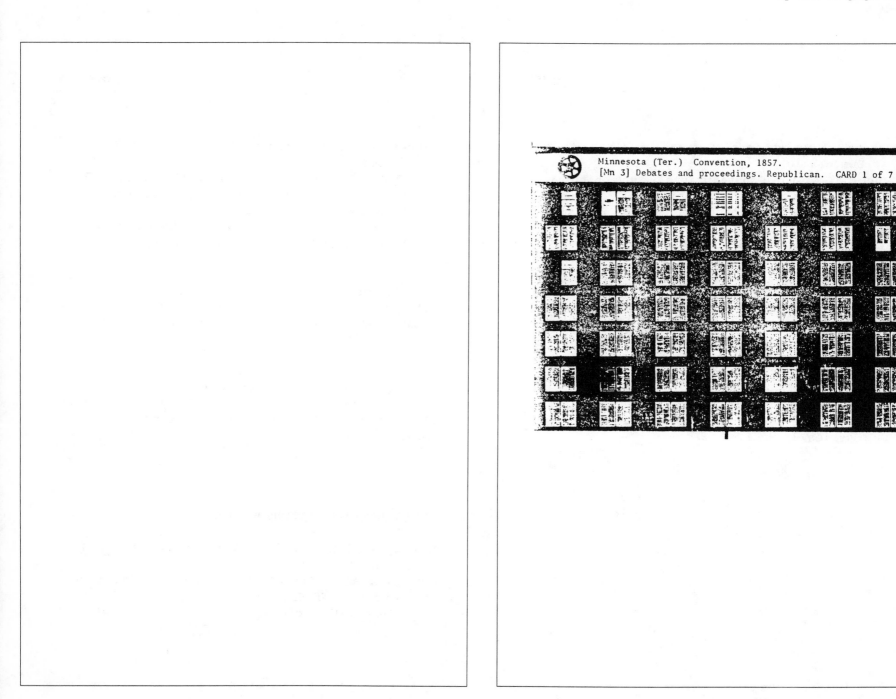

Example 452

```
Minnesota. Constitutional Convention (1857 : Re-
     publican).
     Debates and proceedings of the Constitutional
Convention for the territory of Minnesota, to form
a state constitution preparatory to its admission
into the Union as a state [microform] / T.F.
Andrews, official reporter to the convention. --
Saint Paul : G.W. Moore, printer, 1858.
     7, xviii, [9]-624 p. ; 26 cm.

     Microfiche. [Westport, Conn.] : G[reenwood]
P[ress, 1973]. 7 microfiches ; 11 x 15 cm. ([State
constitutional conventions ; series 2], Mn 3).
Title on header: Debates and proceedings, Republi-
can.


     I. Andrews, T. F. (Theodore F.).   II. Title.
III. Title: Debates and proceedings, Republican.
IV. Series: State constitutional conventions ;
series 2, Mn 3.
```

Example 453

```
Minnesota. Constitutional Convention (1857 : Re-
     publican).
     Debates and proceedings, Republican [micro-
form] / Minnesota (Ter.) Convention,1857.
-- [Westport, Conn.] : G[reenwood] P[ress, 1973].
     7 microfiches ; 11 x 15 cm. ([State constitu-
tional conventions ; series 2], Mn 3).

     Title on header.
     Microreproduction of: Debates and proceedings
of the Constitutional Convention for the territory
of Minnesota, to form a state constitution pre-
paratory to its admission into the Union as a
state / T.F. Andrews, official reporter to the
convention. Saint Paul : G.W. Moore, printer,
1858. 7, xviii, [9]-624 p. ; 26 cm.


     I. Andrews, T. F. (Theodore F.).   II. Title.
III. Title: Debates and proceedings of the Consti-
tutional Convention for the territory of Minnesota
...   IV. Series: State constitutional conventions
; series 2, Mn 3.
```

Using a uniform title, the heading would be:

```
Minnesota. Constitutional Convention (1857, Repub-
     lican)
     [Debates and proceedings of the Constitu-
tional Convention for the territory of Minnesota
...]
     Debates and proceedings, Republican ...
```

ILLUSTRATED HISTORY

AND

Descriptive and Biographical Review

OF

KANDIYOHI COUNTY

MINNESOTA

Published by Victor E. Lawson and J. Emil Nelson

Publication of the Willmar Tribune, Willmar, Minn.

Compiled and arranged under the direction of

VICTOR E. LAWSON

MARTIN E. TEW

Author of Early and Political History and Joint Compiler

J. EMIL NELSON

Promoter and Manager

St. Paul, Minnesota
Pioneer Press Manufacturing Departments
1905

Example 454

Illustrated history and descriptive and biographi-
    cal review of Kandiyohi County [microform] /
    compiled and arranged under the direction of
    Victor E. Lawson ; Martin E. Tew, author of
    early and political history and joint com-
    piler ; J. Emil Nelson, promoter and manager
    -- [Willmar, Minn.] : Published by Victor E.
    Lawson and J. Emil Nelson, 1905 (St. Paul,
    Minn. : Pioneer Press Manufacturing Depart-
    ments).
    446 p. : ill., maps, ports. ; 47 cm.

    Microfilm. [Tucson, Ariz. : Americana Unlim-
ited, between 1974 and 1979]. on reel 8 of 17
microfilm reels ; 35 mm. Book 36, of a microfilm
collection with title: Minnesota local history.

    I. Lawson, Victor E. (Victor Emanuel), 1871-
1960. II. Tew, Martin E., 1869-   . III. Nelson, J. Emil (Johan Emil), 1871-   .

Example 455

Illustrated history and descriptive and biographical
    review of Kandiyohi County [microform] /
    compiled and arranged under the direction of
    Victor E. Lawson ; Martin E. Tew, author of
    early and political history and joint com-
    piler ; J. Emil Nelson, promoter and manager
    -- [Tucson, Ariz. : Americana Unlimited,
    between 1974 and 1979].
    on reel 8 of 17 microfilm reels : ill., maps,
ports, ; 16 mm.

    Title from first frame of item.
    Book 36 of a microfilm collection with title:
Minnesota local history.
    Microreproduction of original published:
[Willmar, Minn.] : Published by Victor E. Lawson
and J. Emil Nelson, 1905 (St. Paul, Minn. : Pioneer Press Manufacturing Departments). 446 p. ; 47
cm.

    I. Lawson, Victor E. (Victor Emanuel), 1871-
1960. II. Tew, Martin E., 1869-   III. Nelson,
J. Emil (Johan Emil), 1871-

81-0858   MINNESOTA HEALTH PROFILES : KANDIYOHI
COUNTY /
DEPARTMENT OF HEALTH. CENTER FOR
HEALTH STATISTICS.
1981?
MINNESOTA STATE DOCUMENT DEPOSITORY
SYSTEM.   001

Example 456

Kandiyohi County [microform]. -- [Minneapolis, MN]
    : Minnesota Dept. of Health, Minnesota Center
    for Health Statistics, [1981?].
    23 leaves ; 28 cm. -- (Minnesota health pro-
files)

    Cover title.
    Microfiche. [Saint Paul, Minn.] : Minnesota
State Document Depository System, [1981?]. 1
microfiche ; 11 x 15 cm. Title on header: Minnesota health profiles. Kandiyohi County. Minnesota
Legislative Reference Library document no.: 81-
0858.

    I. Minnesota Center for Health Statistics.
II. Series.

Example 457

Minnesota health profiles. Kandiyohi County [mi-
    croform] / Department of Health, Center for
    Health Statistics. -- [Saint Paul, Minn.] :
    Minnesota State Document Depository System,
    [1981?].
    1 microfiche ; 11 x 15 cm.

    Title from header.
    Minnesota Legislative Reference Library docu-
ment no.: 81-0858.
    Microreproduction of: Kandiyohi County. [Min-
neapolis, MN] : Minnesota Department of Health,
Minnesota Center for Health Statistics, [1981?].
23 leaves ; 28 cm. (Minnesota health profiles).
Cover title.

    I. Minnesota Center for Health Statistics.
II. Series: Minnesota health profiles.

Using a uniform title, the heading would be:

Kandiyohi County (Minnesota Center for Health
    Statistics).
    Minnesota health profiles ...

Example 458

A SURNAME INDEX
OF
PEDIGREE CHARTS
OF
THE SOUTHERN GENEALOGIST'S EXCHANGE SOCIETY,
INC.
(A non-profit genealogical society with
headquarters in Jacksonville, Florida)

Mailing Address
The Southern Genealogist's Exchange Society,
Inc.
P. O. Box 2801
Jacksonville, Florida 32203

MICROFILMED
BY
GENERAL
MICROFILM
JAX.FLA

FIRST THOUSAND PEDIGREE CHARTS

16mm microfilm

The Southern Geneologist's Exchange Society, Inc.
P. O. Box 2801 • Jacksonville, Florida 32203

A Surname index of pedigree charts of the Southern
   Genealogist's Exchange Society, Inc. [micro-
   form]. -- Jacksonville, Fla. : The Society,
   [19--] (Jax [i.e. Jacksonville], Fla. :
   Microform filmed by General Microfilm).
   1 microfilm reel ; 16 mm.

   Title on container: First thousand pedigree
charts.
   Summary: A collection of genealogical charts
submitted to the society by its members.

   I. Southern Genealogist's Exchange Society.
II. Title: First thousand pedigree charts.

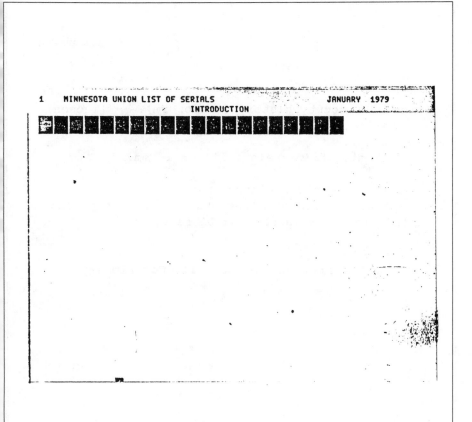

Example 459

Minnesota union list of serials [microform]. --
    2nd ed., rev. -- Minneapolis, Minn. : MIN-
    ITEX, 1979.
    18 microfiches ; 11 x 15 ca.

    "January 1979."

    I. MINITEX (Program).

Container label

```
┌──────────────────────────────────────────────┐
│                                                │
│  Minnesota County History          MICROFILM   │
│                                        247      │
│  Book 1 thru 4                         r. 1     │
│                                                │
└──────────────────────────────────────────────┘
```

Example 460

```
Minnesota county history [microform]. -- [Tucson,
    Ariz.: Americana Unlimited, between 1974 and
    1979].
    17 microfilm reels : ill. ; 16 mm.

    Title from container.
    Reproduction of Minnesota state, county, and
local histories in the Cox Library.


    I. Americana Unlimited.   II. Cox Library.
```

YALE UNIVERSITY LIBRARY
PHOTOGRAPHIC SERVICES *Feb 17 - 54*

Departmental (or other) charge____ _____

Name of individual____ *Father Shannon*_____

Address_____

Delivery Instructions (mail, will call, telephone no. _____)

Title (1)__ *Catholic pamphlets*_____

(2)_____

(3)_____

INSTRUCTIONS: *neg film*

Photostats
  Negatives_____ Positives_____   ___ at $
  Negatives_____ Positives_____   ___ at $ _____
  Negatives_____ Positives_____   ___ at $ _____
  Enlargements____ Reductions_____ ___ at $0.10   _____
  Combinations_____ ___ at $0.10   _____

Microfilms (Minimum charge $1.00)
  Negative exposures   ___ at $ _____
  Service charge (change of sequence or forms)
                                  ___ at $0.10   _____

Photographs
  Negatives 5 x 7 _____   ___ at $1.00   _____
          8 x 10_____   ___ at $1.50   _____
  Contact prints 5 x 7_____   ___ at $0.25   _____
              8 x 10_____   ___ at $0.40   _____
  Enlargements: size _____   ___ at $ _____

Special charges _____   _____
                                           tax   _____
                                       postage   _____
                                         Total   _____

Example 461

Catholic pamphlets [microform]. -- (New Haven,
    Conn.] : Yale University Library, Photodupli-
    cation Service, 1954.
    1 microfilm reel : negative, ill. ; 35 mm.

    Contents: Minnesota, its resources and prog-
ress. 1872 -- Catholic colonization in Minnesota.
1880 -- Emigration versus enforced migration / by
Alexander Sullivan ... [et al.]. [1883?] --
Catholic colonization in Minnesota. Rev. ed. 1879
-- Official report of the Board of Irish Immigration for St. Louis, Mo., for the four months
ending Aug. 15, 1874. 1874 -- "What brings so
many Irish to America!" / by Hibernicus. 1945 --
...

EARLY AMERICAN

IMPRINTS

1639-1800

Dr. Clifford K. Shipton, Editor

Evans Numbers

1 - 415

American Antiquarian Society

Worcester, Mass.

A READEX MICROPRINT

Early American Imprints   Evans Numbers
1639-1800   1-4.

American Antiquarian Society. Worcester, Mass. 1962.
A Readex Microprint.

Example 462

Early American imprints, 1639-1800 [microform]. --
     Worcester, Mass. : American Antiquarian
     Society, 1962-1968.
        microopaques ; 23 x 15 cm.

     Title from header.
     Editor: Clifford K. Shipton.
     "A Readex microprint."
     Microreproduction of items 1-39162 in: Ameri-
can bibliography / by Charles Evans.

     I. Shipton, Clifford K. (Clifford Kenyon),
1902-1973. II. Evans, Charles, 1850-1935. American bibliography. III. American Antiquarian
Society.

EARLY AMERICAN

IMPRINTS

1639-1800

Dr. Clifford K. Shipton, Editor

Evans Numbers

38751 - 39162

American Antiquarian Society

Worcester, Mass.

A READEX MICROPRINT

Early American Imprints   Evans Numbers
1639-1800.   Supplement   39163-39173

American Antiquarian Society. Worcester, Mass. 1968.
A Readex Microprint.

Example 463

Early American imprints, 1639-1800. Supplement
     [microform]. -- Worcester, Mass. : American
     Antiquarian Society, 1968.
        microopaques ; 23 x 15 cm.

     Title from header.
     Editor: Clifford K. Shipton.
     "A Readex microprint."
     Microreproduction of items 39163-49197 in:
Supplement to Charles Evans' American bibliography
/ by Roger P. Bristol.

     I. Shipton, Clifford K. (Clifford Kenyon),
1902-1973. II. Bristol, Roger P. (Roger Pat-
trell). Supplement to Charles Evan's American
bibliography. III. American Antiquarian Society.

SAINT PAUL

DIRECTORY.

For 1864.

INCLUDING

A COMPLETE DIRECTORY OF THE CITIZENS,

A BUSINESS DIRECTORY,

AND AN

APPENDIX,

CONTAINING A LIST OF CITY, COUNTY, STATE AND FEDERAL OFFICERS
LITERARY, BENEVOLENT, AND OTHER ASSOCIATIONS:
CHURCHES: SCHOOLS AND MUCH OTHER
VALUABLE INFORMATION.

VOLUME TWO.

SAINT PAUL:
GROFF & BAILEY, PUBLISHERS.
1864.

ST.PAUL

CITY DIRECTORY

1879-80

COMPRISING

AN ALPHABETICALLY ARRANGED LIST OF BUSINESS FIRMS AND
PRIVATE CITIZENS—A CLASSIFIED LIST OF ALL TRADES,
PROFESSIONS AND PURSUITS—A MISCELLANEOUS
DIRECTORY, CITY AND COUNTY OFFICERS,
TERMS OF COURT, PUBLIC AND PRIVATE
SCHOOLS, CHURCHES, BANKS, IN-
CORPORATED INSTITUTIONS,
SECRET AND BENEVO-
LENT SOCIETIES, &c.

R.L. POLK & CO. AND A.C. DANSER, PUBLISHERS

PRINCE BLOCK, 122 EAST THIRD STREET
1879.

RALPH L. POLK   JACOB W. WEEMS

Example 464

```
Saint Paul directory for ... [microform]. -- Vol.
    2 (1864). -- Saint Paul : Groff & Bailey,
    1864.
    1 v. : ill. ; 24 cm.

    "Including a complete directory of the citi-
zens, a business directory, and an appendix..."
    Continues: A. Bailey's Saint Paul directory
for ...
    Continued by: St. Paul directory for ...
    Microfilm. New Haven, Conn. : Research Publi-
cations, [197-]. on 1 reel of 4 microfilm reels ;
35 mm. On reel 1 of a microfilm collection with
title: United States city directories, 1861-1881.
St. Paul, Minn.


    I. Groff & Bailey.
```

Example 465

```
Saint Paul directory for ... [microform]. -- Vol.
    2 (1864). -- New Haven, Conn. : Research Pub-
    lications, [197-].
    on reel 1 of 4 microfilm reels : ill. ; 35
mm.

    Title from first frame of item.
    "Including a complete directory of the citi-
zens, a business directory, and an appendix..."
    On reel 1 of a microfilm collection with
titles: United States city directories, 1861-1881.
St. Paul, Minn.
    Microreproduction of original published:
Saint Paul : Groff & Bailey, 1864. 1 v. ; 24 cm.


    I. Groff & Bailey.
```

Example 466

St. Paul city directory [microform]. -- 1879-80--
    1888-9. -- [Saint Paul, Minn.] : R.L. Polk &
    Co. and A.C. Danser, 1879-1888.
    10 v. : ill. ; 24 cm.

    Annual.
    Continued by: R.L. Polk & Co.'s St. Paul city
directory.
    Vols. for 1880-81--1881-82 published: [Saint
Paul, Minn.] : R.L. Polk & Co. & J.D. Leonard.
Vols. for 1883-84--1888-9 published: [Saint Paul,
Minn.] : R.L. Polk & Co.
    Microfilm. 1879-80--1880-81. New Haven, Conn.
: Research Publications, [197-]. on 2 reels of 4
microfilm reels ; 35 mm. on reels 3 and 4 of a
microfilm collection with title: United States
city directories, 1861-1881. St. Paul, Minn.

    I. R.L. Polk & Co.   II. Danser, A.C.   III.
Leonard, J.D.

Example 467

St. Paul city directory [microform]. -- 1879-80--
    1888-9. -- New Haven, Conn. : Research Publi-
    cations, [197-].
    on 2 reels of 4 microfilm reels : ill. ; 35
mm.

    On reels 3 and 4 of a microfilm collection
with title: United States city directories, 1861-
1881. St. Paul, Minn.
    Microreproduction of original published:
1879-80--1888-9. [Saint Paul, Minn.] : R.L. Polk &
Co. and A.C. Danser, 1879-1888. 10 v. : ill. ; 24
cm. Annual. Continued by: R.L. Polk & Co.'s St.
Paul city directory. Vols. for 1880-81--1881-82
published: [Saint Paul, Minn.] : R.L. Polk & Co. &
J.D. Leonard. Vols. for 1883-84--1888-9 published:
[Saint Paul, Minn.] : R.L. Polk & Co.

    Microfilm. 1879-80--1880-81. New Haven, Conn.
: Research Publications, [197-]. on 2 reels of 4
microfilm reels ; 35 mm. on reels 3 and 4 of a
microfilm collection with title: United States
city directories, 1861-1881. St. Paul, Minn.

    I. R.L. Polk & Co.   II. Danser, A.C.   III.
Leonard, J.D.

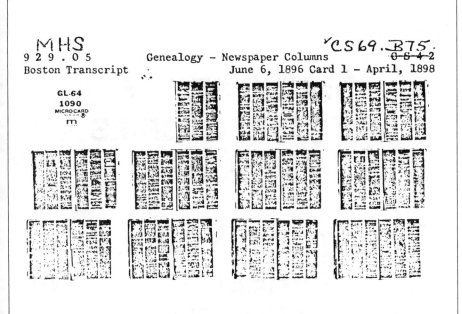

Example 468

Genealogy, newspaper columns [microform] / Boston
    transcript. -- [United States] : Micro Card,
    [1952-1964].
    670 microopaques on 642 : ill. ; 8 x 13 cm.

Reproduction of newspaper columns published
in the Boston evening transcript, June 6, 1894-
Apr. 30, 1941.
    Title from header.
    Publisher's no.: GL-64 1090--GL-64 1117 (June
6, 1894-Apr. 18, 1904) ; Ge-54 326--Ge-54 484
(Jan. 1, 1904-Dec. 30, 1912) ; Ge-52 203--Ge-52
657 (Jan. 1, 1913-Apr. 30, 1941).

    I. Boston evening transcript (1872).

UNITED STATES
CITY DIRECTORIES
1861 - 1881

ST. PAUL, MINN.
REEL 1
1861-1871

microfilmed by **rp** new haven, conn. 06525
Research **rp** publications, inc.

Example 469

United States city directories, 1861-1881. St.
    Paul, Minn. [microform]. -- New Haven, Conn.
    : Research Publications, [197-].
    4 microfilm reels : ill. ; 35 mm.

    Microreproduction of various Saint Paul city
directories.

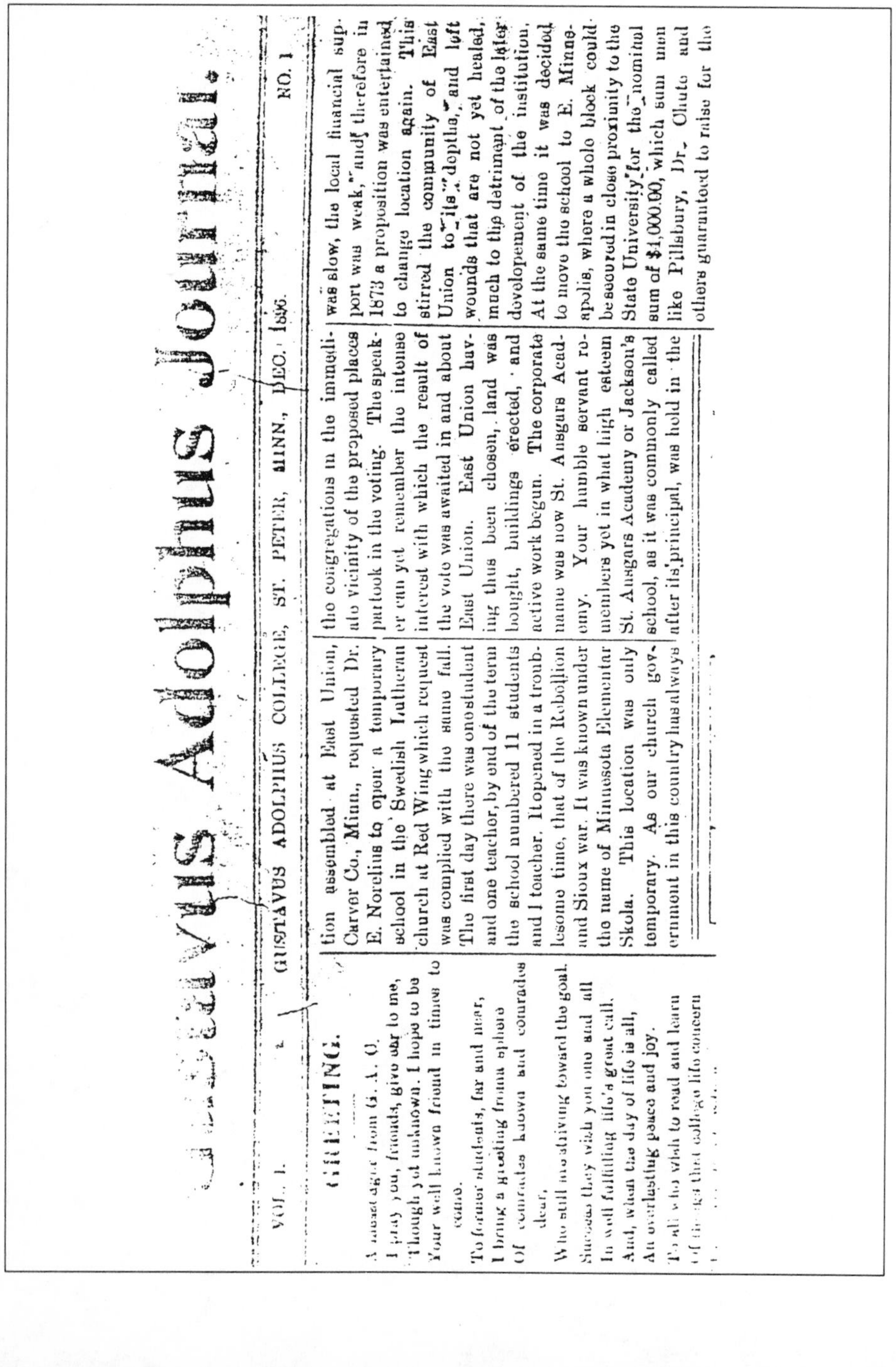

Gustavus Adolphus Journal.

VOL. I. GUSTAVUS ADOLPHUS COLLEGE, ST. PETER, MINN., DEC. 1896. NO. 1

GREETING.

A message from G. A. C.
I pray you, friends, give ear to me,
Though yet unknown. I hope to be
Your well known friend in times to come.
To former students, far and near,
I bring a greeting from a sphere
Of comrades known and comrades dear,
Who still are striving toward the goal.
Success they wish you one and all
In well fulfilling life's great call.
And, when the day of life is all,
An everlasting peace and joy.
To all who wish to read and learn
Of things that college life concern

tion assembled at East Union, Carver Co., Minn., requested Dr. E. Norelius to open a temporary school in the Swedish Lutheran church at Red Wing which request was complied with the same fall. The first day there was one student and one teacher, by end of the term the school numbered 11 students and 1 teacher. It opened in a troublesome time, that of the Rebellion and Sioux war. It was known under the name of Minnesota Elementar Skola. This location was only temporary. As our church government in this country has always the congregations in the immediate vicinity of the proposed places partook in the voting. The speaker can yet remember the intense interest with which the result of the vote was awaited in and about East Union. East Union having thus been chosen, land was bought, buildings erected, and active work begun. The corporate name was now St. Ansgars Academy. Your humble servant remembers yet in what high esteem St. Ansgars Academy or Jackson's school, as it was commonly called after its principal, was held in the was slow, the local financial support was weak, and therefore in 1873 a proposition was entertained to change location again. This stirred the community of East Union to its depths, and left wounds that are not yet healed, much to the detriment of the later developement of the institution. At the same time it was decided to move the school to E. Minneapolis, where a whole block could be secured in close proximity to the State University for the nominal sum of $4,000.00, which sum men like Pillsbury, Dr. Chute and others guaranteed to raise for the

MINNESOTA HISTORICAL SOCIETY START GUSTAVUS ADOLPHUS JOURNAL

DEC 1896 T H R U MAY 1901

Example 470

Gustavus Adolphus journal [microform]. -- Vol. 1,
    no. 1 (Dec. 1896)-   . -- St. Peter, Minn.
    Gustavus Adolphus College, 1896-
        v. : ill. ; 45 cm.

    Caption title.
    Issues for Dec. 1896-Apr. 1900 published in
two issues a month, with continuous numbering, the
second issue each month in Swedish and with title:
Gustaf Adolfs journalen. Monthly, in English only,
May 1900-
    Microfilm. [Vol. 1, no. 1] (Dec. 1896) to [v.
5, no. 5] (May 1901). [Saint Paul, Minn.] : Minnesota Historical Society, 1981. 1 microfilm reel ;
35 mm. Publisher's no.: 27--6-1981.

    I. Gustavus Adolphus College.   II. Title:
Gustaf Adolfs journalen.

Example 471

Gustavus Adolphus journal [microform]. -- [Vol. 1,
    no. 1] (Dec. 1896) thru [v. 5, no. 5] (May
    1901]. -- [Saint Paul, Minn. : Minnesota His-
    torical Society, [1981].
    1 microfilm reel : ill. ; 35 mm.

    Publisher's no.: 27--6-1981.
    Microreproduction of: Vol. 1, no. 1 (Dec.
1896)-   .   St. Peter, Minn. Gustavus Adolphus
College, 1896-   . v. ; 45 cm. Caption title.
Issues for Dec. 1896-Apr. 1900 published in two
issues a month, with continuous numbering, the
second issue each month in Swedish and with title:
Gustaf Adolfs journalen. Monthly, in English only,
May 1900-

    I. Gustavus Adolphus College.   II. Title:
Gustaf Adolfs journalen.

CATHOLIC AID NEWS

No.

OFFICIAL ORGAN AND ASSESSMENT NOTICE OF THE CATHOLIC AID ASSOCIATION

VOLUME 72 NO. 1   1878 — EIGHTY-NINTH YEAR — 1966   ALBANY, MINN., OCTOBER 22, 1966

Hierarchy Gratefully Receives Gifts For Holy Father

'67 Delegate Convention Set For August 20-22

Apostolic Delegation
United States of America
3339 Massachusetts Avenue
Washington, D. C. 20008

September 21, 1966

Right Reverend Msgr. Joseph A. Ettel
Spiritual Director
Catholic Aid Association Women's Council
605 No. State Street
New Ulm, Minnesota

Right Reverend and dear Monsignor:

I wish to acknowledge with sincere thanks your kind letter of September 16th enclosing a check in the amount of $400.00 representing the annual offering to the Holy Father from the Women's Council of the Catholic Aid Association.

Archdiocese of St. Paul
226 Summit Avenue
Saint Paul, Minnesota 55102

September 30, 1966

Mr. R. G. Baetz
The Catholic Aid Association
49 West Ninth Street
St. Paul, Minnesota 55102

Dear Mr. Baetz:

I thank you for your letter of September 29 forwarding a check in the amount of $396.00, an offering for the Holy Father for the Catholic Aid Association.

It is most comforting to have this evidence of the loyalty and devotion of the members of the Catholic Aid Association to His Holiness, Pope Paul VI.

The Grand Council at its October meeting scheduled next year's CAA delegate convention for Monday and Tuesday, August 21st and 22nd. The meetings of the Women's and Men's Council will, therefore, begin on the preceding day, Sunday, August 20th.

This action was taken at the suggestion of Msgr. Terrance Murphy, president of St. Thomas College, who will host our three day session. The 1965 delegate convention was also held at St. Thomas.

Further details as arranged and approved by the Grand Council will be published in future issues of the Catholic Aid News.

MINNESOTA
HISTORICAL SOCIETY
START
CATHOLIC AID
NEWS

OCT 22   THUR   DEC 1978

Example 472

Catholic aid news [microform]. -- [Vol. 72, no. 11
    (Oct. 22, 1966) thur [i.e. thru v. 84, no.
    12] (Dec. 1978)-   . -- [Saint Paul, Minn. :
    Minnesota Historical Society, 1980-
     microfilm reels : ill. ; 35 mm.

    Publisher's no.: 138-2-1980,
    Microreproduction of: Catholic aid news =
Vereins-Bote : official organ and assessment
notice of the Catholic Aid Association of Minnesota. Vol. 53, no. 10 (Jan. 20, 1948)-   . St.
Paul, Minn. ; The Association, 1948-   . v. ; 38-
41 cm. Monthly. Issues for Feb. 22, 1951-   issued without parallel title. Subtitle varies.
Continues: Vereins-Bote. Issues for July 22nd,
1955-   published: Catholic Aid Association.

    I. Catholic Aid Association of Minnesota.
II. Catholic Aid Association. III. Title: Vereins-Bote.

Example 473

Catholic aid news [microform] = Vereins-Bote :
    official organ and assessment notice of the
    Catholic Aid Association of Minnesota. --
    Vol. 53, no. 10 (Jan. 20, 1948)-   . -- St.
    Paul, Minn. ; The Association, 1948-
        v. : ill. ; 38-41 cm.

    Monthly.
    Issues for Feb. 22, 1951-   lack parallel
title.
    Subtitle varies.
    Continues: Vereins-Bote.
    Volume numbering somewhat irregular.
    Issues for July 22nd, 1955-   published:
Catholic Aid Association.
    Microfilm. Vol. 72, no. 1 (Oct. 22, 1966)-
. [Saint Paul, Minn.] : Minnesota Historical
Society, 1980-   .   microfilm reels ; 35 mm.
Publisher's no.: 138-2-1980,

    I. Catholic Aid Association of Minnesota.
II. Catholic Aid Association. III. Title: Vereins-Bote.

**MINNESOTA
HISTORICAL
SOCIETY**

START

**MINNESOTA
LEADER**

**NOV 18
1974**   THRU   **JUL 25
1977**

Example 474

```
Minnesota leader (Minneapolis, Minn. : 1974).
    The Minnesota leader [microform]. -- Vol. 1,
no. 1 (Nov. 18, 1974)-v. 2, no. 7 (July 25, 1977).
-- Minneapolis, Minn. : A. Wroblewski, 1974-1977.
    2 v. : ill. ; 36 cm.

    Triweekly (Nov. 18, 1974-May 6, 1975), Ir-
regular (June 30, 1975-July 25, 1977).
    Microfilm. [Saint Paul, Minn.] : Minnesota
Historical Society, 1981. 1 microfilm reel ; 35
mm. Publisher's no.: 89--6-1981.


    I. Wroblewski, Al.
```

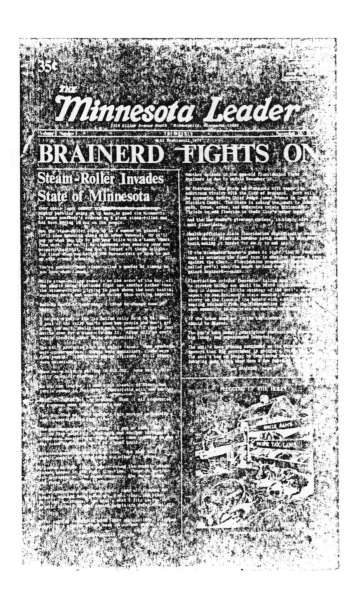

Example 475

Minnesota leader (Minneapolis, Minn. : 1974).
     The Minnesota leader [microform]. -- [Vol. 1,
no. 1] (Nov. 18, 1974) thru [v. 2, no. 7] (Jul[y]
25, 1977). -- [Saint Paul, Minn.] : Minnesota
Historical Society, 1981.
     1 microfilm reel : ill. ; 35 mm.

     Publisher's no.: 89--6-1981.
     Microreproduction of: Minneapolis, Minn. : Al
Wroblewski, 1974-1977. 2 v. ; 36 cm. Triweekly
(Nov. 18, 1974-May 6, 1975), Irregular (June 30,
1975-July 25, 1977).

     I. Wroblewski, Al.

THE EPISTLE

OF

PAUL THE APOSTLE

TO THE

ROMANS

WITH NOTES, COMMENTS, MAPS AND ILLUSTRATIONS

BY

Rev. LYMAN ABBOTT

AUTHOR OF "DICTIONARY OF RELIGIOUS KNOWLEDGE," "JESUS OF NAZARETH," AND

A SERIES OF COMMENTARIES ON THE NEW TESTAMENT

COPYRIGHT, 1888

A.S. BARNES & COMPANY

NEW YORK AND CHICAGO.

Example 476

Bible. N.T. Romans. English. Authorized. 1888.
     Epistle of Paul the Apostle--Romans [micro-
form] / L. Abbott. -- Chicago, Ill. : Photographed
for the American Theological Library Association
Microtext Project by University of Chicago, Joseph
Regenstein Library, Dept. of Photoduplication,
1973.
     1 microfilm reel : ill. ; 35 mm. -- (ATLA ;
bk. 371)
     Contains no maps.
     Microreproduction of the original published
as: The Epistle of Paul the apostle to the Romans.
New York : A.S. Barnes, c1888. viii, 230 p.

     I. Abbott, Lyman, 1835-1922. II. Title.
III. Title: The Epistle of Paul the apostle to the
Romans.

D: 11.1B1, 11.1C1, 11.1F1, 11.4C1, 11.4D1, 11.4F1, 11.5B1, 11.5C2,
     11.5D4, 11.6B1, 11.7B, 1.7A3
ME: 21.13C, 21.37A, 25.17, 25.18A2, 25.18A3, 25.18A10, 25.18A11,
     25.18A13
AE: 21.13C, 21.30J

     Library of Congress has decided not to follow AACR2 when
cataloging microform reproductions of original works. It will continue to
catalog the reproductions according to the originals and add notes concerning the microreproductions.

Type: a Bib lvl: m Govt pub: Lang: eng Source: d illus:
Repr: a Enc lvl: I Conf pub: 0 Ctry: ilu Dat tp: r M/F/B: 00
Indx: 0 Mod rec: Festschr: 0 Cont:
Desc: a Int lvl: Dates: 1973,1888

     010
     040   XXX $c XXX
     007   h $b $c $d $e $f u--- $g b $h u $i c $j u
     041 1   eng $h grc
     090
     049   XXXX
     130 00 Bible. $p N.T. $p Romans. $l English. $s
Authorized. 1888.
     245 10 Epistle of Paul the Apostle--Romans $h
microform / $c L. Abbott.
     260 0   Chicago, Ill. : $b Photographed for the
American Theological Library Association Microtext
Project by University of Chicago, Joseph Regenstein
Library, Dept. of Photoduplication, $c 1973.
     300   1 microfilm reel : $b ill. ; $c 35 mm.
     490 0   ATLA ; $v bk. 371
     500   Contains no maps.
     500   Microreproduction of the original pub-
lished as: The Epistle of Paul the apostle to the
Romans. New York : A.S. Barnes, c1888. viii, 230 p.
     700 10 Abbott, Lyman, $d 1835-1922.
     740 41 The Epistle of Paul the apostle to the
Romans.

Chapter 13

SERIALS

Introduction

This chapter is based on *A Manual of AACR 2 Examples for Serials* by Julia Blixrud, second edition, with examples added from several other manuals.

The bibliographic records are in augmented level one description. This is in accordance with the Library of Congress decision on the level of description for serials as stated in its rule interpretation for *AACR 2* 1.0D (*CSB* 13, p. 3).

The Library of Congress produces no records exactly at the first level description; records for serials are generally at the first level, augmented principally as follows:

> GMD (when required by the options decision)
> Parallel title(s)
> First statement of responsibility (always, no matter what the
>   choice of main entry heading)
> First place of publication, etc.
> Other physical details; dimensions
> Series area

Record also:

> Other title information when it includes a statement of responsibilitry
>   and the statement is an integral part of the other title information
>   (cf. 1.1E4)
> Other title information when it contains the form of the title reflected
>   in the full form vs. acronym or initialism question

> Other title information when 1.1E6 must be applied
> Subsequent statement of responsibility when it contains an entity
>   needed as an added entry

LEVEL OF DESCRIPTION FOR SERIALS

Title proper [gmd when required by options decision] = parallel title(s) / first statement of responsibility. -- Edition statement. -- Numeric and/or alphabetic, chronological or other designation. -- First place of publication, etc. : first publisher, etc., date of publication, etc.
Extent of item : other physical details ; dimensions. -- (Series. Subseries)

Note(s)
Standard number.

Rule numbers listed are those for chapter 12. Serial catalogers should be aware, however, that in *AACR 2* these rule will often refer back to, or need to be used in conjunction with, rules from other chapters.

Most of these examples were cataloged from the issue in hand. Library of Congress practice has been followed regarding punctuation in area 4 and for the order of notes. Other sources for additional bibliographic information were not usually consulted, but the following exceptions were made for most examples:

> If the publication was related to another serial, the
> CONSER database was searched to verify relationship dates.
> The CONSER database was also searched for beginning
> dates of publication when cataloging from other than the first
> issue.
> Headings have been checked against the Library of
> Congress Name Authority File.
> ISSNs were verified in the CONSER databases.

Some of the titles cataloged have ceased publication since these examples were originally prepared. That information is noted, but, in most cases, cataloging was not changed to reflect the ending date of publication.

The Library of Congress rule interpretations for rule 25.5B provide a means of establishing a uniform title for a serial or series whose title proper is the same as the title proper of another serial or series. Various types of qualifiers are provided for, among them:

(1) corporate body, where the title proper consists solely of elements indicating a type of publication, periodicity, or subject content, or a combination of these elements;

(2) place of publication, where the criteria in (1) do not apply. As an exception to this, qualification is by corporate body if the place is not sufficient to distinguish between works because more than one work with the same title proper was published in the same place;

(3) place and date, or corporate body and date, where the addition of only one of the elements is insufficient to distinguish between two or more works;

(4) date alone, where the title proper already includes the place or the corporate body that would be used as the qualifier.

Examples also are provided of the rule interpretations for additions to uniform titles for serials; of changes in the qualifier that require a new record and those that do not require a new record; of uniform titles for serials entered under a name heading; and of uniform titles for serials whose titles consist solely of the name of a corporate body.

Lengthy Library of Congress rule interpretations (LCRIs) for serials have been issued through the *Cataloging Service Bulletin (CSB)*.

LAKE SUPERIOR
PORT CITIES
Spring 1984 / Volume 5, Issue 4

The Quotable Bede:
J. Adam Bede of Duluth

Part I of a two-part article on "one of the most original and humorous characters to ever walk" Duluth streets

by Steve Keillor

LAKE SUPERIOR
PORT CITIES
A quarterly journal of contemporary and historical events around Lake Superior.

Part II —
The Quotable Bede:
J. Adam Bede
of Duluth *by* Steve Keillor

Example 477

Keillor, Steven J. (Steven James).
    The quotable Bede : J. Adam Bede of Duluth / by Steve Keillor. -- p. 13-16, 71, p. 5-9 : ill. ; 28 cm.

    In Lake Superior port cities. -- Vol. 5, issue 4 (spring 1984); v. 6, issue 1 (summer 1984).
    Title from caption.

    I. Title.

An article from a serial cataloged as an "In" analytic.

Type: a Bib lvl: a Govt pub: Lang: eng Source: d Illus: a
Repr: Enc lvl: I Conf pub: 0 Ctry: mnu Dat tp: s M/F/B: 10b
Indx: 0 Mod rec: Festschr: 0 Cont:
Desc: a Int lvl: Dates: 1984,

    010
    040   XXX $c XXX
    043   n-us-mn
    052   4144 $b D9
    090
    049   XXXX
    100 10 Keillor, Steven J. $q (Steven James).
    245 14 The quotable Bede : $b J. Adam Bede of Duluth / $c by Steve Keillor.
    260 | $c
    300   p. 13-16, 71, p. 5-9 : $b ill. ; $c 28 cm.
    500   Title from caption.
    773 0 $7 nnas $t Lake Superior port cities. $v Vol. 5, issue 4 (spring 1984); v. 6, issue 1 (summer 1984). $w (OCoLC)5972863

NAMES

JOURNAL OF THE AMERICAN NAME SOCIETY

VOL. III, No. 2   June 1955

Literature on Personal Names in English, 1954

ELSDON O. SMITH

NAMES

JOURNAL OF THE AMERICAN NAME SOCIETY

VOL. V, No. 2   June 1957

Literature on Personal Names in English, 1956

ELSDON C. SMITH

Example 478

Smith, Elsdon C. (Elsdon Coles), 1902-
    Literature on personal names in English ... /
Elsdon O. [i.e. C.] Smith. -- 1954-1956.

    <u>In</u> Names. -- Vol. 3, no. 2 (June 1955) -- v.
5, no. 2 (June 1957).
    Annual.
    Title from caption.
    Continued by: Smith, Elsdon C. (Elsdon
Coles), 1902-   . Bibliography of personal names
...

    I. Title.

```
Type: a Bib lvl: b Govt pub:    Lang: eng Source: d S/L ent: 0
Repr:   Enc lvl: I Conf pub: 0 Ctry: mnu Ser tp: m Alphabt: a
Indx: 0 Mod rec:   Festschr: 0 Cont:b    Frequn: a Publ st: d
Desc: a Cum ind: u Titl pag: u ISDS:      Regulr: r Dates: 1954,1956
```

```
    010
    040    XXX $c XXX
    043    n-us-mn
    090
    049    XXXX
    110 10 Smith, Elsdon C. $q (Elsdon Coles), $d 1902-
    245 10 Literature on personal names in English ...
/ $c Elsdon O. [i.e. C.] Smith.
    260 ||  $c
    310    Annual
    362 0  1954-1956.
    500    Title from caption.
    773 0    $7 nnas $t Names. $g Vol. 3, no. 2 (June
1955)--v. 5, no. 2 (June 1957). $w (OCoLC)nnnnnnn
    785 00 Smith, Elsdon C. (Elsdon Coles), 1902-    .
$t Bibliography of personal names ... $w (OCoLC)nnnnnnn
```

    This is an example of a serial within a serial cataloged as an "In"
analytic; it also changed its title!

NAMES

JOURNAL OF THE AMERICAN NAME SOCIETY

VOL. VI, No. 4   December 1958

Bibliography of Personal Names, 1957

ELSDON C. SMITH

Example 479

Smith, Elsdon C. (Elsdon Coles), 1902-
    Bibliography of personal names ... / Elsdon
C. Smith. -- 1957-

    In Names. -- Vol. 6, no. 4 (Dec. 1958)-
    Annual.
    Continues: Smith, Elsdon C. (Elsdon Coles),
1902-   . Literature on personal names in English ...

    I. Title.


```
Type: a Bib lvl: b Govt pub:    Lang: eng Source: d S/L ent: 0
Repr:    Enc lvl: I Conf pub: 0 Ctry: nyu Ser tp: m Alphabt: a
Indx: u Mod rec:    Festschr: 0 Cont: b    Frequn: a Publ st: c
Desc: a Cum ind: u Titl pag: u ISDS:    Regulr: r Dates: 1957,9999

    010
    040    XXX $c XXX
    090
    049    XXXX
    110 10 Smith, Elsdon C. $q (Elsdon Coles), $d 1902-
    245 10 Bibliography of personal names ... / $c
Elsdon C. Smith.
    260 |    $c
    310    Annual
    362 0  1957-
    773 0    $7 nnas $t Names. $g Vol. 6, no. 4 (Dec.
1955)-    . $w (OCoLC)nnnnnnn
    785 00 Smith, Elsdon C. (Elsdon Coles), 1902-
$t Literature on personal names in English ... $w
(OCoLC)nnnnnnn
```

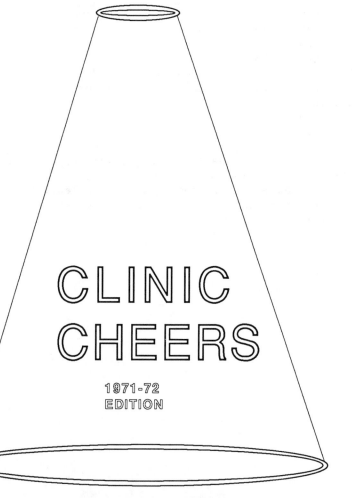

NATIONAL CHEERLEADERS
ASSOCIATION

CLINIC
CHEERS

1971-72
EDITION

BY L.R. HERKIMER
and ROBERT J. SHIELDS

HOW TO USE THIS BOOK

This book of photographically illustrated yells has been designed and compiled in order to simplify the learning of the various yells contained in this book. Where it is impossible to show every single motion, the author has attempted to show the main positions of each yell motion as the rhythm of the yell dictates. The success of, and the perfection of the yell routines illustrated in this book are mainly dependent upon how one moves from one of the illustrated positions to another. The snap and the vigorousness of each motion is very important.

...

It will be easier for you to learn the yells in this book if you have at least one other person who can look at the picture and say the different parts of the yell for you as you go into one position and move to the next. The one with the book can also criticize, or tell you how well or poorly you are doing the motion. After you have mastered the different positions and movements, you can "polish up" the yell routine by putting more expression into the actions as well as personality and pep.

Another outstanding publication by
THE NATIONAL CHEERLEADERS ASSOCIATION
11766 Valleydale Drive, Dallas, Texas 75230

Example 480

Herkimer, L. R.
    Clinic cheers / by L.R. Herkimer and Robert
J. Shields. --   -1973-74 ed. -- Dallas, Tex.
: National Cheerleaders Association,   -c1973.
        v. : ill. ; 28 cm.

    Annual.
    Description based on: 1971-72 ed.; title from
cover.
    Authors: -1971-72 ed., L. R. Herkimer
and Robert J. Shields; 1972-73 ed.-1973-74 ed.,
L.R. Herkimer and Gene W. Cason.
    Continued by: Herkimer, L. R. Clinic cheers
and pom-pon routines.
    Contains "photographically illustrated cheer
routines with complete directions and explanations
for easy comprehension."

    I. Shields, Robert J. II. Cason, Gene W.
III. National Cheerleaders Association (U.S.).
IV. Title.

D: 12.1B1, 12.1F1, 12.3F, 12.4, 12.4F3, 12.5, 12.7B1, 12.7B3,
      12.7B6, 12.7B7, 12.7B18, 12.7B22
C: 21.1A1, 21.1A2, 21.6C1
F: 22.1A, 22.1B (RI), 22.5A
AE: 21.30B, 21.30E, 21.30J
F: 22.1A, 22.5A, 24.1

Type: a Bib lvl: s Govt pub: Lang: eng Source: d S/L ent: 0
Repr: Enc lvl: I Conf pub: 0 Ctry: txu Ser tp: Alphabt: a
Indx: u Mod rec: Phys med: Cont: Frequn: a Pub st: d
Desc: a Cum ind: u Titl pag: ISDS: Regulr: r Dates: 19uu-1974

    010
    040   XXX $c XXX
    090
    049   XXXX
    100 10 Herkimer, L. R.
    245 10 Clinic cheers / $c by L.R. Herkimer and
Robert J. Shields.
    260 01 Dallas, Tex. : $b National Cheerleaders
Association, $c   -c1973.
    300   v. : $b ill. ; $c 28 cm.
    570   Authors: -1971-72 ed., L.R. Herkimer
and Robert J. Shields; 1972-73 ed.-1973-74 ed., L.R.
Herkimer and Gene W. Cason.
    520   Contains "photographically illustrated cheer
routines with complete directions and explanations for
easy comprehension."
    500   Description based on: 1971-72 ed.; title
from cover.
    700 10 Shields, Robert J.
    700 10 Cason, Gene W.
    710 20 National Cheerleaders Association (U.S.)
    785 00 Herkimer, L. R. $t Clinic cheers and pom-pon
routines $w (OCoLC)nnnnnnn

NATIONAL CHEERLEADERS ASSOCIATION
1974-75 EDITION

CLINIC CHEERS

AND

POM-PON ROUTINES

BY

L.R. HERKIMER

and GENE W. CASON

23 PHOTOGRAPHICALLY ILLUSTRATED CHEER AND POM-PON ROUTINES WITH COMPLETE DIRECTIONS AND EXPLANATIONS FOR EASY COMPREHENSION.

TABLE OF CONTENTS

1974 SUMMER CHEERS   PAGE

BOOGIE DOWN 2
COLONELS ARE NUMBER ONE 3
FIGHT, COUGARS, FIGHT 4
YOU BIT OFF MORE THAN YOU CAN CHEW 5
GREAT IS BETTER THAN GOOD 6
GO, FIGHT, WIN
GET GONE
HEY EVERYBODY SAY SCORE
CATS ARE MOVIN' ON
PUSH AHEAD
EASE ON IN
GATORS IN ACTION
LET'S RALLY
THE TIME IS RIGHT
HEY YOU, HEY RAIDERS
WIN TODAY

POM PON ROUTINES
SCORPIO
KING HEROD'S SONG
ROCK AROUND THE CLOCK
W.S.C. MEDLEY

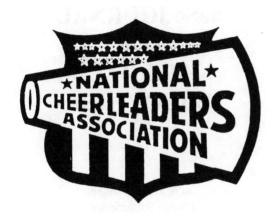

Another outstanding publication by
THE NATIONAL CHEERLEADERS ASSOCIATION
Box 30674, Dallas, Texas 75230

Example 481

```
Herkimer, L. R.
     Clinic cheers and pom-pon routines / by L.R.
Herkimer and Gene W. Cason. -- 1974-75 ed.-
-- National Cheerleaders Association, c1974-
          v. : ill. ; 28 cm.


     Annual.
     Title from cover.
     Continues: Herkimer, L. R. Clinic cheers.
     Contains "photographically illustrated cheer
and pom-pon routines with complete directions and
explanations for easy comprehension."


     I. Cason, Gene W.  II. National Cheerleaders
Association.   III. Title.
```

D: 12.1B1, 12.1F1, 12.3C1, B.5, 12.4, 1.4F6, 12.5, 12.7B1, 12.7B3, 12.7B7, 12.7B18
C: 21.1A1, 21.1A2, 21.6C1
F: 22.1A, 22.1B (RI), 22.5A
AE: 21.30B, 21.30E, 21.30J
F: 22.1A, 22.5A, 24.1

Serials are rarely entered under personal author. The choice of entry in this case was based on cataloger judgment.

FALL 1978
VOLUME XV NO. 1

aaSe

THE
JOURNAL
FOR
SPECIAL
EDUCATORS

Formerly
•**Journal for Special Educators of the Mentally Retarded**
•**Journal for Special Children**
•**The Retarded Adult**

aaSe
**American Association of
Special Educator, Inc.**

PUBLISHERS OF

aaSe JOURNAL
FOR
SPECIAL
EDUCATORS

aaSe Membership &
Journal Subscriptions
aaSe JFSE — Business Office
Joseph Prentsky
179 Sierra Vista Lane
Valley Cottage, NY 10989

aaSe JFSE-Editorial Office
Dr. Alfred Lazar
100 Via Capay
Palos Verdes Estates, CA 90274

aaSe Journal for Special Education solicits original articles concerned with the education, broadly defined,
of the handicapped. Articles concerned with pilot studies, classroom work and innovations at the local level
are encouraged. Papers should be submitted to the Editorial Office. See address above.

From The Editors

Good News...The Triple Merger

We are happy to announce that Special Children, The Retarded Adult and The Journal for Special Educators of the Mentally Retarded are now merged into one major enlarged Journal under the aegis of the A.A.S.E., with a brand new name:

aaSe THE JOURNAL FOR SPECIAL EDUCATORS

You may subscribe for the Journal alone. However, for the same fee, you can join the aaSe (American Association of Special Education) and receive the Journal in addition. With aaSe membership, you will receive:

- aaSe   The Journal for Special Educators plus newsletters
- aaSe   Membership certificate (suitable for framing)
- aaSe   Membership card
- aaSe   Free Professional listing in our forthcoming Directory of Special Educators
- aaSe   Free Facility listing in forthcoming Directory for Special Children
- aaSe   Fellowship Honors Certificate Award to selected aaSe members of 5 or more years (advanced payment up to 5 years accepted).
- aaSe   Publication at reduced cost. Regularly sold for $3.50 each. With membership, $2.50 each:
    Dictionary of Special Education Terminology
    Special Educators Question & Answer Book
    Special Educators Handboks, Vol. 1; Vol. 2
    Directory of Special Educators - to be published in 1979-80
    Directory for Special Children - to be published in 1979-80
- aaSe   Special Education Conference:
    Dallas, Texas — April 25-27, 1979
- aaSe   Job Mart. The Journal will offer aaSe members a free platform of visibility for their job openings and their situation wanted positions.
- aaSe   Membership:
    Professional Individual Membership
    $10.00 per year which includes the Journal ($12 Foreign)
    Institutional Journal Subscription
    $15.00 per year, Journal included. ($17.00 Foreign)
    (Universities, Boards of Education, Libraries, Institutions, etc.)

Use handy subscription blank or your own leter. Include check or Purchase Order for Schools, Libraries, Universities & Institutions. Note: Articles for Publication in the Journal. Submit 3 copies, typed, double spaced on 8 1/2x11" paper. Send to:

Dr. Alfred Lazar, Editorial Office,
Journal for Special Educators, 100 Via Capay,
Palos Verdes Estates, CA 90274

Example 482

```
The Journal for special educators / American Asso-
    ciation of Special Educators. -- Vol. 15, no.
    1 (fall 1978)-    . -- [Palos Verdes Estates,
    Calif. : The Association], c1978-
        v. ; 22 cm.


    Title from cover.
    Merger of: Special children ; Retarded adult
; and, Journal for special educators of the men-
tally retarded.
    Also available on microfilm from University
Microfilms International.
    ISSN 0197-5323.



    I. American Association of Special Educators.
```

Cross reference

```
aaSe journal for special educators
    see
The Journal for Special educators.
```

D:	12.1B1, A.4D, 12.1F1, 12.3C4, 1.4D4, 1.4F6, 12.5, 12.7B3, 12.7B7, 12.7B16, 12.8B1
C:	21.1C
AE:	21.30E
F:	24.1

The abbreviation aaSe was considered a logo rather than part of the title proper, and a cross reference was made according to 26.1

CURRENT PERIODICAL SERIES

PUBLICATION NO: 2543.02

TITLE: JOURNAL FOR SPECIAL EDUCATORS
Index

VOLUME: 15   **ISSUES:**   1-3

DATE: Fall 1978 - Spring 1979

University Microfilms International, Ann Arbor, Mich.

MICROFILMED — 1979

Example 483

Journal for special educators [microform]. --
    Vol. 15, no. 1 (fall 1978)-   . -- [Palos
    Verdes Estates, Calif. : The Association],
    c1978-
       v. ; 22 cm.

    Title from cover.
    Merger of: Special children ; Retarded adult
; and, Journal for special educators of the mentally retarded.
    Microfilm. Ann Arbor, Mich. : University
Microfilms International, 1979-   .   microfilm
reels ; 35 mm. (Current periodical series; no.
2543.02).

    I. American Association of Special Educators.
II. Series: Current periodical series; no.
2543.02.

D: 11.0A, 12.1B1, A.4D, 12.1C, 12.1F1, 12.3C4, 1.4D4, 1.4F6, 12.5,
     12.7B3, 12.7B7, 12.7B19, 11.7B22
C: 21.1C
AE: 21.30E
F: 24.1

Library of Congress practice for cataloging microforms.

Type: a Bib lvl: s Govt pub: Lang: eng Source: d S/L ent: 0
Repr: a Enc lvl: I Conf pub: 0 Ctry: miu Ser tp: p Alphabt: a
Indx: u Mod rec: Phys med: Cont: Frequn: u Pub st: c
Desc: a Cum ind: u Titl pag: u ISDS: Regulr: u Dates: 1978-9999

   010
   040   XXX $c XXX
   007   h $b d $d $e $f u--- $g b $h u $i c $j u
   022   0197-5323
   090
   049   XXXX
   245 04 The Journal for special educators $h micro-
form / $c American Association of Special Educators.
   260 00 Palos Verdes Estates, Calif. : $b The Asso-
ciation, $c c1978-
   300   v. ; $c 22 cm.
   362 0 Vol. 15, no. 1 (fall 1978)-
   500   Title from cover,
   710 20 American Association of Special Educators.
   533   Microfilm. $b Ann Arbor, Mich. : $c University Microfilms International, $d 1979-   . $e
microfilm reels ; 35 mm. $f (Current periodical series ;
no. 2543.02)
   580   Merger of: Special children ; Retarded adult
; and, Journal for special educators of the mentally
retarded.
   780 14 $t Special children $w (OCoLC)nnnnnnn
   780 14 $t Retarded adult $w (OCoLC)nnnnnnn
   780 14 $t Journal for special educators of the
mentally retarded $w (OCoLC)nnnnnnn
   830 0 Current periodical series ; $v no. 2543.02.

Governor's Office of Volunteer Services

VOLUME 1   MARCH, 1976   NUMBER 1

GOVERNOR'S OFFICE OF VOLUNTEER SERVICES

This is the first issue of the Governor's Office of Volunteer Services' newsletter. It is designed to share information and resources relevant to volunteer activities in Minnesota.

Established on June 30, 1975, the Governor's Office of Volunteer Services (G.O.V.S.) is now well underway.

Laura Lee M. Geraghty, a former Coordinator of Volunteer Services for the Ramsey County Welfare Department, was named Director of the Office.

G.O.V.S. was created to provide services to local volunteer programs. In the initial months of operation, G.O.V.S. staff has been gathering information from a wide range of volunteer programs. We have been working with volunteer groups providing services in schools, residential treatment facilities, nursing homes, state and private hospitals, scout programs among others. The scope of volunteer activity is broad and the task of collecting information on these programs is extensive.

G.O.V.S. is currently conducting a survey of Minnesota public agencies as a formal step toward determining the extent of volunteerism in our state. The survey will also identify existing volunteer services and problem areas, in order that G.O.V.S. can provide services to more adequately meet the needs of community volunteer programs. We appreciate the time and efforts of those completing the surveys and providing us with this valuable information.

We will be sharing the results of the surveys through this newsletter. We also solicit your input, ideas, suggestions and articles for future issues of the G.O.V.S. newsletter.

At a meeting discussing the establishment of the Governor's Office of Volunteer Services are (left to right) Laura Lee M. Geraghty, Director of G.O.V.S.; Governor Wendell R. Anderson; and Lois Wollan, Director of the Minnesota ACTION Office, the federal agency funding G.O.V.S.

NATIONAL CONGRESS, '76

Preparations are in progress for the National Congress on Volunteerism and Citizenship, 1976 (NCVC, '76), scheduled for November 19-23, 1976. An official Bicentennial event, the Congress is being convened by the National Center for Voluntary Action (NCVA). Created in 1969, NCVA is a private, non-profit organization dedicated to stimulating and strengthening volunteer services and voluntary organizations.

Beginning with the American Revolution, volunteers have made major contributions to the growth and development of the United States. It is fitting that their efforts and potential be recognized in this significant Bicentennial activity.

NCVC, '76 will provide an opportunity for volunteers to speak out and be heard on matters that concern them and their communities. As a volunteer, you can be involved in the National Congress through a four-step process — a series of meetings at the local, U.S. Congressional District, National and state levels.

The process begins with the Local Forums, where volunteers will meet to identify community problems, and determine how voluntary action can contribute to their solutions. The topics are determined by you, whether it's crime in the streets, the need for increased volunteer benefits, or the need to expand existing volunteer services.

Local Forums can be initiated by either individuals or organizations within a community. Meetings may be formal or informal, large or small. There may be several Local Forums in one community, convened by different groups.

According to NCVC, '76 guidelines Local Forums should be completed by April 15, 1976, in order to make preparations for the District Forums. Although time is limited, G.O.V.S encourages volunteer leaders to participate in this exciting

cont. pg. 2

page 1

Calendar of Events

March 19 VOLUNTEER LEADERS TRAINING WORKSHOP *Location:* Duluth, MN *Theme:* "So Why Make Things Hard for Yourself." *Topics:* Assertive Use of Student Volunteers; Skills for New Coordinators; Volunteer Services to the Bereaved; Training Designs; Volunteer Benefits. Contact: Charlene Kramer, Voluntary Action Center, 402 Ordean Bldg., Duluth, MN 55802, (218) 777-7447.

March 23 PERSPECTIVES ON VOLUNTEERISM *Location:* Rochester, MN *Topics:* motivation and benefits of volunteers. Contact: Phyllis Acker, Information and Volunteer Center of Olmsted County, 913 SE 3rd Avenue, Rochester, MN 55901.

March 29 to June 12 VOLUNTEERS II *Location:* Minneapolis Campus, U of M. An advanced course in training and supervision for volunteer administrators. Instructor: Don Hadfield. Sp. Qtr. Contact: U of M, Continuing Education and Extension, Minneapolis, MN 55455.

March 29 to June 12 DYNAMICS OF VOLUNTARISM *Location:* Duluth, MN. A course designed for those who wish to more effectively utilize volunteer help in social programs. Instructor: Gene Hooyman. Sp. Qtr. held each Thursday evening (7 p.m.). Contact: Continuing Education and Extension, 431 Administration Bldg., U of M, Duluth, MN 55812 or (218) 726-8113.

March 31 VOLUNTEERISM, 1976: HUMAN RESOURCES UTILIZATION *Location:* Radisson Central, Minneapolis, MN (9-11 a.m.). *Purpose:* to provide tools and information by which professional staff in human service agencies can fully and effectively utilize the skills of volunteer staff. A session of the Minnesota Social Service Association Conference. (M.S.S.A.) open to the public.

April 9-10 N.O.W. STATE TASK FORCE ON RAPE *Location:* Camp Courage, Buffalo, MN. A working weekend to train teams of workers who can assess and improve local rape services. Contact: State Task Force on Rape, 2851 E. Lake of the Isles, Minneapolis, MN 55408.

April 23 3rd ANNUAL CONFERENCE FOR HEALTH CARE JR. VOLUNTEERS *Location:* Nolte Center, Minneapolis Campus, U of M. Sponsored by the Minnesota Council of Directors of Health Care Volunteers, this conference is designed for youth volunteers in health care facilities. Contact: Barb Thomasson, Jr. Volunteer Coordinator, Fairview Hospital, 2312 S. 6th, Minneapolis, MN 55454.

April 29-30 MINNESOTA ASSOCIATION OF VOLUNTEER DIRECTORS SPRING CONFERENCE *Location:* Duluth, MN. Contact: Conrad Jones, Student Activity Center, U of M, 317 17th Ave., SE, Minneapolis, MN 55455.

May 14 THE FUTURE IS MAYBE? *Location:* Minneapolis Auditorium (9:30-11:30 a.m.). A review of the external forces affecting hospitals and their impact on volunteer service programs, presented by Sylvia Schaer. An open session of the Upper Midwest Hospital Conference. Contact: Mrs. Dell Poppenberger, Director of Volunteers, St. John's Hospital, 403 Maria Ave., St. Paul, MN 55106.

May 16-22 NATIONAL VOLUNTEER WEEK

June 3-4 HUMANISM — THE RIGHT TO BE *Location:* St. Paul. A two-day skill improvement workshop, focusing on inter-personal relationships and volunteer administrators. Part 1 of a 3 part series. Contact: Maggi Davern, Voluntary Action Center of St. Paul, Inc., 65 E. Kellogg Blvd., St. Paul, MN 55101.

June 14-25 WORKSHOP FOR VOLUNTEER COORDINATORS *Location:* Marshall, MN. Two week workshop, college credits available, as well as certificates for skill mastery. Contact: Keigh Hubel, Southwest State University, Marshall, MN 56258.

August 19 STATE-WIDE YOUTH VOLUNTEER RECOGNITION DAY

Information on national and regional conferences, held outside Minnesota, can be obtained by writing or calling the Governor's Office of Volunteer Services.

If your organization has an upcoming event that would be of interest to volunteers and volunteer coordinators, please contact G.O.V.S.

Governor's Office of Volunteer Services
130 State Capitol
St. Paul, MN 55155

Address Correction Requested

Bulk Rate
U.S. Postage
PAID
Permit No. 171
St. Paul, MN

Please Post for others to read.

Example 484

Governor's Office of Volunteer Services : [news-
    letter]. -- Vol. 1, no. 1 (Mar. 1976)-
    -- [St. Paul, MN : The Office]. 1976-
        v. : ill. ; 28 cm.

Quarterly.
Title from caption.

    I. Minnesota. Governor's Office of Volunteer
Services.

D: 1.1B3, 1.1E6, 12.3C4, 1.4C3, B.14, 1.4D4, 12.4F1, 12.5, 12.7B1,
      12.7B3
C: 21.1C
AE: 21.30E
F: 24.18(type 3)

Type: a Bib lvl: s Govt pub: s Lang: eng Source: d S/L ent: 0
Repr: Enc lvl: I Conf pub: 0 Ctry: mnu Ser tp: p Alphabt: a
Indx: u Mod rec: Phys med: Cont: Frequn: q Pub st: c
Desc: a Cum ind: u Titl pag: u ISDS: Regulr: r Dates: 1976-9999

    010
    040   XXX $c XXX
    090
    049   XXXX
    245 00 Governor's Office of Volunteer Services :
[newsletter].
    260 00 St. Paul, MN : $b The Office. $c 1976-
    265   130 State Capitol, St. Paul, MN 55155
    300   v. : $b ill. ; $c 28 cm.
    362 0 Vol. 1, no. 1 (Mar. 1976)-
    500   Title from caption.
    710 10 Minnesota. $b Governor's Office of Volunteer
Services.

VOLUME 1, NUMBER I   MARCH 1974

The Minnesota Higher Education Coordinating Commission expects to provide loans for up to 25,000 students in the next 18 months following the successful sale of $29.4
                      million in revenue bonds to finance the new State Loan Program. The
$29.4 MILLION   low bid of 4.82% interest rate was submitted by a syndicate headed
STUDENT LOAN   by BancNorthwest of Chicago. Sale of student loan bonds was combined
BONDS SOLD   with the sale of $600,000 in bonds for the rural practice medical
                      loan program. Announcement of the bond sale was made by Governor
Wendell Anderson in a ceremony at his office February 26 featuring legislators, five
student leaders and Commission members. Applications can be obtained from financial
aid offices at more than 200 public and private post-secondary institutions eligible
for the program in Minnesota. Any person registered or accepted for enrollment at an
eligible institution in Minnesota, or a Minnesota resident who is registered or
accepted for enrollment at an eligible institution in another state can apply for a
loan. The program was authorized by the 1973 State Legislature.

Changing enrollment patterns necessitate consideration of possible consolidation or
merger of institutions of post-secondary education in Minnesota, but policies should
                      not be influenced solely by enrollment criteria, says a preliminary
ENROLLMENT NOT HECC staff report. The Commission last fall instructed the staff to
SOLE CRITERIA   re-examine its guidelines on access to post-secondary education in
FOR MERGING   order to establish new priorities for establishment or possible
                      merging of institutions. Despite the projected decline in high
school graduates by 1980, a wide range of factors must be considered to develop
alternatives for dealing with possible adjustments, the report emphasizes. Concerns
besides enrollment include types of programs offered, their cost and extent to which
they are meeting the needs of the community and its surrounding area.

Renewal of the student reciprocity agreement with Wisconsin for the 1974-75 academic
year has been approved by the Coordinating Commission. The program, designed to
                      provide greater accessibility of post-secondary education and
COMMISSION   improved economy, must be ratified by the University of Minnesota
OKS RENEWAL   Board of Regents, State College Board, State Board for Community
OF RECIPROCITY Colleges and State Board for Vocational Education. Under the agree-
PACT   ment, Minnesota and Wisconsin residents would be able to pay in-
                      state tuition in the neighboring state, but space must be available
in a particular program for a student to enter an institution in the other state.
The education pact is tied to an income tax reciprocity plan. Applications are
available from high school counselors, student service officers at Minnesota institutions or from the Commission's Reciprocity Office, Suite 400, 550 Cedar Street,
St. Paul, Minnesota 55101

VOLUME II, NUMBER 11   JULY 1976

LOAN FUNDS ASSURED   The availability of at least $35 million to meet the demand
UNDER NEW PLAN TO   for student loans during the 1976-77 school year has been
FINANCE STATE PROGRAM assured under a new plan developed to finance the state program.
                          The Board on June 29 sold $37.2 million in advance refunding
bonds to refund outstanding revenue bonds in the program. And the Board sold its
existing portfolio of federally-insured loans to the Student Loan Marketing Association (Sallie Mae), a U. S. Government sponsored corporation created to provide liquid-
ity to a lender by purchasing the lender's student loans. The State Student Loan
Program is self supporting. Funds for all expenses, including those for administration, are generated by the program.

    In a little over two years the Board has made 26,000 loans totaling in excess of
$42 million. Loans, which average $1650, have been made to students attending 526
institutions. Students may borrow up to $2500 per year. The program, approved by
the 1973 Minnesota Legislature, began on April 1, 1974, following the sale of $29.4
million in revenue bonds. When funds were nearly exhausted last fall, the Board--
which is authorized to sell up to $90 million in revenue bonds--attempted to sell
bonds but experienced difficulty due to high interest rates offered. Finally, separate bond sales of $8 million and $10 million were negotiated and provided funds for
the school year. However, future financing of the program remained uncertain because
of the high interest rates, and a new plan had to be developed to assure sufficient
funds at no cost to the state. Proceeds of the sale to Sallie Mae will provide up
to $35 million to meet the demand for 1976-77.

    Sale of $37.2 million in refunding bonds was to a group headed by BancNorthwest
of Chicago, First National Bank of St. Paul and Piper, Jaffray and Hopwood Inc. of
Minneapolis. Interest rate is 5.25 percent for the two year notes which mature on
April 1, 1978. The purpose of the refunding bond issue is to eliminate the existing
long term debt, eliminate existing restrictive covenants in previous bond resolutions
accomplish a vehicle for future issuance of short-term obligations, eliminate administrative costs of maintaining the loans outstanding and complete the anticipated
1976-77 program without having to issue additional bonds. Proceeds of the refunding
bonds, in addition to funds currently on hand, will be placed in an escrow account
maintained by Northwestern National Bank of Minneapolis and will be used to acquire
U. S. Treasury notes and bonds sufficient to repay all the $47,400,000 of principal
and interest on refunded bonds to date of maturity.

    The Board sold its eligible loan notes to Sallie Mae at a discounted price of
97 percent. Net proceeds of the sale, in addition to certain bond funds on hand,
will constitute security for the refunding issue. In order to insure adequate funds
will be available to guarantee payment of the refunding bonds due April 1, 1978,

(continued on Page 6)

Example 485

Mhecb report   September 1976   Page 6

Equipment grants approved

The U.S. Department of Health, Education and Welfare has approved grants totaling $133,135 for use by 17 Minnesota post-secondary institutions in purchasing undergraduate instructional equipment.

Congress appropriated $7.5 million this year for the program (Title VI-A Higher Education Act 1965). HECB reviews and ranks applications for grants according to a state plan and HEW regulations.

Institutions apply for grants under two categories — Category I for general undergraduate equipment and Category II for equipment used for closed circuit televised instruction. The federal share comprises about half the total project costs.

Following are institutions receiving Category I grants and the federal share received:

Normandale Community College $10,000, Lakewood Community College $3,240, Metropolitan State University $4,250, North Hennepin Community College $5,000, Rainy River Community College $828, Rochester Community College $8,400, Bethel College $10,000,

College of St. Benedict $10,000, Hibbing Community College $2,271, College of St. Catherine $7,626, Winona State University $10,000, Augsburg College $5,512, St. John's University $9,981, St. Cloud State University $10,000 and Minneapolis College of Art and Design $4,400.

The following institutions received Category II grants:

St. John's University $9,628, College of St. Teresa $3,375, Hibbing Community College $2,775, St. Cloud State University $9,778 and Metropolitan Community College $1,071.

Hawk is selected

HECB Executive Director Richard C. Hawk has been named to a national advisory committee for a study of state student aid programs and their relationship to federal aid programs.

The project has been established at the Education Commission of the States in Denver by a one-year contract of $157,155 from the U.S. Office of Education. The National Center for Higher Education Management Systems, Boulder, Colorado, will assist in the study.

Staff changes are announced

Several HECB staff changes have occurred this summer.

Dr. Neal Burns, acting associate executive director, resigned to form a private consulting firm.

Deborah Reckinger has been appointed Coordinator of Student Financial Aids. She replaces Gary Symonds who moved to Illinois.

Arlon J. Haupert has accepted a position as Administrative Management Director I. He will manage and direct the agency's fiscal affairs.

Alex Lewis has joined the staff's research and information systems division as a research associate. Dr. Robert Rustad has been named assistant executive director for financial planning and budget review. He heads a new division primarily responsible for budget review.

Donald Underhill has been appointed advising coordinator for the Range regional center. Barry Bain, Merle Singer and Mary Sullivan are adult advising coordinators for the Wadena Center under a CETA grant.

First Class
U.S. Postage
PAID 1 OZ
Permit No. 171
St. Paul, Minn.

Minnesota Higher Education
Coordinating Board
Suite 400 — Capitol Square Building
550 Cedar Street
St. Paul, Minn. 55101
612-296-3974

Financial Aid Office
Room 901
Capitol Square Building
612-296-5715

MHECC report. -- Vol. 1, no. 1 (Mar. 1974)-v. 2, no. 11 (July 1976). -- St. Paul, Minn. : Minnesota Higher Education Coordinating Commission, 1974-1976.

2 v. ; 28 cm.

Monthly.
Title from caption.
"Newsletter of the Minnesota Higher Education Coordinating Commission."
Continued by: Mhecb report.

I. Minnesota Higher Education Coordinating Commission.

D: 12.1B1, A.1, 12.3F, C.1C, 12.4F3, 12.5B2, 2.5D1, 12.7B1, 12.7B3, 12.7B5, 12.7B7
C: 21.1C
AE: 21.30E
F: 24.17, 26.3A7, 26.3A3

```
Type: a  Bib lvl: s  Govt pub: s  Lang: eng  Source: d  S/L ent: 0
Repr:      Enc lvl: I  Conf pub: 0  Ctry: mnu  Ser tp: p  Alphabt: a
Indx: u  Mod rec:     Phys med:     Cont:       Frequn: m  Pub st: d
Desc: a  Cum ind: u  Titl pag: u  ISDS:        Regulr: r  Dates: 1974-1976
```

```
010
040      XXX $c XXX
090
049      XXXX
245 00 MHECC report.
260 00 St. Paul, Minn. : $b Minnesota Higher Educa-
tion Coordinating Commission, $c 1974-1976.
300      2 v. ; $c 28 cm.
362 0   Vol. 1, no. 1 (Mar. 1974)-v. 2, no. 11 (July
1976).
500      Title from caption.
500      "Newsletter of the Minnesota Higher Educa-
tion Coordinating Commission."
710 20 Minnesota Higher Education Coordinating
Commission.
785 00 $t Mhecb report $w (OCoLC)nnnnnnn
```

Range regional project report, page 5

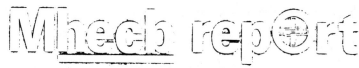

VOLUME III, NUMBER 1   **SEPTEMBER 1976**

Scholarship, grant deadline Feb. 1

The priority deadline to file an application for the Minnesota State Scholarship and Grant-in-Aid Programs for the 1977-78 academic year is February 1, 1977. All application materials must be postmarked on or before that date to receive priority consideration and submitted to the American College Testing Program in Iowa City, Iowa.

Application forms will be mailed this fall to the homes of virtually all high school seniors in the state and renewal candidates. Forms also will be available from high school counselors, post-secondary financial aid officers and from HECB. Submission of one set of completed application forms assures the applicant of consideration for both the Scholarship and Grant-in-Aid Programs. Applicants must complete both the application form and the Family Financial Statement.

HECB awarded Bush grant for library project

A $216,000 grant from the Bush Foundation to HECB will enable libraries in Minnesota and North Dakota to begin developing a computer-based cataloging process.

The grant, largest of 39 announced by the Bush Foundation in July, will help libraries in Minnesota and the region to take advantage of the dramatic, technological changes occurring in library operations.

It will enhance services to Minnesota residents and improve sharing of library resources fostered by the successful statewide MINITEX program (Minnesota Interlibrary Telecommunication Exchange).

The project application was prompted by library leaders who are concerned about rising costs and rapid expansion of printed sources.

The project is aimed at meeting two urgent needs to ensure effective delivery

continued on page 5

HECB planning meeting of state boards

The Coordinating Board will sponsor a special meeting in November for members of the state's post-secondary education boards.

Tentative date for the meeting is November 9. The HECB executive committee is arranging the location, format and other details.

Under a 1976 law HECB is required to sponsor an annual meeting of member representatives of its Board, the Higher Education Facilities Authority, the State Board for Community Colleges, the State University Board, the State Board of Education and the University Board of Regents. Others may be invited.

Purpose of the meeting is to provide an opportunity to discuss issues of mutual concern and to "facilitate coordination and planning of activities deemed beneficial to higher education in the state."

A summary of the discussion and any recommendations approved at the meeting are to be sent to legislative committees.

Southwest citizens report; consultants to speak Sept. 30

Several groups selected to advise the Higher Education Coordinating Board on its study of post-secondary education in southwestern Minnesota are beginning to report their recommendations as the project enters the final two months.

The Citizens' Advisory Committee presented its initial position paper at the HECB August 26 meeting in St. Cloud.

A panel of four out-of-state consultants will report at the Board's September 30 meeting in St. Paul. The Board will meet October 28 in Marshall and will release the study report in early November.

The study staff has refined the 10

Excerpts page 4

alternatives released in June and also has analyzed an additional alternative suggested by the Citizens' Advisory Committee. That alternative involves the transfer of Southwest State University to the University Board of Regents, maintenance of the current liberal arts program, and the addition of programs in agriculture and technology relating to the school's service area. The University of Minnesota at Morris would not be closed.

A study group appointed by the Higher Education Advisory Council is looking at program options which might be desirable

for Southwest State University.

Lew Hudson of Worthington, representing the Citizens' Advisory Committee, told the Board that it must focus on the question of why the enrollment decline at SSU has been so much more precipitous than at any other Minnesota institution. He called this "the single most important and still unanswered question."

Hudson emphasized that the problem is structural, administrative, and programmatic; he said the problem is not demography although demography may at some future time cause problems for all out-state institutions.

An analysis of information from a statewide survey of transfer policies and practices by a transfer study committee is expected to be completed in April.

TRANSFER SURVEY INFORMATION BEING ANALYZED
The committee, appointed in February 1973 by HECC executive director Richard C. Hawk to study the problems of transfer students, consists of two representatives from each of the post-secondary educational systems in the state. The committe chaired by Ralph F. Berdie, expects to meet with representati from post-secondary institutions in May or June to discuss major problems identi in the survey. It hopes to formulate recommendations and forward them to HECC by fall of 1974. In addition, the committee hopes to use the survey information as basis for a handbook that will aid high school and college counselors and studen planning programs which include transfer from one institution to another.

PRIVATE COLLEGE CONTRACT PAYMENT RATE ADOPTED
An adjustment in the method for making payments to institutions under the Privat College Contract Program has been adopted by the Coordinating Commission. A comb tion of significant increases in new resident enrollments at participating institutions, increased grant-in-aid recipients and a limited appropriation make it impossible to allow payme maximum rates allowed under the statutes ($400 for two-year institutions and $500 for four-year institutions.) HECC will proportionately reduce the rate of payment while maintaining the same ratio in tl law. Payments are estimated to be at the rate of $324 for two-year institutions $405 for four-year institutions.

HECC RECEIVES U.S. GRANT FOR HEALTH PLANNING
The Coordinating Commission has received a $7,760 federal grant to prepare mater; for use in improving coordination and information-sharing among persons in state and area-wide health planning. Under the project funded by Noi lands Regional Medical Program, Inc., the HECC staff, with th assistance of seven Community-Based Health Education Councils will design documents of policies, studies, procedures and activities used in health planning. Besides providing area-wi health planners throughout the state with a clearinghouse for sharing informatio and planning activities with HECC, the project is expected to help develop bette communications between the planners and HECC. It is the first time HECC has established relationships with CHECs to share information and as a result it is expected to provide a better picture of who is doing what in health planning in state. Colleen Guilfoile has joined the HECC staff to assist in conducting the w for the project.

Minnesota Higher Education
Coordinating Commission
Suite 400 — 550 Cedar Street
St. Paul, Minn. 55101
296-3974

Example 486

Mhecb report. -- Vol. 3, no. 1 (Sept. 1976)-   . --
    St. Paul, Minn. : Minnesota Higher Education
    Coordinating Board, 1976-
        v. : ill. ; 28 cm.

Monthly.
Title from caption.
Continues: MHECC report.

I. Minnesota Higher Education Coordinating
Board.

D: 12.1B1, A.1, 12.3C4, C.1C, 12.4, 12.5, 12.7B1, 12.7B3, 12.7B7
C: 21.1C
AE: 21.30E

Type: a Bib lvl: s Govt pub: s Lang: eng Source: d S/L ent: 0
Repr: Enc lvl: I Conf pub: 0 Ctry: mnu Ser tp: p Alphabt: a
Indx: u Mod rec: Phys med: Cont: Frequn: m Pub st: c
Desc: a Cum ind: u Titl pag: u ISDS: Regulr: r Dates: 1976-9999

    010
    040   XXX $c XXX
    090
    049   XXXX
    245 00 Mhecb report.
    260 00 St. Paul, Minn. : $b Minnesota Higher Educa-
tion Coordinating Board, $c 1976-
    300   v. : $b ill. ; $c 28 cm.
    362 0 Vol. 3, no. 1 (Sept. 1976)-   .
    500   Title from caption.
    710 20 Minnesota Higher Education Coordinating
Board.
    780 00 $t MHECC report $w (OCoLC)nnnnnnn

Minkus

Stamp Journal

Vol. I
1966

New Faces on American Stamps

No. 1
25¢

Minkus Stamp Journal

A new quarterly publication

JACQUES MINKUS, *Publisher*

CONTENTS

LETTER FROM THE PUBLISHER 3

DESIGNS THAT DIDN'T MAKE IT 4

PROMINENT AMERICANS 5

STAMP PROGRAMS 12

PHILATELIC QUIZ 12

EL GRECO, THE GREEK FROM TOLEDO . . . 13

STAMPS THAT GLOW 23

THE CORAL REEF 35

NEW LISTINGS 38

TOPICAL LISTINGS 66

●

Editorial Board

MINKUS STAMP JOURNAL is published quarterly by Minkus Stamp Journal, Inc. Editorial and Business Offices at 116 West 32nd St., New York, N. Y. 10001. Subscriptions $1.00 a year. Single issue 25¢. Copyright ©1966 by Minkus Stamp Journal. Printed in U. S. A.

Photograph of Virginia Vestoff, Broadway actress, by M. R. Lefkoe, New York City. The stamp portrayed is the Danish Ballet and Music Festival issue of 1965 (Minkus #596, Scott #422).

You are invited to send photographic interpretations of stamps to us. Photo essays accepted for publication will be awarded $10.00. It is not necessary to send a picture of the stamp — simply indicate by Minkus or Scott catalog number. If you wish your photograph returned to you, in the event that it is not accepted for publication, please enclose a self-addressed, stamped envelope. Address entries to: THE MINKUS STAMP JOURNAL, 116 West 32nd St., New York, N. Y. 10001.

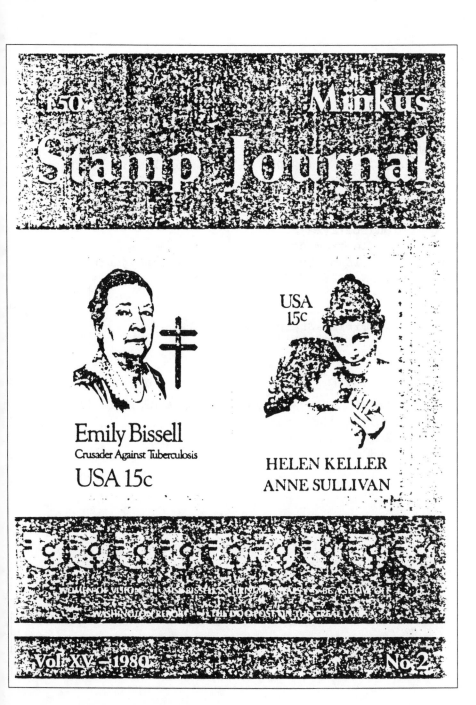

$1.50 **Minkus**

Stamp Journal

Emily Bissell
Crusader Against Tuberculosis
USA 15c

USA 15c

HELEN KELLER
ANNE SULLIVAN

Vol. XV — 1980   No. 2

MSJ

**Minkus
Stamp Journal**

VOL. XV, No. 2 — 1980

Publisher
JACQUES MINKUS

●

Editorial Board

Editor-in-Chief
BELMONT FARIES

Managing Editor
BEATRICE HESSEN

Art Director
SIEGFRIED ROTH

Production Manager
TAD GAITHER

Advertising Manager
LUCILLE FOY

●

Contributing Staff
Harold Adler, Marina Odone, Katie Brooks,
Mariana Kalan, Susan Krabbe, Janet Rotondo,
Robert Oken, George Hamsa

●

We want to hear more from our readers. We invite you to send letters to the editor on: "My Favorite Topic" and "How I Became Interested in Stamp Collecting." You will receive $10 if your letter is published. Send to: Minkus Stamp Journal, 116 West 42nd St., New York, N.Y. 10001.

MINKUS STAMP JOURNAL is published quarterly by Minkus Stamp Journal, Inc. Editorial and Business Offices at 116 West 42nd St., New York, N.Y. 10001. Subscriptions: Subscription rates are $5.00 a year in the United States; $7.00 per year in Canada and all other countries. Single issue $2.50 plus postage. Subscribers: Send changes of address, attaching address label from wrapper, to: Minkus Stamp Journal, 116 West 42nd St., New York, N.Y. 10001. Answers to all correspondence regarding subscriptions will be faster if you enclose your address label. Copyright 1980 by Minkus Stamp Journal, Inc. Printed in U.S.A.

Stamp Journal

WOMEN OF VISION
WASHINGTON REPORT

The whys and wherefores behind a scarce new perforation variety, and a re-engraved Oliver Wendell Holmes.

BE A SHOW OFF

The dramatic story of a famous friendship.

Some advice on how to cure exhibiting fever — economically.

THE DOG POST ON THE GREAT LAKES

A 19th century account of a strange and dangerous postal service linking an isolated frontier.

MISS BISSELL'S CHRISTMAS SEALS

How an idea imported from Denmark — intended to save a small hospital — saved thousands of lives and became a Christmas and philatelic tradition in over 100 countries.

1980 Stamp Program 2
A Letter from the Publisher 3
Miss Bissell's Christmas Seals 5
Women of Vision 9
The Dog Post on the Great Lakes 17
Washington Report 21
Be a Show Off 27
Designs That Didn't Make It 33
Know Your Stamps — A Quiz 35
New Issues Listed by Topics 38
New Issues Index 39
United States New Issues 40
World Wide New Issues 42
There's a Story Behind The Stamp 37
Stamp and Coin Departments and Services 79

Example 487

Minkus stamp journal. -- Vol. 1, no. 1 (1966)- v.
    15, no. 2 (1980). -- [New York, N.Y. : Minkus
    Stamp Journal], 1966-1980.
15 v. : ill. ; 27 cm.

Quarterly.
Title from cover.
Continued by: Minkus stamp & coin journal.
ISSN 0026-5357

I. Title: Stamp journal.

D: 12.1B1, 12.3F, 12.4C1, 12.4D1, 12.4F3, 12.5B2, 12.7B1, 12.7B3,
      12.7B7c, 12.8B1
C: 21.1C
AE: 21.30J

$1.50

Minkus

Stamp & Coin Journal

NEDERLAND
95 C

JULIANA 70

THOSE CONFUSING FARLEYS • THE CORAL REEF • WASHINGTON REPORT
COLLECTING THE ANCIENTS • ROTARY CLUBS • OUR ALL-AMERICAN COIN
STAMP FUN WITH CHILDREN • A HOBBY FOR THE FUN OF IT

Vol. XV – 1980   **No. 3**

**Minkus
Stamp & Coin
Journal**

VOL. XV, No. 3 — 1980

Publisher
JACQUES MINKUS

•

Editorial Board

Editor-in-Chief
BELMONT FARIES

Managing Editor
BEATRICE HESSEN

Art Director
SIEGFRIED ROTH

Production Manager
TAD GAITHER

Advertising Manager
LUCILLE FOY

Circulation Manager
LAURIE POLLACK

•

Contributing Staff
Harold Adler, June A. Zimmer, Katie Brooks,
Marianna Kalan, Susan Krabbe, Janet Rotondo,
Robert Okon, George Hamsa.

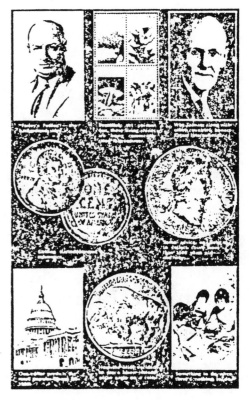

We want to hear more from our read-
ers. We invite you to send letters to the
editor on "My Favorite Topic" and "How
I became interested in Stamp Collecting."
You will receive $10 if your letter is pub-
lished. Send to: Minkus Stamp & Coin
Journal, 116 West 32nd St., New York,
N.Y. 10001.

•

MINKUS STAMP & COIN JOURNAL is published quarterly by Minkus Stamp & Coin, Inc.,
Editorial and Business Offices at 116 West 32nd
St., New York, N.Y. 10001. Subscriptions
for one year, $5.00 for 4 years in the United
States. $7.00 per year of U.S. funds in all
other countries. Single issue $1.50 copy. Six-
month subscribers. Send changes of address
including address label, your magazine, to Minkus Stamp & Coin Journal, 116 West 32nd St.,
New York, N.Y. 10001. Answers to all correspondence regarding subscriptions will be faster if
you enclose your address label. Copyright Spam
by Minkus Stamp Journal, Inc. Printed in U.S.A.

1980 Stamp Program	2
Let's collect coins	5
Those confusing Farleys	9
Collecting the ancients	15
Story behind the stamp	19
Stamp fun with children	21
Washington report	25
All American coin	27
Design that didn't make it	30
Coral reef	33
Rotary International	37
Know your stamps — A quiz	40
New issues listed by topics	41
New issues index	42
United States new issues	43

Our special thanks to Mr. Robert Krajewski, our General Manager,
Coin Division, for his original logo design.

Example 488

Minkus stamp & coin journal. -- Vol. 15, no. 3
     (1980)-   . -- [New York, N.Y. : Minkus Stamp
     Journal], 1980-
         v. : ill. ; 27 cm.

     Quarterly.
     Title from cover.
     Continues: Minkus stamp journal.

     I. Title: Stamp & coin journal. II. Title:
Minkus stamp and coin journal.

D: 12.1B1, 12.3C4, 12.4, 12.5, 12.7B1, 12.7B3, 12.7B7
C: 21.1C
AE: 21.30J(RI)

Type: a Bib lvl: s Govt pub: Lang: eng Source: d S/L ent: 0
Repr: Enc lvl: I Conf pub: 0 Ctry: nyu Ser tp: p Alphabt: a
Indx: u Mod rec: Phys med: Cont: Frequn: q Pub st: d
Desc: a Cum ind: u Titl pag: u ISDS: Regulr: r Dates: 1966-1980

     010
     040   XXX $c XXX
     090
     049   XXXX
     245 00 Minkus stamp journal.
     246 30 Stamp journal.
     260 00 [New York, N.Y. : $b Minkus Stamp Journal],
$c 1966-1980.
     300   15 v. : $b ill. ; $c 27 cm.
     362 0 Vol. 1, no. 1 (1966)-v. 15, no. 2 (1980).
     785 00 $t Minkus stamp & coin journal $w
(OCoLC)nnnnnnn

Vol.5, No.4, February 1980

MINITEX MESSENGER

Minnesota Interlibrary Telecommunications Exchange 30 Wilson Library,
309 19th Avenue S., University of Minnesota Minneapolis, Minnesota 55455

A Program of the Minnesota Higher Education Coordinating Board

RESOURCE SHARING AND INTERLIBRARY LOAN

The sharing of material among libraries isn't a new idea anymore, and it hasn't been for a long time. But the decade just ended witnessed an evolution, still in process, of the ways in which we think about it. As the universe of information resources has expanded, the changing concept of librarianship as providing access to information itself, rather than simple collection and retrieval of documents, has stretched some of the original assumptions of resource sharing.

Beyond librarianship, societal changes also make an impact. Extension of the idea of formal education to lifelong learning, increased consumer demand for responsive services, a widespread need for information to cope with information, inflation, limited resources, and many other things influence the environment in which library service is provided. Once faculty or graduate level research was the only acceptable criterion for an interlibrary loan request. Libraries now use more liberal resource sharing agreements among formally aligned libraries to obtain material needed for the purpose of study, instruction, information, or research.

But the more things change, the more they stay the same, and the local library continues to be the crucial agency for the practice of effective librarianship. To satisfy library users, each library accepts responsibility for maintaining collections of information that meet the predictable needs of its particular community. Only unusual information needs precipitate requests for aid from another library. When this occurs, however, established protocols among cooperating libraries can,

within reason and practicality, permit access to most of what any individual library user really needs.

When interlibrary loan is part of responsive service to individual library users, the librarian has an extra ability to analyze the nature of a particular need and to devise a strategy for appropriate solution to it. Bibliographic displaying holdings of other libraries help this strategy formulation tremendously. And the ability to access other collections to meet users' needs can make the practice of librarianship very satisfying.

The American Library Association library Loan Committee is currently revising the code that regulates lending transactions between research libraries and between libraries operating outside and consortia. Offering a draft of a more liberal code in the December Issue of American Libraries, the Committee states that "the effectiveness of a national system of interlibrary lending is related to the equitable distribution of costs among all the libraries involved. It is understood that every library maintain an appropriate balance between source sharing and responsibility to primary clientele." (p.649)

At this time, librarians engaged in resource sharing arrangements generally a sense of responsibility for all library users served by the cooperating libraries. But if, for any reason, requests from libraries interfere with the ability of a library to serve its primary clientele, foundations of resource sharing quickly crack.

Example 489

MINITEX messenger. -- Minneapolis, Minn. : Minnesota
  Interlibrary Telecommunications Exchange,
     v. : 28 cm.

  Irregular.
  Description based on: Vol. 5, no. 4 (Feb.
1980); title from masthead.
  Began publication in 1974.
  ISSN 0276-0487.

  I. MINITEX (Program).

D: 12.1B1, A.1, 1.4C3, 12.4D1, 12.5B1, 12.5D1, 12.7B1, 12.7B3,
    12.7B8, 12.7B22, 12.8B1
C: 21.1C
AE: 21.30E

Type: a Bib lvl: s Govt pub: s Lang: eng Source: d S/L ent: 0
Repr: Enc lvl: I Conf pub: 0 Ctry: mnu Ser tp: p Alphabt: a
Indx: u Mod rec: Phys med: Cont: Frequn: Pub st: c
Desc: a Cum ind: u Titl pag: u ISDS: Regulr: r Dates: 1974-9999
    010
    040   XXX $c XXX
    022   0276-0487
    090
    049   XXXX
    245 00 MINITEX messenger.
    260 00 Minneapolis, Minn. : $b Minnesota Interli-
brary Telecommunications Exchange,
    265   MINITEX, 30 Wilson Library, 309 - 19th Ave.
So., University of Minnesota, Minneapolis, MN 55455
    300   v. ; $c 28 cm.
    310   Irregular.
    362 1 Began publication in 1974.
    500   Description based on: Vol. 5, no. 4 (Feb.
1980); title from masthead.
    710 20 MINITEX (Program).

HRD

Human Resource Development
An International Journal

Human Resource Development   Volume 4 Number 1 1980

Effective Use of Human Resources
Ronald Lippitt

Training Negotiations
John Carlisle

Effective Team-Building
Gordon Lippitt

Higher Degrees as Management Training
R.W. Pearson

Training for International Operations
Judy Lowe

Inside cover

**Copyright © 1980 MCB Publications Limited: Human Resources
Distributed by MCB Publications Limited: 198/200 & 210 Keighley
Road
Bradford, West Yorkshire, England BD94JQ**

ISSN 0143 77 12

**Printed by Drogher Press Ltd., Airfield Way, Christchurch, Dorset
BH23 3TB**

From the editorial page

... In the United States of America the journal will be known as **Human Resources Development (HRD)** while elsewhere it will continue to be published as the **Journal of European Industrial Training (JEIT)**. Each journal will carry identical contents with contributions from all over the world. We look forward to an interesting and exciting year and trust that you will find the new Journal of interest and value in your work. ...

Example 490

Human resources development : HRD. -- Vol. 4, no.
   1 (1980)-   . -- Bradford, West Yorkshire :
   MCB Publications, c1980-
      v. : ill. ; 30 cm.

   Title from cover.
   Continues: Journal of European industrial
training.
   In countries other than U.S. this journal will
continue to be published as: Journal of European
industrial training.
   ISSN 0143-7712.

   I. Journal of European industrial training.
II. Title: HRD.

D: 12.1B1, 12.1E1, 12.3C4, 12.4, 1.4F6, 12.5, 12.7B3, 12.7B7b,
      12.7B7h, 12.8B1
C: 21.1C
AE: 21.30G, 21.30J

Type: a Bib lvl: s Govt pub: Lang: eng Source: d S/L ent: 0
Repr: Enc lvl: I Conf pub: 0 Ctry: enk Ser tp: p Alphabt: a
Indx: u Mod rec: Phys med: Cont: Frequn: u Pub st: c
Desc: a Cum ind: u Titl pag: u ISDS: Regulr: u Dates: 1980-9999

     010
     040   XXX $c XXX
     022   0143-7712
     090
     049   XXXX
     245 00 Human resource development : $b HRD.
     246 33 HRD
     246 33 Journal of European industrial training
     260 00 Bradford, West Yorkshire : $b MCB Publica-
tions, $c 1980-
     265   MCB Publications Ltd., 198/200 & 210
Keighley Rd., Bradford, West Yorkshire, England BC94JQ
     300   v. : $b ill. ; $c 30 cm.
     362 0 Vol. 4, no. 1 (1980)-
     580   In countries other than U.S. this journal
will continue to be published as: Journal of European
industrial training.
     730 01 Journal of European industrial training
     780 10 $t Journal of European industrial training
$w (OCoLC)nnnnnnn

Revista Latin
de Música American
Latino Music
Americana Review

Volume 1, Number 1 : Spring/Summer 1980

University of Texas Press

Volume 1 : Number 1 : Spring/Summer 1980   ISSN 0163-0350

Revista Latin
de Música American
Latino Music
Americana Review

Editor:
Gerard Behague
Institute of Latin American
Studies
Sid W. Richardson Hall, 1.325
University of Texas
Austin, Texas 78712

Review Editor
Sharon Girard
Department of Music
San Francisco State University
1600 Holloway Avenue
San Francisco, Calif. 94132

Assistant to the Editor:
Susan Rodriguez

Verso of editor page

**Latin American Music Review/
Revista de Música Latinoamericana**
The *Latin American Music Review* is published twice a year (spring and fall) by the University of Texas Press, and publishes original articles in the field of musicology and ethnomusicology, broadly defined, applied to Latin American musical expressions. The views expressed are the authors' and reviewers' and not those of the editors or the officers of the University of Texas Press. Articles and communications should be sent to the editor. Books and records for review should be sent to the review editor. Inquiries pertaining to subscriptions and advertising should be directed to the Journals Department, University of Texas Press, Box 7819, Austin, Texas 78712.

Manuscripts must be typed on one side of the sheet only with ample margins. Two copies should be submitted, along with a short abstract and a brief biographical sketch of the author. Formats for footnotes and bibliography are those of the Chicago *Manual of Style* or of the social science publications, such as *Current Anthropology*. Musical examples should be copied on a separate sheet of music manuscript paper with indication of their location in the main body of the paper. Papers and reviews may be submitted in English, Spanish, or Portuguese.

Manuscripts and editorial correspondence:
Gerard Béhague
Institute of Latin American Studies
Sid W. Richardson Hall, 1.323
University of Texas
Austin, Texas 78712

Book reviews:
Sharon Girard
Department of Music
San Francisco State University
1600 Holloway Avenue
San Francisco, California 94132

Subscriptions:
Individuals: $10.00/year
Institutions: $15.00/year
Foreign: $2.00 additional per subscription
Single copies: $6.00 each

LAMR
Journals Department
University of Texas Press
Box 7819
Austin, Texas 78712

Gerard Béhague   **Editorial Note**

Latin American Music Review—Revista de Música Latinoamericana succeeds the *Yearbook for Inter-American Musical Research,* so ably edited by Gilbert Chase in the 1960's and 1970's. Contrary to the *Yearbook,* however, LAMR is designed to fill a long-felt need for a periodical that focuses exclusively on all of Latin America's varied oral and written musical traditions. The journal will juxtapose scholarly work from many countries and disciplines in as stimulating and carefully refereed a forum as possible. Studies on all aspects of Latin American and Caribbean music are welcomed, including the music of Mexican Americans, Puerto Ricans, Cubans, Spaniards, and Portuguese in the United States and Canada. Diverse theoretical and methodological approaches will be stressed in historical, musicological, and ethnomusicological studies.

Contributions are particularly invited from musicians, musicologists, anthropologists, linguists, folklorists, historians, and literary and art critics.

This first issue of LAMR is dedicated to the memory of Charles Seeger (1886-1979), who maintained a vivid interest in Latin American music throughout his life and supported all along the thought of a specialized journal on Latin American music.

Example 491

Latin American music review = Revista de música
    latino americana. -- Vol. 1, no. 1 (spring/
    summer 1980)-   . -- [Austin, Tex. : Univer-
    sity of Texas Press], 1980-
        v. : music ; 23 cm.

Semiannual.
English, Spanish, or Portuguese.
Title from cover.
Also called: LAMR.
Continues: Yearbook for inter-American musi-
cal research.
    ISSN 0163-0350.

    I. Title: Revista de música latino americana.
II. Title: LAMR.

D: 1.1B8, 12.AD1, 12.3C4, 12.4, 1.4F6, 2.5C2, 12.7B1, 12.7B2,
      12.7B3, 12.7B4, 12.7B7, 12.8B1
C: 21.1C
AE: 21.30J

Type: a Bib lvl: s Govt pub: Lang: eng Source: d S/L ent: 0
Repr: Enc lvl: I Conf pub: 0 Ctry: txu Ser tp: p Alphabt: a
Indx: u Mod rec: Phys med: Cont: o   Frequn: f Pub st: c
Desc: a Cum ind: u Titl pag: u ISDS: Regulr: r Dates: 1980-9999

    010
    040   XXX $c XXX
    022   0163-0350
    041 0   engporspa
    090
    049   XXXX
    245 00 Latin American music review = $b Revista
de música latino americana.
    246 31 Revista de música latino americana
    246 33 LAMR
    260 00 [Austin, Tex. : $b University of Texas
Press], $c 1980-
    265   Journals Department, University of Texas
Press, Box 7819, Austin, TX 78712
    300   v. : $b music; $c 23 cm.
    362 0   Vol. 1, no. 1 (spring/summer 1980)-
    546   English, Spanish, or Portuguese.
    500   Title from cover.
    500   Also called: LAMR.
    780 00 $t Yearbook for inter-American musical
research $w (OCoLC)nnnnnnn

1979
Vol. II No. 1&2

GRADUATE RESEARCH IN URBAN EDUCATION AND RELATED DISCIPLINES

School of Education

The City College

The City University of New York

SCHOOL OF EDUCATION
THE CITY COLLEGE
THE CITY UNIVERSITY OF NEW YORK

Robert E. Marshak, President
The City College

Doyle Bortner, Dean
School of Education

David J. Fox, Director
Research and Evaluation
    Services

Ruth Adams, Associate Dean
School of Education

GRADUATE RESEARCH IN URBAN EDUCATION AND
RELATED DISCIPLINES
publishes reports of research studies conducted by graduate
students in the School of Education and the College of Liberal
Arts and Science of the City College. General policy for this
journal is established by the Committee on Research and Publication of the School of Education. Studies are nominated
for inclusion by members of the faculty of the City College.
In this publication series, preference is given to studies
which make an original contribution to topics of current
concern in Urban Education. Other than this basic criterion,
no limitations are placed on the topic studied or the
population sampled. Our intent is to present in each issue
in the graduate programs in the School of Education and the
College of Liberal Arts And Science of the City College.

EDITORIAL STAFF
EDITOR: RICHARD RUTKIN, Assistant Professor, The City
        College
Assistant to the Editor: Martha Schachner
                                Helen Kusko

COMMITTEE ON RESEARCH AND PUBLICATION
Herwood Fisher   G. Nicholas Paster
Kristina Leeb-Lundberg   Richard Rutkin,
                                Chairperson

Consulting Editors
Lorraine Diamond, Professor   Sigmund Tobias,
Harold Speilman, Professor   Professor

Graduate Research in Urban Education and Related Disciplines is published by the School of Education of the City
College Semiannually. Annual subscription ($8.00) and
individual issues ($5.00) may be ordered through the
editorial offices. Klapper Hall, The City College, New
York, N.Y. 10031. Address inquiries to Mrs. Martha
Schachner, Assistant to Editor.

Example 492

Graduate research in urban education and related
     disciplines. -- New York, N.Y. : School of
     Education, City College, City University of
     New York,
          v. ; 23 cm.

     Semiannual.
     Continues: Graduate research in education and
related disciplines.
     Description based on: Vol. 11, no. 1 & 2
(1979).

     I. City University of New York. City College.
School of Education.

D: 12.1B1, 1.4D2, 12.5, 12.7B1, 12.7B7, 12.7B22
C: 21.1C
AE: 21.30E
F: 24.13 (type 4), 24.14

The date of the title change is uncertain.

the PLAIN TRUTH

a magazine of understanding

AMERICA THE BEAUTIFUL
AMERICA THE CONDEMNED!

THE PLAIN TRUTH
a magazine of understanding

Vol. 45, No. 8   ISSN 0032-0420   August 1980

ARTICLES

America the Beautiful—America the Condemned!	2
America's Disaster in Iran—Why It Happened	5
Are Prisons the Biblical Way to Deal with Crime?	7
The Pygmies Are Being Saved	10
The Specter of Poison Gas Warfare	13
The Amazing Story Behind Worldwide Weather Upset	14
A Voice Cries Out Amid Religious Confusion (Part 4)	19

FEATURES

Personal from Herbert W. Armstrong	1

IMPORTANT NOTICE

You are reading only an *abbreviated version* of The PLAIN TRUTH magazine. Our regular edition, available only to subscribers, is 48 pages and contains numerous additional articles. For your free subscription, see inside.

ABOUT OUR COVER

Grand Canyon, Arizona a wonder of nature without parallel on earth, symbolizes the unique role of the United States of America in 20th-century human experience. This stormy afternoon photo is witness of foreboding national catastrophe before the morning light of reborn hope appears.

Cover Photo by David Maasch

The Plain Truth is published monthly by Ambassador College, Pasadena, California 91123. Copyright © 1980 Worldwide Church of God. All rights reserved. PRINTED IN U.S.A.

United States: 300 W. Green, Pasadena, California 91123
Canada: P.O. Box 44, Station A, Vancouver, B.C. V6C 2M2
Mexico: Institución Ambassador, Apartado Postal 5-595, Mexico 5, D.F.
Colombia: Apartado Aéreo 11430, Bogotá 1, D.E.
United Kingdom, rest of Europe and Middle East: P.O. Box 111, St. Albans, England AL2 2EG.
Rhodesia: P.O. Box U.A.30, Union Ave., Salisbury
South Africa: P.O. Box 1060, Johannesburg, Republic of South Africa 2000
Ghana: P.O. Box 9617, Kotoka Int. Airport, Accra

Kenya and the rest of East and Central Africa: P.O. Box 47135, Nairobi, Kenya
Mauritius and other Indian Ocean isles: P.O. Box 888, Port Louis, Mauritius
Nigeria: P.M.B. 1006, Ikeja, Lagos State, Nigeria
Australia, India, Sri Lanka and Southeast Asia: P.O. Box 202, Burleigh Heads, Queensland 4220, Australia
New Zealand and Pacific Isles: P.O. Box 2709, Auckland 1, New Zealand
The Philippines: P.O. Box 2603, Manila 2801
Caribbean: P.O. Box 6063, San Juan, Puerto Rico 00936
Switzerland: Case Postale 10, 91, rue de la Servette, CH-1211, Geneva 7
Scandinavia: Box 2513 Solli, Oslo 2, Norway

Be sure to notify us immediately of any change in your address. Please include your old mailing label and your new address.

The Plain Truth— SUPPORTED BY YOUR CONTRIBUTIONS

The Plain Truth has no subscription or newsstand price. This magazine is provided free of charge by the Worldwide Church of God. It is made possible by the voluntary, freely given tithes and offerings of the membership of the Church and others who have elected to support the work of the Church. Contributions are gratefully welcomed and are tax-deductible in the U.S. Those who wish to voluntarily aid and support this worldwide Work of God are gladly welcomed as co-workers in this major effort to publish the gospel to all nations. Contributions should be sent to our office nearest you (addresses below).

Founder and Editor-in-Chief:
HERBERT W. ARMSTRONG

Senior Editor for Copy:
Herman L. Hoeh

Managing Editor:
Dexter H. Faulkner

Senior Editor:
Raymond F. McNair

Associate Editors:
Sheila Graham, John Halford, Rod M... H. Sedliacik, Norman L. Shoaf

Contributing Editors:
Dibar Apartian, Elbert Atlas, Le... Selmer L. Hegvold, Kenneth C. H... Jackson, L. Leroy Neff, Richard F... Rice, Donna R. Robertson, John... Robert C. Smith

Copy Editors:
Peter Moore, Clayton Sleep

Art Staff:
Randall Cole, Ronald F. Grove, Mc...

Photo Files:
Hal Finch

News Editor:
Gene H. Hogberg

News Research Staff:
Jeff Calkins, Werner Jebens, Marc... ald D. Schroeder, Keith Stump

Photography:
Photo Services Director: Warren... Charles Buschmann, Alfred Henn... Scott Smith, Kim Stone

Publishing:
Circulation and Production Dir... ... Lipross; *Circulation Manager:* B... duction Manager: Ron Taylor; Pub... tor: Syd Attenborough; *Internationa...* Brown; *Newsstand Distribution:* Jol...

Business Manager:
Stanley R. Rader

International Editions:
Dutch Language: Bram de Bree... Apartian; *German:* John B. Karlsc... Peter Butler; *Spanish:* Don Walls

Offices:
Auckland, New Zealand: Robert Mc... *Germany:* Frank Schnee; *St. Albans...* Brown; Burleigh Heads, Australia... *Geneva, Switzerland:* Bernard Andrist; *Johannes*burg, *South Africa:* Roy McCarthy; *Manila, Philip*pines: Colin Adair; *San Juan, Puerto Rico:* Stan Bass... *Utrecht, The Netherlands:* Bram de Bree; *Vancouver,* B.C. *Canada:* Leslie McCullough, Mexico City, Mexi... co: Thomas Turk

Example 493

The Plain truth. -- Abbreviated version. --
     Pasadena, Calif. : Ambassador College,
        v. : ill. (some col.) ; 28 cm.

     Monthly.
     Description based on: Vol. 45, no. 8 (Aug.
1980); title from cover.
     "A magazine of understanding."
     Issued by: Worldwide Church of God.
     Editor: Herbert W. Armstrong.
     Began with issue for Feb. 1934.
     ISSN 0032-0420.

     I. Worldwide Church of God.   II. Armstrong,
Herbert W.

D:	12.1B1, A.4D, 12.2B1, 1.4C3, 12.4D1, 12.5B1, 2.5C3, 12.5D1, 12.7B1, 12.7B3, 12.7B5, 12.7B6, 12.7B8, 12.7B22, 12.8B1
C:	21.1C
AE:	21.29D
F:	24.1, 22.1A, 22.4

With augmented level one description, the other title information is
not transcribed in area 1. Here it is included as a note.

American Film

Magazine of the
Film and Television Arts

July-August 1980
$2.00

THE MAZURSKY METHOD

EPIC ANIMATION
AMERICAN POP

BATTLE OF THE
BOSTON TV PARTIES

Paul Mazursky, writer-director of the
new film Willie and Phil.

American Film

Director, The American Film Institute:
Jean Firstenberg

Editor: **Hollis Alpert**

Executive Editor: **Antonio Chemasi**

Senior Editors: **Victoria Venker,
Thomas Wiener**

West Coast Editor: **James Powers**

Assistant Editors: **Kathleen Haser,
Peter Craig**

Contributing Editors: **Bruce Cook,
J. Hoberman, Harlan Kennedy (London),
Ernest Lehman, Patrick McGilligan,
Martin Mayer, Robert Sklar**

Assistant to the Editor: **Kathy Davis**

Editorial Assistant: **Patricia Pancoe**

Art Director: **Victoria Valentine**

Assistant Art Director: **Cynthia Friedman**

Art Assistant: **Kyung-Sook Hillman**

Photography Associate:
Maureen Lambray

Publisher: **Tod Herbers**

Publisher's Assistant: **Winifred Rabbitt**

Circulation: **Donna Naroff, Dir.; Charles
Lean, Fulfillment Mgr.; Lisa Daniels, Asst.**

Membership Services: **Monica Morgan,
Mgr.; Elizabeth Brown, Wendy Stark**

*Advertis' Promotio   se,
Mgr

American Film: Magazine of the Film and Television Arts (ISSN-0361-4751) is published monthly, except combined for January-February and July-August, by The American Film Institute. Signed articles herein do not necessarily reflect official Institute policy. Copyright © 1980 The American Film Institute. All rights reserved. Reproduction in whole or in part without permission is prohibited. Editorial, publishing, and advertising offices: The American Film Institute, The John F. Kennedy Center for the Performing Arts, Washington, DC 20566 (202) 828-4050. Single-copy price of current issue is $2 (back issues $3) plus 50¢ postage and handling for each issue. Subscription price: $20 per year in Washington, DC, metropolitan area, $16 elsewhere in U.S. and possessions, $22 outside U.S., includes membership in The American Film

American Film

Magazine of the Film and Television Arts
Volume V Number 9
July-August 1980

| Features | 26 | **All That Jazz...Swing...Pop...and Rock** | Rex McGee |
American Pop is an animated show business chronicle.

32 **Battle of the Boston TV Parties** — Rory O'Connor
The maelstrom over the fate of WNAC-TV.

36 **News: Television's Bargain Basement** — Laurence Bergreen
Where the networks go to find prestige.

42 **Paul Mazursky and** *Willie and Phil* — James Monaco
A director's personal style examined.

46 **The Wooing of Burt Reynolds** — Julian Smith
How Florida got its native son back.

Dialogue on Film 57 **The AFI-Aspen Conference**
What's the future of film? That was the provocative topic
for a recent gathering of experts from Hollywood and elsewhere. We offer a sampling from the lively debate.

Departments 6 **Letters**

9 **The Video Scene**
Show Time on Cassette — Gary Arlen
A Good BET — Gary Arlen

18 **Lehman at Large** — Ernest Lehman
Hitch

20 **Point of View** — Edwin Diamond
Lou Grant—Too Good, Too True?

53 **Books**
Crime Movies: An Illustrated History by Carlos Clarens
and *Film Noir: An Encyclopedic Reference to the American Style* edited by Alain Silver and Elizabeth Ward. — Leo Braudy
Thirty Seconds by Michael J. Arlen. — Bruce Cook

69 **AFI News** — Edited by Brynda Pappas

72 **Periodicals**

Cover: Photo © 1980 Maureen Lambray

Photo Credits: ABC-TV, Rakshi Productions, Ernest Burns, CBS-TV, Cinemabilia, Columbia Pictures, Mary Corliss, Louis Goldman, Roberta Green, Metro-Goldwyn-Mayer, Museum of Modern Art/Film Stills, NBC-TV, Paramount Pictures, Rogers & Cowan, Inc., Twentieth Century-Fox, United Artists, Universal Pictures, Thomas Victor, Warner Bros.

The American Film Institute is an independent, nonprofit organization serving the public interest, established in 1967 by the National Endowment for the Arts to advance the art of film and television in the United States. The Institute preserves films, operates an advanced conservatory for filmmakers, gives assistance to new American filmmakers through grants and internships, provides guidance to film teachers and educators, publishes film books, periodicals, and reference works, supports basic research, and operates a national film repertory exhibition program.

JULY-AUGUST 1980   3

Example 494

American film. -- [Washington, D.C. : American
    Film Institute],
        v. : ill. (some col.) ; 28 cm.

Monthly, except combined for Jan.-Feb. and
July-Aug.
    Description based on: Vol. 5, no. 9 (July-
Aug. 1980); title from cover.
    "Magazine of the film and television arts."
    Began with issue for Oct. 1975.
    ISSN 0361-4751 = American film.

    I. American Film Institute.

D: 12.1B1, 12.4, 12.5B1, 2.5C3, 12.5D1, 12.7B1, 12.7B3, 12.7B5,
    12.7B8, 12.7B22, 12.8B1, 12.8C1
C: 21.1C
AE: 21.30E
F: 24.1

With augmented level one description, the other title information is
not transcribed in area 1. Here it is included as a note.

Example 495

```
Shell answer book. -- #1-    . -- Houston, Tex. :
     Shell Oil Company, c1976-
        v. : col. ill. : 19 cm.

     Irregular.
     Title from cover.
     Each answer book presents information on a
specific aspect of home, energy, or car care.
     Library has: No. 1-2,7-10,12-13,15,18-23.


     I. Shell Oil Company.
```

D: 1.1B2, 12.3B1, 1.4C3, 12.4D1, 12.4F1, 1.4F6, 12.5B1, 2.5C3,
    12.5D1, 12.7B1, 12.7B3, 12.7B18, 12.7B20
C: 21.1C
AE: 21.30E
F: 24.1

Number One, 1978

Scandinavian Review

SPECIAL ISSUE: MINORITIES

 **The American-Scandinavian Foundation**

Scandinavian Review

Editor
Nadia Christensen

**Editor Emeritus and
Advertising Director**
Erik J. Friis

Art Director
Paul Schiff
Jane Sheppard, Assistant

Circulation Director
Helen U. Meyer

Production Manager
Kathleen Madden

Publishing Assistant
Lynne Calman

Contributing Editors
Bengt Broms
Geoffrey Dodd
Mark Goldsmith
Eiður Guðnason
David Hall
Marie Lien
Martin Peterson

About our cover:
British-born illustrator and graphic artist Peter Blay created the cover especially for this issue. Using the traditional symbol of Nordic unity—five flying swans—Mr. Blay's collage subtly conveys the message that minorities do exist in Scandinavia.

Mr. Blay has lived and worked in Scandinavia for the past 20 years and has been a regular contributor to numerous Scandinavian newspapers and magazines. He has traveled extensively in Iceland and the Faroes, where the depopulation of the out-back areas has affected much of his artwork. Several of his sketches of the Faroe Islands accompany Geoffrey Dodd's article which appears in this issue.

SCANDINAVIAN REVIEW, formerly THE AMERICAN-SCANDINAVIAN REVIEW, is published quarterly in March, June, September and December by The American-Scandinavian Foundation, 127 East 73rd St. New York, N.Y. 10021. ©The American-Scandinavian Foundation 1978. All rights reserved. Reproduction in whole or in part without permission is prohibited. Second class postage paid at New Haven, CT. Single copy price is $3.00; special issue price is $4.95. SCANDI-NAVIAN REVIEW is indexed in *Social Sciences Index* and *P.I.A.S.*

Printed by
Van Dyck Printing Company
North Haven, Connecticut

Vol. 66, No. 1. March 1978

Scandinavian Review

7 Aliens in a Beneficent Land
by Joseph B. Perry, Jr.
Why are the Nordic countries a mecca for immigrant workers? Sweden provides a good example

14 Foreign Workers Live Two Lives
A poem by Murat Alpar
translated by Alexander Taylor

15 The Foreign Workers
A poem by Murat Alpar
translated by Alexander Taylor

17 Finns & Swedes as Minorities in Sweden and Finland
by Erik Allardt

24 Mediterranean? No, Scandinavian
A photo essay by Robert Blanchard

26 Gypsies
by Erik J. Friis

28 Swedish Reindeer Lapps: A Minority Within a Minority
by Eugene Kokot

36 Viktoria Street
A poem by Murat Alpar
translated by Alexander Taylor

38 "It's Too Bad You're Greenlanders"
by Karen Nørregaard
One side of the many-sided "Greenland Question"

44 The Black Experience: Two Blacks Talk About Life in Scandinavia
A *Scan R* interview

47 Action or Assimilation: A Jewish Identity Crisis
by Morton H. Narrowe

53 Beyond Bitter Antagonisms
by Gerd Callesen

55 Prologue to an Uncertain Future
by Geoffrey Dodd
drawings by Peter Blay

60 "What Fine People We Are"
by Gunnar Bull Gundersen and Berit Lofsnes
Norway has done much for its dark-skinned foreign workers. But has it done enough? Are the workers' expectations unrealistic? A self-critical look combined with illuminating interviews

66 Vognmandsmarken — A Copenhagen Ghetto
by Jonathan M. Schwartz
photographs by Lene Åkerlund

74 Memet's Apartment
A poem by Murat Alpar
translated by Alexander Taylor

76 Memet's Children Go to School
A poem by Murat Alpar
translated by Alexander Taylor

78 News of Norden

96 Books

103 Music

105 Art & Design

106 Comments & Queries

Example 496

Scandinavian review. -- [New York, N.Y. : American-Scandinavian Foundation],
  v. : ill. (some col.) ; 24 cm.

Quarterly.
Description based on: Vol. 66, no. 1 (Mar. 1978); title from cover.
Some issues are called special issue and are devoted to a particular topic.
Continues: American-Scandinavian review.
Began with issue for Mar. 1975.
ISSN 0098-857X = Scandinavian review.

I. American-Scandinavian Foundation.

D: 12.1B1, 12.4, 12.5B1, 2.5C3, 12.5D1, 12.7B1, 12.7B3, 12.7B4, 12.7B7, 12.7B8, 12.7B22, 12.8B1, 12.8C1
C: 21.1C
AE: 21.30E
F: 24.1

```
Type: a Bib lvl: s Govt pub:    Lang: eng Source: d S/L ent: 0
Repr:     Enc lvl: I Conf pub: 0 Ctry: nyu Ser tp: p Alphabt: a
Indx: u Mod rec:    Phys med:    Cont:     Frequn: q Pub st:   c
Desc: a Cum ind: u Titl pag: u ISDS:      Regulr: r Dates: 1975-9999
```

```
    010
    040     XXX $c XXX
    022     0098-857X
    090
    049     XXXX
    245 00  Scandinavian review.
    260 00  [New York, N.Y. : $b American-Scandinavian
Foundation],
    265     American-Scandinavian Foundation, 127 E.
73rd St., New York, NY 10021
    300     v. : $b ill. (some col.) ; $c 24 cm.
    362 1   Began with issue for Mar. 1975.
    500     Description based on: Vol. 66, no. 1 (Mar.
1978).
    500     Some issues are called special issue and are
devoted to a particular topic.
    510 0   Social sciences index
    510 0   Public affairs information service
    710 20  American-Scandinavian Foundation.
    780 00  $t American-Scandinavian review $w
(OCoLC)nnnnnnn
    936     Mar. 1975.
```

AMERICAN
THEATRE
ANNUAL

1978-79

covering regional theatre
and
national touring companies
and incorporating the
NEW YORK THEATRE ANNUAL

edited by Catharine Hughes

Gale Research Company • Book Tower • Detroit, Michigan 48226

AMERICAN THEATRE ANNUAL

Linda Hubbard, *Production Editor*
Roger D. Hubbard, *Layout Designer
and Photography Coordinator*
Gordon Tretick and Linda Hubbard
Assistant Editors
Arthur Chartow, *Cover Design*

Copyright © 1980 by Gale Research Company

ISBN 0-8103-0418-X
ISSN 0195-945X

Example 497

American theatre annual ... -- 1978-79-   . --
    Detroit, Mich. : Gale Research Co., c1980-
        v. : ill. ; 29 cm.

    "Covering regional theatre and national tour-
ing companies and incorporating the New York
theatre annual."
    ISSN 0195-945X.

    I. Gale Research Company.

D: 12.1B6, 12.AF3, 12.3C1, 1.4D2, 12.4F, 1.4F6, 12.5, 12.7B5,
      12.8B1
C: 21.1C
AE: 21.30E
F: 24.1

    Mark of omission might be unnecessary if date is not considered
part of the title proper.

    Full stop has been omitted before area 3. See 1.0C, paragraph 8.

    Content of the item indicated this was the first yearbook published.

Type: a Bib lvl: s Govt pub: Lang: eng Source: d S/L: 0
Repr: Enc lvl: I Conf pub: 0 Ctry: miu Ser tp: Alphabt: a
Indx: u Mod rec: Phys med: Cont: v   Frequn: a Pub st: c
Desc: a Cum ind: u Titl pag: u ISDS: Regulr: r Dates: 1979,9999

    010
    040   XXX $c XXX
    022   n-us-- $a n-us-ny
    090
    049   XXXX
    245 00 American theatre annual ...
    260 00 Detroit, Mich. : $b Gale Research Co., $c
1980-
    300   v. : $b ill. ; $c 29 cm.
    362 0 1978-79-
    500   "Covering regional theatre and national
touring companies and incorporating the New York theatre
annual."
    710 20 Gale Research Company.
    787 1 $t New York theatre annual $w (OCoLC)nnnnnnn

A Publication of the Jean Piaget Society

Topics in Cognitive Development

Volume 1
Equilibration: Theory, Research, and Application

Edited by

Marilyn H. Appel

Medical College of Pennsylvania
Philadelphia, Pennsylvania

and

Lois S. Goldberg

Glassboro State College
Glassboro, New Jersey

Plenum Press • New York and London

Topics in Cognitive Development

Marilyn H. Appel, Editor-in-Chief
Medical College of Pennsylvania, Philadelphia

Volume 1   EQUILIBRATION : THEORY, RESEARCH,
AND APPLICATION
Edited by
Marilyn H. Appel, *Medical College of Pennsylvania*
Lois S. Goldberg, *Glassboro State College*

A Continuation Order Plan is available for this series. A continuation order will bring delivery of each new volume immediately upon publication. Volumes are billed only upon actual shipment. For further information please contact the publisher.

Example 498

Topics in cognitive development : a publication of
    the Jean Piaget Society. -- Vol. 1-   . --
    New York : Plenum Press, c1977-
       v. : ill. ; 24 cm.

    Includes official symposium proceedings of
the Jean Piaget Society.

    I. Jean Piaget Society.

D: 12.0B1, 12.1E1, 12.3B1, 12.4, 1.4F6, 12.5, 12.7B18
C: 21.1C
AE: 21.30E
F: 24.1

    Copyright date found on verso of the title page. The proceedings
information was found in the Preface.

Computer Literature Index

Formerly the QUARTERLY BIBLIOGRAPHY OF
COMPUTERS AND DATA PROCESSING

April 1980   Volume 10, Number 1
Covering the period January - March 1980

 Applied Computer Research

Computer Literature Index

A Subject/Author Index to Computer and Data Processing Literature

> **FORMERLY THE QUARTERLY
> BIBLIOGRAPHY OF COMPUTERS
> AND DATA PROCESSING**

Contents

1. Guide to Use 1

Provides a general introduction to the Index including a statement of editorial policy
and instructions on the use of the Subject, Author and Publisher's Indexes.

2. Subject Index 5

The main section of the Index, the Subject Index contains the complete bibliographic
entry, including author, title, citation, and annotation. Organized alphabetically by
subject.

3. Author Index 52

This secondary index provides a cross reference by author's last name with pointers
to the subject classification in which the full entry is listed.

4. Publisher Index 63

Contains a listing of publishers of both books and periodicals, with identification of
the abbreviations used in the Subject Index, full publication name, address, and the
specific issues covered in this edition of the Index.

April, 1980
Volume 10, No. 1
Covering the period
January 1980 - March 1980

Published by

Applied Computer Research
P.O. Box 9280
Phoenix, AZ 85068

Editor/Publisher:	Phillip. C. Howard
Associate Editor:	James F. Christensen
Circulation:	Judith B. Caron
Production:	Gayle Fountain
	Suzanne Blair
	Sandra Casey

The *Computer Literature Index* is published four times a year in January, April, July, and October by Applied Computer Research at Phoenix, Arizona. An annual cumulation is published once each year in April for the previous calendar year. Subscription rates: United States, Canada, and Mexico. $75.00 per year; all other countries, $90.00 per year. Single copies, $20.00. Cumulations, $25.00. Multiple year rates available on request.

The *Computer Literature Index* was formerly published under the name *Quarterly Bibliography of Computers and Data Processing* through the year 1979. The name was changed effective with Volume 10 in 1980. Cumulations ordered for 1979 and prior years will be filled with Quarterly Bibliography editions. The basic subject/author index remains the same.

Example 499

```
Computer literature index. -- Vol. 10, no. 1
     (Jan.-Mar. 1980)-    . -- [Phoenix, AZ] :
     Applied Computer Research, 1980-
          v. : ill. ; 28 cm.

     Quarterly, with annual cumulations.
     Title from cover.
     Continues: Quarterly bibliography of comput-
ers and data processing.
     ISSN 0270-4846.


     I. Applied Computer Research (Firm)
```

D: 12.1B1, 12.3C4, 12.4, B.14, 12.5, 12.7B1, 12.7B3, 12.7B7, 12.8B1
C: 21.1C
AE: 21.30E
F: 24.4B

THE LOW COUNTRIES HISTORY YEARBOOK

Acta Historiae Neerlandicae

1978   XI

MARTINUS NIJHOFF · 1979

lange voorhout 9-11 . 's-gravenhage
korrespondentie te richten aan postbus 566
2501 CN 's-gravenhage
telefoon 070 46 94 60 . telex 34164 nijbu nl
telegramadres: bookshague

 uitgeverij martinus nijhoff bv

The Hague, July 1979

Dear sir/madam,

Please note that as from volume 11 on 'Acta Historicae Neerlandicae' has changed title into 'Low Countries History
Yearbook'. The volumes will appear as yearbooks and will be
numbered as such. The former title 'Acta Historicae Neerlandicae'
will henceforth be used as subtitle.

Please change your records accordingly,

Sincerely yours,

UITGEVERIJ MARTINUS NIJHOFF B.V.

F.M.R. van der Ark

Example 500

The Low Countries history yearbook = Acta histo-
    riae Neerlandicae. -- 11 (1978)-   . -- The
    Hague : M. Nijhoff, 1979-
        v. : ill. ; 25 cm.

Annual.
Title from cover.
Spine title: AHN.
Continues: Acta historicae Neerlandicae.

    I. Title: Acta historiae Neerlandicae. II.
Title: AHN.

D: 12.1B1, 12.1D1, 12.3C4, 12.4, 1.4D4, 12.5, 12.7B1, 12.7B3,
     12.7B4, 12.7B7
C: 21.1C
AE: 21.30J

THE INTERNATIONAL SCIENCE FICTION YEARBOOK

1979

NEW YORK LONDON TOKYO

EDITED BY COLIN LESTER

Example 501

```
The International science fiction yearbook ...
     -- 1979. -- New York : Quick Fox, c1978.
     1 v. : ill. : 20 cm.

     Title from cover.
     Editor: Colin Lester.


     I. Lester, Colin.
```

D: 12.1B6, A.4D, 12.3C1, 12.3F, 12.4, 12.4F3, 1.4F6, 12.5, 12.5B2,
       12.7B1, 12.7B3, 12.7B6
C: 21.1C
AE: 21.30D
F: 22.1A, 22.5A

   Mark of omission might be unnecessary if date is not considered
part of the title proper.

1980
MINNESOTA STATE
INDUSTRIAL DIRECTORY

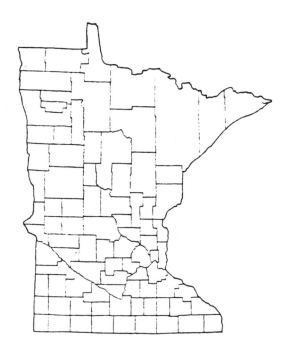

PUBLISHED BY STATE INDUSTRIAL DIRECTORIES CORP.
2 PENN PLAZA, NEW YORK, N.Y. 10121   (212) 564-0340

PRICE $50.00

SIDC AMERICA'S LARGEST PUBLISHER OF STATE INDUSTRIAL DIRECTORIES

Minnesota State Industrial Directory
2 Penn Plaza, New York, N.Y. 10121
(212) 564-0340

Copyright © 1980 by State Industrial Directories Corp.

ISSN 0195-7112
ISBN 0-89910-003-1

Example 502

INTRODUCTION

Our primary concern in preparing this first edition of the MINNESOTA STATE INDUSTRIAL DIRECTORY are completeness and accuracy. Every manufacturer with six or more employees is sent our questionnaire. From this source, from telephone solicitations and inquiries, trade publications, publicity releases, and from state agencies, our listings are prepared.

SIDC is America's largest publisher of industrial directories. We believe that the experience gained in publishing and/or distributing more than 50 directories, here and abroad, is your assurance of a quality directory.

Once again, we wish to thank the manufacturers listed in the directory for replying so readily to our requests for information. Given the scope of a work of this kind, it is impossible to keep pace with the volatility of the industrial community without it's cooperation. Therefore, we welcome your suggestions for new listings and general improvements in future editions.

All manufacturers in the State of Minnesota are listed without charge.

	SIDC
MAY 1980	State Industrial Directories Corp.

```
Minnesota state industrial directory. -- 1980-
     . -- New York, N.Y. : State Industrial
   Directories Corp., 1980-
     v. : maps ; 28 cm.

   Title from cover.
   ISSN 0195-7112.


   I. State Industrial Directories Corp.
```

D: 12.1B1, 12.1B6, 12.3C1, 12.4, 12.5B1, 2.5C2, 12.5D1, 12.7B3, 12.8B1
C: 21.1C
AE: 21.30E
F: 24.1, 24.5C1, B.2, 26.3A3

Stress

The Official Journal of the International Institute of Stress and its Affiliates

Published by
THE HANS SELYE FOUNDATION

Volume 1, No. 1 - Spring 1980

Hans Selye
EDITORIAL

Hans Selye
A SPECIAL REPORT ON THE MONACO SYMPOSIUM
THE SECOND INTERNATIONAL SYMPOSIUM
ON THE MANAGEMENT OF STRESS

Sir Hans Krebs
BIOLOGICAL ASPECTS OF JUVENILE DELINQUENCY

Ronald Melzack
PAIN MECHANISMS AND STRESS

Aelred C. Fonder
THE DENTAL DISTRESS SYNDROME (DDS)

John H. Howard
STRESS AND THE MANAGER

Theron G. Randolph
SPECIFIC ADAPTATION IN THE PRESENCE OF
INDIVIDUAL SUSCEPTIBILITY

ABSTRACTS • REVIEWS • FROM OUR ARCHIVES

Stress

Vol. 1, No. 1   **Spring 1980**

The Official Journal of the International Institute of Stress and its Affiliates
Published quarterly by the Hans Selye Foundation

EDITOR
Rodney Rawlings

ASSISTANT EDITOR
Philip Szporer

EDITORIAL DIRECTOR
Hans Selye, M.D.

EDITORIAL STAFF
Rosie Manickam, M.D.
Cathy Olivieri
Louise Leclerc

SUBSCRIPTIONS
Ginette Larue

STRESS, The Official Journal of International Institute of Stress and its Affiliates, Published quarterly by the Hans Selye Foundation.

Subscription rates are, including postage: $30.00 in Canada (Cdn. funds); $30.00 in U.S. and all foreign countries (U.S. funds). Business communications, remittances and subscriptions should be addressed to the Hans Selye Foundation, 659 Milton Street, Montreal, Canada H2X 1W6.

Books for review, abstracts and meeting notices should be addressed to the Assistant Editor, Philip Szporer, International Institute of Stress, 2900 Edouard Montpetit Blvd., Montreal, Canada H3C 3J7.

Editorial communications and manuscripts should be sent directly to the Editor-in-Chief, Rodney Rawlings, International Institute of Stress, 2900 Edouard Montpetit Blvd., Montreal, Canada H3C 3J7.

The views expressed by authors are their own and not necessarily those of the Institute.

Printed in Canada by SOLOGRAPHIQUE LIMITÉE, Montreal

Example 503

```
Stress: the official journal of the International
    Institute of Stress and its affiliates. --
    Vol. 1, no. 1 (spring 1980)-    . -- Mon-
    treal, Canada : Hans Selye Foundation, 1980-
        v. : ill. ; 23 cm.

    Quarterly.
    Title from cover.
    ISSN 0228-1201.


    I. International Institute of Stress.  II.
Hans Selye Foundation.
```

D: 12.1B1, 12.1E1, 12.3C4, B.9, A.23, 12.4C1, 12.4D1, 12.4F1,
    12.5B1, 12.5C1, 12.5D1, 12.7B1, 12.7B3, 12.8B1
C: 21.1C
AE: 21.30E
F: 24.1

```
Type: a Bib lvl: s Govt pub:    Lang: eng Source: d S/L ent: 0
Repr:    Enc lvl: I Conf pub: 0 Ctry: quc Ser tp: p Alphabt: a
Indx: u Mod rec:    Phys med:    Cont:    Frequn: q Pub st: c
Desc: a Cum ind: u Titl pag: u ISDS:    Regulr: r Dates: 1980-9999

    010
    040    XXX $c XXX
    090
    049    XXXX
    245 00 Stress: $b the official journal of the
International Institute of Stress and its affiliates.
    260 00 Montreal, Canada : $b Hans Selye Foundation,
$c 1980-
    265    Hans Selye Foundation, 659 Milton St.,
Montreal, Que. H2X1W6
    300    v. : $b ill. ; $c 23 cm.
    350    $30.00 per year
    362 0  Vol. 1, no. 1 (spring 1980)-
    710 20 International Institute of Stress.
    710 21 Hans Selye Foundation.
```

Gustavus Adolphus Journal.

VOL. 1.   GUSTAVUS ADOLPHUS COLLEGE, ST. PETER, MINN., DEC. 1896.   NO. 1.

GREETING.

A message from G. A. C.

I pray you, friends, give ear to me,
Though yet unknown, I hope to be
Your well known friend in times to
come.

To former students, far and near,
I bring a greeting from a sphere
Of comrades known and comrades
dear,

Who still are striving toward the goal.
Success they wish you one and all
In well fulfilling life's great call.
And, when the day of life is all,
An everlasting peace and joy.

Each who wish to read and learn
of things that college life concern

tion assembled at East Union, Carver Co., Minn., requested Dr. E. Norelius to open a temporary school in the Swedish Lutheran church at Red Wing which request was complied with the same fall. The first day there was one student and one teacher, by end of the term the school numbered 11 students and 1 teacher. It opened in a troublesome time, that of the Rebellion and Sioux war. It was known under the name of Minnesota Elementar Skola. This location was only temporary. As our church government in this country has always

the congregations in the immediate vicinity of the proposed places partook in the voting. The speaker can yet remember the intense interest with which the result of the vote was awaited in and about East Union. East Union having thus been chosen, land was bought, buildings erected, and active work begun. The corporate name was now St. Ansgars Academy. Your humble servant remembers yet in what high esteem St. Ansgars Academy or Jackson's school, as it was commonly called after its principal, was held in the

was slow, the local financial support was weak," and therefore in 1873 a proposition was entertained to change location again. This stirred the community of East Union to its depths, and left wounds that are not yet healed, much to the detriment of the later developement of the institution. At the same time it was decided to move the school to E. Minneapolis, where a whole block could be secured in close proximity to the State University for the nominal sum of $4,000.00, which same men like Pillsbury, Dr. Ohute and others guaranteed to raise for the

Example 504

```
Gustavus Adolphus journal [microform]. -- Vol. 1,
    no. 1 (Dec. 1896)-    . -- St. Peter, Minn.
    Gustavus Adolphus College, 1896-
        v. : ill. ; 45 cm.

    Caption title.
    Issues for Dec. 1896-Apr. 1900 published in
two issues a month, with continuous numbering, the
second issue each month in Swedish and with title:
Gustaf Adolfs journalen. Monthly, in English only,
May 1900-
    Microfilm. [Vol. 1, no. 1] (Dec. 1896) to [v.
5, no. 5] (May 1901). [Saint Paul, Minn.] : Minne-
sota Historical Society, 1981. 1 microfilm reel ;
35 mm. Publisher's no.: 27--6-1981.


    I. Gustavus Adolphus College.  II. Title:
Gustaf Adolfs journalen.
```

Example 505

```
Gustavus Adolphus journal [microform]. -- [Vol. 1,
    no. 1] (Dec. 1896) thru [v. 5, no. 5] (May
    1901]. -- [Saint Paul, Minn. : Minnesota His-
    torical Society, [1981].
    1 microfilm reel : ill. ; 35 mm.

    Publisher's no.: 27--6-1981.
    Microreproduction of: Vol. 1, no. 1 (Dec.
1896)-    .    St. Peter, Minn. Gustavus Adolphus
College, 1896-    . v. ; 45 cm. Caption title.
Issues for Dec. 1896-Apr. 1900 published in two
issues a month, with continuous numbering, the
second issue each month in Swedish and with title:
Gustaf Adolfs journalen. Monthly, in English only,
May 1900-


    I. Gustavus Adolphus College.  II. Title:
Gustaf Adolfs journalen.
```

CATHOLIC AID NEWS

OFFICIAL ORGAN AND ASSESSMENT NOTICE OF THE CATHOLIC AID ASSOCIATION

VOLUME 72 NO. 1   1878 — EIGHTY-NINTH YEAR — 1966   ALBANY, MINN., OCTOBER 22, 1966

Hierarchy Gratefully Receives Gifts For Holy Father

Apostolic Delegation
United States of America
3339 Massachusetts Avenue
Washington, D. C. 20008

September 21, 1966

Right Reverend Msgr. Joseph A. Eitel
Spiritual Director
Catholic Aid Association Women's Council
905 No. State Street
New Ulm, Minnesota

Right Reverend and dear Monsignor:

I wish to acknowledge with sincere thanks your kind letter of September 16th enclosing a check in the amount of $400.00 representing the annual offering to the Holy Father from the Women's Council of the Catholic Aid Association.

Archdiocese of St. Paul
226 Summit Avenue
Saint Paul, Minnesota 55102

September 30, 1966

Mr. R. G. Baetz
The Catholic Aid Association
49 West Ninth Street
St. Paul, Minnesota 55102

Dear Mr. Baetz:

I thank you for your letter of September 28 forwarding a check in the amount of $396.00, an offering for the Holy Father for the Catholic Aid Association.

It is most comforting to have this evidence of the loyalty and devotion of the members of the Catholic Aid Association to His Holiness, Pope Paul VI.

'67 Delegate Convention Set For August 20-22

The Grand Council at its October meeting scheduled next year's CAA delegate convention for Monday and Tuesday, August 21st and 22nd. The meetings of the Women's and Men's Council will, therefore, begin on the preceeding day, Sunday, August 20th.

This action was taken at the suggestion of Msgr. Terrance Murphy, president of St. Thomas College, who will host our three day session. The 1965 delegate convention was also held at St. Thomas.

Further details as arranged and approved by the Grand Council will be published in future issues of the Catholic Aid News.

MINNESOTA
HISTORICAL SOCIETY
START
CATHOLIC AID
NEWS

OCT 22 T H U R   DEC
                      1978

Example 506

Catholic aid news [microform]. -- [Vol. 72, no. 11
    (Oct. 22, 1966) thur [i.e. thru v. 84, no.
    12] (Dec. 1978)-   . -- [Saint Paul, Minn. :
    Minnesota Historical Society, 1980-
       microfilm reels : ill. ; 35 mm.

    Publisher's no.: 138-2-1980,
    Microreproduction of: Catholic aid news =
Vereins-Bote : official organ and assessment
notice of the Catholic Aid Association of Minnesota. Vol. 53, no. 10 (Jan. 20, 1948)-   . St.
Paul, Minn. ; The Association, 1948-   . v. ; 38-
41 cm. Monthly. Issues for Feb. 22, 1951-   issued without parallel title. Subtitle varies.
Continues: Vereins-Bote. Issues for July 22nd,
1955-   published: Catholic Aid Association.

    I. Catholic Aid Association of Minnesota.
II. Catholic Aid Association. III. Title: Vereins-Bote.

Example 507

Catholic aid news [microform] = Vereins-Bote :
    official organ and assessment notice of the
    Catholic Aid Association of Minnesota. --
    Vol. 53, no. 10 (Jan. 20, 1948)-   . -- St.
    Paul, Minn. ; The Association, 1948-
       v. : ill. ; 38-41 cm.

    Monthly.
    Issues for Feb. 22, 1951-   lack parallel
title.
    Subtitle varies.
    Continues: Vereins-Bote.
    Volume numbering somewhat irregular.
    Issues for July 22nd, 1955-   published:
Catholic Aid Association.
    Microfilm. Vol. 72, no. 1 (Oct. 22, 1966)-
. [Saint Paul, Minn.] : Minnesota Historical
Society, 1980-   .   microfilm reels ; 35 mm.
Publisher's no.: 138-2-1980,

    I. Catholic Aid Association of Minnesota.
II. Catholic Aid Association. III. Title: Vereins-Bote.

volume 12
number 4

ISSN 0022-2240

journal of
library automation

299 Editorial — William D. MATHEWS
300 DOBIS/LIBIS: An Integrated, On-line Library Management System — Caryl McALLISTER, A. Stratton McALLISTER
314 Summary Statistics for Five Years of the MARC Data Base — Martha E. WILLIAMS, Stephen W. BARTH, Scott E. PREECE
338 Expanded Subject Access to Reference Collection Materials — William H. MISCHO
355 The Impact of Technology on Legislation Affecting Libraries — Henriette D. AVRAM
362 The Library and the Computer Center
  362 What the Computer Center Should Do for a Library — Hugh STANDIFER
  366 The Sources of Disharmony — Micki Jo YOUNG, Walt CRAWFORD
  369 The Horror Story — Ken BIERMAN
  372 Negotiating a Workable Relationship — Barbara MARKUSON
  376 A Final Word — William D. MATHEWS
380 Communications
  380 EBCDIC Bibliographic Character Sets— Sources and Uses: A Brief Report — Walt CRAWFORD
  383 A Systems Approach to Label Production through the OCLC System — Christina BOLGIANO
  387 Computing the Effective Length of a MARC Tag — William R. PRINGLE
392 News and Announcements
397 Index to Volume 12
408 Instructions to Authors

december, 1979

jlauay 12(4) 297–408 (1979); j libr automat

journal of
library automation

Editor: William D. Mathews

Communications Editor: Mary A. Madden

Book Review Editor: Katherine King

Advertising Editor: Judith G. Schmidt

Journal of Library Automation is the official publication of the Library and Information Technology Association, a division of the American Library Association, 50 E. Huron St., Chicago, IL 60611; Executive Secretary: Donald P. Hammer. The journal is issued quarterly in March, June, September, and December.

Journal of Library Automation publishes material related to all aspects of library and information technology. Some specific topics of interest are: Automated Bibliographic Control, AV Techniques, Communications Technology, Cable Systems, Computerized Information Processing, Data Management, Facsimile Applications, File Organization, Legal and Regulatory Matters, Library Networks, Storage and Retrieval Systems, Systems Analysis, and Video Technologies. The Journal welcomes unsolicited manuscripts. Submissions should follow the guidelines stated under "Instructions to Authors" on page 408 of this volume.

Manuscripts of articles should be addressed to William D. Mathews, Editor, Journal of Library Automation, 73 E. Linden Ave., Englewood, NJ 07631. Technical communications and news items should be addressed to Mary A. Madden, JOLA Communications, 1605 SW Upland Drive, Portland, OR 97221. Copies of books submitted for review should be addressed to LITA Office, ALA Headquarters, 50 E. Huron St., Chicago, IL 60611. Advertising arrangements should be made with Judith Schmidt, 1408 D St., SE, Washington, DC 20003.

Journal of Library Automation is a perquisite of membership in the Library and Information Technology Association. Subscription price, $7.50, is included in membership dues. Nonmembers may subscribe for $15 per year. Single copies, $4.

Circulation and Production. American Library Association, 50 E. Huron St., Chicago, IL 60611. Please allow six weeks for change of address.

Publication of material in the Journal of Library Automation does not constitute official endorsement by the Library and Information Technology Association or the American Library Association.

Abstracted in Computer & Information Systems, Computing Reviews, Information Science Abstracts, Library & Information Science Abstracts, Referativnyi Zhurnal, Nauchnaya i Tekhnicheskaya Informatsiya, Otdelnyi Vypusk, and Science Abstracts Publications. Indexed in Current Contents, Current Index to Journals in Education, Education, Library Literature, and Quarterly Bibliography of Computers and Data Processing. Microfilm copies available to subscribers from University Microfilms, Ann Arbor, Michigan.

Second-class postage paid at Chicago, Illinois, and at additional mailing offices.

Example 508

```
Journal of library automation. -- [Chicago, IL :
    Library and Information Technology Associa-
    tion].
        v. : ill. ; 24 cm.

    Quarterly.
    Description based on: Vol. 12, no. 4 (Dec.
1979); title from cover.
    Official publication of: Library and Informa-
tion Technology Association, a division of the
American Library Association.
    Began with v. 1, no. 1 (Mar. 1968); ceased
with v. 14, no. 4 (Dec. 1981).
    ISSN 0022-2240 = Journal of library automa-
tion : $15.00 per year ($7.50) to members).


    I. Library and Information Technology Asso-
ciation (U.S.)
```

D: 12.1B1, 12.4C1, B.14, 12.4D1, 12.5B1, 12.5C1, 12.5D1, 12.7B1, 12.7B3, 12.7B6, 12.7B8, 12.7B22, 12.8B1, 12.8C1, 12.8D1, 12.8E1
C: 21.1C
AE: 12.30E
F: 24.1, 24.4C2, 24.12, 26.3A7

Cross reference

```
American Library Association. Library and Informa-
    tion Technology Association
  see
Library and Information Technology Association
    (U.S.)
```

LC does not add terms of availability (12.8D1)

ENERGY
Executive Directory

SPRING 1980

Jack B. Lipton
Editor

Tim R. Kahoe
Assistant Editor

Suzanne Hatcher
Associate Editor

Cynthia R. Kerker
Associate Editor

Paul E. Emig
Art Director

CARROLL PUBLISHING COMPANY
1058 Thomas Jefferson St., NW
Washington, DC 20007
202-333-8620

FRASER/ASSOCIATES
1800 K Street, NW #1006
Washington, DC 20006
202-452-1188

Example 509

```
Energy executive directory. -- Spring 1980-
     -- Washington, DC : Carroll Pub. Co., 1980-
        v. : maps ; 28 cm.


     Three issues yearly.
     Title from cover.
     ISSN 0275-2905.
```

D: 12.1B1, 12.3C1, A.6, 1.4B8, B.5, B.9, B.14, 12.5, 2.5C2, 12.7B1,
    12.7B3, 12.8B1
C: 21.1C

MINNESOTA HISTORICAL SOCIETY

START

MINNESOTA LEADER

NOV 18 1974 **THRU** **JUL 25 1977**

Example 510

Minnesota leader (Minneapolis, Minn. : 1974).
    The Minnesota leader [microform]. -- Vol. 1,
no. 1 (Nov. 18, 1974)-v. 2, no. 7 (July 25, 1977).
-- Minneapolis, Minn. : A. Wroblewski, 1974-1977.
    2 v. : ill. ; 36 cm.

    Triweekly (Nov. 18, 1974-May 6, 1975), Ir-
regular (June 30, 1975-July 25, 1977).
    Microfilm. [Saint Paul, Minn.] : Minnesota
Historical Society, 1981. 1 microfilm reel ; 35
mm. Publisher's no.: 89--6-1981.

    I. Wroblewski, Al.

MLA NEWSLETTER

June/July, 1980   Vol. 7, No. 7

Into the Eighties

434 attendees including 379 registrants and exhibitors and guests con-
verged upon the Sunwood Inn, St. Cloud, for MLA's 85th Annual Conference
May 1-3. Board and membership meeting minutes and sub-unit conference
news may be found inside. Notes on talks by featured speakers will
appear next issue.

MINNESOTA LIBRARY ASSOCIATION
STATE ORGANIZATION SERVICE
11 OAK STREET S.E., SUITE 130
MINNEAPOLIS, MN 55414

ADDRESS CORRECTION REQUESTED

MLA Newsletter

June/July   Vol. 7 No. 7

Jerry Young, President
(612) 780-1463
Adele Panzer Morris, Editor
(612) 432-2833
Lynda Hayes, Production Manager
(612) 373-3170

Published by the Minnesota Library Association,
State Organization Service, 11 Oak Street,
Southeast, Minneapolis, Minnesota 55455

Subscriptions: $12/year (10 issues)
Subscriptions to: Nancy Olson, Memorial Library,
          Mankato State University,
          Mankato, Minnesota 56001
Submissions for the August 1980 issue to:
          AdelePanzer Morris, 16491 Fishing Ave.,
          Rosemount, Minnesota 55068
          by July 27, 1980.

Example 511

```
MLA newsletter (Minnesota Library Association)
     MLA newsletter. -- Minneapolis, Minn. : Min
     nesota Library Association,
          v. : ill. ; 22 cm.

     Ten issues per year.
     Description based on: Vol. 7, no. 7 (June/
July 1980); title from cover.
     Continues: North country librarian.
     Began with issue for July 1974.
     ISSN 0748-9285.



     I. Minnesota Library Association.
```

D: 12.1B1, 1.4C3, 12.4D1, 12.5B1, 12.5C1, 12.5D1, 12.7B1, 12.7B3,
    12.7B7, 12.7B8, 12.7B22, 12.8B1
C: 21.1C
F: 25.5B
AE: 21.30E
F: 24.1

Volume IX   Numbers 2-3   1977

UNIVERSITY OF HARTFORD

Studies in Literature

A Journal of Interdisciplinary Criticism

General Editor
LEONARD F. MANHEIM

Associate Editors
MELVIN GOLDSTEIN   ELEANOR B. MANHEIM

Book Review Editor
RICHARD W. NOLAND (University of Massachusetts)

Assistant Editors
VALERIE GEORGE   EDWARD KLONOSKI

Circulation Assistant
CLIFFORD SCHECHTMAN

HARTFORD STUDIES IN LITERATURE is a journal of literary criticism as informed by any other art, science, or related scholarly discipline. It is published three times a year by the University of Hartford, West Hartford, Connecticut 06117.

Subscription for this annual volume is $4.50 to individuals and $6.00 to institutional subscribers. For foreign postage outside the Western Hemisphere add 10 per cent. Additional charge for air mail subscriptions.

Members of the Board of Advisory Editors are listed on the inside back cover.

IN THIS ISSUE

Editor's Note: The present issue of this inter-disciplinary journal is the first to carry papers devoted to the relationship between Literature and the Law. And probably because this is the first such issue, contributions, all dealing with various phases of the subject, have necessitated the production of a double issue, also the first of its kind which we have issued.

Law and Literature: Introduction and Application...................................vi
    By Richard Weisberg

Literature and the Law: An Interdisciplinary Liberal Arts Course........................83
    By Blair Rouse
A Professor of English at the University of Ar-kansas, Blair Rouse holds degrees through the doctorate from Randolph-Macon College, University of Virginia, and the University of Illinois. He served as an officer in the United States Navy from 1942-46. His fields of interest are varied, taking in English, American, and ...

Example 512

Studies in literature (Hartford, Conn.)
    Studies in literature / University of Hart-ford. -- Vol. 9, no. 2-3 (1977)-   . -- West Hartford, Conn. : The University, c1977-
        v. ; 23 cm.

    Issued 3 times a year.
    Title from cover.
    Running title: Hartford studies in litera-ture.
    "A journal of interdisciplinary criticism."
    Continues: Hartford studies in literature.
    Supplements accompany some volumes.
    ISSN 0196-2280.

    I. University of Hartford. II. Title: Hart-ford studies in literature.

D:	12.1B1, 12.1F1, 12.3C4, 1.4D4, 12.4F, 1.4F6, 12.5, 12.7B1, 12.7B3, 12.7B4, 12.7B5, 12.7B7b, 12.7B7k, 12.8B1
C:	21.1C
F:	25.5B
AE:	21.30E, 21.30J
F:	24.1

With augmented level one description, the other title information is not transcribed in area 1. Here it is included as a note.

Definition for Running title is in Appendix D, Glossary, p. 570.

June 1980 $1.50

Saturday Review

IS JAMES LEVINE WRECKING THE MET?

Saturday Review

June, 1980

SATURDAY REVIEW (ISSN 0361-1655) published monthly by SATURDAY REVIEW MAGAZINE, a wholly owned subsidiary of Macro Commuications Corp., 1290 Avenue of the Americas, N.Y., N.Y. 10019, (212) 246-9700. Subscription price in the U.S. and its possessions one year — $16; two years — $30; three years — $42 (all other countries — additional postage $3 per year). Vol. 7, No. 10, June 1980. Back issues $2.00 each. Controlled circulation postage paid at New York, N.Y., and at Concord, N.H. Canadian postage paid at Montreal, P.Q., Canada © 1980 by SATURDAY REVIEW MAGAZINE CORP. All rights reserved under the Berne and Pan-American copyright conventions. Reproduction in whole or in part of any article (in English or other languages) without permission is prohibited. Printed in the United States of America. Available also in 35mm microfilm and microfiche. SATURDAY REVIEW MAGAZINE CORP. assumes no responsibility for any noncommissioned manuscripts, photographs, drawings, or other material. No such material will be returned unless submitted with a self-addressed envelope and sufficient postage. Send all remittances and correspondence about subscriptions, undelivered copies, and changes of address to Subscription Dept., SATURDAY REVIEW, P.O. Box 10010, Des Moines, Iowa 50340, or call toll-free (800) 247-5470.

Saturday Review

JUNE, 1980

4 Letters
6 Front Runners
10 Editorial by N.C. *Being healthy is not enough*
12 Light Refractions by Thomas H. Middleton *Confusion confo*
14 Top of My Head by Goodman Ace *Humor through adversity*
16 Notes From the Blue Coast by Anthony Burgess *The T-shirt*
17 Guestview by William M. Fine *Letters from my son*
19 Washington by Leonard Reed *Statelessness on trial*
92 The Back Door by Carll Tucker *Writing in the dark*

Issues

22 Is James Levine Wrecking the Met? by Irving Kolodin
*Ill-equipped for the job of music director when he was appointer
ago, Levine threatens to turn the magnificent Metropolitan into
opera company*
28 Gambling Fever: Are Casinos a Bad Bet? by Robert Sam A
*With dollar signs in their eyes, Americans are turning to legaliz
But casinos, built on promises of tax revenues and jobs, may be
propositions for the communities involved*

Pleasures

34 Lookouts *Upcoming events, cultural and literary*
36 Blue Heaven: The Pacific as Paradise   A Special Section
Michener: Man of the Pacific/Man of Asia by Horace Sutta
*him as a chronicler of islands and coral atolls, but James Mich
a master of Asian knowledge as well as a premier collector of its*
40 Memoirs of a Pacific Traveler by James A. Michener
*In a major essay, the author who made the South Pacific come a
personal recollections of favored places, people, and perplexities*
58 Dance by Walter Terry *Ballet West—a new kind of Western*
60 Theater by Stanley Kauffmann *BAM plays the odds of repertc
New York*
62 The Movies by Stephen Harvey *The Fame game*
64 Television by Peter Andrews *How programmers peddle prime*
66 Photography by Owen Edwards *Antonio Mendoza's unsettling
best friend reminds us of its wild side*
67 Books: Arthur Schlesinger, Jr. on Richard Nixon's *The Real Wi
Madsen on Richard Barnet's *The Lean Years*; Michael Brown or
Oppenheimer's *Letters and Recollections*; Marylin Bender on Br
Moynahan's *Airport Confidential*
84 Sporting Life by Jonathan Evan Maslow *Requiem for a sports
Puzzles: Double-Crostic No. 196 (page 91); Literary Crypt No.
Wit Twister No. 166 (page 90); *SR* Competition No 9; Winners of *SR*
Competition No. 6 (page 90)

Cover: Richard Anderson
Cartoonists: Clarence Brown. Thomas W. Cheney, Frank Cotham,
Joseph A. Dawes, William Haefeli, Nick Hobart, Nurit Karlin, Bill Levine,
Robert Mankoff, Henry R. Martin. John A. Ruge, Mick Stevens, Mike Twohy,
P.C. Vey

page 40

SATURDAY REVIEW (ISSN 0361-1655) published monthly by SATURDAY REVIEW MAGAZINE, a wholly owned subsidiary of Macro Communications
Corp. 1290 Avenue of the Americas, N.Y., N.Y. 10019. (212) 246-9700. Subscription price in the U.S. and its possessions: one year—$15.
two years—$33 three years—$42 (all other countries—additional postage $3 per year). Vol 7. No. 10. June 1980. Back issues $2.00 each.
Controlled circulation postage paid at New York, N.Y. and at Concord N.H. Canadian postage paid at Montreal, P.Q. Canada. © 1980 by
SATURDAY REVIEW MAGAZINE Corp. All rights reserved under the Berne and Pan-American copyright conventions. Reproduction in whole or in
part of any article (in English or other languages) without permission is prohibited. Printed in the United States of America. Available also in
35mm microfilm and microfiche. SATURDAY REVIEW MAGAZINE Corp. assumes no responsibility for the noncommissioned manuscripts,
photographs, drawings, or other material. No such material will be returned unless submitted with a self-addressed envelope and sufficient
postage. Send all remittances and correspondence about subscriptions, undelivered copies and changes of address to Subscription Dept.
SATURDAY REVIEW, P.O. Box 10010, Des Moines, Iowa 50340, or call toll-free (800) 247-5470.

Example 513

Saturday review (New York, N.Y. : 1975)
    Saturday review. -- N.Y. [i.e., New York],
N.Y. : Saturday Review Magazine],
        v. : ill. (some col.) ; 28 cm.

    Biweekly, except monthly during Aug. and Dec.
(1975-May 1980), monthly (June 1980-   ).
    Description based on: Vol. 7, no. 19 (June
1980); title from cover.
    Continues: Saturday review/World.
    Began with issue for Jan. 11, 1975.
    Also available in 35mm microfilm and micro-
fiche.
    ISSN 0361-1655 = Saturday review (New York.
1975).

D: 12.1B1, 1.4C1, 1.4C4, 1.4D1, 12.5B1, 2.5C3, 12.5D1, 12.7B1,
     12.7B3, 12.7B7b, 12.7B8, 12.7B16, 12.7B22, 12.8B1, 12.8C1, 8.15
C: 21.1C
F: 25.5B

Example 514

CURRENT PERIODICAL SERIES

PUBLICATION NO: 7972.01

TITLE: SATURDAY REVIEW

VOLUME: 4   **ISSUES:** 1 - 24

DATE: October 1976 - September 1977

NOTICE: This periodical may be copyrighted, in which case
the property of the copyright owner. The microfilm edition
agreement with the publisher. Duplication or resale without perm

University Microfilms International, Ann Arbor, M

MICROFILMED – 1977

Saturday review (New York, N.Y. : 1975)
　　Saturday review　[microform]. -- Vol. 4, no.
1 (Oct. 1976)-　　. -- Ann Arbor, Mich. : University Microfilms International, 1977-
　　microfilm reels : ill. ; 35 mm. -- (Current
periodical series)

　　Microreproduction of original published: N.Y.
[i.e. New York], N.Y. : Saturday Review Magazine,
1975-　　. v. : ill. (some col.) ; 28 cm.
　　"Publication no.: 7972.01."
　　Continues: Saturday review/World.

D:　11.0B1, 11.1B1, 11.1C1, 11.3B, 12.3B1, 12.3C4, 11.4, 11.5B1,S
　　12.5B1, 11.5C2, 11.5D4, 11.6B1, 1.11, 11.7B7, 12.7B7b, 11.7B19
C:　21.1C
F:　25.5B

Example 515

Saturday review (New York, N.Y. : 1975)
    Saturday review [microform]. -- [N.Y. [i.e.,
New York], N.Y. : Saturday Review Magazine],
        v. : ill. (some col.) ; 28 cm.

    Biweekly, except monthly during Aug. and Dec.
(1975-May 1980), monthly (June 1980-   ).
    Description based on: Vol. 7, no. 19 (June
1980); title from cover.
    Continues: Saturday review/World.
    Began with issue for Jan. 11, 1975.
    Microfilm. Ann Arbor, Mich. : University
Microfilms International, 1979-   .   microfilm
reels ; 35 mm. (Current periodical series)
    "Publication no.: 7972.01."

D: 11.0A, 12.AB1, 12.1C1, 1.4C1, 1.4C4, 1.4D1, 12.5B1, 2.5C3,
      12.5D1, 12.7B1, 12.7B3, 12.7B7, 12.7B8, 12.7B19, 11.7B22,
      12.7B22, B.15
C: 21.1C
F: 25.5B

This record shows the Library of Congress practice for cataloging
microforms.

Type: a Bib lvl: s Govt pub: Lang: eng Source: d S/L ent: 0
Repr: a Enc lvl: I Conf pub: 0 Ctry: miu Ser tp: p Alphabt: a
Indx: u Mod rec: Phys med: Cont: Frequn: a Pub st: c
Desc: a Cum ind: u Titl pag: u ISDS: Regulr: r Dates: 1976-9999

    010
    040   XXX $c XXX
    007   h $b d $d a $e f $f u--- $g b $h u $i c $j u
    090
    049   XXXX
    245 00 Saturday review $h microform
    260 00 Ann Arbor, Mich. : $b University Microfilms
International, $c 1977-
    300   microfilm reels : $b ill. ; 35 mm.
    362 0 Vol. 4, no. 1 (Oct. 1976)-
    490 0 Current periodical series
    500   Microreproduction of original published:
N.Y.[i.e. New York], N.Y. : Saturday Review Magazine,
1975-   .   v. : ill. (some col.) ; 28 cm.
    500   "Publication no.: 7972.01."
    780 00 $t Saturday review/World $w (OCoLC)nnnnnnn

News Letter

GOVERNOR'S PLANNING AND ADVISORY COUNCIL ON DEVELOPMENTAL DISABILITIES & THE DEVELOPMENTAL DISABILITIES OFFICE OF THE STATE PLANNING AGENCY

Vol. 1, No. 1   November, 1975

New laws affect disabled

During the 1975 Mn. Legislative Session, numerous bills of benefit to DD persons were passed. Highlights of some of these bills are summarized below.

SPECIAL EDUCATION. The budget adopted for special education provides $38,600,000 for 1976 and $46,750,000 for 1977, representing an increase of some $37.7 million for the coming biennium. The Omnibus School Aid bill includes the following provisions:

• Payment by the state of 65% of the salary of essential personnel in special education, not to exceed $10,000, for the normal school year for a full-time employee.

• Permissive summer programs for handicapped children, both residents and those temporarily placed in the district.

• Permissive instruction and services through the school year during which the pupil reaches age 25 for trainable mentally retarded pupils who have attended public school fewer than 9 years prior to September, 1975.

• State payment of 80% of the excess cost over 128% of the 1974 fiscal year actual net operating cost per eligible handicapped pupil for transportation during fiscal year 1976; and 80% of the excess cost over 134% of same for transportation during the fiscal year 1977.

• Publication by the State Board of Education of rules assuring the safe and efficient transportation of handicapped pupils, with particular attention to standards for vehicles used in transporting handicapped pupils, equipment to assure the safety of the pupils and the qualifications of the drivers and aids providing transportation services.

Legislation to p. 4

Council plans work program

Federal legislation passed in October, 1970 (P.L. 91-517) authorized the establishment in each state and territory of a Planning and Advisory Council on Developmental Disabilities. In Mn., this policy-making body was organized in 1971 and is currently comprised of 29 members. Council members include representatives of principal state and local agencies and nongovernmental organizations and groups concerned with services for the DD population. At least one-third of the members

Council to p. 6

News Letter fills communication gap

DD News Letter will be published quarterly during the coming year by the State DD Council and the DD Office of the State Planning Agency. The goal of this publication is to keep the various people working in the field of developmental disabilities in Mn. in touch with one another.

In addition to timely news items and announcements, DD News Letter will also include longer articles on State DD Council activities, Regional Councils, service projects, analysis of current issues, columns by the State Council chairperson and DD Office director, invited articles, and occasional notes on research in progress or just completed.

DD News Letter will be disseminated to approximately 1,000 persons throughout the state and to leaders of DD programs in other states.

INSIDE:

• New DD Act becomes reality, p. 3.
• Financial benefits for disabled, p. 9.
• Legal Advocacy Project has far-reaching impact, p. 10.

Regions from p. 8

programs for developmentally disabled persons. They should decide whether a need exists for coordinating regional planning for developmentally disabled persons and determine who is most appropriate to be the coordinator. The Regional Councils should also work with the State DD Council to conduct an integrated, statewide planning effort.

Several activities are underway in response to these recommendations. The State DD Council has formed a task force to more clearly define the mission and relationships of the State and Regional DD Councils; regional planners and Regional Council members will be a part of this task force.

In September, the State Council decided to form small teams to visit each regional DD program. Each team will consist of 1 DD Office staff member and 2 State Council members. The team will meet with the regional planners and Regional Council members to share information and improve communication between the state and regional programs.

Other areas of need iden-

tified by the regions may be addressed by the DD Office through Requests for Proposal. Possible areas include needs assessment, alternative planning processes, implementation plans, evaluation, and agency coordination.

DD Dateline

11/6-7 - - "Living in the Community; Problems the Retarded Child Will Face;" Child Development Section, St. Paul Ramsey Hospital; St. Paul Assoc. for Retarded Citizens; East Metropolitan Day Activity Center Council; School of Social Work, Dept. of Conferences, U. of Mn., Nolte Center for Continuing Education; Mpls., Mn.

11/8 - - Annual Meeting, Mn. Epilepsy League, Inc., Health Sci. Bldg. A. U. of Mn., Mpls., Mn.

11/13 - - Workshop on Early and Periodic Screening, Diagnosis and Treatment; Mn. Dept. of Welfare and Mn. Dept. of Health assisted by Region 9 DD Council; Holiday Inn, Mankato, Mn.

11/13-15 - - "The Need is Special," Mn. Assoc. for Children with Learning Disabilities Conference, Leamington Hotel, Mpls., Mn.

11/17-19 - - "Sexuality and the Retarded," Planned Parenthood of Mn. and Central Mn. Regional DD Council, Holiday Inn, Brainerd, Mn.

12/5-6 - - "The Puzzling Child: Autism," College of Education and Dept. of Conferences, St. Paul Campus, U. of Mn., St. Paul, Mn.

1/19-22 - - 5th National Conference on the Epilepsies, Epilepsy Foundation of America, Washington Hilton Hotel, Washington, D.C.

DD News Letter is a publication of the Governor's Planning and Advisory Council on Developmental Disabilities and the DD Office of the State Planning Agency.
Jane Belau,
DD Council Chairperson
Robert Bruininks,
DD Planning Office Director
Linda Baucom,
Editor

Developmental Disabilities News Letter
550 Cedar Street, Room 110
St. Paul, Minnesota 55101

Return
Postage
Guaranteed

Example 516

News letter (Minnesota. Governor's Planning and
    Advisory Council on Developmental Disabili-
    ties)
    News letter / Governor's Planning and Advi-
sory Council on Developmental Disabilities & the
Developmental Disabilities Office of the State
Planning Agency. -- Vol. 1, no. 1 (Nov. 1975)-
. -- St. Paul, Minn. : The Council, 1975-
        v. : ill. ; 28 cm.

    Quarterly.
    Title from cover
    Also called: DD news letter ; and, Develop-
mental disabilities new letter.

    I. Minnesota. Governor's Planning and Advi-
sory Council on Developmental Disabilities. II.
Minnesota State Planning Agency. Developmental
Disabilities Office. III. Title: DD news letter.
IV. Title: Developmental disabilities news letter.

D: 12.1B1, 1.1F4, 12.3C4, 1.4D4, 1.4D5, 1.4F1, 12.5, 12.7B1, 12.7B3,
       12.7B4
C: 21.1C
F: 25.5B
AE: 21.30E, 21.30J
F: 24.18(type 3), 24.13(type 2), 26.3A7

```
Type: a Bib lvl: s Govt pub: s Lang: eng Source: d S/L ent: 0
Repr:   Enc lvl: I Conf pub: 0 Ctry: mnu Ser tp: p Alphabt: a
Indx: u Mod rec:   Phys med:   Cont:     Frequn: q Pub st:  c
Desc: a Cum ind: u Titl pag: u ISDS:     Regulr: r Dates: 1975-9999
```

  010
  040   XXX $c XXX
  090
  049   XXXX
  130 00 News letter (Minnesota. Governor's Planning
and Advisory Council on Developmental Disabilities)
  245 00 News letter / $c Governor's Planning and
Advisory Council on Developmental Disabilities & the
Developmental Disabilities Office of the State Planning
Agency.
  246 33 DD news letter
  246 33 Developmental disabilities new letter
  260 00 St. Paul, Minn. : $b The Council, $c 1975-
  300   v. : $b ill. ; $c 28 cm.
  362 0 Vol. 1, no. 1 (Nov. 1975)-
  500   Title from cover.
  500   Also called: DD news letter ; and, Developmental disabilities new letter.
  710 10 Minnesota. $b Governor's Planning and Advi-
sory Council on Developmental Disabilities.
  710 20 Minnesota State Planning Agency. $b Develop-
mental Disabilities Office.

Left title page

ADVANCES IN PSYCHOLOGY

2

Editors
G. E. STELMACH
P. A. VROON

NORTH-HOLLAND PUBLISHING COMPANY
AMSTERDAM • NEW YORK • OXFORD

Right title page

PERSONALITY AND ADAPTATION

P. J. HETTEMA
Tilburg University
Tilburg, The Netherlands

1979

NORTH-HOLLAND PUBLISHING COMPANY
AMSTERDAM • NEW YORK • OXFORD

Example 517

Advances in psychology (Amsterdam, Netherlands)
    Advances in psychology. -- Amsterdam ; New
York : North-Holland Pub. Co. ; New York : sole
distributors for the U.S.A. and Canada, Elsevier
North-Holland,
        v. : ill. ; 24 cm.

    Description based on: 2, published 1979.
    ISSN 0166-4115.

D: 12.0B1, 12.1B1, 1.4C5, 1.4D3, 12.5, 12.7B22, 12.8B1
C: 21.1C
F: 25.5B

    In this example of a unique serial identifier in a main entry heading,
the qualifier for the title is the place of publication.

    The distribution statement was taken from the verso of the title
page.

```
Type: a Bib lvl: s Govt pub:    Lang: eng Source: d S/L ent: 0
Repr:     Enc lvl: I Conf pub: 0 Ctry: ne  Ser tp: m Alphabt: a
Indx: u Mod rec:    Phys med:    Cont:      Frequn:    Pub st:  c
Desc: a Cum ind: u Titl pag: u ISDS:       Regulr: x Dates:    1979-9999

    010
    040    XXX $c XXX
    090
    049    XXXX
    130 00 Advances in psychology (Amsterdam, Nether-
lands)
    245 00 Advances in psychology.
    260 00 Amsterdam ; $a New York : $b North-Holland
Pub. Co. ; $a New York : $b sole distributors for the
U.S.A. and Canada, Elsevier North-Holland,
    300    v. : ill. ; 24 cm.
    500    Description based on: 2, published 1979.
```

THE REGIONAL SCIENCE ASSOCIATION

PAPERS

VOLUME THIRTEEN, 1964

Edited By

Morgan D. Thomas

University of Washington

Published Annually by the Regional Science Association

The Regional Science Association is an international association devoted to the free exchange of ideas and viewpoints with the objective of fostering the development of theory and method in regional analysis and related spatial and areal studies. Address inquiries to the Regional Science Association, the Wharton School, University of Pennsylvania, Philadelphia, Pennsylvania 19104, U.S.A.

The Graduate School of the University of Washington provided a grant for editorial assistance on this volume.

Printed by the International Academic Printing Co., Ltd., Tokyo, Japan.

Example 518

```
Papers (Regional Science Association)
    Papers / the Regional Science Association. --
Philadelphia, Pa. : The Association,
        v. ; 25 cm.

    Annual.
    Description based on: Vol. 13 (1964).


    I. Regional Science Association.
```

D:	12.1B1, 12.1F1, 1.4D4, 12.5, 12.7B1, 12.7B22
C:	21.1C
F:	25.5B
AE:	21.29B, 21.30E
F:	24.1

In this example of a unique serial identifier in a main entry heading, the qualifier for the title is the issuing body.

THE *FORUM*

A newsletter for bank card customers

This month the BankCard Center is introducing a new service, a monthly newsletter which we are calling the forum. The Forum is designed to provide you with information on credit card usage and money management.

We believe the need for this service grew out of your changing needs. A few years ago, the majority of our customers just used their cards at Christmas and for vacations. That's changed. Today, bank cards are used all year long. This means you need to know as much as you can about credit card usage. That's what this newsletter is all about.

You will be receiving a copy of the Forum in each of your monthly statements.

Volume 1 Number 1   September 1980

Example 519

```
Forum (BankCard Center)
     The forum. -- Vol. 1, no. 1 (Sept. 1980)-
. -- [United States] : BankCard Center, 1980-
       v. : ill. ; 18 cm.

     Monthly.
     Title from cover.
     "A newsletter for bank card customers."


     I. BankCard Center.
```

D: 12.1B1, 12.3C4, B.9, 1.4C6, 12.4D1, 12.4F1, 12.5, 12.7B1, 12.7B3, 12.7B5
C: 21.1C
F: 25.5B
AE: 21.30E
F: 24.1

In this example of a unique serial identifier in a main entry heading, the qualifier for the title is the issuing body.

Proceedings
of

the Seventh Symposium
on
Operating Systems Principles

10-12 December 1979

Asilomar Conference Grounds
Pacific Grove, California

Special Interest Group on Operating Ssytems (SIGOPS)
Association for Computing Machinery (ACM)

ACM ORDER NO. 534790

The Association for Computing Machinery, Inc.
1133 Avenue of the Americas
New York, New York 10036

ISBN 0-89791-009-5

Additional copies may be ordered prepaid from:

ACM Order Department	Price:	
P.O. Box 54145	Members	$ 8.00
Baltimore, MD 21264	Non-members	$ 12.00

Example 520

Symposium on Operating Systems Principles.
    Proceedings of the ... Symposium on Operating
Systems Principles. -- New York, N.Y. : Special
Interest Group on Operating Systems, Association
for Computing Machinery,
        v. : ill. ; 28 cm.

    Description based on: 7th (10-12 Dec. 1979).

    I. Association for Computing Machinery. Spe-
cial Interest Group on Operating Systems. II.
Title.

D: 12.1B1, 12.1B6, 12.4, 12.5, 12.7B22
C: 21.1B2(d)
F: 24.1
AE: 21.30E, 21.30J
F: 24.13(type 1)

Type: a Bib lvl: s Govt pub: Lang: eng Source: d S/L ent: 0
Repr: Enc lvl: I Conf pub: 1 Ctry: nyu Ser tp: Alphabt: a
Indx: u Mod rec: Phys med: Cont: Frequn: u Pub st: c
Desc: a Cum ind: u Titl pag: u ISDS: Regulr: r Dates: 19uu-9999

    010
    040   XXX $c XXX
    090
    049   XXXX
    111 20 Symposium on Operating Systems Principles.
    245 10 Proceedings of the ... Symposium on Operat-
ing Systems Principles.
    260 00 New York, N.Y. : $b Special Interest Group
on Operating Systems, Association for Computing Machinery,
    300   v. : $b ill. ; $c 28 cm.
    500   Description based on: 7th (10-12 Dec. 1979).
    710 20 Association for Computing Machinery. $b
Special Interest Group on Operating Systems.

MINUTES

OF

THE EIGHTY-SIXTH
ANNUAL MEETING

OF THE

**CONGREGATIONAL CHRISTIAN CONFERENCE OF
MINNESOTA**

AND THE

FIFTEENTH ANNUAL MEETING

OF THE

CONGREGATIONAL WOMEN
OF MINNESOTA, INC.

HELD AT

PILGRIM CHURCH
DULUTH

MAY 15-17, 1941

CONGREGATIONAL CHRISTIAN CONFERENCE OF MINNESOTA

FIFTEENTH ANUAL REPORT

OF THE

CONGREGATIONAL WOMEN OF MINNESOTA, INCORPORATED

• •

1941

• •

Minnesota Woman's Home Missionary Union
Organized 1872.

■

Minnesota Branch of the Woman's Board of
Missions of the Interior Organized
October 12, 1877.

■

Merged April 28, 1926.

Minutes

of

The One Hundred Seventh Annual Meeting

of the

**CONGREGATIONAL CONFERENCE
OF MINNESOTA**

and the

**Thirty-Sixth Annual Meeting
Congregational Women of Minnesota**

held at

**FIRST CONGREGATIONAL CHURCH
Minneapolis**

MAY 8-10, 1962

CONGREGATIONAL CONFERENCE OFFICE
122 West Franklin Avenue
Minneapolis 4, Minnesota
Phone Federal 2-2571

THIRTY-SIXTH
ANNUAL REPORT

of the

Congregational Women of Minnesota
INCORPORATED

1962

MINNESOTA WOMEN'S HOME MISSIONARY UNION
Organized 1872

MINNESOTA BRANCH OF THE WOMEN'S BOARD OF
MISSIONS OF THE INTERIOR
Organized October 12, 1877

Merged April 28, 1926

Example 521

Congregational Women of Minnesota, Incorporated.
     Annual report of the Congregational Women of
Minnesota, Incorporated. -- 15th (1941)-36th
(1962).

     Vol. for 1941 in: Congregational Conference
of Minnesota. Meeting. Minutes of the ... Annual
Meeting of the Congregational Christian Conference
of Minnesota ... -- 86th (May 15-17, 1941) ; vols.
for 1942-1962 in: Congregational Conference of
Minnesota. Meeting. Minutes of the ... Annual
Meeting of the Congregational Conference of Minne-
sota ... 87th (May 14-15, 1942)-107th (May 8-10,
1962).
     Annual.
Continues: Minnesota Congregational Woman's
Missionary Society. Annual report of the Minnesota
Congregational Woman's Missionary Society.

     I. Title.

This is a serial within a serial.

Type: a Bib lvl: b Govt pub: Lang: eng Source: d S/L ent: 0
Repr: Enc lvl: I Conf pub: 1 Ctry: mnu Ser tp: Alphabt: a
Indx: u Mod rec: Phys med: Cont: Frequn: a Pub st: d
Desc: a Cum ind: u Titl pag: u ISDS: Regulr: r Dates: 1941,1962

     010
     040   XXX $c XXX
     043   n-us-mn
     090
     049   XXXX
     110 20 Congregational Women of Minnesota, Incorpo-
rated.
     245 10 Annual report of the Congregational Women of
Minnesota, Incorporated.
     260 | $c
     310   Annual.
     362 0 15th (1941)-36th (1962).
     580   Vol. for 1941 in: Congregational Conference
of Minnesota. Meeting. Minutes of the ... Annual Meeting
of the Congregational Christian Conference of Minnesota
... -- 86th (May 15-17, 1941) ; vols. for 1942-1962 in:
Congregational Conference of Minnesota. Meeting. Minutes
of the ... Annual Meeting of the Congregational Conference of Minnesota ... 87th (May 14-15, 1942)-107th (May
8-10, 1962).
     773 1 $7 c2as $a Congregational Conference of
Minnesota. Meeting. $t Minutes of the ... Annual Meeting
of the Congregational Christian Conference of Minnesota
... $g 86th (May 15-17, 1941) $w (OCoLC)nnnnnnn
     773 1 $7 c2as $a Congregational Conference of
Minnesota. Meeting. $t Minutes of the ... Annual Meeting
of the Congregational Conference of Minnesota ... $g
87th (May 12-15, 1942)-107th (May 8-10, 1962). $w
(OCoLC)nnnnnnn
     780 00   Minnesota Congregational Woman's Mis-
sionary Society. $t Annual report of the Minnesota Con-
gregational Woman's Missionary Society $w (OCoLC)nnnnnnn

CARNEGIE MUSEUM OF NATURAL HISTORY

1979 ANNUAL REPORT

Example 522

```
Carnegie Museum of Natural History.
    Annual report / Carnegie Museum of Natural
History. -- [Pittsburgh. Pa.] : The Museum,
        v. : ill. ; 23 cm.

    Description based on: 1979; title from cover.


    I. Title.
```

D: 12.1B1, 12.1F1, 12.4, 12.5, 12.7B3, 12.7B22
C: 21.1B2(a)
F: 24.1
AE: 21.30J

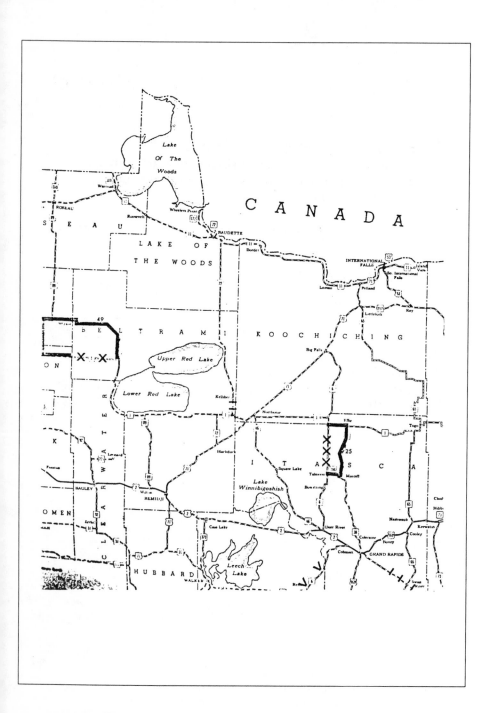

STATE OF
MINNESOTA
TRUNK HIGHWAY SYSTEM

ISSUED BY THE
DEPARTMENT OF HIGHWAYS
JAMES C. MARSHALL, COMMISSIONER

WEEKLY
ROAD CONDITION MAP
JUNE 11, 1963

SAFETY MAKES SENSE AND SAVES DOLLARS TOO.

Example 523

Minnesota. Dept. of Highways.
     Weekly road condition map. -- Scale
1:1,013,760 and ca. 1:1,520,640. --   -Nov. 13,
1967. -- [Saint Paul, Minn. : Minnesota Dept. of
Highways],   -1967.
          maps : col. ; 56 x 43 cm. and 76 x 65 cm.

     Weekly (May-Nov.) (varies)
     Description based on: June 11, 1963.
     Issues for   -Nov. 21, 1966, are red over-
printings on: State of Minnesota trunk highway
system / issued by the Department of Highways.
Issues for May 22-Nov. 13, 1967, are blue overprinting on: Minnesota : official road map /
issued by the Minnesota Department of Highways.
     Continued by: Minnesota. Dept. of Highways.
Monthly road condition map.

     I. Title.

D: 0.25; 3.3B6; 12.5B1, 3.5B1; 12.5C1, 3.5C3; 12.5D1, 3.5D1;
       12.7B1; 3.7B7

     This example is of a serial map, so needs rules from chapters 3 and
12 for cataloging.

Type: a Bib lvl: s Lang: eng Source: d Form: Relief:
RecG: c Enc lvl: I Ctry: mnu Dat tp: m Govt pub: s Indx: 0
Desc: a Mod rec: Base: Dates: 1966, 1967

     010
     040   XXX $c XXX
     034 2   a $b 1013760 $b 1520640
     052   4140
     090
     049   XXXX
     100 2   Minnesota. $b Dept. of Highways.
     245 10 Weekly road condition map.
     255   Scale 1:1,013,760 and ca. 1:1,520,640.
     260 0   [Saint Paul, Minn. : $b Minnesota Dept. of
Highways], $c   -1967.
     300   maps : $b col. ; $c 56 x 43 cm. and 76 x
65 cm.
     315   Weekly (May-Nov.) (varies)
     362 0   -Nov. 13, 1967.
     500   Description based on: June 11, 1963.
     500   Issues for   -Nov 21, 1966, are red over-
printings on: State of Minnesota trunk highway system /
issued by the Department of Highways. Issues for May 22-
Nov. 13, 1967, are blue overprinting on: Minnesota :
official road map / isued by the Minnesota Department of
Highways.
     500   Continued by: Minnesota. Dept. of Highways.
Monthly road condition map.

     This example shows how the record would be input to the OCLC
database. However, fields 362 and 315 in the maps format do not print. In
order to have the cards print as shown, it is necessary to reformat the record
after inputting and edit it as follows before producing cards:

     255   Scale 1:1,013,760 and ca. 1:1,520,640. --
-Nov. 13, 1967.
     500   Weekly (May-Nov.) (varies)

Example 524

Treated as an individual publication:

```
Saint Paul Public Library.
    St. Paul Library [microform] : [catalog].
-- Mar. 1982. -- [Saint Paul, Minn. : Saint Paul
Public Library], 1982 (Monterey Park, Calif. :
Autographics, Inc.)
    126 microfiches ; 11 x 15 cm.

    Title from header.


    I. Title.
```

Example 525

Treated as a serial publication:

```
Saint Paul Public Library.
    St. Paul Library [microform] : [catalog].
-- [Jan. 1981]-    . -- [Saint Paul, Minn. :
Saint Paul Public Library, 1981-    (Monterey Park,
Calif. : Autographics, Inc.)
        microfiches ; 11 x 15 cm.

    Quarterly (somewhat irregular).
    Title from header.
    Each issue supersedes the previous one.


    I. Title.
```

Chapter 14

"IN" ANALYTICS

Introduction

This chapter is based on *A Manual of AACR 2 Examples for "In" Analytics,* by Edward Swanson, with examples added from several other manuals.

The *Anglo-American cataloguing rules,* second edition (AACR 2), defines analysis as "the process of preparing a bibliographic record that describes a part or parts of a larger item" (p. 270). In this way access can be provided to a smaller part of an item than would be possible if only the larger item were cataloged.

Chapter 13 of AACR 2 deals with the rules for analysis. Five methods are given. Of these, multilevel description generally is used only in national bibliographies and in those cataloging agencies that need a single record showing both the primary work and its component parts.

Three other methods -- the use of the series area to record the larger work for a monographic series or multipart monograph, the recording of the parts in a note (generally a contents note), and the use of analytic added entries -- are familiar to most librarians.

The method we are concerned with in this chapter is less often used in most libraries. That is the use of the "in" analytic. For an "in" analytic, the part being analyzed is described, followed by a short citation for the larger work. Rule 13.5 gives the instructions for the preparation of an "in" analytic.

It is the intention of this chapter to give examples of some of the common types of "in" analytics. Two forms of the analytic are given for many of the examples, one in traditional catalog card format and one in the MARC format.

Now that the MARC format allows for creating "in" analytics in machine-readable form, this format also is given. The praticular format used is that followed by OCLC, but the general principles are the same in any machine environment that uses the MARC format. (Note that the symbol "$" is used to represent the delimiter ( ), which should be used when actually inputting a record. In subfield $w, "nnnnnnn" would be replaced by the actual number, e.g., $w (OCoLC) 10702191)

Examples are included in this book for following types of materials: printed materials; maps; manuscripts; music; sound recordings; videorecordings; graphics; computer files; and realia. Among these are several examples of serial "in" analytics, and several examples of "in" analytics that themselves are parts of "in" analytics.

The choice of examples is intended to illustrate various differences in describing a particular type of "in" analytic. For example, in the most common form, the citation of the location with the larger item is given in terms of the inclusive paging, e.g.

```
p. 81-104 ...

v. 1, p. 4 ...
```

In cases where the part is located on nonconsecutive pages, the exact paging is given:

```
p. 34-37, 89-94, 200-207 ...

p. 24-34, 36-37, 40-41 ...
```

For parts that are in more than one issue of a serial, for example, the paging of each part is given, separated by commas, and the first page number in each part preceded by "p.":

```
p. 1-3, p. 3, p. 3, p. 3 ...

p. 13-16, 71, p. 5-9 ...
```

Other physical description details are also given:

```
    p. [232]-269, [6] leaves of plates : ill.,
maps ; 24 cm.
```

For items described in terms of a specific material designation, this is given together with the location within the larger item, e.g.:

```
    no. 3 on 2 of 2 stereograph reels ...

    on side 1 of 1 sound cassette ...

    on side 2 of 1 sound disc ...

    on record 3, side 2, of 6 sound discs ...

    1 map, on 1 leaf facing p. 26 ...

    on 1 computer disk ...

    1 sample, mounted on sheet inside front
cover ...

    1 picture, on p. 213 ...

    1 technical drawing, on p. [12] ...
```

In some cases, the location within the larger item is included in a note:

```
    1 map : col. ; ...
Note:  Inset E on: [details of larger item]
```

For serials, the numeric and/or alphabetic, etc., designation is given instead of the physical description:

```
    15th (1941)-36th (1962).


    1957-
```

The larger item is described in terms of its main entry uniform title (if any), title proper, and publication, etc,.detaills.

```
    In Keillor, Garrison, 1942-    . The
selected verse of Margaret Haskins Durber.
-- Lake Wobegon, Minn. : Jack's Press
[i.e., Saint Paul, Minn. : Minnesota Pub-
lic Radio], 1979.


    In Captain & Tennille.  Love will keep
us together. -- Beverly Hills, Calif. : A
& M Records, p1975.
```

If the larger item is a serial publication, the numeric and/or alphabetic, etc., designation of the issue is given instead of the publication, etc., details:

```
    In Minnesota.  [Laws, etc. (Session
laws : 1858-1891)].  General and special
laws of the state of Minnesota. -- 6th
(1864).


    In The Canadian historical review. --
Vol. 64, no. 1 (Mar. 1983).
```

If the item extends to more than one issue of a serial publication, the citations of the individual issues are separated by a semicolon-space:

<u>In</u> Historical whisperings. -- Vol. 9, no. 2 (July 1982); v. 9, no. 3 (Oct. 1982); v. 9, no.4 (Jan. 1983); v. 10, no. 1 (Apr. 1983).

The extension of the MARC formats to include "in" analytics included four major changes to existing formats. One is the addition of two values for bibliographic level, "a" indicating component part, monographic, in all formats except Serials, and "b" indicating component part, serial, in the Maps and Serials formats.

Second is the addition of field 018 in the Books and serials formats for recording the Copyright Article-Fee Code:

018   0008-3755/83/0300-0003$01.25/0

This information is recorded if it is found on the piece being cataloged, but it does not appear as a part of the eye-readable cataloging record.

Third is the addition of field 773 for recording details about the larger work. The field begins with control subfield $7, which gives information about the type of the author name in subfield $a and the type-of-record and bibliographic level of the larger work.

Control subfield $7 is composed of up to four characters. The first indicates whether the heading in field 773 subfield $a is a personal name, a corporate name, a meeting name, or a uniform title, or if there is no subfield $a. The second character indicates the type of personal, corporate, or meeting name coded in the first position. The third position indicates the type-of-record code of the larger work, and the fourth position the bibliographic level of the larger work.

$7 p0am $a Liliuokalani, Queen of Hawaii, ...

$7 p1am $a Neuberg, Victor E.

$7 p1cm $a Larson, LeRoy.

$7 p1jm $a Harvey, Anne-Charlotte.

$7 p1aa $a Brower, J. V. (Jacob Vradenberg), 1844-1905.

$7 c1as $a Minnesota.

$7 c2as $a Library of Congress.

$7 c2jm $a Captain & Tennille (Musical duo).

$7 m2am $a Conference on Underwater Archaeology (1963 : Saint Paul, Minn.)

$7 unam $a Lord's prayer. Polyglot.

$7 unas $a Collection of the Minnesota Historical Society (1898).

$7 nnas $t Historical whisperings.

$7 nnam $t Hollywood speaks!

$7 nnmm $t Apple barrel II.

Finally, field 580 was extended to all formats for those cases in which the details of the larger item cannot adequately be specified by a single 773 field. In such a case, the details are entered in natural-language form in the 580 field. The information also is entered in one or more 773 fields, but the first indicator of each 773 field is set to "1" indicating that a note is not to be printed from it.

```
580     Vol. for 1941 in: Congregational Con-
ference of Minnesota.  Meeting.  Minutes of
the ... Annual Meeting of the Congrgational
Christian Conference of Minnesota ... -- 86th
(May 15-17, 1941) ; vols. for 1942-1962 in:
Congregational Conference iof Minnesota.
Meeting.  Minutes of the ... Annual Meeting or
the Congregational Conference of Minnesota ...
-- 87th (May 14-15, 1942)-107th (May 8-10,
1962).
```

```
773 1   $7 c2as $a Congregational Conference of
Minnesota.  Meeting.  $t Minutes of the ...
Annual Meeting of the Congregational Christian
Conference of Minnesota ... $g 86th (May 15-
17, 1941).
```

```
773 1   $7 c2as $a Congregational Conference of
Minnesota.  Meeting.  $t Minutes of the ...
Annual Meeting of the Congregational Confer-
ence of Minnesota ... $g 87th (May 14-14,
1942)-107th (May 8-10, 1962).
```

```
580     Inset E on: National Geographic Society
(U.S.).  Cartographic Division.  Hawaii. --
[Washington, D.C. : The Society], 1960. --
(Atlas plate ; 15).
```

```
773 1   $7 c2em $a National Geogrpahic Society
(U.S).  Cartographic Division.  $t Hawaii.  $d
[Washington, D.C. : The Society], 1960.  $k
Atlas plate ; 15.
```

"In" analytics can provide access to information that the library user ordinarily would not find because the only record available is that for the larger work. It is hoped that more libraries will begin using this method to enable their users to find all the riches that their collections contain.

LAKE WOBEGON

SUMUS QUID SUMUS

THE SELECTED VERSE OF
MARGARET HASKINS DURBER

 Jack's Press
Lake Wobegon, Minnesota

TWO-NINE-ONE-NINE-ONE-NINE-OH

Example 526

Keillor, Garrison, 1942-
    Two-nine-one-nine-one-nine-oh. -- p. [8-9] ; 22
cm.

    <u>In</u> Keillor, Garrison, 1942-   . The selected
verse of Margaret Haskins Durber. -- Lake Wobegon,
Minn. : Jack's Press [i.e., Saint Paul, Minn. :
Minnesota Public Radio], 1979.

    I. Title.

Type: a Bib lvl: a Govt pub: Lang: eng Source: d Illus:
Repr: Enc lvl: I Conf pub: 0 Ctry: mnu Dat tp: s M/F/B: 00
Indx: 0 Mod rec: Festschr: 0 Cont:
Desc: a Int lvl: Dates: 1979,

```
010
040     XXX $c XXX
090
049     XXXX
100 10  Keillor, Garrison, $d 1942-
245 10  Two-nine-one-nine-one-nine-oh.
260 |   $c
300     p. [8-9] ; $c 22 cm.
773 0   $7p1am $a Keillor, Garrison, 1942-    . $t
The selected verse of Margaret Haskins Durber. $d Lake
Wobegon, Minn. : Jack's Press [i.e., Saint Paul, Minn. :
Minnesota Public Radio], 1979. $w (OCoLC)nnnnnnn
```

PRIVATE LIBERAL ARTS COLLEGES IN MINNESOTA:

Their History and Contributions

By MERRILL E. JARCHOW

Minnesota Historical Society • St. Paul • 1973

8   MACALESTER COLLEGE

Presbyterians Found a College

18   MACALESTER COLLEGE

The Golden Key

33   MACALESTER COLLEGE

Metamorphosis

Example 527

Jarchow, Merrill E. (Merrill Earl), 1910-
    Macalester College. -- p. 34-37, 89-94, 200-
207 : ill. ; 27 cm.

    In Jarchow, Merrill E. (Merrill Earl), 1910-
. Private liberal arts colleges in Minnesota. --
St. Paul : Minnesota Historical Society, 1973. --
(Publications of the Minnesota Historical Soci-
ety).

    Title from caption.
    Illustrative material between p. 142 and 143.
    Contents: Presbyterians found a college
[1850-1900] -- The golden key [1900-1940] -- Metamorphosis [1940-1970].

    I. Title.

Type: a Bib lvl: a Govt pub: s Lang: eng Source: d Illus: a
Repr: Enc lvl: I Conf pub: 0 Ctry: mnu Dat tp: s M/F/B: 10
Indx: 0 Mod rec: Festschr: 0 Cont:
Desc: a Int lvl: Dates: 1973,

    010
    040   XXX $c XXX
    043   n-us-mn
    052   4144 $b S4
    090
    049   XXXX
    100 10 Jarchow, Merrill E. $q (Merrill Earl), $d
1910-
    245 10 Macalester College.
    260 | $c
    300   p. 34-37, 89-94, 200-207 : $b ill. ; $c 27
cm.
    500   Title from caption.
    500   Illustrative material between p. 142 and
143.
    505 0 Presbyterians found a college [1850-1900] --
The golden key [1900-1940] -- Metamorphosis [1940-1970].
    773 0 $7 p1am $a Jarchow, Merrill E. (Merrill
Earl), 1910-   . $t Private liberal arts colleges in
Minnesota. $d St. Paul : Minnesota Historical Society,
1973. $K Publications of the Minnesota Historical Soci-
ety $z 0-87351-081-X. $w (OCoLC)nnnnnnn

MIKE STEEN

———

HOLLYWOOD SPEAKS!

An Oral History

G. P. Putnam's Sons, New York

The Leading Lady

ROSALIND RUSSELL

Example 528

Russell, Rosalind, 1913-1976.
    The leading lady / Rosalind Russell. -- p.
[71]-103 ; 22 cm.

    In Hollywood speaks!. -- New York : Putnam,
1974.
    Interview with Mike Steen, recorded Aug. 4-6,
1971.

    I. Steen, Mike. II. Title.

Type: a Bib lvl: a Govt pub: Lang: eng Source: d Illus: a
Repr: Enc lvl: I Conf pub: 0 Ctry: mnu Dat tp: s M/F/B: 10
Indx: 0 Mod rec: Festschr: 0 Cont:
Desc: a Int lvl: Dates: 1977,

    010
    040   XXX $c XXX
    043   n-us--- $a n-us-ca
    090
    049   XXXX
    110 10 Russell, Rosalind, $d 1913-1976.
    245 14 The leading lady / $c Rosalind Russell.
    260 | $c
    300   p. [71]-103 ; $c 22 cm.
    500   Interview with Mike Steen, recorded Aug. 4-
6, 1971.
    700 10 Steen, Mike.
    773 0 $7 nnam $t Hollywood speaks!. $d New York :
Putnam, 1974. $w (OCoLC)nnnnnnn

VICTOR E. NEUBERG

The Penny Histories

A study of chapbooks for young readers over two centuries

Illustrated with facsimiles of seven chapbooks

HARCOURT, BRACE & WORLD, INC.
New York

THE

HISTORY

OF

GUY, Earl of Warwick.

Printed and Sold in Aldermary Church Yard, London

Example 529

Guy of Warwick (Romance).
     The history of Guy, Earl of Warwick. -- p. 81-
104 : ill. ; 18 cm.

     In Neuberg, Victor E. The Penny histories.
-- 1st American ed. -- New York : Harcourt, Brace &
World, 1969, c1968.
     Facsim. of: London : Printed and sold in Alder-
mary Church Yard, [1750?]. 24 p.

     I. Title.

Type: a Bib lvl: a Govt pub: Lang: eng Source: d Illus: a
Repr: Enc lvl: I Conf pub: 0 Ctry: nyu Dat tp: r M/F/B: 00
Indx: 0 Mod rec: Festschr: 0 Cont:
Desc: a Int lvl: Dates: 1969, 1750

     010
     040   XXX $c XXX
     090
     049   XXXX
     130 00 Guy of Warwick (Romance).
     245 14 The history of Guy, Earl of Warwick.
     260 | $c
     300   p. 81-104 : $b ill. ; $c 18 cm.
     500   Facsim. of: London : Printed and sold in
Aldermary Church Yard, [1750?]. 24 p.
     773 0 $7 p1am $a Neuberg, Victor E. $t The penny
histories. $b 1st American ed. $d New York : Harcourt,
Brace & World, 1969, c1968 $w (OCoLC)nnnnnnn

FOUR PLAYS BY HOLBERG

THE FUSSY MAN
THE MASKED LADIES
THE WEATHERCOCK
MASQUERADES

TRANSLATED FROM THE DANISH BY
HENRY ALEXANDER

1946

PRINCETON UNIVERSITY PRESS
PRINCETON, NEW JERSEY

FOR THE AMERICAN-SCANDINAVIAN FOUNDATION
NEW YORK

The Masked Ladies

[De Usynlige]

A COMEDY IN THREE ACTS

1725

Example 530

Holberg, Ludwig, Baron, 1684-1754.
    [Usynlige. English]
    The masked ladies : a comedy in three acts :
1725. -- p. [63]-97 ; 20 cm.

    In Holberg, Ludwig, Baron, 1684-1754. [Plays.
Selections. English. 1946]. Four plays by Holberg.
-- Princeton, N.J. : Princeton University Press
for the American Scandinavian Foundation, New
York, 1946.
    Translation of: De usynlige.

    I. Title.

Type: a Bib lvl: a Govt pub: Lang: eng Source: d Illus:
Repr: Enc lvl: I Conf pub: 0 Ctry: nju Dat tp: s M/F/B: 00
Indx: 0 Mod rec: Festschr: 0 Cont:
Desc: a Int lvl: Dates: 1946,

```
010
040     XXX $c XXX
041 1   eng $h swe
090
049     XXXX
100 10  Holberg, Ludwig, $c Baron, $d 1684-1754.
240 10  Usynlige. $l English
245 10  The masked ladies : $b a comedy in three
acts : 1725.
260 |   $c
300     p. [63]-97 ; $c 20 cm.
500     Translation of: De usynlige.
773 0   $7 plam $a Holberg, Ludwig, Baron, 1684-
1754. $s Plays. Selections. English. 1946. $t Four plays
by Holberg. $d Princeton, N.J. : Princeton University
Press for the American Scandinavian Foundation, New
York, 1946. $w (OCoLC)nnnnnnn
```

SUBJECT
KEYWORD INDEX
TO THE
LIBRARY OF CONGRESS
CLASSIFICATION
SCHEDULES
1974

(CONTAINED IN SIX VOLUMES)

Volume One
Aabenra-Coin Tricks

compiled by

Nancy B. Olson

SET V OF THE COMBINED INDEXES TO THE
LIBRARY OF CONGRESS CLASSIFICATION
SCHEDULES, 1974 (IN 15 VOLUMES)

THE U.S. HISTORICAL
DOCUMENTS INSTITUTE, INC.
WASHINGTON, D.C.
1974

iii

THE LIBRARY OF CONGRESS CLASSIFICATION SYSTEM, ITS HISTORY AND DEVELOPMENT

BY

GEORGE ALAN MORGAN, Ph.D.
Cataloging Department, Mankato State College Library

The history of the United States Congress' library is quite generally known, and several detailed accounts of its landmarks exist. The present author has folowed the general outlines given by Dr. John Phillip Immroth, Professor of Library and Information Science at the State University of New York at Geneseo. Professor Immroth's *A Guide to the Library of Congress Classification*[1] begins with a brief history of the Library, treats the purpose and format of the scheme, and then goes into as lengthy a discussion of the individual schedules and their tables as his space allows.

Example 531

Morgan, George Alan.
    The Library of Congress classification system
: its history and development / by George Alan
Morgan. -- v. 1, p. xxi-xxxii ; 28 cm.

    In Olson, Nancy B. Subject keyword index to
the Library of Congress classification schedules,
1974. -- Washington, D.C. : U.S. Historical Documents Institute, 1974. -- (Combined indexes to the
Library of Congress classification schedules ; set
5).

    I. Title.

REPORT

OF THE

LIBRARIAN OF CONGRESS

FOR THE

FISCAL YEAR ENDING JUNE 30, 1902.

WASHINGTON:
GOVERNMENT PRINTING OFFICE.
1902.

Appendix VI

BIBLIOGRAPHY

OF

COOPERATIVE CATALOGUING

AND THE

PRINTING OF CATALOGUE CARDS

WITH INCIDENTAL REFERENCES TO INTERNATIONAL BIBLIOGRAPHY
AND THE UNIVERSAL CATALOGUE

(1850-1902)

BY

TORSTEIN JAHR

AND

ADAM JULIUS STROHM

109

Example 532

Jahr, Torstein, 1871-1931.
    Bibliography of cooperative cataloguing and
the printing of catalogue cards : with incidental
references to international bibliography and the
universal catalogue, 1850-1902 / by Torstein Jahr
and Adam Julius Strohm. -- p. 109-224 ; 26 cm.

    In Library of Congress. Report of the Librar-
ian of Congress. -- 1902.
    Originally presented to the University of
Illinois, June 1903, "in partial fulfillment of
the requirements for the degree of B.L.S. ...
Revised and brought up to date" by Jahr and Theodore W. Koch.

    I. Strohm, Adam Julius, 1870-   II. Koch,
Theodore W. (Theodore Wesley). 1871-   III.
Title.

Type: a Bib lvl: a Govt pub: f Lang: eng Source: d Illus:
Repr: Enc lvl: I Conf pub: 0 Ctry: dcu Dat tp: s M/F/B: 00
Indx: 0 Mod rec: Festschr: 0 Cont: b
Desc: a Int lvl: Dates: 1902,

```
010
040     XXX $c XXX
090
049     XXXX
100 10 Jahr, Torstein, $d 1871-1931.
245 10 Bibliography of cooperative cataloguing and
the printing of catalogue cards : $b with incidental
references to international bibliography and the univer-
sal catalogue, 1850-1902 / $c by Torstein Jahr and Adam
Julius Strohm.
260 |    $c
300     p. 109-224 ; $c 26 cm.
500     Originally presented to the University of
Illinois, June 1903, "in partial fulfillment of the
requirements for the degree of B.L.S. ... Revised and
brought up to date" by Jahr and Theodore W. Koch.
700 10 Strohm, Adam Julius, $d 1870-
700 10 Koch, Theodore W. $q (Theodore Wesley), $d
1871-
773 0    $7 c2as $a Library of Congress, $t Report
of the Librarian of Congress. $g 1902. $w (OCoLC)nnnnnnn
```

MINUTES

OF

THE EIGHTY-SIXTH
ANNUAL MEETING

OF THE

**CONGREGATIONAL CHRISTIAN CONFERENCE OF
MINNESOTA**

AND THE

FIFTEENTH ANNUAL MEETING

OF THE

CONGREGATIONAL WOMEN
OF MINNESOTA, INC.

HELD AT

PILGRIM CHURCH
DULUTH

MAY 15-17, 1941

CONGREGATIONAL CHRISTIAN CONFERENCE OF MINNESOTA

FIFTEENTH ANUAL REPORT

OF THE

CONGREGATIONAL WOMEN OF MINNESOTA, INCORPORATED

• •

1941

• •

Minnesota Woman's Home Missionary Union
Organized 1872.

■

Minnesota Branch of the Woman's Board of
Missions of the Interior Organized
October 12, 1877.

■

Merged April 28, 1926.

Minutes

of

The One Hundred Seventh Annual Meeting

of the

**CONGREGATIONAL CONFERENCE
OF MINNESOTA**

and the

**Thirty-Sixth Annual Meeting
Congregational Women of Minnesota**

held at

**FIRST CONGREGATIONAL CHURCH
Minneapolis**

MAY 8-10, 1962

CONGREGATIONAL CONFERENCE OFFICE
122 West Franklin Avenue
Minneapolis 4, Minnesota
Phone Federal 2-2571

THIRTY-SIXTH
ANNUAL REPORT

of the

Congregational Women of Minnesota
INCORPORATED

1962

MINNESOTA WOMEN'S HOME MISSIONARY UNION
Organized 1872

MINNESOTA BRANCH OF THE WOMEN'S BOARD OF
MISSIONS OF THE INTERIOR
Organized October 12, 1877

Merged April 28, 1926

Example 533

Congregational Women of Minnesota, Incorporated.
     Annual report of the Congregational Women of
Minnesota, Incorporated. -- 15th (1941)-36th
(1962).

     Vol. for 1941 in: Congregational Conference
of Minnesota. Meeting. Minutes of the ... Annual
Meeting of the Congregational Christian Conference
of Minnesota ... -- 86th (May 15-17, 1941) ; vols.
for 1942-1962 in: Congregational Conference of
Minnesota. Meeting. Minutes of the ... Annual
Meeting of the Congregational Conference of Minnesota ... 87th (May 14-15, 1942)-107th (May 8-10,
1962).
     Annual.
     Continues: Minnesota Congregational Woman's
Missionary Society. Annual report of the Minnesota
Congregational Woman's Missionary Society.

     I. Title.

Type: a Bib lvl: b Govt pub: Lang: eng Source: d S/L ent: 0
Repr: Enc lvl: I Conf pub: 1 Ctry: mnu Ser tp: Alphabt: a
Indx: u Mod rec: Phys med: Cont: Frequn: a Pub st: d
Desc: a Cum ind: u Titl pag: u ISDS: Regulr: r Dates: 1941,1962

     010
     040   XXX $c XXX
     043   n-us-mn
     090
     049   XXXX
     110 20 Congregational Women of Minnesota, Incor-
porated.
     245 10 Annual report of the Congregational Women
of Minnesota, Incorporated.
     260 | $c
     310   Annual.
     362 0   15th (1941)-36th (1962).
     580   Vol. for 1941 in: Congregational Confer-
ence of Minnesota. Meeting. Minutes of the ... Annual
Meeting of the Congregational Christian Conference of
Minnesota ... -- 86th (May 15-17, 1941) ; vols. for
1942-1962 in: Congregational Conference of Minnesota.
Meeting. Minutes of the ... Annual Meeting of the
Congregational Conference of Minnesota ... 87th (May
14-15, 1942)-107th (May 8-10, 1962).
     773 1 $7 c2as $a Congregational Conference of
Minnesota. Meeting. $t Minutes of the ... Annual
Meeting of the Congregational Christian Conference of
Minnesota ... $g 86th (May 15-17, 1941) $w
(OCoLC)nnnnnnn
     773 1 $7 c2as $a Congregational Conference of
Minnesota. Meeting. $t Minutes of the ... Annual
Meeting of the Congregational Conference of Minnesota
... $g 87th (May 12-15, 1942)-107th (May 8-10, 1962).
$w (OCoLC)nnnnnnn
     780 00   Minnesota Congregational Woman's
Missionary Society. $t Annual report of the Minnesota
Congregational Woman's Missionary Society $w
(OCoLC)nnnnnnn

AN
EXPLANATION
OF THE FASHION
AND USE OF THREE
and fifty Instruments of
CHIRURGERY.

Gathered out of *Ambrosius Pareus*, the
famous *French* Chirurgion, and done into
English, for the behoofe of young Practitioners
in Chirurgery, by *H.C.*

London Printed for *Michael Sparke*, 1634.

Example 534

Paré, Ambroise, 1510?-1590.
   An explanation of the fashion and use of
three and and fifty instruments of chirurgery /
gathered out of Ambrosius Pareus, the famous
French chirurgion, and done into English, for the
behoofe of young practitioners in chirurgery, by
H.C. -- London : Printed for Michael Sparke, 1634.
-- [3] leaves, 117 p. ; ill. (woodcuts) ; 20 cm.
(8vo).

   In: Σοματογραπηια αντηροπινε / Helkiah Crooke.
London : Printed by Tho. Cotes, and are to be sold
by Michael Sparke at the blew Bible in Greene
Arbor, 1634, [1]-117 (second group)
   Translated by Helkiah Crooke--Cf. Catalogue
of printed books in the Wellcome Historical Medical Library, v. 1, p. 88.

   I. Crooke, Helkiah, 1576-1635. II. Title.
III. Title: The fashion and use of three and fifty
instruments of chirurgery.

D: 13.5B
ME: 21.1A, 22.3B2

Cross references

Pareus, Ambrosius, 1501?-1590.
H. C. (Helkiah Crooke), 1576-1635.
C., H. (Helkiah Crooke), 1576-1635.

Diving into the Past

Theories, Techniques, and Applications of Underwater Archaeology

The Proceedings of a Conference on UnderWater Archaeology
Sponsored by the Minnesota Historical Society, St. Paul
April 26-27, 1963. Edited by JUNE DRENNING HOLMQUIST
and ARDIS HILLMAN WHEELER

THE MINNESOTA HISTORICAL SOCIETY
AND THE COUNCIL OF UNDERWATER ARCHAEOLOGY

Some Legal Problems in the Field of Underwater Archaeology

WALTER N. TRENERRY

Example 535

```
Trenerry, Walter N.
     Some legal problems in the field of underwater
archaeology / Walter N. Trenerry. -- p. 37-43 ; 28
cm.

     In Conference on Underwater Archaeology (1963 :
Saint Paul, Minn.). Diving into the past. -- [Saint
Paul, Minn.] : Minnesota Historical Society and the
Council of Underwater Archaeology, 1963.
     Title from caption.


     I. Title.


Type: a Bib lvl: a Govt pub: s Lang: eng Source: d Illus:
Repr:    Enc lvl: I Conf pub: 1 Ctry: mnu Dat tp: s M/F/B: 10
Indx: 0 Mod rec:    Festschr: 0 Cont:
Desc: a Int lvl:    Dates: 1963,

     010
     040     XXX $c XXX
     090
     049     XXXX
     110 10 Trenerry, Walter N.
     245 10 Some legal problems in the field of underwa-
ter archaeology / $c Walter N. Trenerry.
     260 |    $c
     300     p. 37-43 ; $c 28 cm.
     500     Title from caption.
     773 0    $7 m2am $a Conference on Underwater Archae-
ology (1963 : Saint Paul, Minn.). $t Diving into the
past. $d [Saint Paul, Minn.] : Minnesota Historical
Society and the Council of Underwater Archaeology, 1963.
$w (OCoLC)nnnnnnn
```

The Making of a Code

The Issues Underlying AACR2

Papers Given at the International Conference on AACR2

held March 11-14, 1979

in

Tallahassee, Florida

Sponsored by the School of Library Science

Florida State University

Edited by

Doris Hargrett Clack

Chicago
American Library Association
1980

Implementation of AACR2 at the Library of Congress

BEN TUCKER

Example 536

Tucker, Ben, 1935-
    Implementation of AACR2 at the Library of Congress / Ben Tucker. -- p. 191-206 ; 23 cm.

    In International Conference on AACR2 (1979 : Florida State University). The making of a code. -- Chicago : American Library Association, 1980.

    I. Title.

Type: a Bib lvl: a Govt pub: s Lang: eng Source: d Illus:
Repr: Enc lvl: I Conf pub: 0 Ctry: ilu Dat tp: s M/F/B: 10
Indx: 0 Mod rec: Festschr: 0 Cont:
Desc: a Int lvl: Dates: 1980,

    010
    040   XXX $c XXX
    090
    049   XXXX
    110 10 Tucker, Ben, $d 1935-
    245 10 Implementation of AACR2 at the Library of Congress / $c Ben Tucker.
    260 | $c
    300   p. 191-206 ; $c 23 cm.
    773 0 $7 m2am $a International Conference on AACR2 (1979 : Florida State University). $t The making of a code. $d Chicago : American Library Association, 1980. $w (OCoLC)nnnnnnn

THE DOCUMENTS OF VATICAN II

GUILD PRESS • NEW YORK

AMERICA PRESS • ASSOCIATION PRESS

Pastoral[1] Constitution[2] on the Church in the Modern World

Paul, Bishop
Servant of the Servants of God
Together with the Fathers of the Sacred Council
For Everlasting Memory

PREFACE

THE INTIMATE BOND BETWEEN THE CHURCH
AND MANKIND

1. The joys and the hopes, the griefs and the anxieties of the men of this age, especially those who are poor or in any way

1. An explanatory note was appended to the title of the text in order to satisfy the misgivings of some Fathers of the Council concerning the application of the term "constitution" to a document that of its nature does not define or decree immutable dogma. Though a special vote revealed that a majority of the Council Fathers approved use of the term "pastoral constitution," several hundred voted variously to substitute the terms "declaration," "letter," "exposition," or similar designations.

2. *The pastoral constitution "De Ecclesia in Mundo Huius Temporis" is made up of two parts; yet it constitutes an organic unity.*

Example 537

Vatican Council (2nd : 1962-1965).
    [Constitutio pastoralis de ecclesia in mundo
huius temporis. English]
    Pastoral constitution on the Church in the
modern world. -- p. [199]-308 ; 18 cm.

    In Vatican Council (2nd : 1962-1965). The
documents of Vatican II. -- New York : Guild Press
: America Press : Association Press, 1966. -- (An
angelus book)
    Title from caption.
    Translation of: Constitutio pastoralis de
ecclesia in mundo huius temporis.
    "A response," by Robert McAfee Brown: p.
[309]-316.

    I. Brown, Robert McAfee, 1920- Response.
1966. II. Title.

```
Type: a Bib lvl: a Govt pub:   Lang: eng Source: d Illus:
Repr:   Enc lvl: I Conf pub: 0 Ctry: nyu Dat tp: s M/F/B: 00
Indx: 0 Mod rec:   Festschr: 0 Cont:
Desc: a Int lvl:   Dates: 1980,

   010
   040    XXX $c XXX
   041 1  eng $h lat
   090
   049    XXXX
   111 20 Vatican Council $n (2nd : $d 1962-1965).
   240 10 Constitutio pastoralis de ecclesia in mundo
huius temporis. $l English
   245 10 Pastoral constitution on the Church in the
modern world.
   260 |   $c
   300    p. [199]-308 ; $c 18 cm.
   500    Title from caption.
   700    Translation of: Constitutio pastoralis de
ecclesia in mundo huius temporis.
   700    "A response," by Robert McAfee Brown: p.
[309]-316.
   700 10 Brown, Robert McAfee, $d 1920- $t Response.
$f 1966.
   773 0   $7 m2am $a Vatican Council (2nd : 1962-
1965). $t  The documents of Vatican II. $d New York :
Guild Press : America Press : Association Press, 1966. -
- (An angelus book) $w (DLC)   6620201 (OCoLC)nnnnnnn
```

MINNESOTA REPORTS

VOL. 51

CASES ARGUED AND DETERMINED

IN THE

SUPREME COURT OF MINNESOTA

JULY-NOVEMBER, 1892

CHARLES C. WILLSON

REPORTER

ST. PAUL
WEST PUBLISHING CO.
1894

Ramsey County *vs*. Macalester College.

Argued Nov. 1, 1892.   Decided Dec. 1, 1892.

College Grounds Exempt from Taxation—Extent of.

    A college owns 40 acres of land, on which the college buildings are situated. On a part of the tract, near the college buildings, the college has erected several houses as places of residence for the professors or faculty, such as premises being used for no other purpose. *Held*, that the premises used for that purpose are within the statutory exemption from taxation.

Example 538

Minnesota. Supreme Court.
     Ramsey County vs. Macalester College. -- p.
437-443 ; 25 cm.

     In Minnesota. Supreme Court. Minnesota re-
ports. -- Vol. 51 (July-Nov. 1892).
     Title from caption.
     "Argued Nov. 1, 1892. Decided Dec. 1. 1892."
     Decision signed: Dickinson. J.
     Also published as: 53 N.W. Rep. 704.

     I. Dickinson, Daniel A., 1839-1902. II.
Ramsey County (Minn.). III. Macalester College.
IV. Title.

```
Type: a Bib lvl: a Govt pub: s Lang: eng Source: d Illus:
Repr:   Enc lvl: I Conf pub: 0 Ctry: mnu Dat tp: s M/F/B: 00
Indx: 0 Mod rec:   Festschr: 0 Cont: w
Desc: a Int lvl:   Dates: 1892,

     010
     040     XXX $c XXX
     043     n-us-mn
     052     4143 $b R2
     052     4143 $b S4
     090
     049     XXXX
     110 10  Minnesota. $b Supreme Court.
     245 10  Ramsey County vs. Macalester College.
     260 |   $c
     300     p. 437-443 ; $c 25 cm.
     500     Title from caption.
     500     "Argued Nov. 1, 1892. Decided Dec. 1. 1892."
     500     Decision signed: Dickinson. J.
     500     Also published as: 53 N.W. Rep. 704.
     700 10  Dickinson, Daniel A., $d 1839-1902.
     710 10  Ramsey County (Minn.).
     710 20  Macalester College.
     773 0   $7 c1as $a Minnesota. Supreme Court. $t
Minnesota reports. $g Vol. 51 (July-Nov. 1892). $w
(OCoLC) nnnnnnn
```

GENERAL AND SPECIAL LAWS

OF THE

STATE OF MINNESOTA,

PASSED DURING THE

Sixth Session of the State Legislature,

COMMENCING JANUARY FIFTH, ONE THOUSAND EIGHT
HUNDRED AND SIXTY-FOUR, AND TERMINATING MARCH
FOURTH, ONE THOUSAND EIGHT HUNDRED AND SIXTY-FOUR

TOGETHER WITH THE

JOINT RESOLUTIONS AND REPORT OF STATE TREASURER.

5,000 Copies Ordered Printed.

SAINT PAUL:
FREDERICK DRISCOLL, STATE PRINTER
PRESS PRINTING COMPANY
1864.

---

354   SPECIAL LAWS

CHAPTER LXXXVI.

*An Act to amend an act entitled "an act to incorporate the Baldwin
School in the City of Saint Paul, approved February twinty-sixth,
eighteen hundred and fifty-three," and also to authorize the
Board of Trustees of the College of St. Paul to transfer and
convey its property and franchises to the same.*

Example 539

Minnesota.
    [Laws, etc. (Session laws : 1858-1891 : Special laws). 1864, Chapter 86]
    An Act to Amend an Act Entitled "An Act to Incorporate the Baldwin School in the City of Saint Paul, Approved February Twenty-Sixth, Eighteen Hundred and Fifty-Three" ... -- p. 354-355 ; 22 cm.

    In Minnesota. [Laws, etc. (Session laws : 1858-1891)]. General and special laws of the state of Minnesota. -- 6th (1864).
    At head of title: Chapter LXXXVI.
    "Approved March 3, 1864."--P. 355.

    I. Minnesota. Laws, etc. (Session laws, : 1858-1891 : Special laws). 1853, Chapter 13. II. Title.

Type: a Bib lvl: a Govt pub: s Lang: eng Source: d Illus:
Repr: Enc lvl: I Conf pub: 0 Ctry: mnu Dat tp: s M/F/B: 0
Indx: 0 Mod rec: Festschr: 0 Cont:
Desc: a Int lvl: Dates: 1864,

```
010
040       XXX $c XXX
043       n-us-mn
052       4144 $b S4
090
049       XXXX
100 10 Minnesota.
240 10 Laws, etc. (Session laws : 1858-1891 :
Special laws). $n 1864, Chapter 86
245 13 An Act to Amend an Act Entitled "An Act to
Incorporate the Baldwin School in the City of Saint
Paul, Approved February Twenty-Sixth, Eighteen Hundred
and Fifty-Three" ...
300       p. 354-355 ; $c 22 cm.
500       At head of title: Chapter LXXXVI.
500       "Approved March 3, 1864."--P. 355.
710 11 Minnesota. $t Laws, etc. (Session laws :
1858-1891 : Special laws). $n 1853, Chapter 13.
773 0     $7 c1as $a Minnesota. $s Laws, etc. (Ses-
sion laws : 1859-1891). $t General and special laws of
the state of Minnesota. $g 6th (1864). $w (OCoLC)nnnnnnn
```

COLLECTIONS

OF THE

MINNESOTA

HISTORICAL   SOCIETY

—

VOLUME VIII.

—

ST. PAUL, MINN.
PUBLISHED BY THE SOCIETY.
1898.

PREHISTORIC MAN AT THE HEADWATERS OF THE MISSISSIPPI RIVER.*

BY HON. J. V. BROWER.

I.

PRELIMINARY REFERENCES.

At pages 123 and 124, Vol. VII., Minnesota Historical Collections, prepared and submitted by me in 1889-93, the following appears:

Concerning the presumable fact, that, antedating the first known visit of white men at Lac La Biche, French voyageurs may have reached the basin, no reliable statement in writing is known to exist describing such visit. In the absence of any known record as to the movements of the French fur traders and voyageurs who first established themselves in lines of trade and traffic with the Indians across the northern portion of the territory which now constitutes the State of Minnesota, no definite record can be found concerning a mere probability that they may have reached Elk lake. To the writers of the future must be left the task of discovering the record of the manner in which "Lac La Biche" first became known to the French and of any visits they may have made to the locality, if any such record exists, which now seems doubtful. Certain it is that Mr. Morrison's letter is the only record of the first visit to the source of the Mississippi of which we have any knowledge.

Upon page 16 of my report to his Excellency the Governor of Minnesota, for the two years ending Dec. 1, 1894, the following tabulated historical record of the descent of title by possession appears:

*Abridged extract from the Journal of the Manchester (Eng.) Geographical Society, vol. XI., pp. 1-80, 1895; to which is appended an addendum, relating to the early visits of Mr. Julius Chambers and Rev. J. A. Gilfillan to Itasca lake, prepared for the Minnesota Historical Society by Mr. Brower.

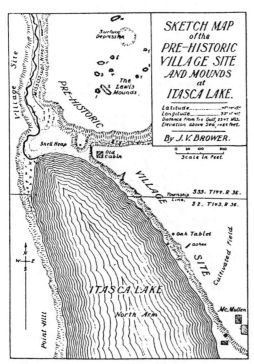

MAP OF THE LEWIS MOUNDS AND PREHISTORIC VILLAGE SITE AT
THE NORTH END OF ITASCA LAKE

Example 540

Brower, J. V. (Jacob Vradenberg), 1844-1905.
    Sketch map of the pre-historic village site
and mounds at Itasca Lake [map] / by J.V. Brower.
-- Scale [ca. 1:3,250]. -- 1 map, on 1 leaf facing
p. 248 ; 15 x 10 cm.

    <u>In</u> Brower, J. V. (Jacob Vradenberg), 1844-
1905. Prehistoric man at the headwaters of the
Mississippi River. -- (Collections of the Minnesota Historical Society (1898) ; v. 8).
    Caption title: Map of the Lewis mounds and
prehistoric village site at the north end of
Itasca Lake.

    I. Title. II. Title: Map of the Lewis mounds
and prehistoric village site at the north end of
Itasca Lake.

```
Type: e Bib lvl: a Lang: eng Source: d Form:      Relief: b
RecG: a Enc lvl: I Ctry: mnu Dat tp: s Govt pub: s Indx: 0
Desc: a Mod rec:    Base:     Dates: 1898,
```

```
   010
   040      XXX $c XXX
   007      a $b j $d c $e a $f n
   034 1    a $b 3,250
   043      n-us-mn
   052      4142 $b I82
   090
   049      XXXX
   110 10 Brower, J. V. $q (Jacob Vradenberg), $d
1844-1905.
   245 10 Sketch map of the pre-historic village site
and mounds at Itasca Lake [map] / $c by J.V. Brower.
   255      Scale [ca. 1:3,250].
   260 |    $c
   300      1 map, on 1 leaf facing p. 248 ; 15 x 10 cm.
   500      Caption title: Map of the Lewis mounds and
prehistoric village site at the north end of Itasca
Lake.
   773 0    $7 p1aa $a Brower, J. V. (Jacob Vraden-
berg), 1844-1905. $t Prehistoric man at the headwaters
of the Mississippi River. -- $k Collections of the Min-
nesota Historical Society (1898) ; v. 8 $w
(OCoLC)nnnnnnn
```

248   MINNESOTA HISTORICAL SOCIETY COLLECTIONS.

5. Length forty-three feet, width sixteen feet at the west end, twenty-four feet at the east end, height two feet, about the shape of an egg cut in two lengthwise, and the half shell turned down.

6. Diameter twenty-six feet, height three feet.

7. Diameter twenty-two feet, height three feet.

8. An elliptical mound, length twenty-eight feet, height two and one-half feet.

9. Diameter sixteen feet, height two and one-half feet.

10. An embankment, forty-four feet in length, eighteen feet in width and two and one-half feet in height.

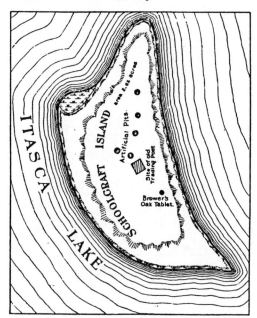

FIG. 1. SKETCH MAP OF SCHOOLCRAFT ISLAND, ITASCA LAKE.

Example 541

Brower, J. V. (Jacob Vradenberg), 1844-1905.
    Sketch map of Schoolcraft Island, Itasca Lake
[map]. -- Scale indeterminable. -- 1 map, on p.
248 ; 13 x 11 cm.

    In Brower, J. V. (Jacob Vradenberg), 1844-
1905. Prehistoric man at the headwaters of the
Mississippi River. -- (Collections of the Minnesota Historical Society (1898) ; v. 8).
    Title from caption under map. At head of
title: Fig. 1.
    Drawn by J.V. Brower.

    I. Title.

Type: e Bib lvl: a Lang: eng Source: d Form: Relief: b
RecG: a Enc lvl: I Ctry: mnu Dat tp: s Govt pub: s Indx: 0
Desc: a Mod rec: Base: Dates: 1898,

    010
    040   XXX $c XXX
    007   a $b j $d c $e a $f n
    043   n-us-mn
    052   4142 $b 182
    090
    049   XXXX
    100 10 Brower, J. V. $q (Jacob Vradenberg), $d
1844-1905.
    245 10 Sketch map of Schoolcraft Island, Itasca
Lake $h map
    255   Scale indeterminable.
    260 | $c
    300   1 map, on p. 248 ; $c 13 x 11 cm.
    500   Title from caption under map. At head of
title: Fig. 1.
    500   Drawn by J.V. Brower.
    773 0 $7 p1aa $a Brower, J. V. (Jacob Vraden-
berg), 1844-1905. $t Prehistoric man at the headwaters
of the Mississippi River. $k Collections of the Minne-
sota Historical Society (1898) ; v. 8 $w (OCoLC)nnnnnnn

205

Milwaukee Dec 2nd 1864

Edward Bliss Esq
100 Broadway New York

Dear Sir: In
mailing my explanatory letter to you
of 10th inst. I omitted to enclose
the little sketch and extract from
letters of Wessington from [illegible]
Claxton, [illegible] [illegible] [illegible]
forward them [illegible]

Very respectfully yours,
[illegible]

Example 542

Cogswell, Jno. B. D. (John Bear Doane), 1829-1889.
     [Letter], 1864 Dec. 12, Milwaukee, [Wis., to]
Edward Bliss, New York [manuscript] / Jno. B.D.
Cogswell. -- p. 205 ; 28 cm.

     In Cogswell, Jno. B. D. (John Bear Doane),
1829-1889. [Letterpress book, 1861-1865].
     Holograph signed (letterpress copy).
     Encloses materials he neglected to send with
his letter of 1864 Dec. 10.

```
Type: b Bib lvl: a Lang: eng Source: d
Repr:   Enc lvl: I Ctry: wiu Dat tp: s
Desc: a Mod rec:      Dates: 1864,

    010
    040    XXX $c XXX
    090
    049    XXXX
    100 1  Cogswell, Jno. B. D. $q (John Bear Doane),
$d 1829-1889.
    245 00 [Letter], 1864 Dec. 12, Milwaukee, [Wis.,
to] Edward Bliss, New York $h manuscript / $d Jno.
B.D. Cogswell.
    260    $c
    300    p. 205 ; 28 cm.
    500    Holograph signed (letterpress copy).
    520    Encloses materials he neglected to send
with his letter of 1864 Dec. 10.
    773 0  $7 p1bm $a Cogswell, Jno. B. D. (John
Bear Doane), 1829-1889. [Letterpress book, 1861-1865].
$w (OCoLC)nnnnnnn
```

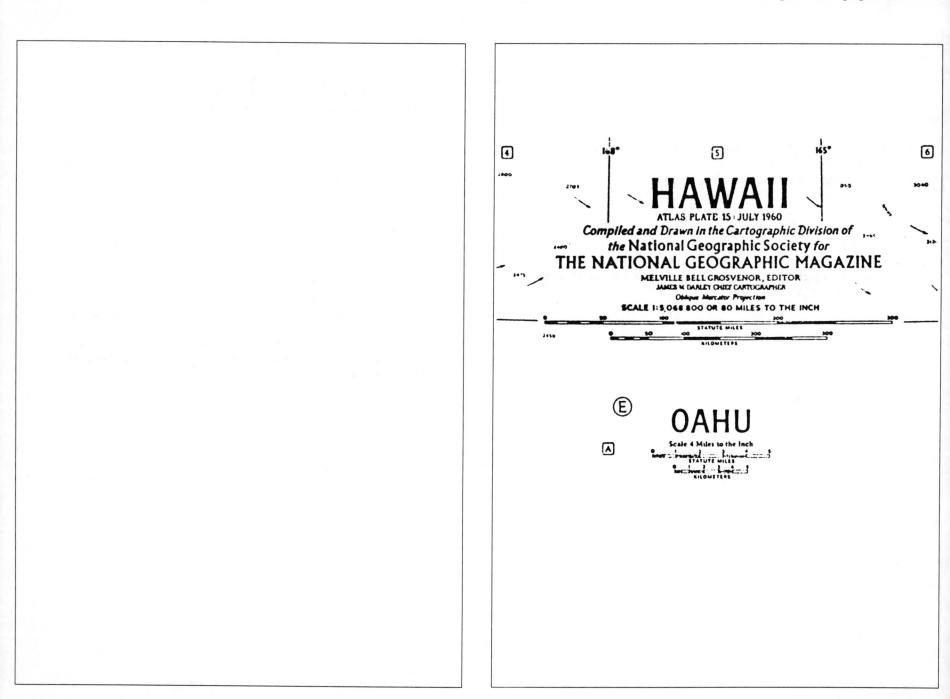

Example 543

National Geographic Society (U.S.). Cartographic
    Division.
    Oahu [map] / compiled and drawn in the Carto-
graphic Division of the National Geographic Society ... -- Scale [1:253,440]. 4 miles to the inch
; oblique Mercator proj. (W 158°30'/W 157° 30'--N
22° 45'/N 22° 10'). -- 1 map : col. ; 24 x 30 cm.,
on sheet 96 x 64 cm.
    Inset E on: National Geographic Society
(U.S.). Cartographic Division. Hawaii. -- [Wash-
ington, D.C. : The Society], 1960. -- (Atlas plate
; 15).

    I. Title.

Type: e Bib lvl: a Lang: eng Source: d Form: Relief: b
RecG: a Enc lvl: I Ctry: dcu Dat tp: s Govt pub: I Indx: 0
Desc: a Mod rec: Base: bd Dates: 1960,

    010
    040   XXX $c XXX
    007   a $b j $d c $e a $f n
    034 1   a $b 253,440 $d W1583000 $e W1573000 $f
N0224500 $g N0221000
    043   n-us-hi
    052   9702 $b 02
    090
    049   XXXX
    110 2   National Geographic Society (u.S.). $b
Cartographic Division.
    245 10 Oahu $h map / $c compiled and drawn in the
Cartographic Division of the National Geographic Society
...
    255   Scale [1:253,440]. 4 miles to the inch ; $b
oblique Mercator proj. $c (W 158°30'/W 157° 30'--N 22°
45'/N 22° 10').
    260 0 $c
    300   1 map : col. ; $c 24 x 30 cm., on sheet 96 x
64 cm.
    580   Inset E on: National Geographic Society
(U.S.). Cartographic Division. Hawaii. -- [Washington,
D.C. : The Society], 1960. -- (Atlas plate ; 15).
    773 1 $7 c2em $a National Geographic Society
(U.S.). Cartographic Division. $t Hawaii. $d [Washing-
ton, D.C. : The Society], 1960. $k Atlas plate ; 15 $w
(0CoLC)nnnnnnn

SVENSKA TURISFÖRENINGENS RESEHANDBÖCKER. XIII.

SKÅNE

UTGIFVEN AF

SVENSKA TURISTFÖRENINGEN

ANDRA UPPLAGAN

MED 52 ILLUSTRATIONER, 7 ÖFVERSIKTSKARTOR
OGH 8 STADSPLANER

STOCKHOLM
WAHLSTRÖM & WIDSTRAND
(1 DISTRIBUTION)

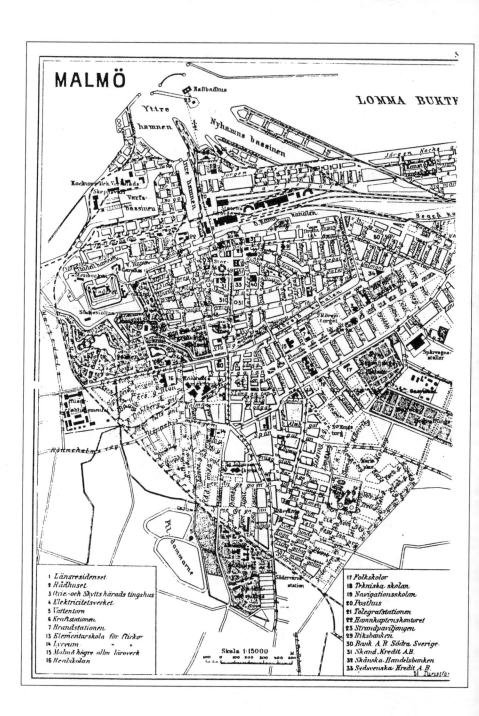

Example 544

Svenska turistföreningen.
    Malmö [map] / Svenska turistföreningen. --
Scale 1:15,000. -- 1 map, on 1 leaf facing p. 26 :
col. ; 30 x 25 cm. folded to 16 x 9 cm.

    In Skåne. -- 2:da uppl. -- Stockholm :
Wahlstrom & Wikstrand, [1912]. -- (Svenska
turistföreningens resehandböcker ; 13).
    Date on map: 1911.
    Index on verso.

    I. Title.

```
Type: e Bib lvl: a Lang: swe Source: d Form:     Relief:
RecG: a Enc lvl: I Ctry: sw  Dat tp: s Govt pub: f Indx: 1
Desc: a Mod rec:   Base:     Dates: 1912,

    010
    040     XXX $c XXX
    007     a $b j $d c $e a $f n
    034 1   a $b 15,000
    043     e-sw---
    052     6954 $b M3
    090
    049     XXXX
    110 2   Svenska turistf¨oreningen.
    245 10  Malm¨o $h map / $c Svenska
turistf¨oreningen.
    255     Scale 1:15,000.
    260 |   $c
    300     1 map, on 1 leaf facing p. 26 : $b col. ; $c
30 x 25 cm. folded to 16 x 9 cm.
    500     Date on map: 1911.
    500     Index on verso.
    773 0   $7 nnam $t Sk°ane. $  2:da uppl. $d Stock-
holm : Wahlstrom & Widstrand, [1912]. $  (Svenska
turistf¨oreningens resehandb¨ocker ; 13). $w
(0CoLC)nnnnnnn
```

*Scandinavian
Old Time
Music Book I*

Waltzes   Schottisches   Polkas

"Å Jänta Å Ja"
"Hälsa dem därhemma"

As Recorded By

**THE MINNESOTA
SCANDINAVIAN ENSEMBLE**

Collected and Edited by LeRoy Larson

HÄLSA DEM DÄRHEMMA
"Greet Them At Home"

Music by Elith Worsing
Text by Ch. Bengtsson
Translation by L. L.

Ed. by LeRoy Larson

Example 545

Worsing, Elith.
    Hälsa dem därhemma [music] / music by Elith
Worsing ; text by Ch. Bengtsson ; translation by
L.L. ; ed[ited] by LeRoy Larson. -- v. 1, p. 4 ;
28 cm.

    In Larson, LeRoy. Scandinavian old time
music book ... -- [Minneapolis, Minn. : Banjar
Publications, 1979].

    I. Bengtsson, Ch. Hälsa dem därhemma. 1979.
II. Larson, LeRoy.   III. Title.

Type: c Bib lvl: a Lang: swe Source: d Accomp mat:
Repr: Enc lvl: I Ctry: mnu Dat tp: s MEBE: 1
         Mod rec: Comp: fm Format: Prts:
Desc: a Int lvl: LTxt: n   Dates: 1979,

    010
    040   XXX $c XXX
    041 0   sweeng
    090
    049   XXXX
    100 10   Worsing, Elith.
    245 10   Hälsa dem därhemma $h music / $c music by
Elith Worsing ; text by Bengtsson ; translation by
L.L. ; ed[ited] by LeRoy Larson.
    260 | $c
    300   v. 1, p. 4 ; $c 28 cm.
    700 12   Bengtsson, Ch. $t Hälsa dem därhemma. $f
1979.
    770 10   Larson, LeRoy.
    773 0 $7 plcm $a Larson, LeRoy. $t Scandi-
navian old time music book ... $d [Minneapolis, Minn.
: Banjar Publications, 1979]. $w (OCoLC)nnnnnnn

MEMORIES

OF

SNOOSE

BOULEVARD

ANNE-CHARLOTTE

HARVEY

• SONGS OF THE SCANDINAVIAN - AMERICAN •

OLLE I SKRATTHULT PROJECT
presents:
"MEMORIES OF SNOOSE BOULEVARD"
SONGS OF THE SCANDINAVIAN-AMERICANS
sung by ANNE-CHARLOTTE HARVEY
(accompanied by E. Craig Ruble,
Stephen Gammell and Maury Bernstein)

STEREO
33 1/3 RPM
SP-223

SIDE 2
MMS7225 B
(19473)

1. CHIKAGO (2:05)
2. NIKOLINA (2:25)
3. HOLY YUMPIN' YIMINY (1:50)
4. FLICKAN PÅ BELLMANSRO (2:25)
5. JÄNTBLIG (1:30)
6. OLEANA (3:25)
7. TRYGGARE KAN INGEN VARA (1:20)
8. HÄLSA DEM DÄRHEMMA (3:55)

All selections Traditional -
Arr. Harvey

Example 546

Worsing, Elith.
    Hälsa dem därhemma [sound recording]. -- on side 2 of 1 sound disc (3 min., 55 sec.) : analog, 33 1/3 rpm, stereo. ; 12 in.

    In Harvey, Anne-Charlotte. Memories of Snoose Boulevard. -- Minneapolis, MN : Olle i Skratthult Project, [1972?].
    Music by Elith Worsing ; words by Ch. Bengtsson.

    I. Bengtsson, Ch. Hälsa dem därhemma. [Sound recording]. 1972. II. Harvey, Anne-Charlotte.

```
Type: c Bib lvl: a Lang: swe Source: d Accomp mat:
Repr:    Enc lvl: I Ctry: mnu Dat tp: s MEBE: 0
         Mod rec:    Comp: fm  Format: n Prts: n
Desc: a Int lvl:     LTxt: n    Dates: 1972,
```

```
     010
     040    XXX $c XXX
     007    s $b d $d b $e s $f m $g e
     090
     049    XXXX
     100 10 Worsing, Elith.
     245 10 H¨alsa dem d¨arhemma $h sound recording
     260 |    $c
     300    on side 2 of 1 sound disc (3 min., 55
sec.) : $b analog, 33 1/3 rpm, stereo. ; $c 12 in.
     500    Music by Elith Worsing ; words by Ch.
Bengtsson.
     511 0  Sung by Anne-Charlotte Harvey.
     700 12 Bengtsson, Ch. $t H¨alsa dem därhemma. $h
Sound recording $f 1972?
     770 10 Harvey, Anne-Charlotte. $4 prf
     773 0   $7 pljm Harvey, Anne-Charlotte. $t Memo-
ries of Snoose Boulevard. $d Minneapolis, MN : Olle i
Skratthult Project, [1972?]. $w (OCoLC)nnnnnnn
```

THE

CHURCH HYMNARY

REVISED EDITION

Authorized for Use in Public Worship

by

THE CHURCH OF SCOTLAND
THE UNITED FREE CHURCH OF SCOTLAND
THE PRESBYTERIAN CHURCH IN IRELAND
THE PRESBYTERIAN CHURCH OF ENGLAND
THE PRESBYTERIAN CHURCH OF WALES
THE PRESBYTERIAN CHURCH OF AUSTRALIA
THE PRESBYTERIAN CHURCH OF NEW ZEALAND
THE PRESBYTERIAN CHURCH
OF SOUTH AFRICA

With Music

LONDON
OXFORD UNIVERSITY PRESS
Glasgow   Melbourne
12 R. Staff

Example 547

Parry, C. Hubert H. (Charles Hubert Hastings),
     1848-1918.
     Jerusalem [music] / Charles Hubert Hastings
Parry ; [words by] William Blake. p. 780-784 ; 19
cm.

     In The church hymnary. -- London : Oxford
University Press, [1927?].
     at head of title: 640. National hymns.

     I. Blake, William, 1757-1827. Jerusalem.
1927? II.Title.

Type: c Bib lvl: a Lang: eng Source: d Accomp mat:
Repr: Enc lvl: I Ctry: enk Dat tp: s MEBE: 1
         Mod rec: Comp: hy Format: Prts:
Desc: a Int lvl: LTxt: n   Dates: 1927.

    010
    040   XXX $c XXX
    090
    049   XXXX
    100 10 Parry, C. Hubert H. $q (Charles Hubert
Hastings), $d 1848-1918.
    245 10 Jerusalem $h music / $c Charles Hubert
Hastings Parry ; [words by] William Blake.
    260 | $c
    300   p. 780-784 ; $c 19 cm.
    500   At head of title: 640. National hymns.
    700 12 Blake, William, $d 1757-1827. $t Jerusa-
lem. $f 1927?
    773 0 $7 nncm $t The church hymnary, $d London
: Oxford University Press, [1927?]. $w (OCoLC)nnnnnnn

GOLDEN
HOUR

60
Minutes
Guaranteed
Playing
Time

Golden Hour Presents

The Choir Of
Winchester Cathedral

Conductor: Martin Neary

Record label

GH 629
SPEED 331/2 RPM
STEREO

GOLDEN
HOUR

SIDE 1 GH 629-A

GOLDEN HOUR
PRESENTS

THE CHOIR OF
WINCHESTER CATHEDRAL

1. JERUSALEM (Parry)
2. MAGNIFICAT AND NUNC DIMITIS ING
(Stanford)
3. CRIMOND
(Arr David Grant Re Arr Baird Ross)
4. MISERERE (Psalm 51) (Allegri)
5. BE NEAR MY LORD WHEN DYING
(St. Matthew Passion) (Bach)
6. CHORALE PRELUDE (Bach)

THE CHOIR OF
WINCHESTER CATHEDRAL
THE WAYNFLETE SINGERS
THE ACADEMY OF THE BBC
(Leader: COLIN SAUER)
Solo Organist: MARTIN NEARY
Sub-Organist: JAMES LANCELOT
Conductor: MARTIN NEARY

Produced by David Calme
Recording Engineer: RAY PRICKETT

PATERSON'S PUB (MCPS) (3)

℗ 1976

Example 548

Parry, C. Hubert H. (Charles Hubert Hastings),
    1848-1918.
    Jerusalem [sound recording] / Parry. -- on
side 1 of 1 sound disc : analog, 33 1/3 rpm,
stereo. ; 12 in.

In Winchester cathedral. Choir. Golden Hour
presents the Choir of Winchester Cathedral. --
[England] : Golden Hour, p1976.

    Words by William Blake.
    Choir of Winchester Cathedral, Martin Neary,
conductor ; Waynflete Singers ; Academy of the
BBC, Colin Sauer, leader.

    I. Blake, William, 1757-1827. Jerusalem.
[Sound recording]. 1976. II. Neary, Martin. III.
Sauer, Colin. IV. Waynflete Singers. V. Academy
of the BBC. VI. Title.

Type: j Bib lvl: a Lang: eng Source: d Accomp mat:
Repr: Enc lvl: I Ctry: enk Dat tp: s MEBE: 1
         Mod rec: Comp: hy Format: Prts:
Desc: a Int lvl: LTxt: n   Dates: 1927.

    010
    040   XXX $c XXX
    090
    049   XXXX
    100 10 Parry, C. Hubert H. $q (Charles Hubert
Hastings), $d 1848-1918.
    245 10 Jerusalem $h sound recording / $c Parry
    260 | $c
    300   on side 1 of 1 sound disc ; $b analog, 33
1/3 rpm. ; $c 12 in.
    300   Words by William Blake.
    511 0   Choir of Winchester Cathedral, Martin
Neary, conductor ; Waynflete Singers ; Academy of the
BBC, Colin Sauer, leader.
    700 12 Blake, William, $d 1757-1827. $t Jerusa-
lem. $h Sound recording $d 1976.
    700 10 Neary, Martin. $4 prf
    700 10 Sauer, Colin. $4 prf
    700 20 Waynflete Singers. $4 prf
    700 20 Academy of the BBC. $4 prf
    773 0 $7 c2jm $a Winchester Cathedral. Choir.
$t Golden Hour presents the Choir of Winchester Cathe-
dral $d [England] : Golden Hour, p1976. $w
(OCoLC)nnnnnnn

Record label

A Columbia Musical Treasury

FESTIVAL!
A TREASURY
OF CLASSICAL HITS
"CARNIVAL"

1. HAYDN: "SURPRISE" SYMPHONY NO. 94 - 2ND MOVEMENT
The Cleveland Orchestra
George Szell, Conductor
2. PROKOFIEV: ROMEO AND JULIET BALLET - "THE MONTAGUES AND THE
CAPULETS"
New York Philharmonic
Dimitri Mitropoulos, Conducting

P3 6209   SIDE 2
STEREO   P3 62092
                                                   ℗ 1974 CBS Inc.

3. IVES: FOURTH OF JULY FROM "SYMPHONY HOLIDAYS"
New York Philharmonic
Leonard Bernstein, Conducting
4. BERLIOZ: ROMAN CARNIVAL OVERTURE
New York Philharmonic
Leonard Bernstein, Conducting
5. GILBERT AND SULLIVAN: OVERTURE TO "THE PIRATES OF PENZANCE"
The Royal Philharmonic Orchestra
Kenneth Allwyn, Conducting

PRODUCER BETSY COHEN
ENGINEER FRANK DECKER

A Product of
COLUMBIA HOUSE

Example 549

Sullivan, Arthur, Sir, 1842-1900.
   [Pirates of Penzance. Overture]
   Overture to "The pirates of Penzance" [sound recording] / Gilbert and Sullivan.-- on record 3, side 2, of 6 sound discs : analog, 33 1/3 rpm, stereo. ; 12 in.

   In Festival! -- [New York, N.Y.] : Columbia, p1974.

   Royal Philharmonic Orchestra, Kenneth Alwyn, conductor.

   I. Gilbert, W. S. (William Schwencke), 1836-1911. Pirates of Penzance. Overture. [Sound recording]. 1974. II. Alwyn, Kenneth. III. Royal Philharmonic Orchestra. IV. Title.

Type: j Bib lvl: a Lang: eng Source: d Accomp mat:
Repr: Enc lvl: 1 Ctry: enk Dat tp: s MEBE: 1
         Mod rec: Comp: hy Format: n Prts: n
Desc: a Int lvl: LTxt: Dates: 1976,

  010
  040   XXX $c XXX
  007   s $b d $d b $e s $f m $g e
  090
  049   Sullivan, Arthur, $c Sir, $d 1842-1900.
  240 10 Pirates of Penzance. $p Overture
  245 10 Overture to "The pirates of Penzance" $h sound recording / $c Gilbert and Sullivan.
  260 | $c
  300   on record 3, side 2, of 6 sound discs : $b analog, 33 1/3 rpm, stereo. ; $c 12 in.
  511 0 Royal Philharmonic Orchestra, Kenneth Alwyn, conductor.
  700 12 Gilbert, W. S. $q (William Schwencke), $d 1836-1911. $t Pirates of Penzance. $p Overture. $h Sound recording $f 1974.
  700 10 Alwyn, Kenneth. $4 prf
  700 20 Royal Philharmonic Orchestra. $4 prf
  773 0 $7 nnjm $t Festival! $d [New York, N.Y.] : Columbia, p1974. $w (OCoLC)nnnnnnn

1 AUDIO-CASSETTE • STEREO   CAEDMON
DOLBY SYSTEM   CP 1713

T.S. Eliot

OLD POSSUM'S BOOK
of PRACTICAL CATS

performed by

Sir John Gielgud
and Irene Worth

Cassette label

CAEDMON	T. S. Eliot
	OLD POSSUM'S BOOK OF PRACTICAL CATS
CP 1713	performed by
	SIR JOHN GIELGUD and IRENE WORTH

16:37

1

CREDITS:

Cover:
Cover illustration: Reproduced by permission of Faber and Faber Ltd.
from the illustrated edition of Old Possum's Book of Practical Cats by T.S. Eliot
with drawings by Nicolas Bentley © 1940
Library of Congress #: 82-740116
© 1983 Caedmon
Directed by Ward Botsford
Recorded at Caedmon Studios, New York   •   Tape Editor: Daniel A. Wolfert
SOURCE: The Words of OLD POSSUM'S BOOK OF PRACTICAL CATS by
T.S. Eliot are recorded by kind permission of
Mrs Valerie Eliot and Faber and Faber Ltd., Copyright © 1939 by T.S. Eliot.
Copyright renewed © 1967 by Esme Valerie Eliot. (Published by Harcourt Brace
Jovanovich, Inc., New York, and Faber and Faber Ltd., London).

Dolby and the "Double D" symbol are trademarks of Dolby Laboratories
Patented: Raytheon Company, Lexington, Mass.

Made in U.S.A.   ISBN # 0-89845-068-3   Fait aux Etats-Unis

Example 551

Eliot, T. S. (Thomas Stearns), 1888-1965.
    The naming of cats [sound recording]. -- on
side 1 of 1 sound cassette : analog, mono.

    In Eliot, T. S. (Thomas Stearns), 1888-1965.
Old Possum's book of practical cats. -- New York,
N.Y. : Caedmon, 1983.

    Title from container.
    Read by Sir John Gielgud and Irene Worth.

    I. Gielgud, John, 1904- II. Worth, Irene,
1916- III. Title.

Type: i Bib lvl: a Lang: eng Source: d Accomp mat:
Repr: Enc lvl: 1 Ctry: nyu Dat tp: s MEBE: 0
         Mod rec: Comp: nn Format: n Prts: n
Desc: a Int lvl: LTxt: p   Dates: 1983,

    010
    040   XXX $c XXX
    007   s $b s $d l $e m $f n $g j $h l $i c
    100 10 Eliot, T. S. $q (Thomas Stearns), $d 1888-
1965.
    245 14 The naming of cats $h sound recording
    260 | $c
    300   on side 1 of 1 sound cassette : $b analog,
mono.
    500   Title from container.
    511 0 Read by Sir John Gielgud and Irene Worth.
    700 10 Gielgud, John, $d 1904- $4 prf
    700 10 Worth, Irene, $d 1916- $4 prf
    773 0 $7 plim $a Eliot, T. S. (Thomas Stearns),
1888-1965. $t Old Possum's book of practical cats. $d
New York, N.Y. : Caedmon, 1983. $x 0-89845-068-3. $w
(OCoLC)nnnnnnn

Album cover

THE CAPTAIN & TENNILLE

Love
Will
Keep us
Together

**LOVE WILL
KEEP US TOGETHER
The Captain & Tennille**

1. **God Only Knows** 2:32
(Brian Wilson - Tony Asher) Irving Music Inc. (BMI)
2. **Honey Come Love Me** 2:50
(Toni Tennille - Daryl Dragon) Moonlight and Magnolias Music (BMI)
3. **Feel Like A Man** 3:14
(Toni Tennille - Daryl Dragon) Moonlight and Magnolias Music (BMI)
4. **Broddy Bounce** 2:32
(Daryl Dragon) Moonlight and Magnolias Music (BMI)
5. **Gentle Stranger** 3:45
(Toni Tennille) Moonlight and Magnolias Music (BMI)
6. **I Write The Songs** 3:26
(Bruce Johnston) Southern Hemisphere Music (ASCAP)

SP-3405/Stereo (SP-3410)

Produced & Arranged by The Captain
Associate Producer Toni Tennille for
Moonlight And Magnolias Productions
℗ 1975 A & M Records, Inc.

2

Example 550

Johnston, Bruce.
    I write the songs [sound recording] / Bruce Johnston. -- on side 2 of 1 sound disc (3 min., 26 sec.) : analog, 33 1/3 rpm, stereo. ; 12 in.

    <u>In</u> Captain & Tennille (Musical duo). Love will keep us together. -- Beverly Hills, Calif. : A & M Records, p1975.

    Performed by The Captain & Tennille.

    I. Captain & Tennille (Musical duo). II. Title.

Type: j Bib lvl: a Lang: eng Source: d Accomp mat: shi
Repr: Enc lvl: 1 Ctry: cau Dat tp: s MEBE: 1
       Mod rec: Comp: pp Format: n Prts: n
Desc: a Int lvl: LTxt: Dates: 1975,

   010
   040   XXX $c XXX
   007   s $b d $d b $e s $f m $g e
   090
   049   XXXX
   100 10 Johnston, Bruce.
   245 10 I write the songs $h sound recording / $c Bruce Johnston.
   260 | $c
   300   on side 2 of 1 sound disc (3 min., 26 sec.) : $b analog, 33 1/3 rpm, stereo. ; 12 in.
   511 0 Performed by The Captain & Tennille.
   710 20 Captain & Tennille (Musical duo). $4 prf
   773 0 $7 c2jm $a Captain & Tennille (Musical duo). $t Love will keep us together. $d Beverly Hills, Calif. : A & M Records, p1975. $w (OCoLC)nnnnnnn

AMOS N' ANDY

Example 552

Meal ticket [videorecording] / directed by Charles
    Barton. -- on 1 videocassette (VHS) (28 min.)
    : sd., b&w ; 1/2 in.

    In Amos n' [sic] Andy. -- [United States? :
s.n., 198-?].

    Originally broadcast ca. 1952 on: The Amos 'n
Andy show.
    Credits: Script, Bob Ross, Dave Schwartz ;
photographer, Robert de Grasse ; editor, Daniel A.
Nathen.
    Cast: Spence Willliams, Jr. (Andy), Tim Moore
(Kingfish).
    Includes commercials for Blatz Brewing Com-
pany and Schenley Industries, Inc.

    I. Barton, Charles. II. Amos 'n Andy show
(Television program).

Type: g Bib lvl: m Govt pub: Lang: eng Source: d Leng: 028
       Enc lvl: I Type mat: v Ctry: us   Dat tp: r MEBE: 0
Tech: 1 Mod rec: Accomp mat:
Desc: a Int lvl: g Dates: 1980,1952

    010
    040   XXX $c XXX
    007   v $b f $d b $e b $f a $g h $h o
    090
    049   XXXX
    245 00 Meal ticket $h videorecording] / $c directed
by Charles Barton.
    260     $c
    300   on 1 videocassette (VHS) (28 min.) : $b sd.,
b&w ; $c 1/2 in.
    500   Originally broadcast ca. 1952 on: The Amos
'n Andy show.
    508   Script, Bob Ross, Dave Schwartz ; photogra-
pher, Robert de Grasse ; editor, Daniel A. Nathen.
    511 1 Spence Willliams, Jr. (Andy), Tim Moore
(Kingfish).
    500   Includes commercials for Blatz Brewing
Company and Schenley Industries, Inc.
    500 11 Barton, Charles.
    730 01 Amos 'n Andy show (Television program).
    773 0 $7 nngm $a Amos n' [sic] Andy. $d [United
States? : s.n., 198-?]. $w (OCoLC)nnnnnnn

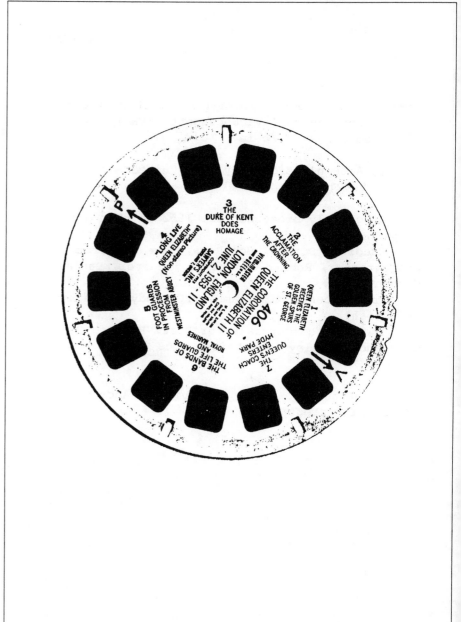

Example 553

```
The Duke of Kent does homage [slide]. -- no. 3 on 2
    of 2 stereograph reels (Viewmaster) (1 double
    fr.) : col.

    In The coronation of Queen Elizabeth II. --
Portland, Or. : Sawyer's Inc., 1953.
    Title from picture caption.
```

```
Type: g Bib lvl: a Govt pub:   Lang: eng Source: d Leng: ---
       Enc lvl: I Type mat: s Ctry: oru Dat tp: s MEBE: 0
Tech: n Mod rec:       Accomp mat:
Desc: a Int lvl: e Dates: 1953,

    010
    040    XXX $c XXX
    007    g $b z $d c $e n $h z
    043    e-uk---
    045 0    $b 19530602
    090
    049    XXXX
    245 04 The Duke of Kent does homage $h slide
    260      $c
    300      no. 3 on 2 of 2 stereograph reels (Viewmaster)
(1 double fr.) : $b 1.
    500    Title from picture caption.
    773 0    $7 nngs $t The coronation of Queen Elizabeth
II. $d Portland, Or. : Sawyer's Inc., 1953.
```

A HISTORY

OF THE

CITY OF SAINT PAUL,

AND OF THE

COUNTY OF RAMSEY,

MINNESOTA.

By J. Fletcher Williams,

SECRETARY OF THE MINNESOTA HISTORICAL SOCIETY; COR. SEC. OF THE OLD
SETTLERS ASSOCIATION OF MINNESOTA; SEC. OF THE RAMSEY
COUNTY PIONEER ASSOCIATION, &C., &C.

[COLLECTIONS OF THE MINNESOTA HISTORICAL SOCIETY: VOL. IV]

SAINT PAUL:

Published by the Society.
1876.

---

house, on Bench street. next Sunday. (to-morrow,) at 11 o'clock in the morning."

" The Galena *Advertiser* says there is a prospect of a heavy immigration to Minnesota the present season. We learn that whole colonies are on the move to Minnesota, from the Middle and Eastern States, and from Canada."

" While we are writing. a Sioux Indian has dropped into our office.

REV. EDWARD D. NEILL.

to look at the printing press. He expresses a great deal of curiosity and surprise."

" Mr. RICE, a gentleman equally distinguished for his liberality and enterprise, returned to Saint Paul on the steamboat ' Senator.' last Tuesday. Mr. RICE received a most cordial welcome. He is very much identified with the growth and prosperity of Saint Paul."

RAPID GROWTH OF THE TOWN.

Immigration poured in very rapidly for a few months,

Example 554

Rev. Edward D. Neill [picture] / Photo Eng. Co.
N.Y. -- 1 picture, on p. 213 : engraving, b&w
; 9 x 9 cm.

In Williams, J. Fletcher (John Fletcher),
1834-1895. A history of the city of Saint Paul and
of the county of Ramsey, Minnesota. -- Saint Paul
: Published by the Society, 1876. -- (Collections
of the Minnesota Historical Society (1872) ; vol.
4)
Title from picture caption.

Type: k Bib lvl: a Govt pub: Lang: eng Source: d Leng: ---
        Enc lvl: I Type mat: i Ctry: mnu Dat tp: s MEBE: 0
Tech: n Mod rec: Accomp mat:
Desc: a Int lvl: e Dates: 1876,

```
010
040      XXX $c XXX
007      k $b i $d b $e o
043      n-us-mn
245 00 Rev. Edward D. Neill $h picture / $c Photo Eng.
Co. N.Y.
260      $c
300      1 picture, on p. 213 : $b engraving, b&w ; $c 9
x 9 cm.
500      Title from picture caption.
773 0    $7 p1am $a Williams, J. Fletcher (John
Fletcher), 1834-1895. $a A history of the city of Saint Paul
and of the county of Ramsey, Minnesota. $d Saint Paul :
Published by the Society, 1876. $k Collections of the Minne-
sota Historical Society (1872) ; vol. 4 $w (0CoLC)nnnnnnn
```

Macalester College

THE WINSLOW HOUSE in Minneapolis where the Baldwin School opened in 1874 as the preparatory department of Macalester College.

Example 555

The Winslow House in Minneapolis where the Baldwin
    School opened in 1874 as the preparatory de-
    partment of Macalester College [picture]. --
    1 photo., on p. [11] following p. 142 : b&w ;
    7 x 10 cm.

    In Jarchow, Merrill E. (Merrill Earl), 1910-
. Private liberal arts colleges in Minnesota. --
St. Paul : Minnesota Historical Society, 1973. --
(Publications of the Minnesota Historical Soci-
ety).
    Title from picture caption.
    The picture actually was taken sometime be-
tween 1881 and 1887, after the building had been
sold by the college to the Minnesota College
Hospital.

Type: K Bib lvl: a Govt pub: Lang: eng Source: d Leng: nnn
         Enc lvl: I Type mat: i Ctry: mnu Dat tp: s MEBE: 0
Tech: n Mod rec: Accomp mat:
Desc: a Int lvl: e Dates: 1973,

    010
    040   XXX $c XXX
    007   k $b i $d b $e o
    043   n-us-mn
    052   4144 $b M5
    090
    049   XXXX
    245 04 The Winslow House in Minneapolis where the
Baldwin School opened in 1874 as the preparatory department of Macalester College $h picture
    260 | $c
    300   1 photo., on p. [11] following p. 142 : $b
b&w ; $c 7 x 10 cm.
    500   Title from picture caption.
    500   The picture actually was taken sometime
between 1881 and 1887, after the building had been sold
by the college to the Minnesota College Hospital.
    773 0 $7 p1am $a Jarchow, Merrill E. (Merrill
Earl), 1910-   . $t Private liberal arts colleges in
Minnesota. -- $d St. Paul : Minnesota Historical Soci-
ety, 1973. $k Publications of the Minnesota Historical
Society $w (OCoLC)nnnnnnn

HAWAII'S STORY

BY

HAWAII'S QUEEN

LILIUOKALANI

ILLUSTRATED

BOSTON
LEE AND SHEPARD PUBLISHERS
1898

BODY OF KING KALAKAUA LYING IN STATE

Example 556

Body of King Kalakaua lying in state [picture]. --
    1 photo., on 1 leaf facing p. 216 : b&w ; 11
    x 18 cm.

    In Liliuokalani, Queen of Hawaii, 1838-1917.
-- Hawaii's story. -- Boston : Lee and Shepard,
1898.
    Title from caption under picture.

    Summary: Shows coffin of King Kalukaua, sur-
rounded with kahilis, in the Throne Room of Iolani
Palace. Queen Kapiolani and Queen Liliuokalani are
seated beside it.

Type: k Bib lvl: a Govt pub: Lang: eng Source: d Leng: ---
        Enc lvl: I Type mat: i Ctry: mau Dat tp: s MEBE: 0
Tech: n Mod rec: Accomp mat:
Desc: a Int lvl: e Dates: 1898,

    010
    040   XXX $c XXX
    007   k $b i $d b $e o
    043   n-us-hi
    045 0
    090
    049   XXXX
    245 00 Body of King Kalakaua lying in state $h
picture
    260      $c
    300   1 photo., on 1 leaf facing p. 216 : $b b&w ;
$c 11 x 18 cm.
    500   Title from caption under picture.
    520   Shows coffin of King Kalakaua, surrounded
with kahilis, in the Throne Room of Iolani Palace. Queen
Kapiolani and Queen Liliuokalani are seated beside it.
    730 0 $7 p0am $a Liliuokalani, Queen of Hawaii,
1838-1917. $t Hawaii's story. $d Boston : Lee and Shepard, 1898. $w (OCoLC)nnnnnnn

THE QUEEN
& HER ROYAL
RELATIONS

A Who's Who of The Royal Families of Europe

By Conrad Miller-Brown

RUPERT HART-DAVIS
36 Soho Square London W1

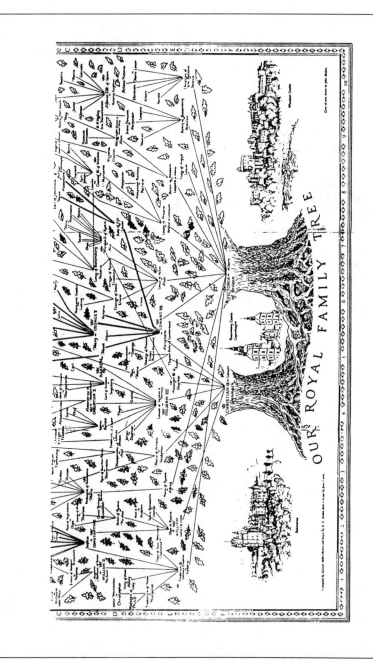

Example 557

Jordan, K. C.
    Our royal family tree [chart] / compiled by
Conrad Miller-Brown and drawn by K.C. Jordan from
a design by Joan Viner ; coats of arms drawn by
John Skelton. -- 1 chart, mounted inside front
cover : col. ; 47 x 52 cm. folded to 24 x 18 cm.

    In Miller-Brown, Conrad. The Queen and her
royal relations. -- London : Hart-Davis, [1952 or
3].
    "Family tree I."

    I. Miller-Brown, Conrad. II. Viner, Joan.
III. Skelton, John. IV. Title.

```
Type:  k Bib lvl: a Govt pub:   Lang: eng Source: d Leng: ---
       Enc lvl: I Type mat: n Ctry: enk Dat tp: s MEBE: 1
Tech:  n Mod rec:        Accomp mat:
Desc:  a Int lvl:   Dates: 1952,

    010
    040     XXX $c XXX
    007     k $b n $d c $e o
    090
    049     XXXX
    100 10  Jordan, K. C.
    245 10  Our royal family tree $h chart / $c compiled by
Conrad Miller-Brown and drawn by K.C. Jordan from a design
by Joan Viner ; coats of arms drawn by John Skelton.
    260     $c
    300     1 chart, mounted inside front cover : $b col. ;
$c 47 x 52 cm. folded to 24 x 18 cm.
    500     "Family tree I."
    700 20  Miller-Brown, Conrad.
    700 10  Viner, Joan.
    700 10  Skelton, John.
    733 0   $7 p2am $a Miller-Brown, Conrad. $t The Queen
and her royal relations. $d London : Hart-Davis, [1952 or
3]. $w (OCoLC)nnnnnnn
```

MINNESOTA HISTORICAL
SOCIETY
Pamphlet Collection.
UNIVERSITY OF MINNESOTA

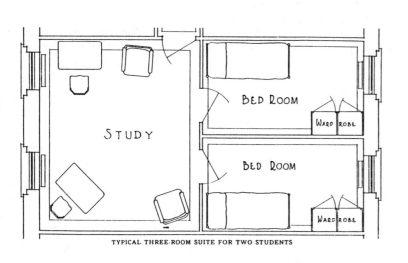

TYPICAL THREE-ROOM SUITE FOR TWO STUDENTS

Example 558

Typical three-room suite for two students [technical
     drawing]. -- 1 technical drawing, on p. [12] ;
     13 x 20 cm.

     In Pioneer Hall. -- [Minneapolis, Minn.] :
University of Minnesota, [193-].
     Title from caption under drawing

Type: k Bib lvl: a Govt pub: Lang: eng Source: d Leng: ---
        Enc lvl: I Type mat: l Ctry: mnu Dat tp: q MEBE: 0
Tech: n Mod rec: Accomp mat:
Desc: a Int lvl: e Dates: 1930,1939

     010
     040   XXX $c XXX
     007   k $b l $d b $e o
     043   n-us-mn
     052   4144 $b M5:2U5
     090
     049   XXXX
     245 00 Typical three-room suite for two students $h
technical drawing
     260     $c
     300   1 technical drawing, on p. [12] ; 13 x 20
cm.
     500   Title from caption under drawing.
     773 0 $7 nnam $t Pioneer Hall. $d [Minneapolis,
Minn.] University of Minnesota, [193-]. $w
(OCoLC)nnnnnnn

Screen 1

Example 559

```
                    APPLE BARREL II
                   THE MONEY BARREL
                       FROM CDS

                     MASTER MENU

                   1  CHECKBOOK

                   2  LOAN CALCULATOR

               3  FUTURE VALUE CALCULATOR

                4  DAYS BETWEEN DATES

                     5  CALENDAR
```

Dynamite [computer file]. -- no. 17 on 1 computer
    disk ; 5 1/4 in.

    In Apple Barrel II. -- Logan, Utah : Soft-
WareHouse, Inc., 1981.
    System requirements: Apple II.
    Title form title screen.
    Summary: Game for one player, in which player
and computer alternately remove up to three sticks
of dynamite at a time, the one taking the last
stick being the loser.

Screen 4

```
                    APPLE BARREL II
                   THE MONEY BARREL
                       FROM CDS

                     MASTER MENU

                     16  THINK

                    17  DYNAMITE

                  18  LUNA C T OR L

                    19  MOUNTAIN

                     20  ALIEN
```

WHAT WOOD IS THAT?

A Manual of Wood Identification

with
40 actual
wood samples
and
79 illustrations
in the text

Herbert L. Edlin

A STUDIO BOOK
THE VIKING PRESS
NEW YORK

9 Bird's-eye Maple *Acer saccharum*

F. Erable œil d'oiseau   G. Vogelaugenahorn
I. Acero occhiolinato   S. Arce ojo de pájaro
FAMILY: Maple (Aceraceae)   KEY: A4   SOURCE: Eastern Canada, Eastern USA

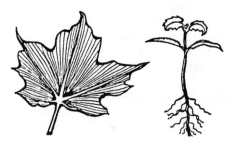

Fig. 31   Bird's-eye maple: leaf and seedling

104

9   BIRD'S-EYE MAPLE

Example 560

Bird's-eye maple [realia]. -- 1 sample, mounted
    on sheet inside front cover ; 22 x 76 x 1 mm.

    In Edlin, Herbert L. (Herbert Leeson), 1913-
1976. -- What wood is that? -- New York : Viking
Press, 1969. -- (A Studio book)

    Title from label on sample.
    At head of title: 9.
    Description of bird's-eye maple on p. 104-
105.

```
Type: r Bib lvl: a Govt pub:    Lang: eng Source: d Leng: ---
        Enc lvl: I Type mat: r Ctry: nyu Dat tp: s MEBE: 0
Tech: n Mod rec:          Accomp mat:
Desc: a Int lvl: f Dates: 1969,

    010
    040    XXX $c XXX
    090
    049    XXXX
    245 00 Bird's eye maple $h realia
    260    $c
    300    1 sample, mounted on sheet inside front cover
; $c 22 x 76 x 1 mm.
    500    At head of title: 9.
    500    Description of bird's eye maple on p. 104-105.
    773 0  $7 plam $a Edlin, Herbert L. (Herbert Lee-
son), 1913-1976. $t What wood is that? $d New York: Viking
Press, 1969. $k A Studio book $w (OCoLC) 23135.
```

MYCOTAXON

Vol. VII, No. 1, pp. 1-9   April-June 1978

MORPHOLOGICAL AND MATING SYSTEM STUDIES OF
A NEW TAXON OF HERICUM (APHYLLOPHORALES,
HERICIACEAE) FROM THE SOUTHERN APPALACHIANS

H. H. Bursdall, Jr., O. K. Miller, Jr.
and K. A. Nishijima

First and thrid authors, Center for Forest Mycology Research, U. S. Department of Agriculture, Forest service, Forest Products Laboratory, Madison, Wis. 53705; and second author,
Virginia Polytechnic Institute and State University, Blacksburg, Va. 24061, U.S.A.

SUMMARY

A new subspecies, Hericium erinaceum
ssp. erinaceo-abietis, is described and
illustrated. It is interfertile with
H.erinaceum   and H. abeitis.

MORPHOLOGICAL AND MATING SYSTEM STUDIES
OF A NEW TAXON OF HERICIUM
(APHYLLOPHORALES, HERICIACEAE)
FROM THE SOUTHERN APPALACHIANS

H. H. Bursdall, Jr.
O. K. Miller, Jr.
and
K. A. Nishijima

Reprinted from MYCOTAXON 7(1) : 1-9. 1978

Published April 1, 1978

Example 561

Burdsall, H. H. (Harold H.)
    Morphological and mating system studies of a
new taxon of Hericium (Aphyllophorales, Hericiaceas) from the southern Appalachians / H.H.
Burdsall, Jr., O.K. Miller, Jr., and K.A.
Nishijima. -- p. 1-9 : ill. ; 23 cm.

    In Mycotaxon. -- Vol. 7, no. 1 (Apr.-June
1978).

    Title from caption.
    "Literature cited": p. 9.
    Summary: A new subspecies, Hericium erinaceum
ssp. erinaceo-abietis, is described and illustrated. It is interfertile with H. erinaceum and
H. abeitis. P. [1]

    I. Miller, O. K. (Orson K.)   II. Nishijima,
K. A.   III. Title.

Type: a Bib lvl: a Govt pub: Lang: eng Source: d Illus: a
Repr: Enc lvl: I Conf pub: 0 Ctry: wiu Dat tp: s M/F/B: 10
Indx: 0 Mod rec: Festschr: 0 Cont: t
Desc: a Int lvl: Dates: 1978,
    010
    040   XXX XXX
    090
    049   XXXX
    100 10 Burdsall, H. H. $q (Harold H.) $u Center for
Forest Mycology Research, Forest Products Laboratory,
U.S. Forest Service
    245 10 Morphological and mating system studies of a
new taxon of Hericium (Aphyllophorales, Hericiaceas)
from the southern Appalachians / H.H. Burdsall, Jr.,
O.K. Miller, Jr., and K.A. Nishijima.
    260 | $c
    300   p. 1-9 : $b ill. ; $c 25 cm.
    302   9
    500   Title from caption.
    504   "Literature cited": p. 9. $b 4
    520   A new subspecies, Hericium erinaceum ssp.
erinaceo-abietis, is described and illustrated. It is
interfertile with H. erinaceum and H. abeitis. $z P. [1]
    700 10 Miller, O. K. $q (Orson K.) $u Virginia
Polytechnic Institute and State University.
    700 10 Nishijima, K. A. $u Center for Forest Mycol-
ogy Research, Forest Products Laboratory, U.S. Forest
Service
    773 0 $7 nnas $t Mycotaxon. $g Vol. 7, no. 1
(Apr.-June 1978). $w (OCoLC)nnnnnnn
    775 0 Burdsall, H. H. (Harold H.). $t Morphologi-
cal and mating system studies of a new taxon of Hericium
(Aphyllophorales, Hericiaceas) from the southern Appala-
chian $c ([Washington, D.C.] : U.S. G.P.O., 1978) $w
(OcoLC)nnnnnnn

IN PLACE OF the regular "The Editor's Page" feature in this issue, Minnesota History herewith presents in full the short speech given by Charles A. Lindbergh on a historic occasion — the dedication of the Lindbergh State Park Interpretive Center on September 30, 1973. Well over a thousand people turned out on a beautiful day to hear the famous aviator, author, scientist, and conservationist reminisce at the place where he grew up along the Mississippi River near Little Falls, Minnesota. He was introduced by Russell W. Fridley, director of the Minnesota Historical Society. — Ed.

Some Remarks at Dedication of Lindbergh State Park Interpretive Center

Charles A. Lindbergh

LADIES AND GENTLEMEN: I wonder if I can convey to you the pleasure I find in taking part in this ceremony — here in the state of Minnesota, where my grandparents immigrated over a hundred years ago. I am deeply appreciative of your coming to join in opening an interpretive center so closely related to my family, and especially to my father. I feel that I cannot sufficiently thank the Minnesota Historical Society for its part in establishing this center, and in maintaining so ably the historical integrity of the park and buildings.

In a sense, this is a dual ceremony. Opening the Lindbergh State Park Interpretive Center coincides with the publication of a biography about my father by Professor Bruce Larson. The title is *Lindbergh of Minnesota*. It is a book of accuracy and perception to which Professor Larson has devoted many years of research, and which incorporates data my family has been assembling for well over half a century. Personally, I want to honor the book along with the center to which it is so closely related. [The second chapter of the book, which will be reviewed in a forthcoming issue, was published in the Spring, 1973, issue of *Minnesota History*. — Ed.]

Obviously, this park means a great deal to me because of associations extending back more than seventy years. As a boy, I spent wonderful days here with my father and mother. During World War I, while I was still below military age, I ran as a farm what is now the nucleus of the park. But the park means even more to me because of its preservation for future generations of the wildness and natural beauty I lived in as a child. With each year that passes I feel more convinced of the essential need of preserving man's natural environment. I find extraordinary satisfaction in knowing that my family has contributed to this preservation.

I wish my father could have known that the land he chose, largely because of its beauty, would eventually become a park, thereby implementing his vision and early interest in the conservation of nature and natural resources. He would have been delighted to see deer

CHARLES A. LINDBERGH *delivers his remarks from the porch of his former home at Little Falls. At left is his sister, Eva Lindbergh Christie Spaeth. Photo by Lila M. Johnson.*

THE EDITOR'S PAGE

Example 562

Lindbergh, Charles A. (Charles Augustus).
     Some remarks at dedication of Lindbergh State
Park interpretive center / Charles A. Lindbergh.
-- p. 275-276 : ill. ; 28 cm.

     In Minnesota history. -- Vol. 43, no. 7 (fall
1973).

     "The editor's page."

     I. Title.

Other forms of main entry

Lindbergh, Charles A., 1902-1974.

Lindbergh, Charles A. (Charles Augustus), 1902-
1974.

D: 13.5A, A.23
ME: 22.16
O: 22.18, 22.16, 22.18

VOLUME 9   Washington County, Minnesota   **JULY 1982**   **Number 2**

WILDWOOD AMUSEMENT PARK: The Valleyfair of Yesteryear

By Mark P. Becker

"Hey, Grandma, can I borrow twenty dollars?"

"Twenty dollars? What do you need that

OCTOBER 1982   HISTORICAL WHISPERINGS   PAGE 3

shall often recall as we see others in city churches or cathedrals when we listen to deep organ tones accompanying vested choirs in chancels fragrant with Christmas greens.

TO BE CONTINUED

memory of our late friend Norman Peterson who spent many hours maintaining and improving the Hay Lake site. We plan to hold our October board meeting in the Hay Lake school - maybe to see what

those who prepared the Way for our 'traveling'.

LeRoy H. Klaus

✠✠✠✠✠✠

Wildwood Amusement Park

Part 2

By: Mark P. Becker

On Sundays there were always special programs given which included baseball in the water, water polo, diving exhibitions

Gasoline launches leave Wildwood Park dock at frequent intervals for last trips, stopping at St. Paul Auto Club at Lake

at the dance pavilion around the lake, serenading the residents. He recalls that often the residents would bring a bottle of liquor or something down to the shore and give it to the musicians as a thank you. Hanselman was also White Bear Lake's first water skier.

TO BE CONTINUED

The Nelson School Townhouses

January 1983   HISTORICAL WHISPERINGS   PAGE 3

Wildwood Amusement Park

Part 3

By: Mark P. Becker

Of all the structures so far discussed, there is none as well remembered as the brick dance pavilion. In 1908 the original Wildwood pavilion burned to the ground, so in 1909 a huge 90-foot x 180-foot brick pavilion was constructed for $29,741, with subsequent expenditures for awnings, lights, a lunch counter and a fountain. The new pavilion had a large hardwood dance

back to town on the streetcar. Muriel Baughn mentions in her taped interview with Mrs. Wright and Mrs. Smith, the authors of "Mahtomedi Memories", that the employees got along well with each other, too.

Since the Wildwood Park-Mahtomedi area was only twelve miles from St. Paul, yet very rural, it was a haven for mobsters

Board Seeks Broader Input

At a special meeting December 2, WCHS board members began an intensive study of membership rolls with a view to recruiting people to serve on an expanded list of committees. With Carolyn Fredell as moderator, discussion produced the following major projects headings: building, maintenance, financial, budget, fund raising, publicity, public relations, community outreach (traveling exhibits, speakers, slide tape presentations), living history (displays and demonstrations),

April 1983   HISTORICAL WHISPERINGS   PAGE 3

Wildwood Amusement Park

Part 4

By: Mark P. Becker

At the end of the year in order to maintain good attendance, the park had special weekends where they offered balloon ascent rides, diving ponies which would walk up a ramp and jump into a tank of water on command, a man that would dive into a burning tank, or other

between their beach and lawn.

The park still plays a significant role in the community. Some of the people who now live where the park once existed have gathered old pictures and mementoes from the park and many of the "old timers" around the community can still

President's Corner

By Charles Woodward

It has been my privilege and honor to serve as your president for the past two years, for which I thank you. It was not my intention to serve a third term. However, at our organization meeting, when officers are named for the ensuing year, things just didn't develop as expected. Our vice

---

Example 563

Becker, Mark P.
    Wildwood Amusement Park : the Valleyfair of yesteryear / by Mark P. Becker. -- p. 1-3, p. 3, p. 3, p. 3 : ill. ; 28 cm.

    In Historical whisperings. -- Vol. 9, no. 2 (July 1982); v. 9, no. 3 (Oct. 1982); v. 9, no. 4 (Jan. 1983); v. 10, no. 1 (Apr. 1983).
    Title from caption.

    I. Title.

Type: a Bib lvl: a Govt pub: Lang: eng Source: d Illus: a
Repr: Enc lvl: I Conf pub: 0 Ctry: mnu Dat tp: m M/F/B: 10
Indx: 0 Mod rec: Festschr: 0 Cont:
Desc: a Int lvl: Dates: 1982,1983

   010
   040   XXX $c XXX
   043   n-us-mn
   052   4144 $b M27
   090
   049   XXXX
   100 10 Becker, Mark P.
   245 10 Wildwood Amusement Park : $b the Valleyfair of yesteryear / $c by Mark P. Becker.
   260 | $c
   300   p. 1-3, p. 3, p. 3, p. 3 : $b ill. ; $c 28 cm.
   500   Title from caption.
   773 0 $7 nnas $t Historical whisperings. $g Vol. 9, no. 2 (July 1982); v. 9, no. 3 (Oct. 1982); v. 9, no. 4 (Jan. 1983); v. 10, no. 1 (Apr. 1983). $w (OCoLC)nnnnnnn

HISTORY

48/1   SPRING 1982

THE QUARTERLY OF THE MINNESOTA HISTORICAL SOCIETY

MINNESOTA PROFILES

Spring 1982   13

REFLECTED GLORY

The Story of Ellen Ireland

Patricia Condon Johnston

Example 564

Johnston, Patricia Condon.
    Reflected glory : the story of Ellen Ireland /
Patricia Condon Johnston. -- p. 13-23 : ill., ports.
; 28 cm.

    In Minnesota history. -- 48/1 (spring 1982).
    Title from caption.
    Includes bibliographical references.

    I. Title.

Type: a Bib lvl: a Govt pub: s Lang: eng Source: d Illus: ac
Repr: Enc lvl: I Conf pub: 0 Ctry: mnu Dat tp: m M/F/B: 10b
Indx: 0 Mod rec: Festschr: 0 Cont: b
Desc: a Int lvl: Dates: 1982,

    010
    040   XXX $c XXX
    018   0026-5497/B2/0013-13$01.75/0
    043   n-us-mn
    052   4144 $b S4
    090
    049   XXXX
    100 10 Johnston, Patricia Condon.
    245 10 Reflected glory : $b the story of Ellen
Ireland / $c Patricia Condon Johnston.
    260 | $c
    300   p. 13-23 : $b ill., ports. ; $c 28 cm.
    500   Title from caption.
    504   Includes bibliographical references.
    773 0 $7 nnas $t Minnesota history. $g 48/1
(spring 1982). $w (OCoLC)nnnnnnn

Spring 1984 / Volume 5, Issue 4

The Quotable Bede:
J. Adam Bede of Duluth

by Steve Keillor

Part I of a two-part article on "one of the most original and humorous characters to ever walk" Duluth streets

LAKE SUPERIOR
PORT CITIES

A quarterly journal of contemporary and historical events around Lake Superior.

Part II —
The Quotable Bede:
J. Adam Bede
of Duluth *by* Steve Keillor

Example 565

Keillor, Steven J. (Steven James).
    The quotable Bede : J. Adam Bede of Duluth / by
Steve Keillor. -- p. 13-16, 71, p. 5-9 : ill. ; 28
cm.

    In Lake Superior port cities. -- Vol. 5, issue
4 (spring 1984); v. 6, issue 1 (summer 1984).
    Title from caption.

    I. Title.

Type: a Bib lvl: a Govt pub: Lang: eng Source: d Illus: a
Repr: Enc lvl: I Conf pub: 0 Ctry: mnu Dat tp: s M/F/B: 10b
Indx: 0 Mod rec: Festschr: 0 Cont:
Desc: a Int lvl: Dates: 1984,

    010
    040   XXX $c XXX
    043   n-us-mn
    052   4144 $b D9
    090
    049   XXXX
    100 10 Keillor, Steven J. $q (Steven James).
    245 14 The quotable Bede : $b J. Adam Bede of
Duluth / $c by Steve Keillor.
    260 | $c
    300   p. 13-16, 71, p. 5-9 : $b ill. ; $c 28 cm.
    500   Title from caption.
    773 0 $7 nnas $t Lake Superior port cities. $v
Vol. 5, issue 4 (spring 1984); v. 6, issue 1 (summer
1984). $w (OCoLC)5972863

ARCHITECTURE
MINNESOTA

Official publication of the Minnesota Society American Institute of Architects

**Volume 3 Number 4
July-August 1977**

**STYLE-HISTORY OF ARCHITECTURE
IN MINNESOTA**

Charles W. Nelson

Example 566

```
Nelson, Charles W. (Charles Winfred), 1945-
    Style-history of architecture in Minnesota /
Charles W. Nelson. -- p. 24-34, 36-37, 40-41 : ill.
; 29 cm.

    In Architecture Minnesota. -- Vol. 3, no. 4
(July-Aug. 1977).
    Title from caption.


    I. Title.




Type: a Bib lvl: a Govt pub:    Lang: eng Source: d Illus: a
Repr:    Enc lvl: I Conf pub: 0 Ctry: mnu Dat tp: s M/F/B: 10
Indx: 0 Mod rec:    Festschr: 0 Cont:
Desc: a Int lvl:    Dates: 1977,

    010
    040    XXX $c XXX
    043    n-us-mn
    090
    049    XXXX
    110 10 Nelson, Charles W. $q (Charles Winfred), $d
1945-
    245 10 Style-history of architecture in Minnesota /
$c Charles W. Nelson.
    260 |    $c
    300    p. 24-34, 36-37, 40-41 : $b ill. ; $c 29 cm.
    500    Title from caption.
    773 0    $7 nnas $t Architecture Minnesota. $g Vol.
3, no. 4 (July-Aug. 1977). $w (OCoLC)2253666
```

NAMES

JOURNAL OF THE AMERICAN NAME SOCIETY

VOL. III, No. 2   June 1955

Literature on Personal Names in English, 1954

ELSDON O. SMITH

NAMES

JOURNAL OF THE AMERICAN NAME SOCIETY

VOL. V, No. 2   June 1957

Literature on Personal Names in English, 1956

ELSDON C. SMITH

Example 567

Smith, Elsdon C. (Elsdon Coles), 1902-
    Literature on personal names in English ... /
Elsdon O. [i.e. C.] Smith. -- 1954-1956.

    In Names. -- Vol. 3, no. 2 (June 1955) -- v.
5, no. 2 (June 1957).
    Annual.
    Title from caption.
    Continued by: Smith, Elsdon C. (Elsdon
Coles), 1902-   . Bibliography of personal names
...

    I. Title.

Type: a Bib lvl: b Govt pub: Lang: eng Source: d S/L ent: 0
Repr: Enc lvl: I Conf pub: 0 Ctry: mnu Ser tp: m Alphabt: a
Indx: 0 Mod rec: Festschr: 0 Cont:b   Frequn: a Publ st: d
Desc: a Cum ind: u Titl pag: u ISDS: Regulr: r Dates: 1954,1956

    010
    040   XXX $c XXX
    043   n-us-mn
    090
    049   XXXX
    110 10 Smith, Elsdon C. $q (Elsdon Coles), $d 1902-
    245 10 Literature on personal names in English ...
/ $c Elsdon O. [i.e. C.] Smith.
    260 | $c
    310   Annual
    362 0   1954-1956.
    500   Title from caption.
    773 0 $7 nnas $t Names. $g Vol. 3, no. 2 (June
1955)--v. 5, no. 2 (June 1957). $w (OCoLC)nnnnnnn
    785 00 Smith, Elsdon C. (Elsdon Coles), 1902-   .
$t Bibliography of personal names ... $w (OCoLC)nnnnnnn

THE MAYO ALUMNUS

April 1982/Volume 18 Number 2

A WOMAN PIONEER
IN A NEW PROFESSION,
MEDICAL EDITING

by Louis B. Wilson

Example 568

Wilson, Louis B. (Louis Blanchard), 1866-1943.
A woman pioneer in a new profession, medical editing / by Louis B. Wilson. -- p. 20-23 : port. ; 29 cm.

In The Mayo alumnus. -- Vol. 18, no. 2 (Apr. 1982).
Reprint. Originally published: In Proceedings of the staff meetings of the Mayo Clinic. Vol. 8, no. 51 (Dec. 20, 1933). Supplement.
Title from caption.
Portrait is of Dr. Wilson.

I. Title.

Type: a Bib lvl: a Govt pub: Lang: eng Source: d Illus: c
Repr: Enc lvl: I Conf pub: 0 Ctry: mnu Dat tp: r M/F/B: 10b
Indx: 0 Mod rec: Festschr: 0 Cont:
Desc: a Int lvl: Dates: 1982, 1933

```
  010
  040    XXX $c XXX
  043    n-us-mn
  052    4144 $b R6
  090
  049    XXXX
  110 10 Wilson, Louis B. $q (Louis Blanchard), $d
1866-1943.
  245 12 A woman pioneer in a new profession, medical
editing / $c by Louis B. Wilson.
  260 |    $c
  300    p. 20-23 : $b port. ; $c 29 cm.
  500    Reprint. Originally published: In Proceed-
ings of the staff meetings of the Mayo Clinic. Vol. 8,
no. 51 (Dec. 20, 1933). Supplement.
  500    Title from caption.
  500    Portrait is of Dr. Wilson.
  773 0    $7 nnas $t The Mayo alumnus. $g Vol. 18,
no. 2 (Apr. 1982). $w (OCoLC)1756894
```

Canadian Historical Review

VOLUME LXIV NUMBER 1 MARCH 1983

C.J. TAYLOR

*Some Early Problems of
the Historic Sites and
Monuments Board of
Canada*

Canadian Historical Review, LXIV, 1, 1983
0008-3755/83/0300-0003 $01-25/0 © University of Toronto Press

Example 569

Taylor, C. J.
    Some early problems of the Historic Sites and
Monuments Board of Canada / C.J. Taylor. -- p. [3]-
24 : ill. ; 25 cm.

    In The Canadian historical review. -- Vol. 64,
no. 1 (Mar. 1983).
    Title from caption.

    I. Title.


```
Type: a Bib lvl: a Govt pub:    Lang: eng Source: d Illus: a
Repr:    Enc lvl: I Conf pub: 0 Ctry: onc Dat tp: s M/F/B: 10
Indx: 0 Mod rec:    Festschr: 0 Cont:
Desc: a Int lvl:    Dates: 1983,

    010
    040      XXX $c XXX
    018      0008-3755/83/0300-0003$01.25/0
    043      n-cn---
    090
    049      XXXX
    110 10 Taylor, C. J.
    245 10 Some early problems of the Historic Sites
and Monuments Board of Canada / $c C.J. Taylor.
    260 |    $c
    300      p. [3]-24 : $b ill. ; $c 25 cm.
    500      Title from caption.
    773 0    $7 nnas $t The Canadian historical review.
$g Vol. 64, no. 1 (Mar. 1983). $w (OCoLC)nnnnnnn
```

LIBRARY RESOURCES & TECHNICAL SERVICES --

WINTER

1962

Problems in Serials

A GLANCE AT THE numerous entries in *Library Literature* under the two headings "Periodicals" and "Serials" will show that these can

---

Serials in a Public Library Katherine C. Dwyre

Head, Processing & Personnel, Free Public Library, Worcester, Mass.

Serials have been called hard names by many people; they have been called dirty, messy, frustrating, diabolical. But I do not remember ever ...

Volume 6, Number 1, Winter, 1962   • 85 •

Example 570

Problems in serials. -- p. 79-92 ; 24 cm.

   In Library resources & technical services. --
Vol. 6, no. 1 (winter 1962).
   Title from caption.
   "From the papers presented at the April 30,
1959, meeting of the Boston Regional Group of
Catalogers and Classifiers ... edited by Helen G.
Kurtz."--P. 79.

   I. Kurtz, Helen G.   II. Boston Regional Group
of Catalogers and Classifiers.

```
Type: a Bib lvl: a Govt pub:    Lang: eng Source: d Illus:
Repr:   Enc lvl: I Conf pub: 0 Ctry: ilu Dat tp: s M/F/B: 00
Indx: 0 Mod rec:   Festschr: 0 Cont:
Desc: a Int lvl:    Dates: 1962,

   010
   040     XXX $c XXX
   090
   049     XXXX
   245 00 Problems in serials.
   260  |   $c
   300     p. 79-92 ; $c 24 cm.
   500     Title from caption.
   500     "From the papers presented at the April 30,
1959, meeting of the Boston Regional Group of Catalogers
and Classifiers ... edited by Helen G. Kurtz."--P. 79.
   700 10 Kurtz, Helen G.
   710 20 Boston Regional Group of Catalogers and
Classifiers.
   773 0   $7 nnas $t Library resources & technical
services. $g Vol. 6, no. 1 (winter 1962). $w
(OCoLC)nnnnnnn
```

The Lord's Prayer

IN THE

Principal Languages, Dialects and Versions of the World

EDITED BY

TYPE AND VERNACULARS OF THE DIFFERENT NATIONS

COMPILED AND PUBLISHED BY

G.F. BERGHOLZ

CHICAGO, ILLINOIS

1884

The Lord's Prayer.

HAWAIIAN.
(SANDWICH ISLANDS, PACIFIC OCEAN.)

He Pule He Akua.

E ko makou Makua iloko o ka lani, e hoanoia kou inoa. E hiki mai kou aupuni; e malamaia kou makemake ma ka honua nei, e like me ia i malamaia ma ka lani la; E haawi mai ia makou i keia la i ai na makou no neia la; E kala mai hoi ia makou i ka makou lawehala ana, me makou e kala nei i ka poe i lawehala i ka makou. Mai hookuu oe ia makou i ka hoowalewaleia mai; e hoopakele no nae ia makou i ka ino; no ka mea, nou ke aupuni, a me ka mana, a me ka hoonaniia, a mau loa aku. Amene.

Example 571

Lord's prayer. Hawaiian.
    He pule ke akua. -- p. 88 ; 20 cm.

    In Lords' prayer. Polyglot. The Lord's prayer in
the principal languages, dialects, and versions of
the world. -- Chicago, Ill. : G.F. Bergholz, 1884.

    At head of title: Hawaiian (Sandwich Islands,
Pacific Ocean).

    I. Title.

Type: a Bib lvl: a Govt pub: Lang: eng Source: d Illus:
Repr: Enc lvl: I Conf pub: 0 Ctry: ilu Dat tp: s M/F/B: 00
Indx: 0 Mod rec: Festschr: 0 Cont:
Desc: a Int lvl: Dates: 1884,

    010
    040   XXX $c XXX
    090
    049   XXXX
    130 00 Lord's prayer. $l Hawaiian.
    245 10 He pule ke akua.
    260 | $c
    300   p. 88 ; $c 20 cm.
    500   At head of title: Hawaiian (Sandwich Islands,
Pacific Ocean).
    773 0 $7 unam $a Lords' prayer. Polyglot. $t The
Lord's prayer in the principal languages, dialects, and
versions of the world. $d Chicago, Ill. : G.F. Bergholz,
1884. $w (OCoLC)nnnnnnn

Chapter 15

LEGAL MATERIALS

Introduction

This chapter is based on *A Manual of AACR 2 Examples for Legal Materials* by Phyllis Marion, with examples added from several other manuals.

This chapter is intended to familiarize the reader with the cataloging of legal materials under AACR 2 through these of examples that illustrate selected rules. It does not intend to be exhaustive, but rather to cover those materials that might be handled by catalogers who, as part of their responsibility, catalog American legal manuals.

There have been major changes made in the "legal rules" between AACR and AACR 2. The rule changes reflect the decision to abandon form subheadings, the extension of the collective uniform title to primary legal materials, the elimination of the concept of corporate authorship in favor of the concept of corporate emanation, and the decision to make AACR 2 an international code. The changes require the cataloger to familiarize her/himself with the basic philosophy of the new rules as well as with the particular rules for choice of access point and form of entry that traditionally have occupied the law cataloger.

It would be good news if one could say that the new rules have made the cataloging of legal materials easier. They do not in all respects. There is a certain ease to the fact that most legal materials are not cataloged any differently than any other materials. But in some areas the waters have certainly been muddied by an attempt to provide rules that reflect the legal system of the jurisdiction being considered. Much work remains to be done on clarifying the language used in such areas as regulations and court rules.

All examples are cataloged according to AACR 2 as interpreted by the Library of Congress. These rule interpretations have been published in the *Cataloging Service Bulletin* published by the Library of Congress Processing Services. (The interpretations have been cited as CSB no. , p. .) It is noted when LC has decided to apply an option instead of the rule as given.

Most items are cataloged only as to choice of main access point, access points, and cross references. Descriptive cataloging past the title proper has been provided for selected examples.

Rule numbers used to formulate the cataloging are given with one exception, that of rules for formulating the names of personal authors.

When formulating headings, information found on the title page was used unless otherwise indicated. This means that the forms of entry found in these examples might differ from the forms established by the Library of Congress. The forms, however, do reflect the rules.

30th CONGRESS,
1st SESSION.
S. 152.

[PUB.]

IN THE SENATE OF THE UNITED STATES.

FEBRUARY 23, 1848.

Agreeably to notice, Mr. DOUGLAS asked and obtained leave to bring in the following bill: which was read twice, and referred to the Committee on Territories.

APRIL 20, 1848.

Reported without amendment, and made the special order of the day for Wednesday, April 25, 1848.

A BILL

To establish the territorial government of Minesota.

1   *Be it enacted by the Senate and House of Repre-sentatives*

2   *of the United States of America in Congress assembled*, That,

3   from and after the passage of this act, all that part of the territory

4   of the United States which lies within the following limits to

5   wit: beginning in the Mississippi river at a point where the line

6   of forty-three degrees and thirty minutes of north latitude

7   crosses the same, then running due west on said line, which is

8   the northern boundary of the State of Iowa, to the place where

9   said line intersects the line of ninety-five degrees and thirty

10   minutes of west longitude, according to Nicollet's map; thence

11   on a direct line north of west to the point where the one-

Example 572

United States. Congress (30th, 1st session : 1847-
1848). Senate.
   A bill to establish the territorial government of Minesota [sic] / 30th Congress, 1st session, in the Senate of the United States. --
[Washington? D.C. : s.n., 1848].
   17 p. ; 28 cm. -- (Pub. / 30th Congress, 1st
session ; S. 152)

   Caption title.
   At head of title: February 23, 1848. Agreeably to notice, Mr. Douglas asked and was given
leave to bring in the following bill, which was
read twice, and referred to the Committee on
Territories. April 20, 1848. Reported without
amendment, and made the special order of the day
for Wednesday, April 26, 1848.

   I. Douglas, Stephen Arnold, 1813-1861. II.
Title.

D: 1.0F
ME: 21.31B2; 24.18, type 5; 24.21A; 24.21D
AE: I. 21.30F

Type: a Bib lvl: a Govt pub: f Lang: eng Source: d Illus:
Repr: Enc lvl: I Conf pub: 0 Ctry: dcu Dat tp: S M/F/B: 10
Indx: 0 Mod rec: Festschr: 0 Cont:
Desc: a Int lvl: Dates: 1848,

   010
   040   XXX $c XXX
   043   n-us-mn
   045 0 $b d1848
   090
   049   XXX
   110 10 United States. $b Congress $n (30th, 1st
session : $d 1847-1848). $b Senate.
   245 12 A bill to establish the territorial government of Minesota [sic] / $c 30th Congress, 1st session,
in the Senate of the United States.
   260 0 [Washington? D.C. : $b s.n., $c 1848].
   300   17 p. ; $c 28 cm.
   490 0 Pub. / 30th Congress, 1st session ; $v S.
152
   500   At head of title: February 23, 1848. Agreeably to notice, Mr. Douglas asked and was given leave to
bring in the following bill, which was read twice, and
referred to the Committee on Territories. April 20,
1848. Reported without amendment, and made the special
order of the day for Wednesday, April 26, 1848.
   710 10 Douglas, Stephen Arnold, $d 1813-1861.

AN ACT

ORGANIZING THE TERRITORIAL GOVERNMENT

OF

MINNESOTA,

Approved March 3, 1849.

**MINNESOTA HISTORICAL
SOCIETY**

Example 573

```
Minnesota.
     [Organic Act of Minnesota]
     An act organizing the territorial government
of Minnesota : approved March 3, 1849. -- [Wash-
ington? D.C. : n, 1849?]
     8 p. ; 23 cm.


     Cover title.
     Caption title: An act to establish the terri-
torial government of Minnesota.


     I. United States. Organic Act of Minnesota.
II. Title.  III. Title: An act to establish the
territorial government of Minnesota.
```

ME: 21.31B1; 25.15A2(b); A.20
AE: I. 21.31B1, par. 2; 25.15A2(b)
      II. 21.30J, par. 2

SESSION LAWS

OF THE

STATE OF MINNESOTA

Enacted by the
SIXTY-NINTH LEGISLATURE

AT THE 1976 REGULAR SESSION,
COMMENCING JANUARY 27, 1976
AND
ADJOURNING APRIL 5, 1976

WITH TABLES AND INDEX

———————

Official publication of the State of Minnesota
State Capitol, St.. Paul
Sale and Distribution by the Documents Section
Department of Administration

I

Example 574

Minnesota.
    [Laws, etc. (Session laws : 1915-   )]
    Session laws of the state of Minnesota /
enacted by the … Legislature. -- St. Paul : Sale
and distribution by Documents Section, Dept. of
Administration
        v. ; 24 cm.

    Description based on: 69th (1976 regular
session).
    Annual. Biennial, 1915-1973.
    "Official publication of the state of Minne-
sota."

    I. Title.

D: 12.1B6; 12.3C4; 12.4G1; 12.7B1; 12.7B6; 12.7B22; 12.3B1
ME: 21.1B2(b); 21.31B1; 25.15A1
O: 25.15A1 (CSB 6; 25.5B)

The terms used to modify the uniform title are given in CSB 16, p. 49-50.

GENERAL AND SPECIAL LAWS

OF THE

STATE OF MINNESOTA,

PASSED DURING THE

Sixth Session of the State Legislature,

COMMENCING JANUARY FIFTH, ONE THOUSAND EIGHT
HUNDRED AND SIXTY-FOUR, AND TERMINATING MARCH
FOURTH, ONE THOUSAND EIGHT HUNDRED AND SIXTY-FOUR

TOGETHER WITH THE

JOINT RESOLUTIONS AND REPORT OF STATE TREASURER.

5,000 Copies Ordered Printed.

SAINT PAUL:
FREDERICK DRISCOLL, STATE PRINTER
PRESS PRINTING COMPANY
1864.

---

354   SPECIAL LAWS

CHAPTER LXXXVI.

An Act to amend an act entitled "an act to incorporate the Baldwin School in the City of Saint Paul, approved February twinty-sixth, eighteen hundred and fifty-three," and also to authorize the Board of Trustees of the College of St. Paul to transfer and convey its property and franchises to the same.

Example 575

Minnesota.
    [Laws, etc. (Session laws : 1858-1891 : Special laws). 1864, Chapter 86]
    An Act to Amend an Act Entitled "An Act to Incorporate the Baldwin School in the City of Saint Paul, Approved February Twenty-Sixth, Eighteen Hundred and Fifty-Three" ... -- p. 354-355 ; 22 cm.

    <u>In</u> Minnesota. [Laws, etc. (Session laws : 1858-1891)]. General and special laws of the state of Minnesota. -- 6th (1864).
    At head of title: Chapter LXXXVI.
    "Approved March 3, 1864."--P. 355.

    I. Minnesota. Laws, etc. (Session laws, : 1858-1891 : Special laws). 1853, Chapter 13.   II. Title.

Type: a Bib lvl: a Govt pub: s Lang: eng Source: d Illus:
Repr: Enc lvl: I Conf pub: 0 Ctry: mnu Dat tp: s M/F/B: 0
Indx: 0 Mod rec: Festschr: 0 Cont:
Desc: a Int lvl: Dates: 1864,

```
010
040      XXX $c XXX
043      n-us-mn
052      4144 $b S4
090
049      XXXX
100 10 Minnesota.
240 10 Laws, etc. (Session laws : 1858-1891 :
Special laws). $n 1864, Chapter 86
245 13 An Act to Amend an Act Entitled "An Act to
Incorporate the Baldwin School in the City of Saint
Paul, Approved February Twenty-Sixth, Eighteen Hundred
and Fifty-Three" ...
300      p. 354-355 ; $c 22 cm.
500      At head of title: Chapter LXXXVI.
500      "Approved March 3, 1864."--P. 355.
710 11 Minnesota. $t Laws, etc. (Session laws :
1858-1891 : Special laws). $n 1853, Chapter 13.
773 0    $7 c1as $a Minnesota. $s Laws, etc. (Ses-
sion laws : 1859-1891). $t General and special laws of
the state of Minnesota. $g 6th (1864). $w (OCoLC)nnnnnnn
```

MINNESOTA STATUTES

1978

Printed by the Revisor of Statutes. Embraces laws of a general and permanent nature in force at the close of the 1978 session of the Legislature.

♠

**COMPILED, EDITED, AND PUBLISHED BY
the office of Revisor of Statutes**

**OFFICIAL PUBLICATION
OF THE
STATE OF MINNESOTA**

Example 576

Minnesota.
    [Laws, etc. (Compiled statutes : 1978)]
    Minnesota statutes, 1978 : embraces laws of a general and permanent nature in force at the close of the 1978 session of the Legislature / compiled, edited, and published by the Office of Revisor of Statutes. -- [St. Paul?] : Office of Revisor of Statutes, [1978].
    4 v. (lix, 7606, 644 p.) ; 26 cm.

    "Official publication of the State of Minnesota."

    I. Minnesota. Office of Revisor of Statutes.
II. Title.

ME: 21.1B2(b); 21.31B1; 25.15A1
AE: I. 21.29B; 24.18, type 2; 24.20E
AE: II. 21.30J

NAVAJO TRIBAL CODE

Appendix
Title I through Title 4

On Spine: 1977 edition

Edited and Published by

PUBLISHING CORPORATION
ORFORD, NEW HAMPSHIRE 08777

Example 577

```
Navaho Tribe.
    [Laws, etc.]
    Navajo tribal code ...



    I. Equity Publishing Corporation.   II. Title.
```

Cross references

```
Navajo Tribe.


Navaho Tribe.
    Navajo tribal code.
```

ME: 21.1B2(b); 21.31B1; 25.15A1; 24.1
AE: I. 21.30D; 24.1
AE: II. 21.30J

American Indian nations, although frequently called tribes, are considered to be jurisdictions for the purposes of AACR 2 since these nations have treaty-making power and their laws are often codified in the western tradition. Thus rule 21.31B is applied for choice of entry. Tribal law, as found in the index to AACR 2, sends the cataloger to rule 21.31C. This rule refers to those tribal laws for which there is no possible corporate heading for the tribe.

THE

CHARTER AND ORDINANCES

OF THE

CITY OF ROCHESTER,

TO 1881, INCLUSIVE.

———◇———

COMPILED BY ORDER OF THE COMMON COUNCIL.

———◇———

ROCHESTER:
KELLEY BROS., OFFICIAL PRINTERS
1881.

Example 578

Level 1

Rochester (Minn.).
    [Charter]
    The charter and ordinances of the city of
Rochester to 1881 inclusive / compiled by order
of the Common Council. -- Kelley Bros., official
printers, 1881.
    74, 4, viii p.

    I. Rochester (Minn.). Ordinances. II. Roch-
ester (Minn.). Common Council. III. Title.

Example 579

Level 2

Rochester (Minn.).
    [Charter]
    The charter and ordinances of the city of
Rochester to 1881 inclusive / compiled by order of
the Common Council. -- Rochester, [Minn.] : Kelley
Bros., official printers, 1881.
    74, 4, viii p. ; 23 cm.

    I. Rochester (Minn.). Ordinances. II. Roch-
ester (Minn.). Common Council. III. Title.

D: 1.4G1 ; 2.5B2
ME: 21.31B1; 25.15A1; 24.3E
AE: 21.33; 25.15A2
        24.18, type 5

INTERNAL REVENUE CODE

1980

Complete Text with Index

**Including Legislation Enacted
By The
Ninety-Sixth Congress
First Session**

**ST. PAUL, MINN.
WEST PUBLISHING CO.**

Example 580

```
United States.
    [Internal Revenue Code of 1954]
    Internal Revenue Code, 1980 ...



    I. Title.
```

Cross reference

```
United States.
    [Laws, etc. (U.S. code). Title 26, Internal
Revenue Code.]
```

ME: 21.1B2(b); 21.31B1; 25.15A2
AE: I. 21.30J

The Internal Revenue Code is Title 26 of The U.S. Code (a general collection of laws).

LAWS OF
MARITIME WARFARE

AFFECTING

RIGHTS AND DUTIES
OF BELLIGERENTS

As Existing on August 1, 1914

———

Prepared by
HAROLD H. MARTIN and JOSPEH R. BAKER

MAY, 1918

WASHINGTON
GOVERNMENT PRINTING OFFICE
1918

Example 581

```
Laws of maritime warfare affecting rights and
        duties of belligerents ...



    I. Martin, Harold H.   II. Baker, Joseph R.



ME:  21.31B2; 21.7B
AE:  I & II. 21.7B
```

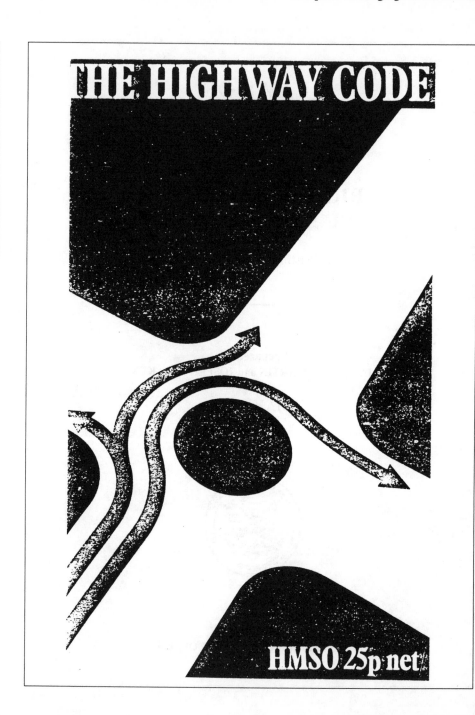

Example 582

Great Britain.
    [Highway code]
    The highway code / [prepared by the Depart-
ment of Transport and the Central Office of Infor-
mation]. -- London : H.M.S.O., 1978.
    69 p. : ill. (some color) ; 19 am.

    ISBN 0-11-550433-8 : £0.25.

    I. Great Britain. Dept. of Transport. II.
Great Britain. Central Office of Information.
III. Title.

D: 1.1F1; 1.8B1; 1.8D1
ME: 21.31 B1; 25.15A2; CSB 6
AE: 24.18, type 1
     24.18, type 2

Type: a Bib lvl: a Govt pub: f Lang: eng Source: d Illus: a
Repr: Enc lvl: I Conf pub: 0 Ctry: enk Dat tp: S M/F/B: 10
Indx: 0 Mod rec: Festschr: 0 Cont: 1
Desc: a Int lvl: Dates: 1978,

  010
  040   XXX $c XXX
  020   0115504338 : $c 0.25
  043   e-uk---
  090
  049   XXX
  110 10 Great Britain.
  240 10 Highway code
  245 14 The highway code / $c [prepared by the
Department of Transport and the Central Office of Infor-
mation].
  260 0   London : $b H.M.S.O., $c 1978.
  300   69 p. : $b ill. (some col.) ; $c 19 ca.
  710 10 Great Britain. $b Dept. of Transport.
  710 10 Great Britain. $b Central Office of Informa-
tion.

Calendar No. 39

94TH CONGRESS
1ST SESSION

H. R. 2166

[Report No. 94–36]

IN THE SENATE OF THE UNITED STATES

FEBRUARY 28 (legislative day, FEBRUARY 21), 1975
Read twice and referred to the Committee on Finance

MARCH 17 (legislative day, MARCH 12), 1975
Reported by Mr. LONG, with amendments

[Strike out all after the enacting clause and insert the part printed in italic]

MARCH 20 (legislative day, MARCH 12), 1975
Recommitted to the Committee on Finance with instructions

MARCH 20 (legislative day, MARCH 12), 1975
Reported by Mr. LONG, with amendments

[Strike out all after the enacting clause and insert the part printed in italic]

AN ACT

To amend the Internal Revenue Code of 1954 to provide for a refund of 1974 individual income taxes, to increase the low income allowance and the percentage standard deduction, to provide a credit for certain earned income, to increase the investment credit and the surtax exemption, and for other purposes.

1   *Be it enacted by the Senate and House of Representa-*
2   *tives of the United Sates of America in Congress assembled,*
3   SECTION 1. SHORT TITLE; TABLE OF CONTENTS.

Example 583

United States. Congress (94th : 1975-1976). Senate.
    An act to amend the Internal Revenue Code of 1954 to provide for a ... purposes. --

    I. Title: An act to amend the Internal Revenue Code of 1954 to provide for a refund of 1974 individual income taxes ...

ME: 21.1B2(c); 21.31B3; 24.18, type 5; 24.21A; 24.21D
AE: I. 21.30J

MINNESOTA BUSINESS CORPORATION ACT

Drafted and Proposed

by

The Minnesota State Bar Association

P.L. Solether, chairman
The State Bar Association Committee
1218 McKnight Building
Minneapolis, Minnesota

January 20, 1933

Example 584

```
Minnesota State Bar Association.
    Minnesota business corporation act ...


    I. Title.
```

ME: 21.1B2(c); 21.31B3; 24.1
AE: I. 21.30J

The Burgundian Code

LIBER CONSTITUTIONUM SIVE LEX GUNDOBADA

CONSTITUTIONES EXTRAVAGANTES

Translated by
KATHERINE FISCHER

Philadelphia
UNIVERSITY OF PENNSYLVANIA PRESS
London: Geoffrey Cumberlege
Oxford University Press
1949

Example 585

```
Lex Burgundionum. English.
     The Burgundian Code ...



     I. Fischer, Katherine.
```

ME: 21.31C; 25.15B; 25.4A; 25.5D
AE: I. 21.30K1

MICHIGAN COMPILED LAWS

Annotated

Under Arrangement of the Official Compiled Laws of Michigan

Volume 8

Sections
125.1 to 144.End

St. Paul, Minn.
WEST PUBLISHING CO.

Example 586

```
Michigan.
     [Laws, etc. (Compiled statutes : 1967)]
     Michigan compiled laws annotated ...



     I. West Publishing Co.   II. Title.
```

Cross reference

```
Michigan.
     Michigan compiled laws annotated.
```

ME: 21.31A; 21.13C; 21.1B2(b); 21.31B1; 25.15A1
AE: I. 21.30F; 24.1
AE: II. 21.30J

COMMENTARIES ON THE
U. P.
Consolidation Of Holdings Act

(U.P. Act No. V OF 1954)

WITH
Rules, Forms and Notifications and full Text of the Amending Acts
(As amended up-to-date)

By
CHANDRA BEHARI
Advocate
*(Author of Civil Procedure Code, Accomplices and Approvers and
Cr. Investigative and Prosecutions)*

5th Edition

HIND PUBLISHING HOUSE
Law Publishers & Booksellers
629, University Road,

Example 587

Behari, Chandra.
    Commentaries on the U.P. Consolidation of
Holdings Act (U.P. Act No. V of 1954) ...

    I. Uttar Pradesh (India). U.P. Consolidation
of Holdings Act.   II. Title.

                                                    Cross reference

Uttar Pradesh (India)
    Consolidation of Holdings Act.

ME: 21.31A; 21.13B
AE: I. 21.13B; 21.31B1; 25.15A2; 23.4B, option 1; 23.4H
AE: II. 21.30J

MINNESOTA STATE REGULATIONS

Rules and Regulations of

CAPITOL AREA ARCHITECTURAL AND PLANNING COMMISSION

**Filed with the Secretary of State
and Commissioner of Administration
November 18, 1975**

Distributed by

**DOCUMENTS SECTION, DEPARTMENT OF ADMINISTRATION
Room 140 Centennial Office Building, St. Paul, Minnesota 55155**

Example 588

```
Minnesota. Capitol Area Architectural and Planning
     Commission.
   Rules and regulations of Capitol Area Archi-
tectural and Planning Commission ...



   I. Title.
```

ME: 21.1B2(b); 21.32A1; 24.18, type 2
AE: I. 21.30J

The rules for entering regulations as found in AACR 2 present the cataloger of legal materials with many problems. Their application is unclear, and many situations are not covered. The examples in this chapter present situations that are fairly straight-forward. The Library of Congress (with the assistance of law catalogers from the United States and Canada) is now working on some explanatory materials that will aid in the use of rule 21.32.

Administrative regulations as used in 21.32A ought to be understood as regulations issued under the authority of a law to provide detailed provisions omitted from the law. If the regulations are the kind formulated by the body for carrying on its own business, the correct rule to apply would be 21.1B2(a).

MINNESOTA STATE REGULATIONS

Rules and Regulations of

THE DEPARTMENT OF PUBLIC SAFETY

DIVISION OF CIVIL DEFENCE

**Filed with the Secretary of State
and Commissioner of Administration
November 29, 1973**

Distributed by

**DOCUMENTS SECTION, DEPARTMENT OF ADMINISTRATION
Room 140 Centennial Office Building, St. Paul, Minnesota 55155**

Example 589

```
Minnesota. Dept. of Public Safety.
    Rules and regulations of the Department of
Public Safety, Division of Civil Defence [sic]. --
St. Paul, Minn. : Distributed by Documents Sec-
tion, Dept. of Administration, [1973?]-
    1 v. (loose-leaf) ; 22 cm. -- (Minnesota
state regulations)

    Cover title.



    I. Minnesota. Division of Civil Defense.  II.
Title.



D:    1.0F; 2.5B9; 2.7B3
ME:   21.32A1; 24.18, type 1
AE:   21.32A1; 24.18, type 1; 24.19
```

Example 590

Minnesota. Secretary of State.
    [Certificate of] incorporation of Minnesota
AACR 2 Trainers, 1980 May 8 [manuscript] / State
of Minnesota, Department of State.
    [1] leaf ; 28 cm.

    In part typescript.
    Signed: Joan Anderson Growe, secretary of
state.
    Seal of the state of Minnesota attached.
    "S 0588."

    I. Minnesota AACR 2 Trainers. II. Growe,
Joan Anderson, 1935-

D: 4.7B1, 4.7B6, 4.7B10
ME: 21.1B2(a), 21.1B4, 24.20E
AE: I. 21.30F
      II. 21.30F

MINNESOTA

LAWS and REGULATIONS

Relating to

GASOLINE TAX

and

PETROLEUM INSPECTION

1962 EDITION

September, 1962

Example 591

```
Minnesota.
    Minnesota laws and regulations relating to
gasoline tax and petroleum inspection …

    I. Title.



ME:  21.32A2
AE:  I. 21.30J
```

There are no special provisions in AACR 2 for collections of laws and regulations when the regulations are not derived from the law(s) or when it is impossible to tell if the regulations are derived from the law(s). While 21.32A2 seems to restrict entry to cases with such derivation, in actual LC practice the rule is not applied that restrictively. No attempt seems to be made to determine the relationship and 21.32A2 is applied in all cases.

REGULATION MADE UNDER

THE FAMILY BENEFITS ACTS

Regulation 287 of Revised
Regulations of Ontario, 1970

as amended by

Ontario Regulation   73/71
Ontario Regulation 153/71
Ontario Regulation 277/71
Ontario Regulation   25/72
Ontario Regulation   59/72
Ontario Regulation   60/72
Ontario Regulation 321/72
Ontario Regulation 381/72
Ontario Regulation 581/72
Ontario Regulation 187/73
Ontario Regulation 380/73
Ontario Regulation 559/73
Ontario Regulation 685/73
Ontario Regulation 715/73
Ontario Regulation 801/73
Ontario Regulation 821/73

Example 592

```
Ontario.
    [Regulation Made Under the Family Benefits
Act (1970)]
    Regulation made under the Family Benefits Act
...


    I. Ontario. Family Benefits Act.   II. Title.
```

Cross reference

```
Ontario.
    Regulation 287/70
```

ME: 21.1B2(b); 21.32B; 21.31B1; 25.15A2
AE: I. 21.32B; 21.31B1; 25.15A2
AE: II. 21.30J

code of federal regulations

7

Agriculture
PARTS 0 TO 52

Revised as of January 1, 1980

CONTAINING
A CODIFICATION OF DOCUMENTS
OF GENERAL APPLICABILITY
AND FUTURE EFFECT

AS OF JANUARY 1, 1980

With Ancillaries

Published by
the Office of the Federal Register
National Archives and Records Service
General Services Administration

as a Special Edition of
the Federal Register

Example 593

```
Code of federal regulations ...


     I. United States.



ME:  21.32C; 21.7B
AE:  21.30F
```

American
History Leaflets

COLONIAL AND CONSTITUTIONAL
EDITED BY
ALBERT BUSHNELL HART AND EDWARD CHANNING -
Of Harvard University.

NO. 8

EXACT TEXT OF THE CONSTITUTION OF THE
UNITED STATES AND THE
ACCOMPANYING DOCUMENTS, 1787-1913
FROM THE ORIGINAL MANUSCRIPTS

PARKER P. SIMMONS Co., Inc.

NEW YORK

Example 594

```
United States.
    [Constitution]
    Exact text of the Constitution of the United
States and the accompanying documents, 1787-1913
from the original manuscripts. -- New York : P.O.
Simmons, c1915.
    28 p. ; 19 cm. -- (American history leaflets
: colonial and constitutional ; no. 8)


    I. Title.  II. Series.



D:    1.6D1
ME:   21.33; 25.15A2
```

CONSTITUTION

OF THE

STATE OF MICHIGAN

———

COMPILED AND PUBLISHED
UNDER THE SUPERVISION OF
COLEMAN C. VAUGHAN
SECRETARY OF STATE

FORT WAYNE PRINTING COMPANY
CONTRACTORS FOR MICHIGAN STATE PRINTING AND BINDING
FORT WAYNE, INDIANA
1919

Example 595

```
Michigan.
     [Constitution (1909)]
     Constitution of the state of Michigan ...


     I. Vaughan, Coleman C.   II. Title.
```

Cross reference

```
Michigan.
     Constitution of the state of Michigan.
```

ME: 21.1B2(a); 21.33A; 25.3A; 25.5C
AE: I. 21.30D
AE: II. 21.30J

Although the constitution of a country certainly qualifies as a legal work, constitutions are not listed as qualifying for type "b" corporate emanation. They do, however qualify for type "a" emanation.

There is not a specific rule for establishing the uniform title for constitutions, charters, and fundamental laws. If the cataloger wishes to establish a uniform title to gather together different manifestations of the constitution, etc., the general rules for uniform titles as found in Chapter 25 should be applied. If there is no one title established as required by 25.3A, and one is applying 25.3B, take note of 25.3B(2). CSB 11, p. 45-46, indicates that such phrases as "of the state of Michigan" and "Konger-iget Norges" are to be treated as statements of responsibility.

It should be noted that the choice of uniform title for materials covered under 21.33 will be in the original language of the document and will not necessarily be the English word "Constitution".

A Consolidation of

THE BRITISH NORTH AMERICA ACTS

1867 to 1952

Prepared by
ELMER A. DRIEDGER, Q.C., B.A., LL.B.
Assistant Deputy Minister and Parliamentary Counsel
Department of Justice
Ottawa

Example 596

```
Canada.
     [British North America Act (Consolidation,
1957)]
     A consolidation of the British North America
Acts, 1867 to 1952 ...


     I. Great Britain. British North America Act.
II. Driedger, Elmer A.   III. Title.
```

Cross references

```
Canada.
     Constitution.

Canada.
     Consolidation of the British North America
Acts, 1867 to 1952
```

```
ME:   21.1B2(a); 21.33A; 25.3A; 25.5C
AE:   I. 21.33A; 21.31B1; 25.15A2
AE:   II. 21.30D
AE:   III. 21.30J
```

OFFICIAL JOURNAL

OF THE PROCEEDINGS OF THE

Constitutional Convention

of 1973

of the

STATE OF LOUISIANA

HELI IN ACCORDANCE WITH ACT 2 OF THE
972 R GULAR SESSION OF THE LEGISLATURE, . S AMENDED

Begun and He d in the City of Baton Rouge, Janu ry 5, 1973

P\ AU 'IORITY

E. L. HENRY
Chairman

MOISE W. DENNERY
Secretary

DAVID R. POYNTER
Chief Clerk

Example 597

Louisiana. Constitutional Convention (1973).
    Official journal of the proceedings of the
Constitutional Convention of 1973 of the state of
Louisiana ...

    I. Title.

ME: 21.1AB2(c); 24.22A
AE: 21.30J

THE

DEBATES AND PROCEEDINGS

OF THE

MINNESOTA CONSTITUTIONAL CONVENTION

INCLUDING THE

ORGANIC ACT OF THE TERRITORY.

WITH THE

ENABLING ACT OF CONGRESS, THE ACT OF THE TERRITORIAL LEGISLATURE RELATIVE TO THE CONVENTION, AND THE VOTE OF THE PEOPLE ON THE CONSTITUTION.

Reported Officially by Francis H. Smith.

SAINT PAUL:

EARLE S. GOODRICH, TERRITORIAL PRINTER.

PIONEER AND DEMOCRAT OFFICE.

1857.

Example 598

```
Minnesota. Constitutional Convention (1857 : Demo-
     cratic)
     The debates and proceedings of the Minnesota
Constitutional Convention ...


     I. Smith, Francis H.   II. Title.
```

ME: 21.1B2(c); 24.22A
AE: I. 21.30F
AE: II. 21.30J

Both the Democratic Party and the Republican Party held constitutional conventions the same year in Minnesota, thus the need to modify.

Note also that this is the constitutional convention held when Minnesota was still a territory. The entry for a territory that becomes a state of the same name is the name of the state. (See CSB 6, p. 18, explaining rule 24.6)

Minnesota (Ter.) Convention, 1857.
[Mn 3] Debates and proceedings. Republican. CARD 1 of 7

Example 599

Minnesota. Constitutional Convention (1857 : Re-
    publican).
    Debates and proceedings of the Constitutional
Convention for the territory of Minnesota, to form
a state constitution preparatory to its admission
into the Union as a state [microform] / T.F.
Andrews, official reporter to the convention. --
Saint Paul : G.W. Moore, printer, 1858.
    7, xviii, [9]-624 p. ; 26 cm.

    Microfiche. [Westport, Conn.] : G[reenwood]
P[ress, 1973]. 7 microfiches ; 11 x 15 cm. ([State
constitutional conventions ; series 2], Mn 3).
Title on header: Debates and proceedings, Republican.

    I. Andrews, T. F. (Theodore F.). II. Title.
III. Title: Debates and proceedings, Republican.
IV. Series: State constitutional conventions ;
series 2, Mn 3.

Example 600

Minnesota. Constitutional Convention (1857 : Re-
    publican).
    Debates and proceedings, Republican [micro-
form] / Minnesota (Ter.) Convention, 1857.
-- [Westport, Conn.] : G[reenwood] P[ress, 1973].
    7 microfiches ; 11 x 15 cm. ([State constitu-
tional conventions ; series 2], Mn 3).

    Title on header.
    Microreproduction of: Debates and proceedings
of the Constitutional Convention for the territory
of Minnesota, to form a state constitution preparatory to its admission into the Union as a
state / T.F. Andrews, official reporter to the
convention. Saint Paul : G.W. Moore, printer,
1858. 7, xviii, [9]-624 p. ; 26 cm.

    I. Andrews, T. F. (Theodore F.). II. Title.
III. Title: Debates and proceedings of the Constitutional Convention for the territory of Minnesota
... IV. Series: State constitutional conventions
; series 2, Mn 3.

Using a uniform title

Minnesota. Constitutional Convention (1857, Repub-
    lican)
    [Debates and proceedings of the Constitu-
tional Convention for the territory of Minnesota
...]
    Debates and proceedings, Republican ...

DEBATES

AND

PROCEEDINGS

OF THE

CONSTITUTIONAL
CONVENTION

FOR THE

TERRITORY OF MINNESOTA,

**TO FORM A STATE CONSTITUTION PREPARATORY
TO ITS ADMISSION INTO THE UNION AS A STATE**

T.F. ANDREWS, Official Reporter to the Convention.

SAINT PAUL:
GEORGE W. MOORE, PRINTER.
MINNESOTIAN OFFICE.
1858.

Example 601

```
Minnesota. Constitutional Convention (1857 :
     Republican)
     The debates and proceedings of the Minnesota
Constitutional Convention for the territory of
Minnesota ...


     I. Andrews, T. F.   II. Title.
```

ME: 21.1B2(c); 24.22A
AE: I. 21.30F
AE: II. 21.30J

MARRIAGE LICENSE.

STATE OF MINNESOTA, } ss.
County of St. Louis.

DISTRICT COURT,
Eleventh Judicial District.

To any Person Lawfully Authorized to Solemnize Marriage within said State:

Know Ye, That License is hereby granted to join together as Husband and Wife

Charles Nilson

of the County of _____ and State of _Minnesota_

and _Mary Borg_

of the County of St. Louis and State of Minnesota, being satisfied by the oath of said _____

Charles Nilson

that there is no legal impediment thereto.

Therefore, This shall be your sufficient authority for solemnizing the Marriage of said parties, and making return thereof as provided by law.

In Testimony Whereof, I have hereunto set my hand and affixed the seal of said District Court, at Duluth, Minnesota, this

_13th_ day of _Dec_ 189_7_

_____ Clerk.

By _____ Deputy Clerk.

To be kept by Party Performing Marriage Ceremony.

Example 602

Minnesota. District Court (Saint Louis County)
    Marriage license, 1897 Dec. 13, for Charles Nilson and Mary Borg [manuscript] / State of Minnesota, County of St. Louis, District Court, Eleventh Judicial District.
    [1] leaf ; 18 x 22 cm.

    In part holograph, signed John Owens, clerk, by W.T. James, deputy clerk.
    Signed at Duluth, Minn.

    I. Nilson, Charles. II. Nilson, Mary Borg.

D: 4.7B1, 4.7B8
ME: 21.1B2(a), 21.4B, 24.23A
AE: I. 21.30F
      II. 21.30F

The second added entry presents an interesting situation. The assumption has been made that the marriage was performed, so the form of name used is her married name. If it had not been performed, the form would be: Borg, Mary.

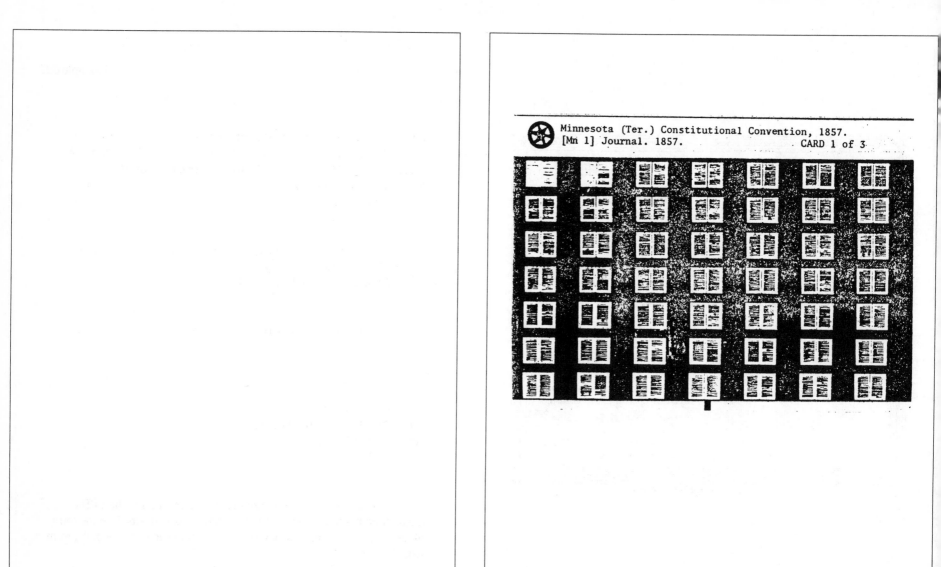

Minnesota (Ter.) Constitutional Convention, 1857.
[Mn 1] Journal. 1857.   CARD 1 of 3

Example 603

Minnesota. Constitutional Convention (1857).
     Journal of the Constitutional Convention of
the territory of Minnesota [microform] : begun and
held in the city of Saint Paul, capital of said
territory, on Monday, the thirteenth day of July,
one thousand eight hundred and fifty-seven. --
Saint Paul : E.S. Goodrich, state printer, 1857.
     209 p. ; 23 cm.

     Microfiche. [Westport, Conn.] : G[reenwood
P[ress, 1973]. 3 microfiches ; 11 x 15 cm. ([State
constitutional conventions ; series 2], Mn 1).
Title on header: Journal.

     I. Title. II. Title: Journal. III. Title:
Journal. IV. Series: State constitutional conventions ; series 2, Mn 1.

Example 604

Minnesota. Constitutional Convention (1857).
     Journal [microform] / Minnesota (Ter.) Con-
stitutional Convention, 1857. -- [Westport, Conn.]
: G[reenwood P[ress, 1973].
     3 microfiches ; 11 x 15 cm. ([State constitu-
tional conventions ; series 2], Mn 1)

     Title on header: Journal.
     Microreproduction of: Journal of the Consti-
tutional Convention of the territory of Minnesota.
Saint Paul : E.S. Goodrich, state printer, 1857.
209 p. ; 23 cm.

     I. Title. II. Title: Journal of the Consti-
tutional Convention of the territory of Minnesota.
III. Series: State constitutional conventions ;
series 2, Mn 1.

Using a uniform title

Minnesota. Constitutional Convention (1857).
     [Journal of the Constitutional Convention of
the territory of Minnesota]
     Journal [microform] ...

DISTRICT COURT OF MINNESOTA

FOURTH JUDICIAL DISTRICT HENNEPIN COUNTY

Special Rules of Practice
and
Registration of Land Title Rules

Effective January 1, 1954

Example 605

```
Minnesota. District Court (4th Judicial District :
     Hennepin County)
     Special rules of practice and registration of
land title rules ...


     I. Minnesota. District Court (4th Judicial
District : Hennepin County). Registration of land
title rules.  II. Title.
```

ME: 21.1B2(a); 21.34A; 24.18, type 6; 24.23A
AE: I. 21.30M; 24.18, type 6; 24.23A
AE: II. 21.30J

The piece in hand does not indicate what body promulgated the rules. This raises the question of how much outside research is to be done to find out such information.

REPUBLIC OF SOUTH AFRICA
_____

RULES AND REGULATIONS

as amended

for

CHIEFS' AND HEADMEN'S CIVIL COURTS
BANTU AFFAIRS COMMISSIONERS' COURTS
BANTU DIVORCE COURTS
and
BANTU APPEAL COURTS

MARCH 1971

STATUTORY LAWS
REPRODUCED UNDER GOVERNMENT PRINTER'S COPYRIGHT
AUTHORITY NO. 3985 OF 9TH APRIL 1968

PUBLISHED BY:

UNITY SECRETARIAL SERVICES
TYPING & DUPLICATING EXPERTS
114/117 KENYA HOUSE
LOVEDAY STREET
OOR. MARSHALL STREET
JOHANNESBURG.

Example 606

South Africa.
    Rules and regulations as amended for chiefs'
and headmen's civil courts ..., March 1971 ...

    I. Title.

ME: 21.1AB2(a); 21.34B; 21.31B1
AE: 21.30J

ALASKA RULES

OF

COURT PROCEDURE

AND

ADMINISTRATION

VOLUME I

**PREPARED AND PROMULGATED BY
ORDER OF THE SUPREME COURT OF
THE STATE OF ALASKA
1963**

WITH CHANGES TO NOVEMBER, 1975

Example 607

```
Alaska. Supreme Court.
    Alaska rules of court procedure and admini-
stration ...


    I. Title.
```

ME: 21.1B2(a); 21.34B; 24.18, type 6; 24.23A
AE: 21.30J

MICHIGAN COURT RULES 1979

MICHIGAN RULES

	Page
General Court Rules	1
Index	363
Administrative Orders	409
Case Information Control System	443
Uniform System of Citations	449
Evidence Rules	459
Index	497
District Court Rules	521
Index	649
Probate Court Rules	675
Forms	753
Juvenile Court Rules	807
Rules of Court of Claims	835
Rules of Circuit Court—Wayne County	839
Administrative Orders	889
Rules of Common Pleas Court of Detroit	895
Rules for Recorder's Court of Detroit	951
Rules of Circuit Court—Oakland County	1005
Administrative Orders	1021
Code of Professional Responsibility and Canons	1041
Code of Judicial Conduct	1071
Rules Concerning the Judicial Conference	1081
Rules Concerning the State Bar	1083
Rules for the Board of Law Examiners	1101

FEDERAL RULES

Rules of Court of Appeals—Sixth Circuit	1107
Index	1121
Rules of United States District Court—Western District of Michigan	1143
Rules of United States District Court—Eastern District of Michigan	1169

WEST PUBLISHING CO.   ST. PAUL, MINN.

Example 608

Michigan court rules, 1979 ...

I. West Publishing Co.

ME: 21.34C; 21.7B
AE: 21.34C; 24.1

FEDERAL RULES OF EVIDENCE

(As Amended through October 28, 1978)

TABLE OF CONTENTS

ARTICLE I. GENERAL PROVISIONS

Rule 101.   Scope.

Rule 102.   Purpose and construction.

Rule 103.   Rulings on evidence:

     (a) Effect of erroneous ruling:
         (1) Objection.
         (2) Offer of proof.
     (b) Record of offer and ruling.
     (c) Hearing of jury.
     (d) Plain error.

Rule 104.   Preliminary questions:

     (a) Questions of admissibility
        generally.
     (b) Relevancy conditioned on fact.
     (c) Hearing of a jury.
     (d) Testimony by accused.
     (e) Weight and credibility.

Rule 105.   Limited admissibility.

Example 609

```
United States.
     Federal rules of evidence ...


     I. United States. Supreme Court. II. Title.
```

ME: 21.1B2(a); explanation as below; 21.31B1
AE: I. 21.30F; 24.18, type 6; 24.23A
AE: II. 21.30J

This set of rules constitutes a code of procedure for all types of federal courts. It is not a collection, it is a single set of rules. It is promulgated by the Supreme Court and passed as a single law by the Congress.

Unfortunately, AACR 2 has no rule to cover a single set of rules, not a collection, governing more than one court of a single jurisdiction (see also 25). Some preliminary papers by the Office for Descriptive Cataloging Policy dealing with this problem suggest that by analogy the cataloger should prefer entry as follows:

1.   Prefer entry as a law if the set of rules is a law. If not,
2.   prefer entry under promulgating agency. If none,
3.   enter under title.

96th Congress   COMMITTEE PRINT   No. 4
1st Session

FEDERAL RULES

OF

APPELLATE PROCEDURE

WITH FORMS

OCTOBER 1, 1979

Printed for the use
of
THE COMMITTEE ON THE JUDICIARY
HOUSE OF REPRESENTATIVES

U.S. GOVERNMENT PRINTING OFFICE
WASHINGTON 1979

Example 610

```
United States. Supreme Court.
    Federal rules of appellate procedure ...


    I. Title.
```

ME: 21.1B2(a); explanation on 24; 24.18, type 6; 24.23A
AE: 21.30J

This set of rules constitutes a code of procedure for all types of federal courts. It is not a collection, it is a single set of rules. It is promulgated by the Supreme Court, but it is not a law.

This set of rules is incorrectly given as an example of rule 21.34B on p. 332 of AACR 2.

TREATIES AND OTHER INTERNATIONAL ACTS
SERIES 1860

UNITED STATES EDUCATIONAL FOUNDATION IN BELGIUM

Agreement between the UNITED STATES OF AMERICA and BELGIUM and LUXEMBOURG

• Signed at Brussels October 8, 1948

• Entered into force October 8, 1948

Note: Treaty between the United States on one side and Belgium and Luxembourg on the other.

Example 611

```
United States.
    [Treaties, etc. 1948 Oct. 8]
    United States Educational Foundation in Bel-
gium ...


    I. Belgium. Treaties, etc. United States,
1948 Oct. 8.  II. Luxemburg. Treaties, etc. United
States, 1948 Oct. 8.  III. Title.
```

Cross reference

```
United States
    United States Educational Foundation in Bel-
gium.
```

ME: 21.1B2(b); 21.35A1(a); 25.16B1
AE: I. 21.35A1; 25.16B1
AE: II. 21.35A1; 25.16B1; 23.2A
AE: III. 21.30J

AIR SERVICE

Facilities in French Territory

**Agreement between the
UNITED STATES OF AMERICA
and FRANCE**

Amending Agreement of June 18, 1946

• **Effected by Exchange of Notes
Signed at Paris May 8 and 17, 1947**

• **Entered into force May 17, 1947**

Example 612

```
France.
     [Treaties, etc. United States, 1947 May 8]
     Air service facilities in French territory
...


     I. United States. Treaties, etc. France, 1947
May 8.   II. Title.
```

ME: 21.1B2(b); 21.35A1(b); 25.16B1
AE: I. 21.35A1; 25.16B1
AE: II. 21.30J

CONVENTION

BETWEEN THE

UNITED STATES OF AMERICA

AND

HIS BRITANNIC MAJESTY,

FOR

DETERMINING BOUNDARIES,

PURSUANT TO THE PROVISIONS CONTAINED IN THE
TREATY OF PEACE OF 1783

CONCLUDED AT LONDON

ON THE 12th OF MAY, 1803,

═══════════

OCTOBER 24th, 1803.

Printed by order of the Senate

Example 613

```
Great Britain.
    [Treaties, etc. United States, 1803 May 12]
    Convention between the United States of Amer-
ica and His Britannic Majesty for determining
boundaries : pursuant to the provisions contained
in the treaty of peace of 1783 : concluded at
London on the 12th of May 1803. -- [Washington,
D.C.] : Printed by order of the Senate, 1803.
    11 p. ; 22 cm. (12mo)
    Dated: October 24th, 1803.
    "Forty copies printed."


    I. United States.Treaties, etc. Great Brit-
ain, 1803 May 12.
```

ME: 21.35A1(b); 25.16B1; 24.3E

Since bilateral treaties are now entered under the name of the nation whose name is first alphabetically, the main entry is under Great Britain with an added entry for United States. This is a case where form subdivision has been dropped and replaced by uniform title. Note also the form of the additions to the uniform title entries.

U.S.-Soviet Commercial Agreements 1972

Texts, Summaries, and Supporting Papers

U.S. DEPARTMENT OF COMMERCE
Peter G. Peterson, Secretary

Andrew E. Gibson, Assistant Secretary
DOMESTIC AND INTERNATIONAL
BUSINESS ADMINISTRATION
BUREAU OF EAST-WEST TRADE

JANUARY 1973

Example 614

```
Soviet Union.
    [Treaties, etc. United States]
    U.S.-Soviet commercial agreements 1972 :
texts, summaries, and supporting papers. -- [Wash-
ington] : U.S. Dept. of Commerce, Domestic and
International Business Administration, Bureau of
East-West Trade, 1973.
    v, 107 p. ; 26 cm.



    I. United States. Treaties, etc. Soviet
Union.  II. United States. Bureau of East-West
Trade.
```

ME: 21.35A1(b); 25.16A; LC decision on Soviet Union as conventional
     name
AE: 21.35A1; 25.16A, 24.18, type 2; 24.19

TREATIES AND OTHER INTERNATIONAL ACTS SERIES 1895

ESTABLISHMENT OF THE INDO-PACIFIC FISHERIES COUNCIL

**Agreement between the
UNITED STATES OF AMERICA
and OTHER GOVERNMENTS**

- **Formulated at Baguio February 26, 1948**

- **Entered into force November 9, 1948**

Example 615

Establishment of the Indo-Pacific Fisheries Coun-
       cil ...

    I. United States. II. Regional Meeting to
Consider the Formation of a Regional Council for
the Study of the Sea (1948 : Baguio, Philippines)

ME: 21.35A2
AE: I. 21.35A2
AE: II:.21.30F; 24.1; 24.7

This example shows entry when uniform titles are not used; see below for use of uniform title.

Example 616

Agreement for the Establishment of the Indo-
           Pacific Fisheries Council ...

    I. United States. Treaties, etc. 1948 Feb.
26. II. Title. III. Regional Meeting to Consider
the Formation of a Regional Council for the Study
of the Sea (1948 : Buguio, Philippines)

ME: 21.35A2; 25.16B2
AE: I. 21.35A2; 25.16B1
AE: II. 21.30F; 24.1; 24.7
AE: III. 21.30J

Treaty was formulated at the Regional Meeting to Consider the Formation of a Regional Council for the Study of the Sea.

TREATIES AND OTHER INTERNATIONAL ACTS SERIES 1886

TRADE

**Application of Most-Favored-Nation
Treatment to Areas of Western Germany
Under Occupation or Control**

**Agreement between the UNITED
STATES OF AMERICA and
OTHER GOVERNMENTS,
WESTERN GERMANY**

**• Dated at Geneva September 14,
1948**

**• Entered into force, with respect to
the United States, October 14, 1948**

Example 617

```
Agreement on Most-Favoured-Nation Treatment for
     Areas of Western Germany under Military Oc-
     cupation (1948)
     Trade application of most-favored-nation
treatment to areas of western Germany under occu-
pation or control ...


     I. United States. Treaties, etc. 1948 Sept.
14.  II. Contracting Parties to the General Agree-
ment on Tariffs and Trade.
```

Cross references

```
United States.
     Agreement on Most-Favoured-Nation Treatment
for Areas of Western Germany Under Military Occu-
pation.

United States.
     Trade application of most-favored-nation
treatment to areas of western Germany under occu-
pation or control ...
```

ME: 21.35A2; 25.16B2
AE: I. 21.35A2; 25.16B1
AE: II. 21.30F; 24.1; 24.7
AE: III. 21.30J

TREATIES AND OTHER INTERNATIONAL ACTS SERIES 1899

HEADQUARTERS OF
THE UNITED NATIONS

Loan for Construction and Furnishing

**Agreement between the
UNITED STATES OF AMERICA
and the UNITED NATIONS**

**• Signed at Lake Success, New York,
March 23, 1948**

• Entered into force August 30, 1948

Example 618

```
United Nations.
     [Treaties, etc. United States. 1948 Mar. 28]
     Headquarters of the United Nations ...


     I. United States. Treaties, etc. United Na-
tions, 1948 Mar. 28.   II. Title.
```

ME: 21.1B2(b); 21.35B; 21.35A1; 25.16B1
AE: I. 21.35A1; 25.16B1
AE: II. 21.30J

Make x-refs. to main entry and a.e.: I.

AGREEMENT BETWEEN THE UNITED NATIONS AND THE INTERNATIONAL CIVIL AVIATION ORGANIZATION

ACCORD ENTRE LES NATIONS UNIES ET L'ORGANISATION DE L'AVIATION CIVILE INTERNATIONALE

UNITED NATIONS
LAKE SUCCESS, NEW YORK
1947

Example 619

```
International Civil Aviation Organization.
     [Treaties, etc. United Nations, 1947 Oct. 1]
     Agreement between the United Nations and the
International Civil Aviation Organization ...


     I. United Nations. Treaties, etc. Interna-
tional Civil Aviation Organization, 1947 Oct. 1.
II. Title.   III. Title: Accord entre les Nations
unies es l'Organisation de l'aviation civile
internationale.
```

ME:21.35A2; 25.16B2
AE: I. 21.35A2; 25.16B1
AE: II. 21.30F; 24.1; 24.7
AE: III. 21.30J

Make x-refs. to main entry and a.e. I.

AGREEMENT

**CREATING AN ASSOCIATION BETWEEN THE
MEMBER STATES OF THE EUROPEAN FREE
TRADE ASSOCIATION AND THE REPUBLIC
OF FINLAND**

**Signed at Helsinki on 27th March, 1961
Entered into force on 26th June, 1961**

**This edition incorporates all amendments
up to 31st January, 1967**

Example 620

```
Agreement Creating an Association Between the
     Member States of the European Free Trade
     Association and the Republic of Finland
     (1961)
     Agreement creating an association between the
member states of the European Free Trade Associa-
tion and the republic of Finland ...


     I. Finland. Treaties, etc. 1961 Mar. 27.  II.
European Free Trade Association.  III. Title
```

ME: 21.35B; 21.35A; 25.16B2
AE: I. 21.35A2; 25.16B1
AE: II. 21.30E

Example 621

GENERAL AGREEMENT
ON TARIFFS AND TRADE

**Between the UNITED STATES of
AMERICA and OTHER
GOVERNMENTS**

**Protocol for the Accession of
Signatories of the Final Act
of October 30, 1947**

• Signed at Geneva September 14, 1948

• Entered into force September 14, 1948

```
General Agreement on Tariffs and Trade (1947).
     Protocols, etc., 1948 Sept. 14.
     General agreement on tariffs and trade ...


     I. United States. Treaties, etc. 1947 Oct.
30. Protocols, etc., 1948 Sept. 14.
```

ME: 21.35E; 25.16B3
AE: 21.35A2; 21.35E; 25.16B3

Example 622

Chippewa Indians.
    [Treaties, etc. United States]
    Treaties and agreements of the Chippewa Indi-
ans. -- Washington, D.C. : Institute for the
Development of Indian Law, [1973?].
    iii, 142 p. ; 28 cm.

    I. United States. Treaties, etc. Chippewa
Indians. II. Institute for the Development of
Indian Law.

ME: 21.1B2(b); 21.35F1; 21.35A1 (and footnote 1); 25.16A
AE: I. 21.35A1; 25.16A
AE: II. 21.30J

Make x-refs. to main entry and a.e. I.

United States Treaties and Other International Agreements

VOLUME 20

IN THREE PARTS

Part I

1969

Example 623

```
United States.
    [Treaties, etc.]
    United States treaties and other interna-
tional agreements ...


    I. Title.
```

ME: 21.1B2(b); 21.35F2; 25.16A
AE: 21.30J

Make x-ref. to main entry.

European Treaties bearing on the History of the United States and its Dependencies to 1648

EDITED BY
FRANCES GARDINER DAVENPORT

GLOUCESTER, MASS.

PETER SMITH

1967

Example 624

```
European treaties bearing on the history of the
        United States and its dependencies to 1648
    ...


    I. Davenport, Frances Gardiner.
```

ME: 21.35F2; 21.7B
AE: 21.7B

REPORTS

FROM

THE COURT OF CLAIMS

PUBLICATION OF THE

HOUSE OF REPRESENTATIVES

DURING THE

SECOND SESSION OF THE THIRTY-SIXTH CONGRESS.

1860-'61

IN THREE VOLUMES.

WASHINGTON:
GOVERNMENT PRINTING OFFICE.
1861.

Example 625

```
United States. Court of Claims.
     Reports from the Court of Claims ...


     I. Title.
```

ME: 21.1B2(b); 21.36A1; 24.18, type 6; 24.23A
AE: 21.30J

CASES ARGUED AND DECIDED

IN THE

SUPREME COURT

OF THE

UNITED STATES

OCTOBER TERM, 1938, IN

305, 306, 307 U. S.

BOOK 83

LAWYERS' EDITION

COMPLETE WITH HEADLINES, HEADNOTES, STATEMENTS OF
CASES, POINTS AND AUTHORITIES OF COUNSEL, FOOTNOTES, AND
PARALLEL REFERENCES

BY

THE PUBLISHER'S EDITORIAL STAFF.

———————

THE LAWYERS CO-OPERATIVE PUBLISHING
COMPANY
ROCHESTER, NEW YORK
1939

Example 626

Cases argued and decided in the Supreme Court of
the United States ...

I. United States. Supreme Court. II. Lawyers
Co-operative Publishing Company.

ME: 21.36A1
AE: I. 21.36A1 (example); 24.18, type 6; 24.23A
AE: II. 21.36A1

MINNESOTA REPORTS

Volume 312

CASES ARGUED AND DETERMINED

IN THE

SUPREME COURT OF MINNESOTA

January 21, 1977—April 15, 1977

(98 Opinions)

RUTH JENSEN HARRIS

REPORTER

REVIEW PUBLISHING COMPANY

ST. PAUL, MINNESOTA

1979

Example 627

```
Minnesota. Supreme Court.
    Minnesota reports ...


    I. Title.
```

ME: 21.1AB2(b); 21.36A1; 24.18, type 6; 24.23A
AE: 21.30J

Rule 21.36A1 states that the reports of one court that are ascribed to a reporter should be entered according to the citation practice of the jurisdiction where the court is located. This involves research into legal citation practice. In Anglo-American law countries, current practice is to city by court, not reporter. In the United States, citation practice changed from reporter to court in the late 19th century. (For further discussion of this situation see P. Marion, "Sources for Determining Citation Practice for Court Reports Throughout the World," *Library Resources & Technical Services,* v. 25 (April 1981), p. 139-148.) This rule also calls for an added entry under the reporter. The compiler believes that most libraries would ignore this added entry for a serial such as this where the reporter might change from year to year.

CASES

ARGUED AND ADJUDGED

IN

THE SUPREME COURT

OF

THE UNITED STATES,

DECEMBER TERM, 1863.

REPORTED BY
JOHN WILLIAM WALLACE.

VOL. I.

WASHINGTON, D.C.:
W.H. & O. H. MORRISON,
LAW PUBLISHERS AND BOOKSELLERS,
1864.

Example 628

```
Wallace, John William.
    Cases argued and adjudged in the Supreme
Court of the United States ...


    I. United States. Supreme Court.  II. Title.
```

ME: 21.36A1
AE: I. 21.36A1; 24.18, type 6; 24.23A
AE: II. 21.30J

United States Supreme Court reports were cited by reporter until 1875.

MINNESOTA REPORTS

VOL. 51

CASES ARGUED AND DETERMINED

IN THE

SUPREME COURT OF MINNESOTA

JULY-NOVEMBER, 1892

CHARLES C. WILLSON

REPORTER

ST. PAUL
WEST PUBLISHING CO.
1894

Ramsey County *vs.* Macalester College.

Argued Nov. 1, 1892.   Decided Dec. 1, 1892.

College Grounds Exempt from Taxation—Extent of.

A college owns 40 acres of land, on which the college buildings are situated. On a part of the tract, near the college buildings, the college has erected several houses as places of residence for the professors or faculty, such as premises being used for no other purpose. *Held,* that the premises used for that purpose are within the statutory exemption from taxation.

Example 629

Minnesota. Supreme Court.
    Ramsey County vs. Macalester College. -- p.
437-443 ; 25 cm.

    In Minnesota. Supreme Court. Minnesota re-
ports. -- Vol. 51 (July-Nov. 1892).
    Title from caption.
    "Argued Nov. 1, 1892. Decided Dec. 1. 1892."
    Decision signed: Dickinson. J.
    Also published as: 53 N.W. Rep. 704.

    I. Dickinson, Daniel A., 1839-1902. II.
Ramsey County (Minn.). III. Macalester College.
IV. Title.

A case heard before the Minnesota Supreme court cataloged as an
"In" analytic.

Type: a Bib lvl: a Govt pub: s Lang: eng Source: d Illus:
Repr: Enc lvl: I Conf pub: 0 Ctry: mnu Dat tp: s M/F/B: 00
Indx: 0 Mod rec: Festschr: 0 Cont: w
Desc: a Int lvl: Dates: 1892,

```
    010
    040    XXX $c XXX
    043    n-us-mn
    052    4143 $b R2
    052    4143 $b S4
    090
    049    XXXX
    110 10 Minnesota. $b Supreme Court.
    245 10 Ramsey County vs. Macalester College.
    260 |    $c
    300    p. 437-443 ; $c 25 cm.
    500    Title from caption.
    500    "Argued Nov. 1, 1892. Decided Dec. 1. 1892."
    500    Decision signed: Dickinson. J.
    500    Also published as: 53 N.W. Rep. 704.
    700 10 Dickinson, Daniel A., $d 1839-1902.
    710 10 Ramsey County (Minn.).
    710 20 Macalester College.
    773 0   $7 clas $a Minnesota. Supreme Court. $t
Minnesota reports. $g Vol. 51 (July-Nov. 1892). $w
(OCoLC) nnnnnnn
```

REPORTS OF CASES

ARGUED AND DETERMINED IN THE

SUPREME COURT,

AND THE

COURT OF ERRORS AND APPEALS

OF THE

STATE OF NEW JERSEY,

FROM JUNE TERM, 1855, TO JUNE TERM, 1856, INCLUSIVE.

—————

ANDREW DUTCHER, Reporter.

—————

VOLUME 1.

SECOND EDITION.

WITH REFERENCES SHOWING WHERE THE CASES HAVE BEEN
CITED, AFFIRMED, OVERRULED, QUESTIONED, LIMITED, ETC.,
DOWN TO VOL. XXXIX, N.J. LAW REPORTS (X VROOM), AND VOL.
XXVIII, N.J. EQUITY REPORTS (I STEW.), INCLUSIVE.

By John Linn, Esq., of the Hudson Co. Bar.

—————

JERSEY CITY:
FREDERICK D. LINN & CO.
1886.

Example 630

Dutcher, Andrew.
    Reports of cases argued and determined in the
Supreme Court and the Court of Errors and Appeals
of the state of New Jersey ...

    I. New Jersey. Supreme Court. II. New Jer-
sey. Court of Errors and Appeals. III. Linn,
John. IV. Title.

ME: 21.36A2
AE   I & II: 21.36A2; 24.18, type 6; 24.23A
AE: III. 21.30C
AE: IV. 21.30J

New Jersey

Miscellaneous Reports

**Containing cases decided in the Court of
Errors and Appeals, Court of Chancery,
Prerogative and Supreme Courts that are
not reported in the New Jersey Law and
Equity Reports.**

**Also important cases decided in the
NewJersey Courts of Common Pleas,
District and Circuit Courts, and by the
Surrogates and Department of Labor.**

**Reported by
the
Publisher's Editorial Staff**

Volume XXVI

SONET & SAGE CO.
Newark, New Jersey
1949

Example 631

```
New Jersey miscellaneous reports...


     I. New Jersey. Court of Errors and Appeals.
II. Soney & Sage Co.



ME:  21.36A2
AE:  I. 21.36A2; 24.18, type 6; 24.23A
AE:  II. 21.36A2; 24.1
```

The term "publisher's editorial staff" does not qualify as a corporate body, and therefore it does not qualify as a reporter. However, it can be taken to indicate that the publisher functions as more than publisher and thus should be given an added entry.

SHEPARD'S
CALIFORNIA CITATIONS

CASES

A COMPILATION OF CITATIONS
TO
CALIFORNIA CASES REPORTED IN THE VARIOUS SERIES OF CALIFORNIA REPORTS,
IN THE PACIFIC REPORTER AND IN THE CALIFORNIA REPORTER

THE CITATIONS

which include affirmances, reversals and dismissals by the California courts and the United States
Supreme Court

APPEAR IN

CALIFORNIA SUPREME COURT REPORTS	LOYOLA OF LOS ANGELES LAW REVIEW
CALIFORNIA APPELLATE REPORTS	PACIFIC LAW JOURNAL
CALIFORNIA REPORTER	SAN DIEGO LAW REVIEW
PACIFIC REPORTER (California Cases)	SANTA CLARA LAW REVIEW
CALIFORNIA UNREPORTED CASES	SANTA CLARA LAWYER
LABATT'S DISTRICT COURT REPORTS	SOUTHERN CALIFORNIA LAW REVIEW
MYRICK'S PROBATE COURT REPORTS	SOUTHWESTERN UNIVERSITY LAW REVIEW
COFFEY'S PROBATE DECISIONS	STANFORD LAW REVIEW
UNITED STATES SUPREME COURT REPORTS	UNIVERSITY OF CALIFORNIA AT LOS
LAWYERS' EDITION UNITED STATES	ANGELES LAW REVIEW
SUPREME COURT REPORTS	UNIVERSITY OF SAN FRANCISCO LAW
SUPREME COURT REPORTER	REVIEW
FEDERAL CASES	COLUMBIA LAW REVIEW
FEDERAL REPORTER	CORNELL LAW QUARTERLY
FEDERAL SUPPLEMENT	CORNELL LAW REVIEW
FEDERAL RULES DECISIONS	GEORGETOWN LAW JOURNAL
OPINIONS OF THE ATTORNEY	HARVARD LAW REVIEW
GENERAL OF CALIFORNIA	LAW AND CONTEMPORARY PROBLEMS
DECISIONS OF THE INDUSTRIAL	MICHIGAN LAW REVIEW
ACCIDENT COMMISSION OF	MINNESOTA LAW REVIEW
CALIFORNIA	NEW YORK UNIVERSITY LAW REVIEW
CALIFORNIA COMPENSATION CASES	NORTHWESTERN UNIVERSITY LAW REVIEW
OPINIONS AND ORDERS OF THE RAIL-	TEXAS LAW REVIEW
ROAD COMMISSION OF CALIFORNIA	UNIVERSITY OF CHICAGO LAW REVIEW
OPINIONS AND ORDERS OF THE PUBLIC	UNIVERSITY OF ILLINOIS LAW FORUM
UTILITIES COMMISSION OF	UNIVERSITY OF PENNSYLVANIA LAW
CALIFORNIA	REVIEW
CALIFORNIA LAW REVIEW	VIRGINIA LAW REVIEW
CALIFORNIA WESTERN LAW REVIEW	WISCONSIN LAW REVIEW
HASTINGS LAW JOURNAL	YALE LAW JOURNAL
JOURNAL OF THE STATE BAR OF	AMERICAN BAR ASSOCIATION JOURNAL
CALIFORNIA	

and in annotations of

LAWYERS' EDITION, UNITED STATES SUPREME COURT REPORTS
AMERICAN LAW REPORTS

also, for California cases reported prior to the Pacific Reporter or not reported in either the California
Reporter or the Pacific Reporter as cited in all units of the National Reporter System and in Vols. 1-283
Illinois Appellate Court Reports, Vols. 1-19 Ohio Appellate Reports and Vols. 1-101 Pennsylvania
Superior Court Reports

SEVENTH EDITION - - - - - - Case Edition Supplement 1970-1978

SHEPARD'S, INC.
of
COLORADO SPRINGS
COLORADO 80901

Example 632

Shepard's California citations, cases ...

I. Shepard's, Inc. of Colorado Springs.

ME: 21.36B
AE: 21.36B; 24.1

ARKANSAS DIGEST

VOLUME 13A

NEGLIGENCE—PAYMENT

COVERING CASES FROM

STATE AND FEDERAL COURTS

ST. PAUL, MINN.
WEST PUBLISHING CO.

ST. PAUL, MINN.
WEST PUBLISHING CO.

Example 633

Arkansas digest ...

    I. West Publishing Co.

ME: 21.36B
AE: 21.36B; 24.1

THE SACCO-VANZETTI CASE

**TRANSCRIPT OF THE RECORD
OF THE TRIAL OF
NICCOLA SACCO AND BARTOLOMEO VANZETTI
IN THE COURTS OF MASSACHUSETTS
AND SUBSEQUENT PROCEEDINGS
1920-7**

VOLUME I
Pages 1 to 1092

**NEW YORK
HENRY HOLT & COMPANY
MCMXXVIII**

Example 634

Sacco, Nicola, 1891-1927.
　　The Sacco-Vanzetti case : transcript of the record of the trial of Nicola Sacco and Bartolomeo Vanzetti in the courts of Massachusetts and subsequent proceedings, 1920-7. -- New York : Holt, 1928-1929.
　　5 v. (5621 p.) : ports., plans ; 25 cm.

　　Sacco and Vanzetti were tried at Dedham, in the Superior Court of Massachusetts for Norfolk County, May 31-July 14, 1921 ...

　　I. Vanzetti, Bartolomeo, 1888-1927.　II. Massachusetts. Superior Court (Norfolk County). III. Title.

Option

Sacco, Nicola, 1891-1927, defendant.
Vanzetti, Bartolomeo, 1888-1927, defendant.

ME:　21.36C1; 21.6C1
AE:　21.36C1; 21.6C1; 21.36C1; 24.23A
O:　　21.36C1; 21.6C1

```
Type: a Bib lvl: a Govt pub:    Lang: eng Source: d illus: ce
Repr:    Enc lvl: I Conf pub: 0 Ctry: nyu Dat tp: m M/F/B: 10
Indx: 0 Mod rec:    Festschr: 0 Cont: v
Desc: a Int lvl:    Dates: 1928-1929

    010
    040    XXX $c XXX
    043    n-us-ma
    045 2  $b d19210531 $b d19210714
    090
    049    XXXX
    100 10 Sacco, Nicola, $d 1891-1927.
    245 14 The Sacco-Vanzetti case : $b transcript of the
record of the trial of Nicola Sacco and Bartolomeo Vanzetti
in the courts of Massachusetts and subsequent proceedings,
1920-7.
    260 0  New York : $b Holt, $c 1928-1929.
    300    5 v. (5621 p.) : $b ports., plans ; $c 25 cm.
    500    Sacco and Vanzetti were tried at Dedham, in the
Superior Court of Massachusetts for Norfolk County, May 31-
July 14, 1921 ...
    700 10 Vanzetti, Bartolomeo, $d 1888-1927.
    710 10 Massachusetts. $b Superior Court (Norfolk
County).
```

THE GING MURDER

— AND THE —

GREAT HAYWARD TRIAL

THE OFFICIAL STENOGRAPHIC REPORT
Containing Every Word of the Wonderful Trial From its Opening to Sentence of Death;
the Rulings of the Court; Speeches of Frank M. Nye, W. W. Erwin
Albert H. Hall and John Day Smith; the Court's
Charge, Etc., Etc.

SUPPLEMENTED BY

A DRAMATIC STORY OF THE GREAT CRIME

— BY —

OSCAR F.G. DAY,
Author of "A Mistaken Identity," "The Devil's Gold," "A Crown of Shame," Etc.

COPYRIGHTED BY

THE MINNESOTA TRIBUNE COMPANY

Example 635

```
Hayward, Harry T.
     The Ging murder and the great Hayward trial
...


     I. Minnesota. District Court (4th Judicial
District : Hennepin County).  II. Day, Oscar F. G.
III. Title.
```

ME: 21.36C1
AE: I. 21.36C1; 24.18, type 6; 24.23A
AE: II. 21.30C
AE: III. 21.30J

Example 636

LURED TO DEATH

OR

THE MINNEAPOLIS MURDER

BEING
AN AUTHENTIC ACCOUNT OF THE TRIAL OF HARRY T. HAYWARD
FOR THE MURDER OF MISS CATHERINE M. GING

WITH
PORTRAITS OF THE PRINCIPAL, ETC., ETC.

BY
STUART C. WADE

———

CHICAGO:
E.A. WEEKS & COMPANY
521-531 WABASH AVE.

```
Wade, Stuart C.
     Lured to death, or, The Minneapolis murder
...


     I. Hayward, Harry T.   II. Title.   III. Title:
The Minneapolis murder.
```

ME: 21.1A2; 1.1B1
AE: I. 21.30F
AE: II. 21.30J
AE: III. 21.30J

This is not an official report of the trial. It is Wade's "authentic account".

THE

TRIAL

OF

Alexander Addison, Esq.

PRESIDENT OF THE COURTS OF COMMON PLEAS, IN THE
CIRCUIT CONSISTING OF THE COUNTIES OF WEST-
MORELAND, FAYETTE, WASHINGTON AND ALLEG-
HENY

ON AN IMPEACHMENT,

BY THE HOUSE OF REPRESENTATIVES.

*BEFORE THE SENATE OF THE COMMONWEALTH
OF PENNSYLVANIA.*

TAKEN IN SHORTHAND BY
THOMAS LLOYD

———————————

Second edition, with additions

———————————

LANCASTER:

PRINTED BY **GEORGE HELMBOLD**, junior,
FOR **LLOYD** AND **HELMBOLD**, junior
1803.
[Copy-right Secured.]

Example 637

```
Addison, Alexander.
     The trial of Alexander Addison, Esq. ...


     I. Pennsylvania. General Assembly. House of
Representatives. II. Pennsylvania. General Assem-
bly. Senate.  III. Lloyd, Thomas.  IV. Title.
```

ME: 21.36C1
AE: I. 21.30E; 24.18, type 5; 24.21A
AE: II. 21.36C1; 24.18, type 5; 24.21A
AE: III. 21.36C1
AE: IV. 21.30J

The rule indicates that the cataloger should not make an added entry
under the jurisdiction bringing the prosecution. However, the compiler
feels that in cases of impeachment, the cataloger should not treat the body
that is impeaching in the same manner as the jurisdiction bringing the
prosecution. Instead, an added entry should be made under the body that
is impeaching.

Example 638

PROCEEDINGS

OF A

GENERAL COURT-MARTIAL,

HELD AT

BRUNSWICK, IN THE STATE OF NEW JERSEY,

BY ORDER OF

HIS EXCELLENCY GEN. WASHINGTON,

COMMANDER-IN-CHIEF OF THE ARMY OF THE UNITED STATES OF AMERICA,

FOR THE TRIAL OF

MAJOR-GENERAL LEE.

JULY 4TH, 1778.

MAJOR-GENERAL LORD STIRLING, PRESIDENT

New York:
PRIVATELY REPRINTED.
1864.

Lee, Charles.
    Proceedings of a general court-martial held
at Brunswick, in the state of New-Jersey, by order
of His Excellency Gen. Washington, commander-in-
chief of the Army of the United States of America,
for the trial of Major-General Lee ...

    I. United States. Army. Court-martial (Lee :
1778). II. Title: Proceedings of a general court-
martial held at Brunswick, in the state of New-
Jersey ...

ME: 21.36C1
AE: I. 21.36C1; 24.18, type 6; 24.23B
AE: II. 21.30J

COURT OF QUEEN'S BENCH, IRELAND

A REPORT

OF

THE PROCEEDINGS

ON AN

INDICTMENT FOR A CONSPIRACY,

IN THE CASE OF

THE QUEEN

V.

DANIEL O'CONNELL,	REV. PETER JAMES TYRRELL,
JOHN O'CONNELL,	RICHARD BARRETT,
THOMAS STEELE,	JOHN OBAY, AND
CHARLES GAVAN DUFFY,	THOMAS MATTHEW BAY
REV. THOMAS TIERNEY.	

IN

MICHAELMAS TERM, 1843, AND HILARY TERM, 1844.

BY

JOHN SIMPSON ARMSTRONG,

AND

EDWARD SHIRLEY TREVOR, Esqrs.,

BARRISTERS AT LAW

DUBLIN
HODGES AND SMITH, 21, COLLEGE-GREEN.
MDCCCXLIV.

Example 639

A Report of the proceedings of an indictment for a
        conspiracy in the case of the Queen v.
        Daniel O'Connell ... : in Michaelmas Term
    ...

    I. Ireland. Court of Queen's Bench. II.
O'Connell, Daniel. III. Armstrong, John Simpson.
IV. Trevor, Edward Shirley.

ME: 21.36C1; 21.6C2
AE: I. 21.36C1; 24.18, type 6; 24.23A
AE: II. 21.36C2
AE: III & IV. 21.36C1

Concerning added entry I.: In the past, LC has used the entry form
"Court of King's Bench" for both the Court of King's Bench and the Court
of Queen's Bench. Under AACR 2, the entry will change as the name of
the court changes. "See also" references should be used to connect them.

SUPREME COURT

Of New-Jersey — Essex Circuit.

═══════════════

THE <u>AMERICAN PRINT WORKS</u> ,

vs.

CORNELIUS W. LAWRENCE.

═══════════════

Proceedings at the Trial of above entitled Cause, at Essex
Circuit, October, 1852

COMPILED FROM NOTES OF REPORTER AT THE TRIAL, AND REVISED
BY THE COUNSEL FOR THE DEFENDANT.

═══════════════

New-York:
COLLINS, DOWNE & CO. PRINTERS,

Stationers' Hall, 174 of 176 Pearl Street.

1852.

Example 640

```
American Print Works.
    The American Print Works vs. Cornelius W.
Lawrence ...


    I. Lawrence, Cornelius W.   II. New Jersey.
Supreme Court (Essex Circuit).   III. Title.
```

ME: 21.36C2; 24.1
AE: I. 21.36C2
AE: II. 21.36C2; 24.18, type 6; 24.23A
AE: III. 21.30J

INDICTMENT

IN THE UNITED STATES DISTRICT COURT

For the Southern District of New York

———

Criminal No. C 128-402

Title 18, Section 1621 U. S. C.

———

UNITED STATES OF AMERICA

Plaintiff

v.

ALGER HISS

Defendant

———

The Grand Jury charges:

1. That on the 15th day of December 1948, at the Southern District of New York and within the jurisdiction of this Court, Alger Hiss, the defendant herein, having duly taken an oath before a competent tribunal, to wit, the Grand Jurors of the United States of America, duly impanelled and sworn in the United States District Court for the Southern District of New York, and inquiring for that District in a case then and there pending before said Grand Jurors in which a law of the United States authorizes an oath to be administered, that he would testify truly, did unlawfully, knowingly and wilfully and contrary to said oath, state material matter which he did not believe to be true, that is to say:

2. That at the time and place aforesaid, the said Grand Jurors, inquiring as aforesaid, were conducting an investigation entitled *United States v. John Doe,* pertaining to possible violations of espionage laws of the United States and any other Federal criminal statutes:

Example 641

Hiss, Alger.
　　Indictment in the United States District
Court for the Southern District of New York ...

　　I. United States. District Court (New York :
Southern District).　II. Title.

ME:　21.36C4; 21.36C1
AE:　I. 21.36C1; 24.18, type 6; 24.23A
AE:　II. 21.30J

OPINION

OF THE

SUPREME COURT OF THE UNITED STATES,

Delivered by Chief Justice Marshall, on the 21st of February, 1807, referred to in the trials of Colonel Burr.

The United States
vs.
Bollman and Swartwout. } *Habeas Corpus*, on a commitment for treason.

The prisoners having been brought before this court on a writ of *habeas corpus*, and the testimony on which they were committed having been fully examined and attentively considered, the court is now to declare the law upon their case.

This being a mere inquiry, which, without deciding upon guilt, precedes the institution of a prosecution, the question to be determined is whether the accused shall be discharged or held to trial; and if the latter, in what place they are to be tried, and whether they shall be confined, or admitted to bail. "If," says a very learned and accurate commentator, "upon this inquiry it manifestly appears that no such crime has been committed, or that the suspicion entertained of the prisoner was wholly groundless, in such cases only it is lawful totally to discharge him; otherwise he must either be committed to prison or give bail."

The specific charge brought against the prisoners is treason, in levying war against the United States.

As there is no crime which can more excite and agitate the passions of men than treason, no charge demands more from the tribunal before which it is made a deliberate and temperate inquiry. Whether this inquiry be directed to the fact or the law, none can be more solemn; none more important to the citizen or to the government; none can more affect the safety of both.

To prevent the possibility of those calamities which result from the extension of treason to offences of minor importance, that great fundamental law which defines and limits the various departments of our Government has given a rule on the subject,

xxxix

Example 642

United States. Supreme Court.
    Opinion of the Supreme Court of the United
States ...

    I. Bollman, Erich.   II. Title.

ME: 21.36C6; 24.18, type 6; 24.23A
AE: I. 21.36C6; 21.36C1
AE: II. 21.30J

CORRECTED OPINION

of

HAROLD R. MEDINA

United States Circuit Judge

in

UNITED STATES OF AMERICA,

Plaintiff,

—*v.*—

HENRY S. MORGAN, HAROLD STANLEY, *et. al.,*
doing business as Morgan Stanley & Co., *et. al.,*

Defendants.

Example 643

```
Medina, Harold R.
    Corrected opinion of Harold R. Medina, United
States circuit judge ...


    I. Morgan, Harry S.  II. United States.  III.
Title.
```

```
ME:  21.36C7
AE:  I & II. 21.36C7
AE:  III. 21.30J
```

This is a civil action, so added entry II. is appropriate.

Depending upon the entries in your catalog, you will want a reference of some sort between Henry S. Morgan and Morgan Stanley & Co.

```
        UNITED STATES COURT OF APPEALS
           FOR THE SECOND CIRCUIT

              _____



        UNITED STATES OF AMERICA,
                                         Appellee

                  against

           ALGER HISS,              Appellant



─────────────────────────────────────────────

             BRIEF FOR APPELLANT

─────────────────────────────────────────────



           Beer, Richards, Lane & Haller
              Attorneys for Appellant


   Robert M. Benjamin,
   Harold Rosenwald,
   Chester T. Lane,
   Kenneth Simon,
        Of Counsel.
```

Example 644

```
Hiss, Alger.
    United States of America, appellee, against
Alger Hiss, appellant ...


    I. Benjamin, Robert M.   II. Title.
```

ME: 21.36C8
AE: I. 21.36C8
AE: II. 21.30J

Since the brief was written by more than three lawyers, the compiler has chosen to use the "rule of three" and make an added entry only under the first one named.

IMPEACHMENT OF WM. W. BELKNAP.

ARGUMENT

OF

HON. MATT. H. CARPENTER

OF COUNSEL FOR RESPONDENT

IN THE

SENATE OF THE UNITED STATES

July 25 and 26, 1876

WASHINGTON
1876

Example 645

```
Carpenter, Matthew H.
     Argument of Hon. Matt. H. Carpenter, of coun-
sel for respondent, in the Senate of the United
States, July 25 and 26, 1876 ...


     I. Belknap, Wm. W. (William W.).   II. Title.
```

ME: 21.36C8; CSB 16, p. 38
AE: I. 21.36C8
AE: II. 21.30J

A

C O L L E C T I O N

OF

THE MOST REMARKABLE

AND

INTERESTING TRIALS

PARTICULARLY

Of the PERSONS who have FORFEITED their LIVES to the injured LAWS of their COUNTRY

IN WHICH

THE MOST REMARKABLE

OF THE

S T A T E T R I A L S

WILL BE INCLUDED

With the DEFENCE and BEHAVIOUR of the CRIMINAL before and after CONDEMNATION

INTENDED

Not only to point out the CRIMES of the GREAT, which are at present but little farther known than their own FAMILIES

BUT

Also those of INFERIOR CRIMINALS, who only are handed down as EXAMPLES TO POSTERITY.

V O L. 1.

Example 646

A Collection of the most remarkable and interesting trials ...

ME: 21.36C9

UNITED STATES DEPARTMENT OF AGRICULTURE

AGRICULTURE DECISIONS

DECISIONS OF THE SECRETARY OF AGRICULTURE

UNDER THE

REGULATORY LAWS ADMINISTERED IN THE
UNITED STATES DEPARTMENT OF AGRICULTURE

(Including Court Decisions)

VOL. 39   No. 1

(Nos. 19,579—19,664)

Pages 1—91

January 1980

Example 647

```
United States. Dept. of Agriculture.
    Agriculture decisions ...


    I. Title.
```

ME: 21.1B2(c); 21.4B; 24.20E; 24.18, type 1
AE: I. 21.30J

The Library of Congress Office for Descriptive Cataloging Policy has indicated that decisions and opinions of administrative agencies may be treated as examples of 21.1B2(c).

UNITED STATES DEPARTMENT OF AGRICULTURE

———————

DIGEST

OF

DECISIONS OF SECRETARY OF AGRICULTURE

UNDER THE

PACKERS AND STOCKYARDS ACT

(7 U.S.C., SECS. 181-229)

Act approved August 15, 1921 (42 Stat. 159)
Act amended May 5, 1926 (44 Stat. 397
[7 U.S.C., sec. 205]), August 14, 1935
(49 Stat. 648 [7 U.S.C., secs. 218-218d]),
and June 29, 1937 (50 Stat. 395, 406).

———————

Including Resumes of Cases Appealed from the Secretary's
Decisions, Cases Testing the Constitutionality and Scope
of the Act, Cases Related to the Packers and Stockyard Act
or to the Secretary's Decision Made under the Act, Criminal
Cases Arising Pursuant to the Provisions of the Act, and
Opinions of the Attorney General Construing Provisions of
the Act, up to June 30, 1940.

———————

Prepared by the Office of the Solicitor

In cooperation with the

Agricultural Marketing Service

Compilation by: Linus R. Fike, Attorney

Washington, D.C.

Example 648

United States. Dept. of Agriculture. Office of the
    Solicitor.
    Digest of decisions of the secretary of agri-
culture under the Packers and Stockyards Act (7
U.S.C., secs. 181-229) ... / United States Department of Agriculture ; prepared by the Office of
the Solicitor, in cooperation with the Agricultural Marketing Service ; compilation by Linus R.
Fike. -- Washington, D.C. : [s.n., 1942].
    viii, 940 p. ; 27 cm.

    Subtitle: Including resumes of cases appealed
from the secretary's decisions, cases testing the
constitutionality and scope of the act, cases
related to the Packers and Stockyards Act or to
the secretary's decision made under the act,
criminal cases arising pursuant to the provisions
of the act, and opinions of the attorney general
construing provisions of the act, up to June 30,
1940.
    "Act approved August 15, 1921 (42 Stat. 159);
Act amended May 5, 1926 (44 Stat. 397 [7 U.S.C.,
sec. 205]), August 14, 1935 (49 Stat. 648 [7
U.S.C., secs. 218-218d]), and June 29, 1937 (50
Stat. 395, 406)."

    I. United States. Agricultural Marketing
Service. II. Fike, Linus R.   III. Title.

D: A.13H; 1.1E3; 1.7B5; A.20
ME: 21.1B2(a); 21.1B4

STATE OF NEW YORK

—————

OPINIONS

of the

ATTORNEY GENERAL

for the

YEAR ENDING DECEMBER 31, 1975

—————

LOUIS J. LEFKOWITZ
Attorney General

Example 649

```
New York (State). Attorney General.
    Opinions of the Attorney General ...


    I. Title.
```

ME: 21.1B2(c); 21.4B, option 2; 23.4B; 24.6B; CSB 6, p. 18; 24.20E;
      24.18, type 3
AE: 21.30J

U.S. MARITIME COMMISSION REPORTS

DIGEST

By

JOHN H. EISENHART, JR.

Member of the Bar of the District of Columbia.
Trial Examiner, U.S. Maritime Commission.

Published by

AMERICAN MARITIME CASES, Inc.
BALTIMORE
1940

Example 650

Eisenhart, John H.
    U.S. Maritime Commission reports digest ...

    I. United States. Maritime Commission. II.
United States. Maritime Commission. Reports. III.
Title.

ME: 21.10; 21.1A2
AE: I. 21.30E; 24.18, type 2
AE: II. 21.28B
AE: III. 21.30J

One might also catalog this by analogy with rule 21.36B.

UNITED STATES DEPARTMENT OF THE INTERIOR

Washington, D.C.　20240

Secretary of the Interior: **Rogers C. B. Morton**
Office of Hearings and Appeals: **James M. Day,** *Director*
Office of the Solicitor: **Kent Frizzell,** *Solicitor*

CUMULATIVE INDEX-DIGEST
OF UNPUBLISHED DECISIONS
FOR THE PERIOD 1943-1954 INCLUSIVE

This Index-Digest covers all the important unpublished Decisions, Letters Memorandums, Memorandum Opinions and Solicitor's Opinions of the Department from 1943 to 1954.

Copies of this Digest may be obtained from the Superintendent of Documents, U.S. Government Printing Office, Washington, D.C. 20402.

CONTENTS

Symbols --- I

Topical Index to Decisions, Letters, Memorandums, Memorandum Opinions
and Solicitor's Opinions--- II

Table of Decisions-- X

Table of Letters-- CXXV

Table of Memorandums--- CXV

Table of Memorandum Opinions-- CXX

Table of Opinions--- XC

INDEX-DIGEST --

Example 651

Cumulative index-digest of unpublished decisions
for the period 1943-1954 inclusive ...

　　　I. United States. Dept. of the Interior.　II.
United States. Dept. of the Interior. Office of
the Solicitor.

ME:　21.10; 21.1C; 21.5A
AE:　I. 21.30E; 24.18, type 1
AE:　II. 21.30E; 24.18, type 2; 24.19; 24.20E

One might also catalog this by analogy with rule 21.36B.

LC will use the abbreviated form "Dept." (CSB 6, p. 23).

OUTER CONTINENTAL SHELF

H E A R I N G S

BEFORE THE

SUBCOMMITTEE ON
MINERALS, MATERIALS, AND FUELS

OF THE

COMMITTEE ON
INTERIOR AND INSULAR AFFAIRS
UNITED STATES SENATE
NINETY-FIRST CONGRESS

SECOND SESSION

ON

ISSUES RELATED TO ESTABLISHMENT OF SEAWARD
BOUNDARY OF UNITED STATES OUTER CONTINENTAL SHELF AND RELATED MATTER,
INCLUDING S. 3070, TO AMEND THE OUTER CONTINENTAL SHELF LANDS ACT

———————

SEPTEMBER 22 AND 23, 1970

———————

PART 3

Printed for the use of the
Committee on Interior and Insular Affairs

———————

U.S. GOVERNMENT PRINTING OFFICE

52-035

WASHINGTON: 1970

Example 652

```
United States. Congress. Senate. Committee on
     Interior and Insular Affairs. Subcommittee
     on Minerals, Materials, and Fuels.
  Outer continental shelf : hearings ...


  I. Title.
```

ME: 21.1B2(b); 21.4B; 24.18, type 5; 24.21C
AE: I. 21.30J

NATIONAL CONSUMER PROTECTION HEARINGS

Federal Trade Commission

November 1968

Example 653

```
National consumer protection hearings...


        I. United States. Federal Trade Commission.
```

ME: 21.1C
AE: I. 21.30E; 24.18, type 4

The Library of Congress Office for Descriptive Cataloging Policy has indicated that administrative hearings may not be considered to fall under 21.1B2 and therefore may not be entered under corporate body.

UNIFORM BUILDING CODE

Preface: enacted by the International Conference of Building Officials

1979 EDITION

Example 654

```
International Conference of Building Officials.
     Uniform building code ...


     I. Title.
```

ME: 21.1B2(c); 24.1
AE: I. 21.30J

The Library of Congress Office for Descriptive Cataloging Policy has indicated that model and uniform codes can be seen as to record the collective thought of the body from which they emanate. Therefore they may be entered under 21.1B2(c).

Example 655

Bijou Theatre (Cloquet, Minn.).
    [Contract] 1909 Dec. 1, between J.J. Ellis-
A.E. Nelson, Bijou Theatre, Cloquet, Minn., and
Rodgers & Marvin [manuscript].
    [2] p. on 1 leaf ; 31 cm.

    In part ms.
    Summary: Contract for Rodgers & Marvin to
perform at the Bijou Theatre for one week beginning Dec. 20, 1909.

    I. Willis, J. J. II. Nelson, A. E. III.
Rodgers & Marvin (Singers).

D: 4.1B1
ME: 21.1B2(a), 21.6C1
AE: I.-II. 21.30F
        III. 21.6C1, 24.4B

Chapter 16

LITURGICAL WORKS

Introduction

This chapter is based on *A Manual of AACR 2 Examples for Liturgical Works,* both the first edition by Irene Schilling and the second edition by Jim Kellen, with examples added from several other manuals. Not every rule in *AACR 2* that deals with religious works is illustrated . This chapter does include some religious works that are not liturgical works or sacred scriptures.

Although the examples in this chapter are primarily of monographic materials, a few examples of other types of materials are included to help illustrate the fact that format does not affect the choice and form of entry or the use of uniform titles.

It should be pointed out that uniform titles are optional. Uniform titles are given in the examples of this chapter whenever prescribed by the rules. Individual libraries, however, must make their own decisions whether or not to use them.

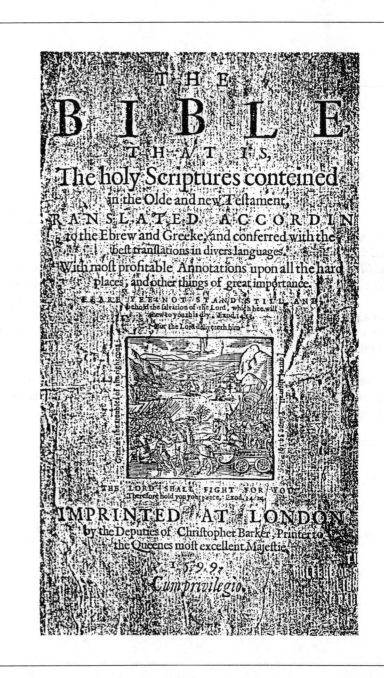

Example 656

Bible. English. Geneva. 1599.
   The Bible : that is, The Holy Scriptures
contained in the Olde and New Testament translated
according to the Ebrew and Greeke, and conferred
with the best translations in divers languages ;
with most profitable annotations upon all the hard
places, and other things of great importance. --
London : Imprinted ... by the deputies of Christo-
pher Barker ..., 1599.
   [4], 474, 122, [14] leaves : ill., 26 cuts, 4
maps, plan. ; 26 cm. (4to)

   First ed. of the Geneva version, the earliest
Bible printed in Roman type, with verse divisions.
Translated by William Whittingham, Anthony Gilby.
Thomas Sampson (and others?) at Geneva. The New
Testament revised from Whittingham's edition
(Geneva, 1557) also published separately in 1599.
   References: British and Foreign Bible Soci-
ety. Historical catalogue of printed Bibles.
   Signatures: ***4, a-z⁴, A-Z⁴, Aa-Zz⁴, Aaaa-
Zzzz⁴, Aaaaa-Bbbbb⁴, AA-ZZ⁴, AAa-LLl⁴.
   Also called the Breeches Bible from the head-
ing "breeches" (for aprons) in Gen. III, 7.
   New Testament has special t.p.: The Newe
Testament of Our Lord, Jesus Christ : conferred
diligently with the Greke, and best approved
translations, in divers languages. [woodcut]
   Books except the Apochrypha, Mark, Luke,
John, John I, and John II preceded by "Argument."
   Woodcut on t.p.

   I. Whittingham, William, d.1579.   II. Gilby,
Anthony, d.1585.   III. Sampson, Thomas, 1517?-
1589.

D: 1.1B1 2.16F 2.18C. 2.7B7 2.7B10
ME: 25.17 25.18A1 25.18A10 25.18A11 25.18A13
X   26.4A1

THE
INTERPRETER'S BIBLE

———

THE HOLY SCRIPTURES

IN THE KING JAMES AND REVISED
STANDARD VERSIONS WITH GENERAL
ARTICLES AND INTRODUCTION, EXEGESIS,
EXPOSITION FOR EACH BOOK OF THE BIBLE

IN TWELVE VOLUMES

VOLUME
1

דבר־אלהינו יקום לעולם

NEW YORK   *Abington Press*   **NASHVILLE**

Example 657

Bible. English. Authorized. 1951.
    The interpreter's Bible : the Holy Scriptures
in the King James and Revised Standard versions
with general articles and introduction, exegesis,
exposition for each book of the Bible / [editorial
board, George Arthur Buttrick ... et al.]. -- New
York, Abingdon, 1951-1957.
    12 v. : ill., maps ; 26 cm.

    Includes bibliographies and indexes.

    I. Buttrick, George Arthur, 1892-   II.
Bible. English. Revised Standard. 1952.   III.
Title.

D: A19J, 1.1F1, 1.1F5, 1.4C5, 1.4F8, 2.5B17, 2.5C2
ME: 21.13C, 21.37A, 25.17, 25.18A10, 25.18A11, 25.18A13
AE: 25.18A11, 21.30D, 22.18, 21.30J

New World Translation
of the
Holy Scriptures

Rendered from the Original Languages
by the
NEW WORLD BIBLE TRANSLATION COMMITTEE
—Revised A.D. 1961—

"THIS IS WHAT THE LORD JEHOVAH [יהוה YHWH]
HAS SAID: '. . .HERE I AM CREATING NEW HEAVENS
AND A NEW EARTH; AND THE FORMER THINGS
WILL NOT BE CALLED TO MIND,
NEITHER WILL THEY COME UP INTO THE HEART.' "
—ISAIAH 65:13, 17; also see 2 Peter 3:13.

Example 658

Bible. English. New World. 1961.
    New World translation of the Holy Scriptures
/ rendered from the original languages by the New
World Bible Translation Committee. -- Rev. A.D.
1961. -- Brooklyn : Watchtower Bible and Tract
Society of New York, 1961.
    1460 p. : maps, plans ; 19 cm.

    I. New World Bible Translation Committee.

D: 1.2B1
ME: 21.37A; 25.18A1; 25.18A10; 25.18A11; 25.18A13
AE: 21.30K1

THE ANCHOR BIBLE

GENESIS

INTRODUCTION, TRANSLATION, AND NOTES
BY
E. A. SPEISER

Doubleday & Company, Inc.

Garden City, New York

1964

Example 659

<u>Whole work</u>

Bible. English. Anchor Bible. 1964.
    The Anchor Bible. -- Garden City, N.Y. : Dou-
bleday, 1964-
    v. ; 25 cm.

    I. Title.

ME: 21.37A; 25.18A1; 25.18A10; 25.18A12; 25.18A13

Example 660

One volume

Bible. O.T. Genesis. English. Speiser. 1964.
    Genesis / introduction, translation and notes
by E.A. Speiser. -- 1st ed. -- Garden City, N.Y. :
Doubleday, 1964.
    lxxvi, 378 p. ; 25 cm. -- (The Anchor Bible;
1)

    I. Speiser, E.A. II. Title. III. Series:
Bible. English. Anchor Bible. 1964 ; 1.

D: 1.6B1
ME: 21.37A; 25.18A1; 25.18A2; 25.18A3; 25.18A10; 25.18A12;
      25.18A13
AE: I. 21.30K1; II. 21.30L

Type: a Bib lvl: m Govt pub: Lang: eng Source: d illus:
Repr: Enc lvl: I Conf pub: 0 Ctry: nyu Dat tp: s M/F/B: 00
Indx: 0 Mod rec: Festschr: 0 Cont: b
Desc: a Int lvl: Dates: 1964,

    010
    040   XXX $c XXX
    041   engheb
    090
    049   XXXX
    130 00 Bible. $p O.T. $p Genesis. $1 English. $s
Speiser. $f 1964.
    245 10 Genesis / $c introduction, translation and
notes by E.A. Speiser.
    250   1st ed.
    260 0 Garden City, N.Y. : $b Doubleday, $c 1964.
    300   lxxvi, 378 p. ; $c 25 cm.
    490 0 The Anchor Bible; $v 1
    700 10 Speiser, E.A.
    830 0 Bible. $1 English. $s Anchor Bible ; $v 1.

THE JERUSALEM BIBLE

DOUBLEDAY & COMPANY, INC.
GARDEN CITY, NEW YORK

GENERAL EDITOR
ALEXANDER JONES
L.S.S., S.T.L., L.C.B.

The list of all those who have helped in the preparation of this Bible is too long to be given in its entirety. The principal collaborators in translation and literary revision were:

Joseph Leo Alston	D. O. Lloyd James
Florence M. Bennett	James McAuley
Joseph Blenkinsopp	Alan Neame
David Joseph Bourke	Hubert Richards
Douglas Carter	Edward Sackville-West
Aldhelm Dean O.S.B.	Ronald Senator
Illtud Evans, O.P.	Walter Shewring
Kenelm Foster, O.P.	Robert Speaight
Ernest Graf, O.S.B.	J. R. R. Tolkien
Prospero Grech, O.S.A.	R. F. Trevett
Edmund Hill, O.P.	Thomas Worden
Sylvester Houédard, O.S.B.	John Wright
Leonard Johnston	Basil Wrighton
Anthony J. Kenny	

Example 661

Bible. English. Jerusalem Bible. 1966.
    The Jerusalem Bible / [general editor, Alexander Jones]. -- Garden City, N.Y. : Doubleday, 1966.
    xvi, 1547, 498 p., [4] p. of plates : 9 maps (some col.) ; 24 cm.

    "The principal collaborators in translation and literary revision were: Joseph Leo Alston ... [et al.]"--Prelim.
    Includes index.

    I. Jones, Alexander, 1906-   II. Title.

D: 1.1F1, 1.4D2, 2.5B2, 2.5B10, 2.5C2 & 2.5C3, 2.5C4, 2.7B6, 1.1F5,
       1.7A3, 2.7B18
ME: 21.37A, 25.17, 25.18A10, 25.18A11, 25.18A13, 25.2A
AE: 21.30D, 22.18, 21.30J

Saint Joseph Edition of

THE NEW AMERICAN BIBLE

Translated from the Original Languages
with Critical Use of All the Ancient Sources

INCLUDING
THE REVISED NEW TESTAMENT

AUTHORIZED BY THE BOARD OF TRUSTEES
of the
CONFRATERNITY OF CHRISTIAN DOCTRINE

and

APPROVED BY THE ADMINISTRATIVE COMMITTEE/BOARD
of the
NATIONAL CONFERENCE OF CATHOLIC BISHOPS
and the
UNITED STATES CATHOLIC CONFERENCE

WITH MANY HELPS FOR BIBLE READING

Vatican II Constitution on Divine Revelation, How to Read the Bible,
Historical Survey of the Lands of the Bible, Bible Dictionary,
Liturgical Index of Sunday Readings, Doctrinal Bible Index,
and over 50 Photographs and Maps of the Holy Land

CATHOLIC BOOK PUBLISHING CO.
NEW YORK

NIHIL OBSTAT:	Stephen J. Hartdegen, O.F.M., S.S.L.
	Christian P. Ceroke, O. Carm., S.T.D.
IMPRIMATUR:	✠ Patrick Cardinal O'Boyle, D.D.
	Archbishop of Washington

July 27, 1970

THE REVISED NEW TESTAMENT

NIHIL OBSTAT:	Stephen J. Hartdegen, O.F.M., S.S.L.
	Censor Deputatus
IMPRIMATUR:	✠ James A. Hickey, S.T.D., J.C.D.
	Archbishop of Washington

August 27, 1986

"Let them remember that prayer should accompany the reading of Sacred Scripture, so that God and man may talk together."
(Dogmatic Constitution on Divine Revelation: Second Vatican Council)

Prayer to the Holy Spirit

COME, Holy Spirit, fill the hearts of your faithful and enkindle in them the fire of your love.

Partial Indulgence. *Enchiridion Indulgentiarum*, 1968 edition, no. 62

A partial indulgence is granted to the faithful who use Sacred Scripture for spiritual reading with the veneration due the word of God. A plenary indulgence is granted if the reading continues for at least one half hour.
(*Enchiridion Indulgentiarum*, 1968 edition, no. 50)

Example 662

Bible. English. New American. 1987.
   Saint Joseph edition of the New American
Bible : including the revised New Testament /
authorized by the Board of Trustees of the Confra-
ternity of Christian Doctrine and approved by the
Administrative Committee/Board of the National
Conference of Catholic Bishops and the United
States Catholic Conference. -- New York : Catholic
Book Pub. Co., c1987.
   1103, 436 p., [25] leaves ofj plates : ill.
(some col.), maps ; 22 cm.

   "Translated from the original languages with
critical use of all the ancient sources."
   "With many helps for Bible reading."
   O.T. copyright 1970; N.T. copyright 1986; all
other materials copyright 1987.
   "Doctrinal Bible index": p. 428-436.

   I. Confraternity of Christine Doctrine. II.
Catholic Church. National Conference of Catholic
Bishops. III. Title. IV. Title: New American
Bible.

ME: 21.37A, 25.17, 25.18A10 , 25.18A11, 25.18A9, 25.18A13
D.:   1.1F1, 1.4D2, 2.5B10, 1.1F15, 1.7A3
AE: 21.30E , 21.30J
exp. ref.: 26.3C1

United States Catholic Conference
   United States Catholic Conference and the National Conference of
Catholic Bishops are the same body; same staff and offices; different
names for tax reasons; USCC is the name used for legal and corporate
affairs; NCCB is the name used for ecclesiastical decisions of the body. --
LC Authority File

United States Catholic Conference
   United States Catholic Conference is a civil entity of the American
Catholic bishops; NCCB is a distinct entity from the USCC; the relation-
ship of the NCCB to the USCC is that of a sponsoring organization. --
Official Catholic Directory, 1986

THE
READER'S
DIGEST
BIBLE

CONDENSED FROM
THE REVISED STANDARD VERSION
OLD AND NEW TESTAMENTS

General Editor
BRUCE M. METZGER
PH.D., D.D., L.H.D., D. Theol.
Princeton Theological
Seminary

THE READER'S DIGEST ASSOCIATION
PLEASANTVILLE, NEW YORK
LONDON, MONTREAL, SYDNEY, CAPE TOWN, HONG KONG

Example 663

Bible. English. Revised Standard. Selections.
    1982.
    The Reader's Digest Bible / condensed from
the Revised Standard Version, Old and New Testa-
ments ; general editor, Bruce M. Metzger. -- 1st
ed. -- Pleasantville, N.Y. : Reader's Digest
Association, c1982.
    xvi, 799 p. ; 24 cm.

    Lacks chapter and verse divisions.
    Includes index.

    I. Metzger, Bruce M. (Bruce Manning).   II.
Reader's Digest Association.   III. Title.

ME: 21.37A, 25.17, 25.18A10, 25.18A11 , 25.18A9, 25.18A13
D: 1.1F1, 1.1B1, 1.2B1, 1.4C3, 2.7B18
AE: 21.30D, 22.16A, 21.30E, 21.30J

The

Interlinear

HEBREW/GREEK
ENGLISH

Bible

Four Volume Edition

Volume One

(Genesis - Ruth)

Jay Green,

general editor and translator

ASSOCIATED PUBLISHERS AND AUTHORS
WILMINGTON, DELAWARE 19808

1976

Example 664

```
Bible. Hebrew-Greek. 1976.
     The interlinear Hebrew/Greek English Bible /
Jay Green, general editor and translator. -- 4 v.
ed. -- Wilmington, Del. (P.O. Box 5103, Wilmington
Del. 19808) : Associated Publishers and Authors,
1976-1979.
     4 v. ; 24 cm.


     I. Green, Jay.  II. Bible. English. Green.
1976.  II. Title.
```

Cross references

```
Bible. O.T. Hebrew ...
     see also
Bible. Hebrew-Greek ...


Bible. N.T. Greek ...
     see also
Bible. Hebrew-Greek ...
```

D: 1.1B1, 1.1F1, 1.2B1, 1.4C7, 1.4F8, 2.5B17
ME: 21.37A, 25.17, 25.18A10a, 25.18A12, 25.18A13
AE: 21.30D, 25.18A10, 25.18A11, 25.18A13, 21.30J
SA: 25.18A10

THE
PSALMS

for
Modern
Man

Today's English Version

Example 665

```
Bible. O.T. Psalms. English. Today's English.
     1970.
     The Psalms for modern man : Today's English
version. -- [New York?] : American Bible Society,
c1970.
     211 p. : ill. ; 19 cm.


     I. American Bible Society.   II. Title.
```

ME: 21.37A, 25.17, 25.18A2, 25.18A3, 25.18A10, 25.18A11, 25.18A13
D: 1.1B1, 1.1F2, 1.4C6
AE: 21.30E, 21.30J

===============================

THE FOUR TRANSLATION NEW TESTAMENT

**KING JAMES
NEW AMERICAN STANDARD BIBLE
WILLIAMS—IN THE LANGUAGE OF THE PEOPLE
BECK—IN THE LANGUAGE OF TODAY**

===============================

**Printed for
DECISION MAGAZINE
by
WORLD WIDE PUBLICATIONS
1313 Hennepin Avenue
Minneapolis, Minnesota 55403**

Example 666

```
Bible. N.T. English. 1966.
    The four translation New Testament : King
James, New American Standard Bible, Williams--in
the language of the people, Beck--in the language
of today. -- Minneapolis, Minn. : Printed for
Decision Magazine by World Wide Publications,
1966.
    xxviii, 739 p. ; 24 cm.


    I. Title.
```

D: A.19L, 1.1F2, 1.4D3a
ME: 21.37A, 25.18A2, 25.18A10, 25.18A12, 25.18A13
AE: 21.30J

THE SONG OF SONGS

A Study, Modern Translation and Commentary

by

R O B E R T G O R D I S

NEW YORK

THE JEWISH THEOLOGICAL SEMINARY OF AMERICA

5714 - 1954

Example 667

Gordis, Robert, 1908-
     The Song of Songs : a study, modern transla-
tion, and commentary / by Robert Gordis. -- New
York : Jewish Theological Seminary of America,
1954.
     xii, 108 p. ; 24 cm. -- (Texts and studies of
the Jewish Theological Seminary of America ; v.
20)

     Date also appears as: 5714.
     Bibliography: p. 99-106.

     I. Bible. O.T. Song of Solomon. English.
Gordis. 1954. II. Title. III. Series.

Cross references

Bible. O.T. Song of Songs.
     see
Bible. O.T. Song of Solomon

Bible. O.T. Canticle of Canticles.
     see
Bible. O.T. Song of Solomon

Bible. O.T. Solomon, Song of.
     see
Bible. O.T. Song of Solomon

ME: 21.13B, 22.1A, 22.18
D: A.19J, 1.4F1, 2.6B1, 1.6G1, 2.7B9, 2.7B18
AE: 21.30G, 25.17, 25.18A2, 25.18A3, 25.18A10, 25.18A11,
      25.18A13, 21.30J, 21.30L
X   25.18A6

GOSPEL PARALLELS

A Synopsis of the First Three Gospels

With alternative readings from the Manuscripts and Noncanonical Parallels

Text used is the Revised Standard Version, 1952

The arrangement follows the Huck-Lietzmann Synopsis, Ninth edition, 1936

Edited by Burton H. Throckmorton, Jr.

THOMAS NELSON & SONS

TORONTO   **NEW YORK**   EDINBURGH

Example 668

```
Bible. N.T. Gospels. English. Revised Standard.
   Selections. 1957.
   Gospel parallels : a synopsis of the first
three Gospels : with alternative readings from the
manuscripts and noncanonical parallels / edited by
Burton H. Throckmorton, Jr. -- 2nd ed., rev. --
New York : Nelson, 1957.
   xxv, 191 p. ; 26 cm.
   "Text used is the Revised Standard Version,
1952. The arrangement follows the Huck-Lietzmann
synopsis, ninth edition, 1936."
   Includes indexes.


   I. Throckmorton, Burton H.   II. Title.
```

D: 1.1E2, 1.1A1, 1.2B1, 2.7B18
ME: 21.37B, 25.17, 25.18A2, 25.18A4, 25.18A10, 25.18A11, 25.18A9, 25.18A13
AE: 21.30D, 21.30J

Tabernacle Pictures

IN FILMSTRIP

"SEEKING THE LOST"

Luke 15

The Sheep - The Coin - The Son

Produced by
GOSPEL SLIDE & FILM SERVICE
Box 1143 - 923 South Eye St.
Tacoma 3, Washington

SEEKING

THE LOST

produced by
Gospel Slide and Film Service

arranged by Adam B. Hunter

Artist - William Fay

Copyright - Adam B. Hunter

Example 669

Bible. N.T. Luke XV. English. Authorized. 1951.
   Seeking the lost [filmstrip] / produced by
Gospel Slide and Film Service ; arranged by Adam
B. Hunter ; artist, William Fay. -- Tacoma, Wash.
: The Service [1951]
   1 filmstrip (35 fr.) : col. ; 35 mm. + 1
script.

   On text and container: Tabernacle Pictures.
   Summary: The parables of the lost sheep, the
lost coin, and the prodigal son are depicted in
pictures with accompanying script in the words of
the Authorized Version of Luke XV.

   I. Hunter, Adam B. II. Fay, William. III.
Gospel Slide and Film Service. IV. Title.

D: 8.1B1, 8.1C1, 8.1F1, 1.4C1, 1.4D4, 8.4F1, 8.5B1, 8.5B2, 8.5C4 ,
     8.5D2, 8.5E1, 8.7B6, 8.7B17
ME: 21.11A, 21.37A, 25.17, 25.18A2, 25.18A3, 25.18A10, 25.18A11,
     25.18A13
AE: 21.30F, 21.30K2, 21.30E, 21.30J

HARMONIA
QVATUOR
EVANGELISTA-
RVM,

E
THEOLOGIS CELEBERRIMIS,
D. MARTINO CHEMNITIO
PRIMUM INCHOATA,

D. POLYCARPO LYSERO
POST CONTINUATA,

ATQVE
D. JOHANNE GERHARDO
tandem feliciffime absoluta.

QVÆ
NVNC PERFECTA, IVSTO COMMENTARIO

TOMUS PRIMUS.

QVI EST CHEMNITII ET LYSERI.

Cum Gratia & Privilegio S. Reg. Maj. Sveciæ &
Electoris Saxoniæ.

FRANCOFVRTI ET HAMBVRGI
Sumtibus Zachariæ Hertelij Bibliopolæ Hamburgensis.
ANNO M. DC. LII.

HARMONIÆ
QVATUOR
EVANGELISTA-
RVM,

A
THEOLOGIS CELEBERRIMIS,
D. MARTINO CHEMNITIO
PRIMUM INCHOATÆ,

D. POLYCARPO LYSERO
POST CONTINUATÆ,

ATQVE
D. JOHANNE GERHARDO
tandem feliciffime abfolutæ, &c.

TOMVS SECUNDUS,

QVI SOLIVS EST JOH. GERHARDI.

Cum Gratia & Privilegio S. Cæfareæ Maj. &
S. Reg. Maj. Sveciæ.

FRANCOFVRTI ET HAMBVRGI
Sumtibus Zachariæ Hertelij Bibliopolæ Hamburgensis.
ANNO M. DC. LII.

Example 670

Bible. N.T. Gospels. Greek. Selections. 1652.
    Harmonia quatuor evangelistarum / a Martino
Chemnitio, primum inchoata ; Polycarpo Lysero,
post continuata ; atque Johanne Gerhardo, tandem
felicissime absoluta. -- Quae nunc perfecta, iusto
commentario illustrata, duobus tomis comprehensa,
multum auctior, juxta & indicibus variis ac neces-
sariis ornata prodit. ... -- Francofurti ; Ham-
burgi : Sumtibus Z. Hertelii, 1652.
    2 v. ; 37 cm. (fol.)
    Signatures: v.1: g^6, gg^6, A^6-Z^6, Aa^6-Zz^6, Aaa^6-
Zzz^6, $Aaaa^6$-$Zzzz^6$, $Aaaaa^6$-$Zzzzz^6$, $Aaaaaa^6$-$Oooooo^4$.
v.2: t^6-ttt^6, A^6-Z^6, Aa^6-Zz^6, Aaa^6-Zzz^6, $Aaaa^6$-$Zzzz^6$,
$Aaaaa^6$-$Zzzzz^6$, $Aaaaaa^6$-$Zzzzzz^6$, $Aaaaaaa^6$-$Eeeeeee^8$,
A^6-Z^6, Aa^6-Zz^6, Aaa^6, a^6-q^6.
    Vol. 1 by M. Chemnitz and P. Leyser; v. 2 by
J. Gerhard.
    In Greek and Latin.
    Vol. 2 has title: Harmoniae quatuor evangis-
tarum. Lacks ed. statement.

    I. Chemnitz, Martin, 1522-1584. II. Leyser,
Polycarp, 1552-1637. III. Gerhard, Johann, 1582-
1610. IV. Bible. N.T. Gospels. Latin. Selections.
1652. V. Title.

D:	21.2B2
ME:	21.37B 21.13D2 25.17 25.18A1-A2 25.18A4 25.18A9 25.18A13 25.18A6
AE:	I-III. 22.3B2
AE:	II. 22.3D
AE:	IV. 25.18A10
x II:	26.2A2

NENE

KARIGHWIYOSTON

TSINIHORIGHHOTEN NE

SAINT JOHN.

THE

GOSPEL

ACCORDING TO

SAINT JOHN.

London: printed for the

BRITISH AND FOREIGN BIBLE SOCIETY

By Phillips & Fardon, George Yard, Lombard Street.

Example 671

Bible. N.T. John. Mohawk. Norton. 1805.
    Nene karighwiyoston tsinihorighhoten ne Saint
John = The gospel according to Saint John. --
London : Printed for the British and Foreign Bible
Society by Phillips & Fardon, 1805.
    125, 125 p. ; 15 cm.

    Translated by John Norton.
    Mohawk and English on opposite pages, the
pages numbered in duplicate.

    I. Bible. N.T. John. English. Authorized.
1805. II. Norton, John. III. Title: The gospel
according to Saint John.

D: 1.1D1; 2.7B2; 1.7B6; 1.7B2; 2.5B13
ME: 21.37A; 25.18A1; 25.18A2; 25.18A3; 25.18A10; 25.18A11;
    25.18A13
AE: 25.18A10; 25.18A1; 25.18A2; 25.18A3; 25.18A11; 25.18A13;
    21.30K1

Type: a Bib lvl: m Govt pub: Lang: moh Source: d illus:
Repr: Enc lvl: I Conf pub: 0 Ctry: enk Dat tp: s M/F/B: 10
Indx: 0 Mod rec: Festschr: 0 Cont:
Desc: a Int lvl: Dates: 1805,

    010
    040   XXX $c XXX
    041 1   moheng $h enggrc
    090
    049   XXXX
    130 00 Bible. $p N.T. $p John. $l Mohawk. $s Nor-
ton. $f 1805.
    245 10 Nene karighwiyoston tsinihorighhoten ne
Saint John = $b The gospel according to Saint John.
    260 0   London : $b Printed for the British and
Foreign Bible Society by Phillips & Fardon, $c 1805.
    300   125, 125 p. ; $c 15 cm.
    500   Translated by John Norton.
    500   Mohawk and English on opposite pages, the
pages numbered in duplicate.
    730 02 Bible. $p N.T. $p John. $l English. $s
Authorized. $f 1805.
    700 10 Norton, John.
    740 41 The gospel according to Saint John.

Die autem natalis herodis saltauit filia hero-
diadis inmedio & placuit herodi. Unde cum
iuramento pollicitus est ei dare quodcumq
postulasset ab eo. At illa premonita a matre
sua. Da mihi inquit hic indisco caput iohannis
baptistae. Et contristatus est rex. Propter iusiuran
dum autem & eos qui pariter recumbebant iussit
dari. Misitq & decollauit iohannem incarcere.
& allatum est caput eius indisco & datum est
puelle & tulit matrisue. Et accedentes discipuli
eius tulerunt corpus & sepelierunt illud.
Et uenientes nunciauerunt ihu.

Quod cum audisset ihs secessit inde innauicula inlocum desertum seorsum. Et cum au
dissent turbe secute sunt eum pedestres de
ciuitatibus. Et exiens uidit turbam multam.
& misertus est eius & curauit languidos eorum.
Vespere autem facto accesserunt adeum disci
puli eius dicentes. Desertus est locus & hora
iam preterit. dimitte turbas ut euntes in
castella emant sibi escas. Ihs autem dixit eis.
Nonhabent necesse ire. date illis uos mandu
care. Responderunt ei. Nonhabemus hic.

nisi quinq panes & duos pisces. Qui ait eis. Afferte
illos mihi huc. Et cum iussisset turbam discubere
sup fenum. Acceptis quinq panibus & duobus
piscibus aspiciens incelum benedixit & fregit
& dedit discipulis panes discipuli autem turbis.
Et manducauerunt omnes & saturati sunt. Et
tulerunt reliquias duodecim cophinos fragmen
torum plenos. Manducantium autem fuit nume
rus quinq milia uiroru exceptis mulieribus & paruulis
Et statim iussit discipulos ascendere innauicula
& precedere eu transfretu donec dimitteret turbas.
Et dimissa turba. Ascendit inmonte solus orare.
Uespere autem facto solus erat ibi. Nauicula autem
inmedio mari iactabatur fluctibus. Erat enim
uentus contrarius. Quarta autem uigilia noctis.
uenit adeos ambulans supmare. Et uidentes
eum supmare ambulantem turbati sunt
dicentes quia fantasma est. Et pretimore cla
mauerunt. Statimq ihs locutus est eis dicens.
Habete fiduciam. Ego sum. nolite timere.
Respondens autem petrus dixit. Dne si tu es.
iube me uenire adte supaquas. At ipse ait.
Ueni. Et descendens petrus denauicula.

Example 672

Bible. N.T. Matthew XIV, 6-29. Latin.
   [Leaf from Gospel of Matthew, chapter 14,
verses 6-29] [manuscript]. -- [10--].
   [2] p. on 1 leaf (23 lines) : parchment ; 29 x
15 cm.

   Ms.
   Title supplied by cataloger.
   Carolingian script, second half of the 11th
century, written almost entirely without abbreviations. Probably from the Low Countries.

D: 1.4F7; 2.5B1; 4.5C1; 4.7B22
ME: 21.37A; 25.18A1, 25.18A2, 25.18A3, 25.18A10

```
Type: b Bib lvl: m Coll st:    Lang: 1st Source: d Illus:
Repr:   Enc lvl: I Con lvl:    Ctry: mnu Dat tp: q Pr st:
Desc: a Mod rec:               File: Dates: 1898,

    010
    040     XXX $c XXX
    090
    090     XXXX
    130 0   Bible. $p N.T. $p Matthew XIV, 6-29. $1
Latin.
    245 00  [Leaf from Gospel of Matthew, chapter 14,
verses 6-29] $h manuscript
    260     $c [10--].
    300     [2] p. on 1 leaf (23 lines) : $b parchment ;
$c 29 x 15 cm.
    500     Ms.
    500     Title supplied by cataloger.
    500     Carolingian script, second half of the 11th
century, written almost entirely without abbreviations.
Probably from the Low Countries.
```

THE EPISTLE

OF

PAUL THE APOSTLE

TO THE

ROMANS

WITH NOTES, COMMENTS, MAPS AND
ILLUSTRATIONS

BY

Rev. LYMAN ABBOTT

AUTHOR OF "DICTIONARY OF RELIGIOUS KNOWLEDGE," "JESUS OF NAZARETH,"
AND

A SERIES OF COMMENTARIES ON THE NEW TESTAMENT

COPYRIGHT, 1888

A.S. BARNES & COMPANY

NEW YORK AND CHICAGO.

Example 673

Bible. N.T. Romans. English. Authorized. 1888.
    Epistle of Paul the Apostle--Romans [micro-
form] / L. Abbott. -- Chicago, Ill. : Photographed
for the American Theological Library Association
Microtext Project by University of Chicago, Joseph
Regenstein Library, Dept. of Photoduplication,
1973.
    1 microfilm reel : ill. ; 35 mm. -- (ATLA ;
bk. 371)
    Contains no maps.
    Microreproduction of the original published
as: The Epistle of Paul the apostle to the Romans.
New York : A.S. Barnes, c1888. viii, 230 p.

    I. Abbott, Lyman, 1835-1922. II. Title.
III. Title: The Epistle of Paul the apostle to the
Romans.

D: 11.1B1, 11.1C1, 11.1F1, 11.4C1, 11.4D1, 11.4F1, 11.5B1, 11.5C2,
     11.5D4, 11.6B1, 11.7B, 1.7A3
ME: 21.13C, 21.37A, 25.17, 25.18A2, 25.18A3, 25.18A10, 25.18A11,
     25.18A13
AE: 21.13C, 21.30J

    Library of Congress has decided not to follow AACR2 when
cataloging microform reproductions of original works. It will continue to
catalog the reproductions according to the originals and add notes concerning the microreproductions.

Type: a Bib lvl: m Govt pub: Lang: eng Source: d illus:
Repr: a Enc lvl: I Conf pub: 0 Ctry: ilu Dat tp: r M/F/B: 00
Indx: 0 Mod rec: Festschr: 0 Cont:
Desc: a Int lvl: Dates: 1973,1888

    010
    040   XXX $c XXX
    007   h $b $c $d $e $f u--- $g b $h u $i c $j u
    041 1 eng $h grc
    090
    049   XXXX
    130 00 Bible. $p N.T. $p Romans. $l English. $s
Authorized. 1888.
    245 10 Epistle of Paul the Apostle--Romans $h
microform / $c L. Abbott.
    260 0 Chicago, Ill. : $b Photographed for the
American Theological Library Association Microtext Proj-
ect by University of Chicago, Joseph Regenstein Library,
Dept. of Photoduplication, $c 1973.
    300   1 microfilm reel : $b ill. ; $c 35 mm.
    490 0 ATLA ; $v bk. 371
    500   Contains no maps.
    500   Microreproduction of the original published
as: The Epistle of Paul the apostle to the Romans. New
York : A.S. Barnes, c1888. viii, 230 p.
    700 10 Abbott, Lyman, $d 1835-1922.
    740 41 The Epistle of Paul the apostle to the
Romans.

THE LIVING BIBLE

PARAPHRASED

TYNDALE HOUSE PUBLISHERS
Wheaton, Illinois

COVERDALE HOUSE PUBLISHERS LTD.
London, England

Distributed to the general book trade by
Doubleday & Company, Inc.

First printing, July 1971
Eighteenth printing, February 1973

Total Living Bibles in print: 7,875,000

The Living Bible is a compilation of the Scripture paraphrases previously published by Tyndale House Publishers under the following titles:
Living Letters, 1962; *Living Prophecies*, 1965; *Living Gospels*, 1966; *Living Psalms and Proverbs*, 1967; *Living Lessons of Life and Love*, 1968; *Living Books of Moses*, 1969; *Living History of Israel*, 1970.

Printed in the United States of America.

Library of Congress Catalog Card Number 78-156898
ISBN 8423-2250-7

Example 674

Taylor, Kenneth Nathaniel.
     The living Bible : paraphrased. -- Wheaton,
Ill. : Tyndale ; [Garden City, N.Y.] : Distributed
to the general book trade by Doubleday, 1971.
     1020 p. ; 23 cm.

     "A compilation of the Scripture paraphrases
previously published ... under the following
titles: Living letters, 1965; Living prophecies,
1965; Living Gospels, 1966; Living Psalms and
Proverbs, 1967; Living lessons of life and love,
1968; Living books of Moses, 1969; Living history
of Israel, 1970."
     ISBN 8423-2259-7.

     I. Bible. English. Taylor. 1971. II. Title.

D: 1.4C3, 1.4D1, 1.4D2, 1.4D3a, 2.7B7, 1.7A3, 1.8B1
ME: 21.10, 21.4A, 22.1A
AE: 21.30G, 25.17, 25.18A10, 25.18A12b, 25.18A13

AN
ANALYTICAL CONCORDANCE
TO THE
REVISED STANDARD VERSION
OF THE
NEW TESTAMENT

BY
CLINTON MORRISON

THE WESTMINSTER PRESS

PHILADELPHIA

Example 675

```
Morrison, Clinton, 1924-
    An analytical concordance to the Revised
Standard Version of the New Testament / by Clin-
ton Morrison. -- 1st ed. -- Philadelphia : West-
minster, 1979.
    xxv, 773 p. : 2 maps ; 28 cm.

    Includes index.
    ISBN 0-664-20773-1.


    I. Bible. N.T. English. Revised Standard.
1973.  II. Title.
```

D: 1.2B1, 2.5C2, 2.5C4, 2.7B18, 1.8B1
ME: 21.28A, 21.28B, 21.4A, 22.18
AE: 21.30G, 25.17, 25.18A2, 25.18A10, 25.18A11, 25.18A13, 21.30J

NEW ONE VOLUME EDITION

COMMENTARY

ON THE WHOLE BIBLE

by

Matthew Henry

———

GENESIS TO REVELATION

Edited by

Rev. Leslie F. Church, Ph.D., F.R.Hist.S.

ZONDERVAN PUBLISHING HOUSE
OF THE ZONDERVAN CORPORATION
GRAND RAPIDS, MICHIGAN 49506

Example 676

Henry, Matthew, 1662-1714.
    Commentary on the whole Bible : Genesis to
Revelation / by Matthew Henry. -- New 1 v. ed. /
edited by Leslie F. Church. -- Grand Rapids, Mich.
: Zondervan, 1961.
    ix, 1986 p. ; 25 cm.

    I. Church, Leslie F.   II. Title.

D: 1.2B1, 1.2C1, 1.4C3
ME: 21.12A, 22.18
AE: 21.12A, 21.30J

Example 677

```
Geier, Martin, 1614-1680.
    Commentarius in Psalmos Davidis, fontium
Ebraeorum mentem et vim vocum phrasiummque sacra-
rum : sensumque adeo genuinum adductis copiose
locis parallelis ... eruens / Martini Geieri. --
Editio altera, plurimus notarum accessionibus, ...
locupletior. -- Dresdae ; Francoforti ; Lipsiae :
Typis Sumptibus C. Bergenii, 1681.
    2654 columns ; 36 cm. (4to)

    In double columns.
    Signatures: ):(², ):( ):(², A⁴-Z⁴, Aa⁴-Zz⁴, Aaa⁴-
Zzz⁴, Aaaa⁴-Zzzz⁴, Aaaaa⁴-Uuuuu⁴, A⁶-C⁶.
    In Latin.
    "Ad finum habentur vocum Ebraicarum, idiotis-
morumque explicatorum, et rerum verborumque
luculenti indices."
    Manuscript notes in margins.


    I. Title.
```

D: 1.1F3, 1.1F7, 2.5B2, 2.14E, 2.14F, 2.17A, Appendix B.6
ME: 21.13

This is a commentary on the Psalms; in Latin with some Greek and Hebrew phrases. It does not contain the text of the Psalms.

REPORT & RECOMMENDATIONS

**of the
Commission for a New Lutheran Church
to
The American Lutheran Church
The Association of Evangelical Lutheran Churches
Lutheran Church in America**

June 25, 1986

Example 678

```
Commission for a New Lutheran Church.
     Report & recommendations of the Commission
for a New Lutheran Church to the American Lutheran
Church, the Association of Evangelical Lutheran
Churches, Lutheran Church in America. -- [Minnea-
polis? Minn.] : Evangelical Lutheran Church in
America, c1986.
     xxiv, 211 p. : port. ; 23 cm.

     "June 25, 1986."

     I. American Lutheran Church (1961-    ).  II.
Association of Evangelical Lutheran Churches.
III. Lutheran Church in America.  IV. Evangelical
Lutheran Church in America.  V. Title.  VI. Title:
Report and recommendations of the Commission for a
New Lutheran Church.
```

ME: 21.1B2c, 24.15A, 24.15A
D.:   1.1F1, 1.4C6, 1.4F5, 1.7A3
AE: 21.30E, 21.30J

THE LORD'S PRAYER

Franklin Watts, Inc.

This book, first impression 1960, published by
Franklin Watts, Inc., 575 Lexington Avenue, New York 22, N.Y.

The autolithographs are by *Charles Mozley*. The text has been handset in Baskerville type. The paper is Tielens Cartridge supplied by Corvey N.V., Amsterdam; printing from the original plates by L. van Leer & Co. N.V., Amsterdam; binding by Van Rijmenam N.V., The Hague, Holland

© illustrations and presentation Rainbird, McLean Ltd 1960

Printed in The Netherlands

Example 679

Lord's prayer. English.
    The Lord's prayer. -- New York, N.Y. : Watts,
1960.
    [23] p. : col. ill. ; 33 cm.

    Picture book.
    "The autolithographs are by Charles Mozley"--
T.p. verso.

    I. Mozley, Charles.

Cross references

Bible. N.T. Matthew VI, 9-13 ...
    see
Lord's prayer ...

Bible. N.T. Luke XI, 2-4 ...
    see
Lord's prayer ...

D: 1.1F2, 2.5B7, 2.5C3, 2.7B1, 2.7B6, 1.7A3
ME: 21.11A, 21.37A, 25.18A7, A19K, 25.18A10
AE: 21.30K2b, 21.30J
x: 25.18A7

The Lord's Prayer

IN THE

Principal Languages, Dialects and Versions of the World

EDITED BY

TYPE AND VERNACULARS OF THE DIFFERENT NATIONS

COMPILED AND PUBLISHED BY

G.F. BERGHOLZ

CHICAGO, ILLINOIS

1884

The Lord's Prayer.

HAWAIIAN.

(SANDWICH ISLANDS, PACIFIC OCEAN.)

He Pule He Akua.

E ko makou Makua iloko o ka lani,
e hoanoia kou inoa. E hiki mai kou
aupuni; e malamaia kou makemake
ma ka honua nei, e like me ia i malamaia ma ka lani la; E haawi mai ia
makou i keia la i ai na makou no
neia la; E kala mai hoi ia makou i ka
makou lawehala ana, me makou e
kala nei i ka poe i lawehala i ka makou.   Mai hookuu oe ia makou i ka
hoowalewaleia mai; e hoopakele no
nae ia makou i ka ino; no ka mea,
nou ke aupuni, a me ka mana, a me
ka hoonaniia, a mau loa aku. Amene.

88

Example 680

Lord's prayer. Hawaiian.
    He pule ke akua. -- p. 88 ; 20 cm.

    In Lords' prayer. Polyglot. The Lord's prayer
in the principal languages, dialects, and versions
of the world. -- Chicago, Ill. : G.F. Bergholz,
1884.

    At head of title: Hawaiian (Sandwich Islands,
Pacific Ocean).

    I. Title.

The Liturgy of the Lutheran Church in America

AUTHORIZED BY THE CHURCHES COOPERATING IN THE COMMISSION ON LITURGY

◆ The Liturgical Choir of Philadelphia, Harold W. Gilbert, director

◆ The Choir of First Lutheran Church, Moline, Ill., Brynolf Lundholm, director

◆ The Choir of Trinity Lutheran Church, Germantown, Philadelphia, Catherine Deisher Baxter, director

EVERYONE is different.

This is not a matter to regret, but rather is a reason for praising the Creator who fashioned each of us with individual care.

Down through the ages groups of these different individuals have been moved to raise a united voice when expressing their most reverent thoughts. To further this unity, these records have been produced as a guide.

As PART of the "one, holy, catholic and apostolic Church," the Lutheran Church inherits the liturgy developed in the Christian household of faith. As symbolized on the cover, the liturgy had its beginning in Asia Minor, flowed to the western end of the Mediterranean, to northern Europe and on to the Western Hemisphere. These recordings present the liturgy as it has survived the centuries and overcome the barriers of language, been purified of unscriptural accretions and enriched with new material.

Specifically, this album contains three settings of The Service and the Offices of Matins and Vespers as authorized by a commission representing the major segment of the Lutheran Church in America. The work was begun in 1945 when eight Lutheran bodies embarked on the venture of a common hymnal. This led to the desire for a common liturgy grounded upon the Common Service (an American form of 1888 established on the Lutheran liturgies of the sixteenth century), and upon other forms significant to American Lutherans, particularly those of

have been "faded" where necessary to complete a setting on one side of a record. The variable parts of The Service are those designated for the Festival of the Holy Trinity.

THE MUSIC of the liturgy at the time of the Reformation was plainchant, most ancient music of the Christian Church. When, as a result of the Reformation, the Latin text was translated into the vernacular, it sometimes failed to fit the accustomed musical phrases. In some cases versification of the texts replaced the original words and these were set to chorale-type melodies. Later when the reformed liturgy was translated for early American use the church accepted, along with the English text, the chant form characteristic of liturgical music in the English church. Thus the liturgy of Lutherans in America reflects three musical traditions—plainsong, the chorale, and English chant.

THE FIRST SETTING and Matins and Vespers are in chant form. They are sung by the Liturgical Choir of Philadelphia directed by Harold W. Gilbert. Intonations are by Edward T. Horn, III. In this setting the "cathedral" pointing evident in the Common Service has been replaced by contemporary pointing wherein the normal accents of the text occur upon the natural accents of the chant.

THE SECOND SETTING is sung by a choir from First Lutheran Church, Moline, Ill., directed by Brynolf Lundholm. Organist is Regina H. Fryxell. The minister's intonations are by Bertil Anderson. Based on the melodic form of the chorale, this music reflects the spirit of continental

FALCKNER RECORDINGS

THE LITURGY OF THE
LUTHERAN CHURCH IN AMERICA
SIDE 1

THE FIRST SETTING
AUTHORIZED BY THE CHURCHES
COOPERATING IN
THE COMMISSION ON LITURGY

MRR 337 A
LONG PLAY • 33 1/3 • MICROGROOVE

Example 681

The Liturgy of the Lutheran Church in America
    [sound recording] / authorized by the
    churches cooperating in the Commission on
    Liturgy. -- [United States] : Falckner Re-
    cordings, [195-?]
    2 sound discs (ca. 100 min.) : analog, 33 1/3
rpm ; 12 in.

    Falckner Recordings: MRR337-MRR338.
    Liturgical Choir of Philadelphia, Harold W.
Gilbert, director ; Choir of First Lutheran
Church, Moline, Ill., Brynolf Lundholm, director ;
Choir of Trinity Lutheran Church, Germantown,
Philadelphia, Catherine Deisher Baxter, director.
    Contents: The first setting -- The second
setting -- The Plain song setting -- Matins,
Vespers.

    I. Commission on the Liturgy.

    In this example "Lutheran Church in America" refers not to a single
corporate body but to several Lutheran bodies that cooperated in the
Commission on the Liturgy. There is no single corporate body whose
name is "Lutheran Church."
    The Library of Congress has determined that "Lutheran Church" is
not an appropriate corporate name heading and should no longer be used.
It will continue to be used for subject purposes. (Letter from LC dated 1
Jan. 1981)

```
Type: j Bib lvl: a Lang: eng Source: d Accomp mat:
Repr:    Enc lvl: 1 Ctry: us  Dat tp: s MEBE:0
         Mod rec:    Comp: cc  Format: n Prts: n
Desc: a Int lvl:    LTxt:       Dates: 1950,1959

    010
    040    XXX $c XXX
    007    s $b d $d b $e e $f m $g e $h n $i n
    028 02 MRR337-MRR338 $b Falckner Recordings
    090
    049    XXXX
    245 04 The Liturgy of the Lutheran Church in Amer-
ica $h sound recording / $c authorized by the churches
cooperating in the Commission on Liturgy.
    260 0  [United States] : $b Falckner Recordings, $c
[195-?]
    300    1 sound disc (ca. 100 min.) : analog, $b 33
1/3 rpm ; $c 12 in.
    306    014000
    511 0  Liturgical Choir of Philadelphia, Harold W.
Gilbert, director ; Choir of First Lutheran Church,
Moline, Ill., Brynolf Lundholm, director ; Choir of
Trinity Lutheran Church, Germantown, Philadelphia, Cath-
erine Deisher Baxter, director.
    505 0  The first setting -- The second setting --
The Plain song setting -- Matins, Vespers.
    710 21 Commission on the Liturgy.
```

LAUDAMUS

**HYMNAL FOR THE ASSEMBLY OF THE
LUTHERAN WORLD FEDERATION**

+

**GESANGBUCH FÜR DIE VOLLVERSAMMLUNG
DES LUTHERISCHEN WELTBUNDES**

+

**PSALMBOK FÖR LUTHERSKA VÄRLDSFÖRBUNDETS
GENERALFÖRSAMLING**

**FIRST EDITION HANNOVER 1952
SECOND EDITION MINNEAPOLIS 1957**

**SCHLÖTERSCHE VERLAGSANSTALT UND BUCHDRUCKEREI
HANNOVER**

Example 682

```
Laudumus [text] : hymnal for the Assembly of the
   Lutheran World Federation = Gesangbuch fur
   die Vollversammlung des Lutherischen Weltbun-
   des = Psalmbok for Lutherska varldforbundets
   generalforsamling. -- 2nd ed. -- Hannover:
   Schluter, 1957.
   259 p. : music ; 18 cm.


   "The second edition ... for use at the Assem-
bly in Minneapolis in 1957 has been prepared
through the Committee on Worship ..."--Postcript.
   Includes index.


   I. Lutheran World Federation. Committee on
Worship.  II. Lutheran World Federation. Assembly
(2nd : 1957 : Minneapolis, Minn.)
```

D: 1.1C2, 1.1E5 (CSB25), 1.1A1, 1.1F2, 1.2B1, 1.4D2, 2.5C2, 2.7B6,
    2.7B18
ME: 21.39A3b, 21.1B3, 21.1C3
AE: 21.30E, 24.13 Type 2, 24.13 Type 5, 24.7B2, 24.7B3, 24.7B4

THE CONSTITUTION

OF

THE UNITED PRESBYTERIAN CHURCH

IN THE

UNITED STATES OF AMERICA

PART I

BOOK OF CONFESSIONS

SECOND EDITION, 1970

OFFICE OF THE GENERAL ASSEMBLY
THE UNITED PRESBYTERIAN CHURCH
IN THE UNITED STATES OF AMERICA
1201 INTERCHURCH CENTER
475 RIVERSIDE DRIVE
NEW YORK, N.Y. 10027

Example 683

United Presbyterian Church in the U.S.A.
     [Book of confessions]
     The Constitution of the United Presbyterian
Church in the United States of America. Part 1,
Book of confessions [text]. -- 2nd ed. -- New
York, N.Y. : Office of the General Assembly, The
Church, 1970, c1967.
     vii, ca. 300 p., [8] p. of plates : col.
ill.; 23 cm.

     Includes index.

     I. Title.   II. Title: Book of confessions.

Cross reference

United Presbyterian Church in the U.S.A.
     Constitution of the United Presbyterian
Church in the United States of America. 1. Book of
Confessions.
     see
United Presbyterian Church in the U.S.A.
     Book of confessions.

D: 1.1B9, A.20,S 1.1C2,S 1.1F13, 1.2B1, 1.4C3, 1.4D4, 1.4F5, 2.5B6,
      2.5B10, 2.5C3, 2.7B18
ME: 21.38, 24.1, 24.5A
UT: 25.6A1
AE: 21.30J
x: 25.6a1, 26.4A2

MISSALE
ROMANUM
EX DECRETO SACROSANCTI
Concilii Tridentini reftitutum,
S. PII V. PONTIFICIS MAX.
JUSSU EDITUM,
CLEMENTIS VIII. & URBANI VIII.
Auctoritate recognitum;
IN QUO MISSÆ NOVISSIMÆ SANCTORUM
Ex Indulto Apoftolico ufque ad
SS. D. N. CLEMENTEM XI.
Editæ accuratè difponuntur.

VENETIIS, MDCCXIX.
Apud Nicolaum Pezzana.

Example 684

```
Catholic Church.
    [Missal]
    Missale Romanum ex decreto sacrosancti Con-
cilii Tridentini restitutum / S. Pii V, Pontificis
max. jussu editum, Clementis VIII & Urbani VIII
auctoritate recognitum, in quo missae novissimae
sanctorum ex indulto apostolico usque ad SS. D.N.
Clementem XI editae accurate disponuntur. --
Venetiis : Nicolaum Pezzana, 1719.
    448, lxxxvii, 28 p. ; 31 cm. (4to)

    Signatures: A⁴-Z⁴, Aa⁴-Ee⁴, aᴵⱽ-fᴵⱽ, A⁷.
    Engraved t.p.


    I. Catholic Church. Pope (1592-1605 : Clement
VIII).  II.  Catholic Church. Pope (1700-1721 :
Clement XI).  III.  Catholic Church. Pope (1566-
1572 : Pius V).  IV.  Catholic Church. Pope (1623-
1644 : Urban VIII).




ME:  21.38A1 25.19
AE:  I-IV. 22.17A2 22.17B 26.3C1, p. 505. 24.27B2
```

One added entry could replace all those for the individual popes:
Catholic Church. Pope.

(24.27B2)

THE MISSAL

OF

ST AUGUSTINE'S ABBEY
CANTERBURY

WITH EXCERPTS FROM THE ANTIPHONARY
AND LECTIONARY OF THE SAME MONASTERY

**EDITED, WITH AN INTRODUCTORY MONOGRAPH,
FROM A MANUSCRIPT IN THE LIBRARY
OF CORPUS CHRISTI COLLEGE, CAMBRIDGE,**

BY
M A R T I N R U L E , M.A.

**CAMBRIDGE:
AT THE UNIVERSITY PRESS.
1896**

Example 685

```
Catholic Church.
    [Missal {St. Augustine Abbey, Canterbury)]
    The Missal of St. Augustine's Abbey, Canter-
bury : with excerpts from the antiphonary and lec-
tionary of the same monastery / edited, with an
introductory monograph, from a manuscript in the
Library of Corpus Christi College, Cambridge, by
Martin Rule. -- Cambridge [Cambridgeshire] :
University Press, 1896.
    clxxxiv, 174 p., [1] leaf of plates : facsim.
, 28 cm.

    Introduction in English; Missal in Latin.
    Rubricated.
    Includes bibliographical references and in-
dexes.


    I. Rule, Martin.  II. St. Augustine's Abbey
(Canterbury, Kent).
```

ME: 21.39A
UT: 25.22A2, 25.5D
D: 1.1F1, 1.4C3, 1.4D2, 2.5B10, 2.7B18, B.9, 2.7B2
AE: 21.30D, 21.30E, 24.4C5, 21.30J1

NIGHT PRAYER

1976
Publications Office
UNITED STATES CATHOLIC CONFERENCE
1312 Massachusetts Avenue, N.W.
Washington, D.C. 20005

Example 686

```
Catholic Church.
    [Night prayer]
    Night prayer. -- Washington, D.C. : Publica-
tions Office, United States Catholic Conference,
1976.
    ix, 86 p. ; 18 cm.


    I. Title.
```

Cross reference

```
Catholic Church.
    Liturgy of the hours. Night prayer.
    see
Catholic Church
    Night prayer
```

ME: 21.39A3a, 21.39A1
UT: 25.23A
AE: 21.30J
x: 25.23A, 26.4A2

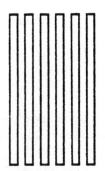
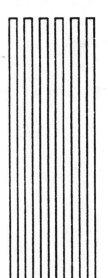

THE ROMAN PONTIFICAL

**REVISED BY DECREE OF THE
SECOND VATICAN ECUMENICAL
COUNCIL AND PUBLISHED BY
AUTHORITY OF POPE PAUL VI**

I

**INTERNATIONAL COMMISSION ON
ENGLISH IN THE LITURGY • 1978**

Example 687

```
Catholic Church.
     [Pontifical. English]
     The Roman pontifical revised by decree of the
Second Vatican Ecumenical Council and published by
authority of Pope Paul VI. -- [Washington] :
International Commission on English in the Lit-
urgy, 1978-
     v. ; 30 cm.


     I. International Commission on English in the
Liturgy.   II. Title.



ME:   21.39A1; 25.19
```

THE RITES

OF THE

CATHOLIC CHURCH

**as Revised by Decree of the
Second Vatican Ecumenical Council
and Published
by Authority of Pope Paul VI**

**English translation
prepared by
The International Commission
on English in the Liturgy**

PUEBLO PUBLISHING CO

New York

Example 688

```
Catholic Church.
    [Ritual. English]
    The rites of the Catholic Church / as revised
by decree of the Second Vatican Ecumenical Council
and published by authority of Pope Paul VI ;
English translation prepared by the International
Commission on English in the Liturgy. -- New York
: Pueblo, 1976.
    xviii, 756 p. : ill. ; 23 cm.

    Includes bibliographical references.


    I. International Commission on English in the
Liturgy.  II. Title.
```

D: 1.1F6, 1.4D2, 2.7B18
ME: 21.39A1
UT: 25.19, 25.5D
AE: 21.30E, 21.30J

𝔖𝔱𝔞𝔱𝔲𝔱𝔢𝔰

of the

𝔇𝔦𝔬𝔠𝔢𝔰𝔢 𝔬𝔣 𝔚𝔦𝔫𝔬𝔫𝔞

Enacted and Promulgated

By

𝔥𝔦𝔰 𝔈𝔵𝔠𝔢𝔩𝔩𝔢𝔫𝔠𝔶

𝔗𝔥𝔢 𝔐𝔬𝔰𝔱 𝔯𝔢𝔳𝔢𝔯𝔢𝔫𝔡 𝔈𝔡𝔴𝔞𝔯𝔡 𝔄. 𝔉𝔦𝔱𝔷𝔤𝔢𝔯𝔞𝔩𝔡, 𝔇.𝔇.

𝔅𝔦𝔰𝔥𝔬𝔭 𝔬𝔣 𝔚𝔦𝔫𝔬𝔫𝔞

in the

FIRST DIOCESAN SYNOD

Convoked on

JUNE FIFTEENTH

NINETEEN HUNDRED AND FIFTY

in the

CHAPEL OF ST. MARY OF THE ANGELS

COLLEGE OF SAINT TERESA   WINONA, MINNESOTA

Example 689

Catholic Church. Diocese of Winona (Minn.).
    Statutes of the Diocese of Winona / enacted
and promulgated by Edward A. Fitzgerald in the
first Diocesan Synod. -- [Winona? Minn. : s.n.],
1950.
    xv, 142. [12] p. ; 24 cm.

    "Convoked on June fifteenth, nineteen hundred
and fifty, in the Chapel of St. Mary of the Angels, College of Saint Teresa, Winona, Minnesota."
    Includes index.

    I. Fitzgerald, Edward A. (Edward Aloysius),
1893-1972. II. Catholic Church. Diocese of Winona
(Minn.). Bishop (1949-1969 : Fitzgerald). III.
Catholic Church. Diocese of Winona (Minn.). Dioce-
san Synod (1st : 1950 : Winona, Minn.). IV.
Title.

ME: 24.27C, 24.27C3, 23.4C
D: 1.1F7d , 1.4C6, 1.4D6, 2.7B5
AE: 21.4D1, 21.30F, 21.30J, 24.27A3, 24.27B1

THE

PAPAL ENCYCLICAL

BY

THE RIGHT REV. THOMAS L. GRACE,

BISHOP OF ST. PAUL.

BEING A PASTORAL LETTER TO THE CLERGY AND LAITY OF THE
DIOCESE, ON OCCASION OF THE PUBLICATION
OF THE JUBILEE.

Tu es Petrus, et super hano petram ædificabe ecelesiam messn.
Matthew, xvi 18.

ST. PAUL,
PIONEER PRINTING COMPANY.
1865.

Example 690

Catholic Church. Diocese of St. Paul (Minn.).
    Bishop (1859-1884 : Grace)
    The papal encyclical : being a pastoral let-
ter to the clergy and laity of the diocese on the
occasion of the publication of the jubilee / by
Thomas L. Grace, Bishop of St. Paul. -- St. Paul :
Pioneer Print. Co., 1865.
    29 p. ; 22 cm.

    I. Grace, Thomas L. (Thomas Langdon), 1814-
1897. II. Title.

D: 1.1F7, 1.1F7(c)
ME: 21.1B2; 21.4D1; 24.27C3; 24.27B1
AE: I. 21.4D1, par. 2

Type: a Bib lvl: m Govt pub: Lang: eng Source: d illus:
Repr: Enc lvl: I Conf pub: 0 Ctry: mnu Dat tp: s M/F/B: 10
Indx: 0 Mod rec: Festschr: 0 Cont:
Desc: a Int lvl: Dates: 1865,

   010
   040   XXX $c XXX
   090
   049   XXXX
   110 20 Catholic Church. $b Diocese of St. Paul
(Minn.). $b Bishop (1859-1884 : Grace)
   245 14 The papal encyclical : $b being a pastoral
letter to the clergy and laity of the diocese on the
occasion of the publication of the jubilee / $c by Tho-
mas L. Grace, Bishop of St. Paul.
   260 0 St. Paul : $b Pioneer Print. Co., $c 1865.
   300   29 p. ; $c 22 cm.
   700 10 Grace, Thomas L. $q (Thomas Langdon), $d
1814-1897.

ENCYCLICAL LETTER
ON
PRIESTLY CELIBACY

SACERDOTALIS
CAELIBATUS

JUNE 24, 1967

POPE PAUL VI

UNITED STATES CATHOLIC CONFERENCE

Example 691

Catholic Church. Pope (1963-1978 : Paul VI)
    [Sacerdotalis caelibatus. English]
    Encyclical letter on priestly celibacy : sac-
erdotalis caelibatus, June 24, 1967 / Pope Paul
VI. -- Washington : United States Catholic Conference, [1967?]
    42 p. ; 22 cm.

    I. Paul VI, Pope, 1897-1978. II. Title.

Cross reference

Catholic Church. Pope (1963-1978 : Paul VI)
    Here are entered works of the Pope acting in
his official capacity. For other works see,

    Paul VI, Pope, 1897-1978.

D: 1.4F7
ME: 21.4D1b, 24.27B2
UT: 25.24A, 25.5D
AE: 21.4D1, 22.17B, 21.30J
exp. ref: 26.3C1

Type: a Bib lvl: a Govt pub: Lang: eng Source: d illus:
Repr: Enc lvl: I Conf pub: 0 Ctry: dcu Dat tp: s M/F/B: 10
Indx: 0 Mod rec: Festschr: 0 Cont:
Desc: a Int lvl: Dates: 1967,

    010
    040   XXX $c XXX
    041 1 eng $h lat
    045 0 $b d19670624
    090
    049   XXXX
    110 20 Catholic Church. $b Pope (1963-1978 : Paul
VI)
    240 10 Sacerdotalis caelibatus. $l English
    245 10 Encyclical letter on priestly celibacy : $b
sacerdotalis caelibatus, June 24, 1967 / $c Pope Paul
VI.
    260 0 Washington : $b United States Catholic
Conference, $c [1967?]
    300   42 p. ; $c 22 cm.
    700 00 Paul $b VI, $c Pope, $d 1897-1978

The

Alternative
Service Book
1980

Services authorized for use in the Church
of England in conjunction with The Book
of Common Prayer

together with The Liturgical Psalter

Clowes
SPCK
Cambridge University Press

Example 692

```
Church of England.
    [Alternative service book]
    The Alternative service book 1980 : services
authorized for use in the Church of England in
conjunction with the Book of common prayer :
together with the liturgical psalter.  -- Beccles
[Suffolk] : Clowes, 1980.
    1292 p. ; 17 cm.

    Includes index.


    I. Title: Book of Common Prayer.  II. Title:
Liturgical Psalter.
```

ME: 21.39A1
UT: 25.19, 24.5A, 25.5D
D: 1.1F2, 1.4C3, 2.7B18
AE: 21.30J, 21.30J1

THE

BOOK OF MORMON

An Account Written by

THE HAND OF MORMON

UPON PLATES

TAKEN FROM THE PLATES OF NEPHI

Wherefore, it is an abridgment of the record of the people of Nephi, and also of the Lamanites—Written to the Lamanites, who are a remnant of the house of Israel; and also to Jew and Gentile—Written by way of commandment, and also by the spirit of prophecy and of revelation — Written and sealed up, and hid up unto the Lord, that they might not be destroyed—To come forth by the gift and power of God unto the interpretation thereof —Sealed by the hand of Moroni, and hid up unto the Lord, to come forth in due time by way of the Gentile—The interpretation thereof by the gift of God.

An abridgment taken from the Book of Ether also, which is a record of the people of Jared, who were scattered at the time the Lord confounded the language of the people, when they were building a tower to get to heaven —Which is to show unto the remnant of the House of Israel what great things the Lord hath done for their fathers; and that they may know the covenants of the Lord, that they are not cast off forever—And also to the convincing of the Jew and Gentile that Jesus is the Christ, the Eternal God, manifesting himself unto all nations—And now, if there are faults they are the mistakes of men; wherefore, condemn not the things of God, that ye may be found spotless at the judgment-seat of Christ.

TRANSLATED BY JOSEPH SMITH, Jun.

PUBLISHED BY
The Church of Jesus Christ of Latter-day Saints
SALT LAKE CITY, UTAH, U. S. A.
1961

Example 693

Book of Mormon.
    The Book of Mormon / an account written by the hand of Mormon upon plates taken from the plates of Nephi ; translated by Joseph Smith, Jun. -- Salt Lake City, Utah : Church of Jesus Christ of Latter-Day Saints, 1961.
    558 p., [8] leaves of plates : col. ill. ; 18 cm.

    I. Smith, Joseph.

D: 1.1F1
ME: 21.37A; 25.17
AE: 21.30K1; 21.37A

The Festal Menaion

translated from the original Greek

by

MOTHER MARY
of the Orthodox Monastery of the Veil of the Mother of God
Bussy-en-Othe, France

and

ARCHIMANDRITE KALLISTOS WARE
Spalding lecturer in Eastern Orthodox Studies
University of Oxford

with an introduction by

ARCHPRIEST GEORGES FLOROVSKY
Emeritus Professor of Eastern Church History
Harvard University

FABER AND FABER
3 Queen Square
London

Example 694

```
Orthodox Eastern Church.
   [Menaion. English]
   The festal Menaion / translated from the
original Greek by Mother Mary and Kallistos Ware ;
with an introduction by George Florovsky. --
London : Faber, 1977, c1969.
   564 p. ; 20 cm.

   ISBN 0-571-11137-8 : $10.95


   I. Mary, Mother.  II. Ware, Kallistos, 1934-
III. Title.
```

Cross reference

```
Mother Mary
   see
Mary, Mother
```

D: 1.4D2, 1.4F5, 1.8B1, 1.8D1
ME: 21.39B, 24.3C2
UT: 25.19, 25.5D
AE: 21.30K1, 22.1C, 22.18, 21.30J
X: 26.2A3

The Lenten Triodion

═══════

translated from the original Greek

by

MOTHER MARY

and

ARCHIMANDRITE KALLISTOS WARE

FABER AND FABER

London & Boston

Example 695

```
Orthodox Eastern Church.
    [Triodion. English]
    The Lenten Triodion / translated from the
original Greek by Mother Mary and Kallistos Ware.
-- London ; Boston : Faber, 1978, c1977.
    699 p. ; 23 cm. -- (The Service books of the
Orthodox Church)

    Uniform with this title: The Festal Menaion.
    Includes bibliographical references.
    ISBN 0-571-11253-6.


    I. Mary, Mother.  II. Ware, Kallistos, 1934-
. III. Title.  IV. Series.
```

Cross reference

```
Mother Mary
    see
Mary, Mother
```

ME: 21.39B, 24.3C2
UT: 25.19, 25.5D
D: 1.4C5, 1.4D2, 1.4F5, 1.0C, 2.6B1, 1.7A3, 1.8B1
AE: 21.30K1, 22.1C , 22.18, 21.30J, 21.30L
X   26.2A3

THE PHILOKALIA

Volume I

THE COMPLETE TEXT
compiled by
ST NIKODIMOS OF THE HOLY MOUNTAIN
and
ST MAKARIOS OF CORINTH

translated from the Greek
and edited by
G. E. H. PALMER

PHILIP SHERRARD

KALLISTOS WARE

with the assistance of
THE HOLY TRANSFIGURATION MONASTERY
(BROOKLINE)

CONSTANTINE CAVARNOS

BASIL OSBORNE

NORMAN RUSSELL

FABER AND FABER
London & Boston

Example 696

Philokalia. English.
    The Philokalia : the complete text / compiled
by St. Nikodimos of the Holy Mountain and St.
Makarios of Corinth ; translated from the Greek
and edited by G.E.H. Palmer, Philip Sherrard,
Kallistos Ware ; with the assistance of the Holy
Transfiguration Monastery (Brookline) ... [et
al.]. -- London ; Boston : Faber, c1979-
        v. ; 23 cm.

    Translation of: Philokalia.
    Includes bibliographical references and in-
dexes.
    ISBN 0-571-11377-X.

    I. Nicodemos, the Hagiorite, Saint, 1748-
1809. II. Makarios, Saint, Metropolitan of
Corinth, 1731-1805. III. Palmer, G.E.H. (Gerald
Eustace Howell), 1904- . IV. Sherrard, Philip.
V. Ware, Kallistos, 1934-   VI. Title.

ME: 25.2A, 25.2A , 25.3A, 25.5D
D: 1.1F5, 1.4C5, 1.4D2, 1.4F8, 1.5B5, 1.8B1, 2.7B18, 2.7B2
AE: 22.13A, A.19C, 21.30J1

THE GOSPEL ACCORDING TO THOMAS

COPTIC TEXT ESTABLISHED AND TRANSLATED

BY

A. GUILLAUMONT, H.-CH. PUECH, G. QUISPEL, W. TILL AND † YASSAH ʿABD AL MASĪḤ

LEIDEN
E. J. BRILL

NEW YORK
HARPER & BROTHERS

Example 697

```
Gospel of Thomas. English & Coptic (Sahidic).
   The Gospel according to Thomas / Coptic text
established and translated by A. Guillaumont ...
[et al.]. -- Leiden : Brill ; New York : Harper,
1959.
   vii, 62 p. ; 25 cm.

   Parallel texts in Coptic and English.
   Bibliography: p. vii.


   I. Guillaumont, Antoine.   II. Title.
```

Cross reference

```
Bible. N.T. Apocryphal books.
   For individual apocryphal books of the New
Testament, see the title of the book, e.g., Coptic
Gospel of Thomas.
```

ME: 21.37A, 25.18A14, 25.5D
D: 1.1F5, 1.4D5, 2.7B2, 2.7B18
AE: 21.30K1, 21.30J
X: 25.18A14

NEW EDITION

OF THE

BABYLONIAN TALMUD

Original Text Edited, Corrected, Formulated, and
Translated into English

BY

MICHAEL L. RODKINSON

First Edition Revised and Corrected

BY

THE REV. DR. ISAAC M. WISE
President Hebrew Union College, Cincinnati, O.

Volume I.

TRACT SABBATH

SECOND EDITION, RE-EDITED, REVISED AND ENLARGED

BOSTON
THE TALMUD SOCIETY
1918

Example 698

Talmud. English.
   New edition of the Babylonian Talmud / original text edited, corrected, formulated, and translated into English by Michael L. Rodkinson ; first
edition revised and corrected by Isaac M. Wise. --
2nd ed., re-edited, rev., and enl. -- Boston :
Talmud Society, 1918.
   20 v. in 10 : facsims. ; 25 cm.

   I. Rodkinson, Michael L. (Michael Levi), 1843
or 4-1904. II. Wise, Isaac M. (Isaac Mayer),
1819-1900. III. Title.

D: 1.1F1, 1.2B1, 2.5B19, 2.5C2, 2.7B6, 1.7A3
ME: 21.12A, 21.37A, 25.17, 25.5D
AE: 21.30D, 21.12A, 22.16A, 22.18, 21.30J

TRACTATE SANHEDRIN

MISHNAH AND *TOSEFTA*

**THE JUDICIAL PROCEDURE OF THE JEWS
AS CODIFIED TOWARDS THE END OF THE
SECOND CENTURY A.D.**

TRANSLATED FROM THE HEBREW WITH BRIEF ANNOTATIONS

BY

HERBERT DANBY, M.A.

SUB-WARDEN OF ST. DEINIOL'S LIBRARY, MAWARDEN

**LONDON:
SOCIETY FOR PROMOTING
CHRISTIAN KNOWLEDGE
NEW YORK: THE MACMILLAN COMPANY
1919**

Example 699

Mishnah. Sanhedrin. English.
    Tractate Sanhedrin : Mishnah and Tosefta :
the judicial procedure of the Jews as codified
towards the end of the second century A.D. /
translated from the Hebrew with brief annotations
by Herbert Danby. -- London : Society for Promoting Christian Knowledge ; New York : Macmillan,
1919.
    xxi, 148 p. ; 19 cm. -- (Translations of
early documents. Series 3, Rabbinic texts ; 5)
    Translation arranged in alternate paragraphs
of the Mishnah and Tosefta.
    Bibliography: xvi-xviii.
    Includes indexes.

    I. Danby, Herbert, 1889-   II. Tosefta.
Sanhedrin. English.   III. Title.

Cross reference

Sanhedrin.
    see
Mishnah. Sanhedrin.
    Tosefta. Sanhedrin.

D: 1.1E2, 1.4B8, 1.6B1, 1.6H1, 1.6H2, 1.6G1, 1.6H5, 2.7B10, 2.7B18
ME: 21.37A, 25.18C, 25.5D
AE: 21.30K1, 22.18, 21.7B, 21.30J
X: 25.18D

Jaina Sutras

Translated from Prakrit by

Hermann Jacobi

in two parts

Part I

The Âkârânga Sûtra

The Kalpa Sûtra

Dover Publications, Inc.
New York

Example 700

Jaina Agama. English. Selections.
    Jaina Sutras / translated from Prakit by
Hermann Jacobi. -- Dover ed. -- New York : Dover,
1968.
    2 v. ; 22 cm.

    Reprint of: Gaina sûtras. Oxford : Clarendon
Press, 1884-1895. (The Sacred books of the East ;
22, 45).
    Includes bibliographical references and in-
dexes.
    Contents: pt. 1. The Akârânga Sutra. The
Kalpa Sûtra -- pt. 2. The Uttarâdhyayana Sûtra.
The Sutrakritânga Sûtra.
    ISBN 486-21156-8-X (pbk.) : 3.50 per vol.

    I. Jacobi, Hermann, 1850-1938. II. Title.
III. Series: Sacred books of the East ; 22, 45.

ME: 21.37A, 25.18J, 25.5D
D.:   1.1F1, 1.1F15, 1.7B22, 1.8D1, 2.5B17, 2.6B1, 1.6G1, 2.7B7,
      2.7B18, 2.8B1, 2.8D2
AE: 21.30K1, 22.16A, 22.18, 21.30J, 21.30L

THE KORÂN

TRANSLATED INTO ENGLISH
FROM THE ORIGINAL ARABIC

BY

GEORGE SALE

WITH EXPLANATORY NOTES
FROM THE MOST APPROVED COMMENTATORS

WITH AN INTRODUCTION
BY
SIR EDWARD DENISON ROSS
C.I.E., Ph.D., ETC.

LONDON
FREDERICK WARNE AND Co. Ltd.
AND NEW YORK

Example 701

Koran. English.
    The Korân / translated into English from the
original Arabic by George Sale ; with explanatory
notes from the most approved commentators ; with
an introduction by Sir Edward Denison Ross. --
London ; New York : Warne, [18--?]
    xiv, 608 p. ; 19 cm.

Includes index.

I. Sale, George, 1697?-1736.

D: 1.1F6, 1.1F7d, 1.4C5, 1.4D2, 1.4F7, 2.7B18
ME: 21.37A, 25.17, 25.5D
AE: 21.30K1, 21.30J1

הגדה וסדר של פסח.

===

FORM OF SERVICE

FOR THE

TWO FIRST NIGHTS

OF THE

FEAST OF PASSOVER

WITH ENGLISH TRANSLATION.

===

NEW ILLUSTRATED EDITION.

===

HEBREW PUBLISHING CO.,

83-85-87 Canal Street,   NEW YORK.

Example 702

Haggadah. English and Hebrew.
                              הגדה וסדר של פסח
= Form of service for the two first nights of the
Feast of Passover / with English translation. --
New illustrated ed. -- New York : Hebrew Pub. Co.,
c1859.
    60 p. : ill. ; 23 cm.

    Title romanized: Haggadah ve-seder shel Pe-
sah.

    I. Title: Form of service for the first two
nights of the Feast of Passover.

D: 2.7B4
ME: 25.21 25.5D

    Jewish liturgical works are now entered under uniform title. AACR
2 has dispensed with form subdivisions in entries.
    Jews. Liturgy and ritual as a heading no longer exists. Since "Jews"
is not a corporate heading like United States, entry then becomes uniform
title. Brackets are not used for uniform title main entries.

An ISRAEL

HAGGADAH

FOR PASSOVER

adapted by Meyer Levin

HARRY N. ABRAMS, INC.   PUBLISHERS

NEW YORK

Example 703

Haggadah. English & Hebrew. Selections.
    An Israel Haggadah for Passover / adapted by
Meyer Levin. -- New York : Abrams, 1970.
    126 p. : ill. (some col.), music ; 29 cm.

English and/or Hebrew.
"Songs": p. 102-126.

    I. Levin, Meyer, 1905-   . II. Title.

D: 1.4D2, 2.5C3, 2.5C2, 2.7B2, 2.7B18
ME: 21.10, 21.39C, 25.21, 25.5D, 25.6B3
AE: 21.30C, 22.18, 21.30J

Example 704

Haggadah (Abravenel)
סדר הגדה של פסח : ,כמנהג אשכנז וספרד, : עם
פירוש ,אברבנאל, ... =

The Amsterdam Haggadah of 1695 / edited, with
commentary, by Isaac Abravanel. -- [New York :
Orphan Hospital Ward of Israel, 1974].
     26 leaves ; 21 cm. -- (Passover Haggadah ; v.
12)

     Cover title.
     Introd. in English and Hebrew by M.I. Fried-
man.
     Title romanized: Seder Haggadah shel Pesah.
     Facsim. of: Amsterdam : A. Anshil, 1695.
26 leaves, 2 leaves of plates : ill. ; 31 cm.
     Historical map of Exodus at end.
     Ceremonial directions are given in Hebrew,
Judeo-German and Judeo-Spanish.
     Original in the library of the family of
Mordecai Hirsch.

     I. Abravenel, Isaac, 1437-1508. II.
Freidman, Murray I., 1926-   . III. Haggadah
(Sephardic, Abravenel). IV. Title: The Amsterdam
Haggadah of 1695. V. Series.

D: 2.7B4 2.6B1 2.7B2 2.7B6 1.11F
ME: 25.21 25.22A3
AE: III. 25.21 25.22A

Publication information on back cover of volume.

Jataka Tales

Edited by Nancy DeRoin
with original
Drawings by Ellen Lanyon

HOUGHTON MIFFLIN COMPANY BOSTON 1975

Example 705

Tipiṭaka. Suttapiṭaka. Khuddakanikāya. Jātaka.
    English. Selections.
    Jataka tales / edited by Nancy De Roin ; with
original drawings by Ellen Lanyon. -- Boston :
Houghton Mifflin, 1975.
    x, 82 p. : ill. ; 23 cm.

    Summary: Retells thirty of the 500 tales told
by the Buddha.
    ISBN 0-395-20281-7

    I. De Roin, Nancy. II. Lanyon, Ellen. III.
Title.

Cross reference

Jātaka.
    see
Tipiṭaka. Suttapiṭaka. Khuddakanikāya.
    Jātaka.

D: 1.1F6, 2.7B17, 1.8B1
ME: 21.37A, 25.18F1, 25.5D, 25.6B3
AE: 21.30D, 21.30K2c, 21.30J
X: 25.18F3

SONGS OF
ZARATHUSHTRA
THE GATHAS
TRANSLATED FROM THE AVESTA

by
DASTUR FRAMROZE ARDESHIR BODE
B.A. (BOMBAY)
Parsi High Priest, Petit Fasali Atash-kadsh (Fire Temple), Bombay

and

PILOO NANAVUTTY

M.A., M. LITT. *(Cantab.)*
Formerly Lecturer in English literature
Wilson College, Bombay

Foreword by
RADHAKRISHNAN

LONDON
GEORGE ALLEN & UNWIN LTD
Ruskin House Museum Street

Example 706

Avesta. Yasna. Gathas. English.
    Songs of Zarathushtra : the Gathas / trans-
lated from the Avesta by Dastur Framroze Ardeshir
Bode and Piloo Nanavutty ; foreword by Radhakrish-
nan. -- London : Allen & Unwin, 1952.
    127 p. ; 19 cm. -- (Ethical and religious
classics of East and West ; no. 6)

    Bibliography: p. 107-110.
    Includes index.

    I. Bode, Dastur Framroze Ardeshir.   II.
Nanavutty, Piloo.   III. Title.

Cross reference

Gathas.
    see
Avesta. Yasna. Gathas.

D: 1.1F6, 1.4D2, 1.6B1, 1.6G1, 2.7B18
ME: 21.37A, 25.18K, 25.5D
AE: 21.30K1, 21.30J
X: 25.18L

Hindu Scriptures

HYMNS FROM THE RIGVEDA
FIVE UPANISHADS
THE BHAGAVADGÍTÁ

EDITED BY
NICOL MACNICOL, M.A., D.LITT., D.D.

FOREWORD BY
RABINDRANATH TAGORE

DENT: LONDON
EVERYMAN'S LIBRARY
DUTTON: NEW YORK

Example 707

Hindu scriptures : hymns from the Ṛgveda, five
  Upanishads, the Bhagavidgītā / edited by
  Nicol Macnicol ; foreword by Rabindranath
  Tagore. -- London : Dent ; New York : Dutton,
  1938.
  xxiv, 293 p. ; 19 cm. -- (Everyman's library
; no. 944)

  The Upanishads are "from Max Müller's translation of the Sacred Books of the East ... The
translation of the Bhagavadgītā is by L.D. Barnett
..."--p. [x]

  I. Macnicol, Nicol, 1879-   . II. Müller,
Max, 1823-1900. III. Barnett, L.D. (Lionel
David), 1871-   . IV. Vedas. Ṛgveda. English.
Selections. IV. Upanishads. English. Selections.
V. Mahābhārata. Bhagavadgītā. English. Selections.

Cross reference

Ṛgveda.
    see
Vedas. Ṛgveda.

D: 1.1E1, 1.1F6, 1.4B8, 1.6B1, 1.6G1, 2.7B2
ME: 21.7B
AE: 21.30D, 21.30K1, 21.30M, 25.18G, 25.18H, 25.17, 25.5D, 25.6B3
X: 25.18L